D0203433

ECONOMY AND SOCIETY IN SCOTLAND AND IRELAND 1500–1939

Economy and Society in Scotland and Ireland 1500–1939

Edited by

ROSALIND MITCHISON

and

PETER ROEBUCK

JOHN DONALD PUBLISHERS LTD

EDINBURGH

John Donald Publishers Ltd., 138 St Stephen Street, Edinburgh, EH3 5AA.

ISBN 0 85976 171 1

Distributed in the United States of America and Canada by Humanities Press Inc., Atlantic Highlands, NJ 07716, USA.

Phototypeset by Quorn Selective Repro Ltd., Loughborough.
Printed in Great Britain by Bell & Bain Ltd., Glasgow.

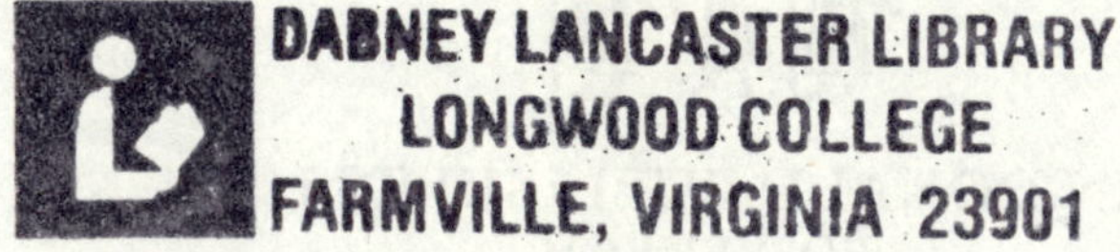

PREFACE

On no less than three occasions in the past decade historians from both sides of the Irish Sea and, indeed, further afield have gathered together to compare the historical development of Scotland and Ireland. Sponsored by the Social Science Research Council, the first two conferences took place at Trinity College, Dublin in 1976 and at the University of Strathclyde in 1981. Their proceedings were subsequently published as L. M. Cullen & T. C. Smout, eds., *Comparative Aspects of Irish and Scottish Economic and Social History, 1600–1900* (Edinburgh, 1977), and T. M. Devine & David Dickson, eds., *Ireland and Scotland, 1600–1850: Parallels and Contrasts in Economic and Social Development* (Edinburgh, 1983). The present volume contains the fruits of the third such conference. With the help of generous support from the Economic and Social Research Council this was held at Magee College, the Londonderry campus of the University of Ulster, in September 1985.

The deliberations of the first two conferences were largely confined to the period from the later seventeenth to the later nineteenth centuries. On each occasion, moreover, discussion was dominated by analysis of the causation and nature of the very different experiences of the two countries in the nineteenth century: why did the Scottish and Irish economies diverge so markedly in the years after c.1780? A number of the contributions which follow continue the search for answers to this central question. In planning the third conference, however, we were anxious to go further. We wished, firstly, to broaden the comparison, not merely by dealing with topics neglected on earlier occasions but also by extending the chronological range of the proceedings; and secondly, to deepen it by commissioning as many explicitly and wholly comparative papers as possible. In the event about half the contributions fell into this latter category.

We were unable to solve some of the problems which we encountered. In the current state of research and in view of the manpower and space available to us, it proved impossible to balance the proceedings as carefully as we would have wished. There is nothing here, for example, about shipbuilding or engineering. More seriously, like its forerunners this volume fails to confront at least one matter of overriding significance — the differing rates of population growth in the two countries in the eighteenth and early nineteenth centuries. Also, in terms of the spatial distribution of the topics covered, there is rather more here on Ulster and on the Scottish Highlands, and correspondingly less on other regions, than is ideal. Despite these imperfections, the volume endeavours to complement its predecessors and to break new ground. It falls into three parts. The first attempts to identify some of the roots of later differences, and is chiefly concerned with the interrelationship between tradition and change in the rural world of the sixteenth and seventeenth centuries. The second examines a series of critical issues — real wages, poverty, alienation, diet and relations between the social strata — in the period during which marked economic divergence first took place. The final section is primarily devoted to industrial and infrastructural developments in the modern period, and in particular to some of the more striking examples of the contrasts (and connections) which emerged in both the private and the public sectors. Prior to publication the papers were revised in the light of discussions at the conference. The volume opens with our reflections on those discussions and on the proceedings as a whole.

We take pleasure in acknowledging the debts which we have accumulated in organising the conference and editing its proceedings. Without the assistance of the Economic and Social Research Council the conference could not have taken place. We are deeply grateful to the staff of Magee College, particularly the Provost, Professor R. J. Gavin, and the Administrative Officer, Miss A. M. Simpson, for providing excellent facilities for the conference; to Gillian Coward and Sean Connolly for tape-recording the proceedings; and to Vivienne Pollock for pre-circulating the papers and for help with a host of matters too numerous to mention. The task of preparing this volume for the press was greatly facilitated by a generous grant from the Muirhead Hanna Publications Fund of the University of Ulster; by the patience and skill of our typist, Morag Stark; and by the advice and assistance of our publisher. Nor do we forget those who preceded us in this endeavour, especially Louis Cullen and Christopher Smout. The plan for a collective comparison of Scotland and Ireland originated with them; and it was they who first determined to execute it.

Rosalind Mitchison and Peter Roebuck
Edinburgh and Coleraine

MEMBERS OF THE CONFERENCE

BARNARD, Dr. T. C.	Hertford College, Oxford.
BARTLETT, Dr. T.	Dept. of Modern History, University College, Galway.
BROWNE, Mr. B. N.	Dept. of Economic & Social History, Queen's University, Belfast.
CLARKSON, Prof. L. A.	Dept. of Economic & Social History, Queen's University, Belfast.
COLLINS, Mrs. B.	Institute of Irish Studies, Queen's University, Belfast.
CONNOLLY, Dr. S. J.	Dept. of History, University of Ulster.
CRAWFORD, Dr. M.	Dept. of Economic & Social History, Queen's University, Belfast.
CRAWFORD, Dr. W. H.	Ulster Folk and Transport Museum, Cultra.
CULLEN, Prof. L. M.	Dept. of Modern History, Trinity College, Dublin.
DALY, Dr. M. E.	Dept. of Modern Irish History, University College, Dublin.
DEVINE, Dr. T. M.	Dept. of History, University of Strathclyde.
DICKSON, Dr. D. J.	Dept. of Modern History, Trinity College, Dublin.
DODGSHON, Dr. R. A.	Dept. of Geography, University College, Aberystwyth.
DURIE, Dr. A.	Dept. of Economic History, University of Aberdeen.
GIBSON, Mr. A.	Dept. of Scottish History, University of St. Andrews.
GILLESPIE, Dr. R.	Dept. of Finance, Dublin.
HARVIE, Prof. C.	Dept. of British Studies, University of Tübingen, F.D.R.
HONDA, Prof. S.	Dept. of Economic History, Osaka University of Economics, Japan.
HOUSTON, Dr. R.	Dept. of Modern History, University of St. Andrews.
JOHNSON, Mr. D. S.	Dept. of Economic & Social History, Queen's University, Belfast.
KIRKHAM, Mr. G. E.	Dept. of History, University of Ulster.
LEE, Prof. J. J.	Dept. of Modern History, University College, Cork.
MACINNES, Dr. A.	Dept. of Scottish History, University of Glasgow.
MANNING, Prof. B. S.	Dean, Faculty of Humanities, University of Ulster.
MITCHISON, Prof. R. M.	Dept. of Economic & Social History, University of Edinburgh.
MOSS, Dr. M.	The Archives, University of Glasgow.
MUNN, Dr. C. W.	Dept. of Economic & Social History, University of Glasgow.
O'BRIEN, Dr. G.	Dept. of History, University of Ulster.
O'DOWD, Dr. M.	Dept. of Modern History, Queen's University, Belfast.
OLLERENSHAW, Dr. P. G.	Dept. of History, University of Ulster.
POLLOCK, Miss V. L.	Dept. of History, University of Ulster.
RICHARDS, Prof. E.	History Discipline, Flinders University, Australia.
ROEBUCK, Prof. P.	Dept. of History, University of Ulster.
SMOUT, Prof. T. C.	Dept. of Scottish History, Univerity of St. Andrews.
SOLAR, Dr. P.	University of Louvain, Belgium.
STEVENSON, Dr. D.	Dept. of History, University of Aberdeen.
TYSON, Dr. R. E.	Dept. of Economic History, University of Aberdeen.
WALKER, Dr. G.	Dept. of History, University of Strathclyde.
WEIR, Dr. R. B.	Dept. of Economics, University of York.
WHYTE, Dr. I. D.	Dept. of Geography, University of Lancaster.
WOODWARD, Dr. D.	Dept. of Economic & Social History, University of Hull.

CONTENTS

LIST OF ABBREVIATIONS

Anal. Hib.	*Analecta Hibernica*
A.P.S.	*Acts of the Parliaments of Scotland*
B.L.	British Library
C.S.P.I.	*Calendar of State Papers, Ireland*
Cullen & Smout	L. M. Cullen and T. C. Smout (eds.), *Comparative Aspects of Scottish and Irish Economic and Social History, 1600–1900* (Edinburgh, 1978)
Devine & Dickson	T. M. Devine and David Dickson (eds.), *Ireland and Scotland, 1600–1850: Parallels and Contrasts in Economic and Social Development* (Edinburgh, 1983)
Ec.H.R.	*Economic History Review*
I.H.S.	*Irish Historical Studies*
I.M.C.	*Irish Manuscripts Commission*
Ir. Ec. & Soc. Hist.	*Irish Economic and Social History*
N.L.I.	National Library of Ireland
N.L.S.	National Library of Scotland
N.S.A.	*New Statistical Account of Scotland*
O.S.A.	*Statistical Account of Scotland* or *Old Statistical Account*
P.P.	Parliamentary Papers
P.R.O.	Public Record Office, London
P.R.O.I.	Public Record Office of Ireland, Dublin
P.R.O.N.I.	Public Record Office of Northern Ireland, Belfast
R.P.C.S.	*Register of the Privy Council of Scotland*
Sc. Ec. & Soc. Hist.	*Scottish Economic and Social History*
S.H.R.	*Scottish Historical Review*
S.R.O.	Scottish Record Office

INTRODUCTION

Rosalind Mitchison and Peter Roebuck

In resuming the search for 'the roots of the visibly different nineteenth-century economies and social structures'[1] of Scotland and Ireland, it seemed appropriate to begin in the rural world of the sixteenth and seventeenth centuries. During this earlier period there were striking similarities in the institutions and cultures of the Scottish Highlands and much of Ireland. In particular the conventions and powers of the system of lordship provided a common framework for much contemporary economic activity. Thus, the conference proceedings commenced with an examination of lordship and its significance in both societies, via papers which approached the subject from complementary points of view: the first was primarily concerned with the evolution of the system and the second with its character and mode of operation. Both contributors stressed the force of continuity and the protracted nature of change.

Lordship, it was argued, was far more resilient and adaptable in the face of changing economic circumstances than was often supposed. In difficult times, for instance, lordly hospitality was readily switched from feasting to the support of the lord's followers. At least for men of fighting age or personal prestige, such flexibility mitigated the absence of a formal system of social welfare and acted as a powerful preservative of tradition. Nor was lordship automatically more vulnerable in areas, like Ireland, which were subject to invasion and colonisation. Throughout the sixteenth century English intentions in Ireland were progressively watered down in practice. Many features of lordship were both familiar and acceptable to Englishmen, and it often proved sensible to utilise and, indeed, to strengthen the system. Nevertheless, in both Ireland and the Scottish Highlands the persistent endeavours of government to reduce the incidence of war, or at least to contain it, had important implications for the old order. Henceforward the life-style of the chiefs was increasingly dependent on the extent of their purchasing power: accordingly they became intent on monetisation and on gaining access to the market. One should not, however, regard the use of money and of money terms as a sure sign of monetisation; nor was monetisation more or less synonymous with modernisation. Historical reality was far more complex than that. In Scotland in 1500 there was already a cash component in some rents 'even in the most isolated islands';[2] yet grain rents survived in the Lowlands till beyond 1700 and there were 'many instances of reversion to victual rents as a means of coping with inflation'[3] in the later decades of the eighteenth century. It was also acknowledged that the sheer size of the areas under consideration posed difficulties of interpretation, for they clearly encapsulated substantial regional and local variations.

Much of the discussion focused on the nature and pace of the process whereby the traditional system was superseded. Lordship, it was suggested, was more vulnerable from above than from below; feasting and generosity waned because, under pressure from external market forces, chiefs gradually adapted to a new system and found 'something better to do with their money'.[4] However, even after a change in economic conditions or activities, social attitudes and relationships might continue. Personal status and connection to a lord were valued items, neither lightly surrendered nor easily eroded. Monetisation of rent in response to lordly pressure might force tenants into contact with external markets so that by the sale of produce or other goods they could acquire cash, but their relationship to their lord could continue in many other ways unchanged. It was at this point, as well as later in discussing the nature of eighteenth-century society, that participants stressed the enduring strength of deference as a social cement.[5]

It was generally agreed that the old system broke down more slowly in the Highlands, which were less fertile and where a pre-market economy persisted for much longer. Gaelic Ireland on the other hand was well-endowed economically and had a market network: it was therefore more vulnerable to the activities of immigrants, adept at exploitation and quite ready in pursuit of profits to sub-let extensively to their fellows.[6] A further key difference between the two areas derived from their relationship to government. In its bid to subdue and 'civilise' Ireland the English Crown exerted much greater pressure on Irish society than either the King or his Privy Council in Scotland brought to bear in the Highlands. The situation in Scotland did alter perceptibly when James VI removed to England: the policy of the Statutes of Iona was one of cultural invasion and was not without effect. Nevertheless, it was only after the '45 that government entirely ceased to tolerate lordly power in the Highlands, and only then that a money economy finally became dominant there, whereas in Ireland the English government pursued explicitly colonial processes from a very early date and with growing success.

Meanwhile, as further papers demonstrated, lordship was everywhere weakened by the Great Rebellion and its aftermath. In Scotland there was the traumatic effect of the military disasters of the 1640s and the ensuing defeat by Cromwell, before which the Scots (in sharp contrast to the English) had never been conquered. Parts of the Highlands suffered extensive physical devastation with the result that the position of many Highland chiefs was subsequently undermined by absenteeism, conspicuous expenditure and crippling debt. Contemporary conditions in Ulster were generally fissiparous, with war, population movement, unpaid rents and heavy taxation combining to produce almost two decades of profound uncertainty. In contrast to this there was considerable continuity in other parts of Ireland, especially in Munster, and by the 1650s Dublin was positively benefiting from the turn of public events. On the other hand the southern provinces were more seriously affected by the Cromwellian land revolution.[7] All these developments eroded traditional structures and values, increased the pace of change, and heightened the power of commercialism.

Much of the discussion was taken up with the evidence which these papers provided, not of negative responses and reactions, but of positive, longer-term developments. Among the latter perhaps the most obvious was the significant increase in the power and influence of central government. Major emphasis was placed on the contribution of the Covenanters who, though in power for only a very short period, rapidly extended central authority, not least in the form of taxation; even local government was tighter on account of the obtrusive behaviour of the presbyteries. In Ireland the revolution appears to have accelerated the demise of the great provincial power blocks, so that following the Restoration Ormond was able to succeed where, in the 1630s, Wentworth had failed. In the interim, significantly, it proved easier to attract people across the Irish Sea. The plantations of the late sixteenth and early seventeenth centuries, officially planned and sponsored and limited in their success, were followed from the late 1640s by spontaneous and more substantial immigration. The fact that the activities of some of these immigrants — for example, the fine weavers from the North of England who settled in the Lagan Valley — proved to be of strategic economic significance was judged to be less important than the impact of the flow overall, which was by no means confined to the northern counties of Ireland. Other developments in Scotland were individually less striking though no doubt cumulative in their effect. In the Highlands chiefly indebtedness prompted some rationalisation of estate management and, in the most serious cases, was alleviated only by the alienation of property to subordinate clan gentry. In the Lowlands various factors progressively weakened the traditional non-economic links between landlords and tenants and, in so doing, may have left both parties free to adopt a more commercial approach to their future relations. Viewed as a whole, the legislative activities of the Covenanters suggest a major shift in attitudes to economic development at an earlier date than we have hitherto supposed.

The remaining papers in Part I were less concerned with attitudes than with performance. Earlier research by Ian and Kathy Whyte had revealed the remarkable extent and stratification of the rural labour force in the seventeenth-century Lowlands.[8] At this conference, on the basis of testamentary evidence from the Panmure estate in Angus, they demonstrated that there was also considerable wealth among some sections of the farming community, and that that wealth was circulated to general advantage. Most will-makers borrowed from other members of the rural community: there was almost no borrowing from nobility, gentry or clergy, and only in the case of the most substantial tenants was credit obtained from the burghs; lending by peasants to burgh dwellers was similarly unimportant. The upper classes, however, were net debtors of their rural subordinates, with at least 35 per cent of all lent capital going to them. It was recognised in discussion that the testamentary material under consideration represented only a very narrow band of evidence, though the Irish contingent expressed envy that even so much had survived; also, the area to which it related could not be regarded as typical — the estate was exceptionally well-managed; it contained very valuable salmon fisheries; and it exported grain through Montrose. Nevertheless, taken in conjunction with other research, these findings clearly lent further support to the view that there was significant agricultural development in the seventeenth-century Lowlands, and that where it occurred change was not merely landlord-led. Proprietors provided the bulk of long-term capital but in the short term tenant farmers could, and did, participate in financing improvement.

Matters were very different in the north of Ireland. In what was virtually a frontier economy tenants with sufficient wherewithal were in short supply and had to be attracted by lease terms which were so generous as to deprive proprietors of close involvement in, and effective control over, the management of their property. In addition the owners of even the largest estates were themselves chronically short of capital. The economic and social conditions responsible for this situation were slow to improve. Ulster remained lowly populated till the turn of the seventeenth century and was plagued by harvest crises for several decades thereafter. Although landowners gradually became both wealthier and more directly engaged with their property after 1750, a deeply entrenched tenurial system was not easily dismantled and much proceeded unreformed into the nineteenth century. In Ulster and, indeed, elsewhere in Ireland the tendency to excessive subdivision was rooted, along with many other agrarian problems, in the landlord-tenant relations of a much earlier age.

Thus, the relatively rapid erosion of the traditional system did not necessarily promote the appearance of a stable and viable alternative. It was this consideration which finally provoked the revision of one conclusion of the Dublin conference of 1976: 'that Ireland seemed to hold more promise of a bright economic future than Scotland at the opening of the eighteenth century'.[9] The faster pace of social change in Ireland was not in dispute; nor the fact that Ireland fed her population better than Scotland in the seventeenth century. Indeed, it was precisely this contrast which was thought to offer a valuable clue to the nature of events. In reality, it was felt, the steadier rate of change in Scotland generated greater future potential because the process of development there was essentially organic. In spite of the variety of the ethnic origins of her people Scotland seems to have been a more homogeneous society than Ireland. Differences in rank and culture did not override similarities in attitude and motivation. Particularly in the Lowlands commercialism was spread primarily by internal forces and slowly permeated the entire economic and social fabric: this was an important element in the ease with which the Scottish labour force adjusted to the needs of new types of farming.[10] In Ireland on the other hand external factors were paramount: largely imposed from above, the new order, though superficially more impressive, was much less securely based.

Much of the conference, inevitably, was concerned with the period and manner in which the Scottish and Irish economies significantly diverged, and a number of issues raised at previous conferences re-emerged. One such was the question of relative poverty and backwardness. Before the eighteenth century economic insecurity in both countries was particularly marked in thinly populated, peripheral areas. In the north-west of Ireland, for example, the difficulties encountered by both landowners and farmers produced an acute shortage of capital until at least the 1750s. Fortunately, the expansion of domestic industry did not require much capital. The spinning of linen yarn reduced the risks involved in farming in a poorly endowed environment and customs records reveal a close connection between peaks of yarn exports and troughs of agricultural distress. Yet the critical question is not what allowed poor farmers to subsist before the mid-eighteenth century but why they multiplied so rapidly thereafter. In this connection Graeme Kirkham took one of the discussions at the Strathclyde conference a stage further by exploring peasant attitudes to economic development.[11] Domestic industry promoted subdivision by significantly relaxing constraints which would have applied more tightly in a purely agricultural economy: but a powerful additional factor was the manner in which farming families strove to retain their holdings within the lineage, even at the cost of progressive fragmentation and a reduction in income. 'Without further evidence on the size and composition of the domestic productive group' not everyone was persuaded of the existence of this 'sort of Chayanovian peasantry'; nor was there much possibility of comparison with Scotland, for the subject of proto-industrialisation 'seems to have passed by Scottish historians'.[12] Nevertheless, the paper suggested further parallels between the Irish periphery and the Scottish Highlands: both witnessed the growth of a destructive tension between economic requirements and concepts of family tenure, whereas in the Lowlands and in much of east-central Ireland tenurial change generally facilitated agricultural improvement.

Comparison of the relative levels of real wages in the two economies provided a further and more dramatic sequel to the Strathclyde conference. Here the application of complex methodology to previously unused data enabled the subject to be moved from the realm of impressions to that of calculation. Though far from definitive, the results of this fresh research tend to confirm the faster pace of economic change in Ireland down to the mid-eighteenth century, as well as the greater homogeneity of contemporary society in Scotland. They also strongly corroborate the view that Ireland was beset by crippling structural disadvantages and that the two economies diverged decisively during the later decades of the eighteenth century. By the turn of the century the gap had become marked. The Scottish economy was far stronger in terms of the skills it had nurtured. Ireland, already possessing a larger zone of poverty, did not benefit on the scale that Scotland did from the changes in organisation which promoted the early stages of the industrial revolution. Nor, of course, did the Scottish Highlands. Indeed, the buoyant tone of the reports from Lowland parishes in the *Statistical Account* is in sharp contrast to the note struck again and again in the Highland reports. From the 1790s and possibly somewhat earlier the greater part of Ireland, and in population terms the lesser part of Scotland, became amongst the most poverty-stricken areas of the British Isles.

This led on to a consideration of the relations between different social strata: it is now accepted that for much of the eighteenth century these were not more divided and antagonistic in Ireland than in Scotland. Yet somehow, throughout the century and even more conspicuously later, Ireland had a reputation for illegality and violence. The conference had a lively discussion of how this came about. English observers, it was suggested, had to find some explanation for the failure of evangelisation and anglicisation.[13] They took for granted forms of protest and disturbance which existed in England — food riots and opposition to excise or to enclosure, for instance, which had developed as partly ritualised and symbolic demonstrations over particular aspects of property rights and power. Violence in Ireland, however, contained distinctly atavistic elements and provoked fears of the kind of order, and disorder, which were thought to have existed in a much earlier age. Similar types of activity were also found in the Scottish Highlands before the drastic suppression of the '45, and were commonly regarded as politically menacing. A further source of apprehension was the ineffectiveness of the machinery of law enforcement and criminal justice in Ireland. Although broadly similar in nature to that in England, this was subject to much greater corruption and malpractice, while the proliferation of capital statutes made juries extremely reluctant to convict. Together with the insistence of the courts on strict legal procedure, these factors produced a very low incidence of capital sentences and executions and a very high rate of acquittal. Ireland was generally regarded as unsafe long before the British government judged it to be a threat to national security.

Westminster was also nervous of unrest in Scotland but with less justification. In the Lowlands, and in the Highlands too once they had become fully open to Lowland penetration, there were strong and interlinked elements which made for a tight system of control. Scotland benefited from a relatively uniform religious adherence, at least in terms of dogma and organisation, and control was exercised through the Church and its courts as well as through the organs of civil government. These instruments were backed by the considerable authority of a relatively small class of landowners: in comparison with any other area undergoing such change, the lack of resistance to the process of agricultural re-organisation in Lowland Scotland is striking. Some groups within the British establishment believed that Scotland as a whole was a security risk in 1745, a view which might more appropriately have been applied to 1725, the year of widespread opposition to changes in the malt tax; but the rapid acceptance of law and order in the Highlands in the second half of the century, which even opened the area to tourism, effectively destroyed this illusion.

Beyond the mid-eighteenth century the growing frequency of collective protest in Ireland caused mounting concern to the political establishment, partly for reasons which had originally promoted the conquest of the country. It was a large area, with elements of a system of local authority and leadership which had ceased to exist in England. The very presence of the Irish Parliament created greater scope for factions and divisions. The contentious issue of Catholic relief was in the air in every decade from the 1750s, and before long Irish disaffection and the threat of invasion became closely associated in the public consciousness in Britain.[14] Furthermore, political expression in Ireland was not confined, as it was in Scotland, to an artificially small and manipulable segment of society. The rapid expansion of the Irish population, and more especially the large size of the Irish popular vote, generated acute political nervousness which, in conjunction with other factors, led to a sharp change of policy. In the 1790s the authorities were understandably fearful that radical groups might, as they had in France, set up a network of organisations outwith the official system. In Scotland radicalism was narrowly based and easily stamped on: few serious disturbances occurred after 1794 except in the form of militia riots.[15] Ireland on the other hand saw the nationalist movement of 1798: but even before then both Dublin Castle and local magistrates abandoned impartiality and began using the law differentially and repressively. Poverty was increasingly complemented by alienation.

The papers which followed demonstrated the inadequacies of the institutional response to the problem of poverty. In Scotland these stemmed in large measure from the manner in which the legal system allowed statute law to be overridden by customary practice, which then gained the authority of law. In Ireland they were partly a result of the diversity of religious organisation, which diminished the voluntary pool of funds for relief; and partly a consequence of the meagre statutory basis for shifting resources to the poor. In discussion it was stressed that poor relief consisted of specific responses to changing concepts of poverty. Both the general incidence of relief and its particular manifestations reflected shifts in the capacity of different groups of contemporaries to recognise poverty for what it was. Indeed, for long it was the effects of poverty rather than its existence which stimulated preventive or remedial action. In Scotland, for example, central government responded negatively to famine in the late sixteenth century and belatedly and incompetently in the early seventeenth century. Urban government, however, was more sensitive to the destitution which arose from harvest failure and associated unemployment, not so much from recognition of poverty as such as of the possible disorder to which it might give rise. Very gradually general awareness was heightened and in practice, until the end of the eighteenth century, the working of the almost entirely voluntary relief system in Ireland was very similar to that of the nominally statute-based one in Scotland. Pauperism was one of the economic weaknesses that the two areas had in common and their respective upper classes adopted a coherent approach to its alleviation.

Indeed, pauperism involved not only poverty but also the concept of a need for intervention. The papers reveal that similar problems arose in getting a poor law to work in the two countries, and that it was particularly difficult to make any poor law effective in regions such as the west of Ireland or the Scottish Highlands where poverty was the social norm. Although there was a firmer statutory base for relief in Scotland which enabled its poor law to provide a better safety net, this did not invest the labouring population with a right to relief. Nevertheless, the stress in crisis years — and these years were different in the two countries — rendered the Irish system, such as it was, more liable to submergence under the weight of vagrancy and a permanently mendicant sub-culture. Moreover — and this harked back to points made earlier — the Irish Poor Law (established by the Act of 1838) was imposed from outside the country and was fashioned by outside interests. Along with other features of public affairs after 1790, it revealed the forces of the central government as directive and as hostile to local solutions. In this case too the hand of power had become lighter in Scotland.

As people became poorer it was quite possible for their food supply to increase and to improve in quality. In Scotland and above all in Ireland the instrument of this paradox was the potato, whose dominance is clearly exhibited in the dietary maps which accompany the paper by Clarkson and Crawford. In terms of any form of measurable income Irish peasants and labourers were very poor. They liked the potato and were right to do so: its yield was abundant, it could be consumed in large quantities, and nutritionally it was better-endowed than almost any other item of mass consumption. Nevertheless, the choice of the potato as a dietary mainstay by one generation effectively restricted the economic choice of later generations. At a time of considerable economic change, when many factors of production (particularly labour) were insufficiently mobile, the potato allowed, perhaps encouraged, peasants and labourers to remain where they were, for at least they enjoyed an adequate diet. In the long run, however, the use of the potato as the basic food resource came to be closely associated with another element of poverty, vulnerability to disaster. Of course all working families in the eighteenth and early nineteenth centuries were vulnerable to features of life — accident, injury, sickness, bereavement — which brought a fairly steady proportion of them to rely on relief. But the vulnerability of populations dependent on the potato was peculiar: they risked the general famines which had long ceased to threaten societies elsewhere.

Another paradox to be considered was that for some sections of populations the risk of destitution grew in severity and extent precisely because economies as a whole experienced rapid growth. Industrialisation had centripetal tendencies and specialisation in one region meant de-industrialisation elsewhere. Thus, although no effective industrial base was ever established in the Scottish Highlands, activity in the kelp, cattle, fishing, linen and woollen industries was heightened by the interregional demands of the late eighteenth century. By the 1820s, however, all but the last had lost their impetus as industrialisation in the south had altered factor rewards on the periphery — where, meanwhile, population had become congested. The failure of the domestic textile industry in the west of the country was similarly implicated in the disaster which struck Ireland in the 1840s. The problems of regional imbalance and failure stemmed partly from natural and long-standing disadvantages in geography, resources and facilities for communication. Evidence of the excess of unskilled labour and the shortage of skills in Ireland, particularly in the rural areas, suggests that economic development there, though capable of creating export surpluses, had always been relatively narrowly based. In some regions in the nineteenth century that base was further eroded as peasant manufacturing declined and imports undermined demand for local products. Yet purely economic considerations, such as relative ease of access to markets and factors relating to the scale of operations, were not the only sources of poverty. Businessmen had views about the quality of labour and about the long-term prospects of investment. Then as now, money was a highly mobile resource, and its availability depended in part at least on opinion as well as on established fact. In the main capital went where skills and markets could be found, and its vagaries pushed some vulnerable areas beyond nil growth into actual decline. Not only did development sometimes result in the growth of population rather than of incomes: not infrequently it also raised costs which were borne outside those regions which developed.[16]

Turning to more modern developments the conference noted firstly that there was a growing interrelationship between the two economies during the course of the nineteenth century, and secondly, that after the first world war the divergent political experiences of the two countries meant that economic trends and their periodisation differed considerably for some forty years. While the nineteenth-century relationship was based primarily on close physical proximity, it was undoubtedly facilitated by political union from 1800 and strengthened by the strong flow of migratory labour from Ireland to Scotland in the middle decades of the century. The number of interconnections also increased as a result of the emergence of Glasgow and Belfast alongside Liverpool as the major ports in the Irish Sea area, though the process was by no means confined to finance, trade and commerce, and shipbuilding. Many of the agents and surveyors who grappled with Irish agrarian problems in the period after 1815 were of Scottish origin. And as Collins and Pollock show here, there were extensive connections between the sewing industries of the two countries in the early nineteenth century; and over a much longer period there developed a particularly close relationship between the Scottish and Irish fishing industries, which shared grounds, harbours, boats, techniques and personnel.

Nevertheless, connection did not mean convergence. In fact in terms of performance some of the economic activities which Scotland and Ireland had in common diverged just as radically as did the two economies as a whole. In sewing, for example, the link with the decline in cotton spinning was weaker, and the numbers involved very much greater, in Ireland. Whereas earnings from sewing provided a useful supplement to rural incomes in Scotland, they constituted a significant hedge against privation in Ireland. Above all, while the Scottish industry declined rapidly from the 1860s, Irish skills were quickly diverted to work on domestic linens and in shirt-making. The linen industry provides another case in point. In the 1780s linen manufacture, though greater in volume and value in Ireland, was in both countries widely dispersed, extremely varied in its product mix, and oriented towards export markets. However, subsequent developments were so different that the two branches of the industry were more complementary than competitive in the 1860s. Both had become more spatially concentrated, in Angus and in east Ulster respectively: but the Scottish industry was much more mechanised and urbanised, and used more full-time labour, than the Irish; the former depended on imported flax while the latter continued to grow most of its own; and one produced largely coarse and the other largely fine linens.

By and large the papers in this section of the conference worked from the supply side of the activities with which they were concerned although, clearly, markets were neither static nor passive. The development of an international taste for herring had a dramatic effect on the viability of the fishing industry; the growth of social groups anxious to display cleanliness and conventionality produced a rapid expansion in exports of shirts and collars; and demand for linen goods fell sharply only after the first world war. This methodological imbalance provoked a discussion of major areas of ignorance in our understanding of nineteenth- and early twentieth-century business history. Many firms were dominated by powerful individuals who did not (and often had no need to) consult others, and who kept no record of their decisions or of the reasons which underlay them. Not infrequently, therefore, major industrial units cannot be examined with any rigour. There is also a spatial aspect to this elusiveness. Belfast, Glasgow and Liverpool not only had close links with each other but were part of a complex international network which stretched from Montreal to Calcutta. Thus, domestic developments were influenced by widely-dispersed events as well as by obscure personal or family concerns. At the other extreme were activities involving very large numbers of poor people and an exceedingly diffuse pattern of control. In these cases, shirtmaking being a prime example, business records of all types are (and were) extremely rare, if only because much of the labour was employed on a part-time, intermittent or seasonal basis. At times sheer complexity militated against record-keeping: fishing commonly involved different activities with different equipment aimed at different markets at different periods of the year.

And yet the production and marketing of goods in both the sewing and the fishing industries necessarily involved large-scale capital enterprise. At some stage or other of most activities the methods by which capital became available were of critical importance. Munn and Ollerenshaw argued persuasively that the banks played a far more dynamic role in this connection than has hitherto been supposed. In the first place banks did not restrict themselves to supplying short-term funds:[17] credit lines operated much like modern overdrafts and were a long-term facility available at short-term rates. Furthermore, despite their deliberately cultivated conservative image, they were flexible and imaginative in their operations, not only responding to need but attempting to anticipate it too. They gathered information systematically; many of their senior employees were involved in industry; they took a good spread of business from all sectors of the economy; they were alive to the effects of seasonal fluctuations in economic activity; and they dealt with new and developing as well as with old-established companies. While there was little change until the 1960s in the normal services offered by banks, there was very considerable development in the adaptation of those services. It is perhaps surprising, given this flexibility, that so many firms came to use accounts with other producers rather than those with their banks. It was also suggested that the lack of new entrants to the banking system allowed complacency, if it did not positively generate it: freedom of entry for new banks virtually ceased in Scotland with the Bank Act of 1845, and by 1914 the market structure of banking in both countries was effectively oligopolistic.[18] The contention in response was that the rapid expansion of branch networks in the later nineteenth century more than compensated for this — as well, incidentally, as being responsible for the diffusion of insurance services throughout the countryside.[19] All this amounted, it was agreed, to a complete reversal of previous views on the role of banking in late nineteenth-century economic development:

but as bank records are also almost exclusively concerned with supply, this too requires confirmation on the demand side.

The main theme underlying discussion of the inter-war period was the relative slowness on both sides of the Irish Sea to enlarge the role of the state in areas which previously had been left to private enterprise. Following partition, the government of the Irish Free State was fully autonomous, whereas policies for both Scotland and Northern Ireland were determined at Westminster. However, particularly in the 1920s, forms of government counted for much less than basic economic realities, and in all three areas the possibility of new policy initiatives was smothered by the weight of economic conservatism. Eventually both the Irish Free State and the United Kingdom used protection as a cure for economic ills, though to markedly differing degrees and in very different ways. Without the six northern counties the Free State was a largely unindustrialised political unit, with only 13.3 per cent of its workforce in the industrial sector in the mid-1920s. It was primarily for this reason that the Fianna Fail government, elected in 1932, espoused protection with such enthusiasm: and indeed its policies produced a significant increase in the number of jobs available in manufacturing industry, albeit at a heavy cost both to the taxpayer and to the consumer. In contrast the tariff system adopted in Britain was more diffuse and was pitched at a lower level. In Scotland and Northern Ireland selective protectionism appealed to neither businessmen nor labour: in view of the orientation of the main industries towards exports, it was irrelevant. And in any case economic issues were rarely considered by the Cabinet in terms of specific regional or local needs: the sole exception to this in Scotland, it was suggested, was the promotion of hydro-electric power.[20] There was sharp disagreement with the contention that a much more vigorous set of promotional and lobbying groups emerged in the Free State than in Scotland. There was, apparently, a huge polemical and planning literature in Scotland,[21] although clearly it had little effect.

While Scotland and Northern Ireland suffered from similar economic problems — much heavy industry was derelict and there was an urgent need for diversification — the political and religious stresses of the day led to the development of very different types of organisation and leadership amongst their workers. The removal of the Irish issue from Scottish politics enabled Labour to draw on both Protestants and Catholics to man its machine, whereas in Northern Ireland partition stunted the growth of class-based politics. Some similarity in religious structures can be detected in the fact that in both Scotland and Northern Ireland (and also in the Free State) there were denominationally distinct birth rates. A critical distinction, however, was that Ulster Protestantism retained an evangelical fervour which prevented the British labour movement from winning the loyalty of the Northern Irish workforce: the general strike of 1926 had a very limited impact in Northern Ireland compared to its long-term effect on political allegiance in Scotland.[22] Nonetheless, despite considerable and varied talents, the Clydeside labour group never exerted more than a limited and ultimately ineffectual influence on the thinking of the Labour Party as a whole. In economic matters it held to an old-fashioned liberalism with a free trade philosophy and thus had little to offer as a solution to the high unemployment of the 1930s. In Scotland it was not just government but also the leaders of labour who thought primarily in national rather than in local or regional terms, and who held the dead hand of economic orthodoxy.

In these circumstances it is scarcely surprising that there was also a failure to develop adequate systems in all regions for the administration of health and welfare. The new Northern Ireland government, for example, operated under clear financial constraints. The decision to maintain parity with the rest of the United Kingdom in some respects left it with little money and less will to achieve parity in others. Health services were fragmentary in provision, cumbersome in structure, and lacking in co-ordination and direction. Medical facilities remained generally unimproved and standards of hygiene (and in particular of ante- and post-natal care) were poor. Consequently, whereas infant mortality rates had declined more rapidly in the north of Ireland than in Britain before the first world war, thereafter Northern Ireland's relative position deteriorated. Earlier trends were re-established only after the onset of another war, which in turn brought with it greater central control.

At that point too a much more fundamental process got underway in Ireland. Hitherto, despite partition, there had been, at least in terms of living standards, one economic nation: per capita incomes in both parts of the country increased by between 13 and 17 per cent during the inter-war period. Beyond 1939, however, the differential impact of war produced considerable divergence: within a decade average per capita income in Northern Ireland was almost 75 per cent higher than in the Republic, and was much closer to the average for the United Kingdom as a whole than had ever previously been the case.[23] Irish neutrality in the war allowed the policies of the 1930s to be pursued for a further two decades. Only when those policies had demonstrably failed and the Whitaker Report of 1958 had mapped out a series of alternatives was a more convergent pattern of economic development resumed.

NOTES

1. Devine & Dickson, p. 261.

2. A comment by Robert Dodgshon during discussion of his own and Mary O'Dowd's papers. As at the last conference, verbal (and often unscripted) comments made by participants and cited here are reproduced from tapes made of the proceedings: these are temporarily deposited in the Film and Sound Resource Unit, Faculty of Humanities, University of Ulster at Coleraine.

3. Eric Richards on the paper by Robert Dodgshon.

4. Sean Connolly on the papers by Mary O'Dowd and Robert Dodgshon.

5. A point emphasised by Sean Connolly, both in discussion and below, p. 123.

6. Raymond Gillespie on Mary O'Dowd's paper. On the other hand the argument that Catholic landowners were less commercially minded than the new Protestant proprietors who replaced them has been challenged in L. M. Cullen, *The Emergence of Modern Ireland, 1600–1900* (Dublin, 1983), pp. 115–120, 124–128.

7. For P. J. Corish's map of the Cromwellian land-confiscation which illustrates this point, see T. W. Moody, F. X. Martin & F. J. Byrne, eds., *A New History of Ireland*, III, *Early Modern Ireland 1534–1691*, p. 358. For a recent debate concerning provincial differences in mid-seventeenth-century Ireland, see N. P. Canny, 'Migration and Opportunity: Britain, Ireland and the New World', *Ir. Ec. & Soc. Hist.* XII (1985), pp. 7–32; R. Gillespie, 'Migration and Opportunity: A Comment' and N. P. Canny, 'A Reply', *Ir. Ec. & Soc. Hist.* XIII (1986), pp. 90–100.

8. Devine & Dickson, pp. 32–45.

9. Cullen & Smout, p. 4.

10. On this point see in particular T. M. Devine, 'Scottish Farm Service in the Agricultural Revolution', in Devine, ed., *Farm Servants and Labour in Lowland Scotland 1780–1914* (Edinburgh, 1984).

11. See Devine & Dickson, p. 264.

12. Rab Houston on Graeme Kirkham's paper.

13. Tom Bartlett on the papers by Sean Connolly and Tom Devine. The excellence of this particular discussion stemmed primarily from Dr. Bartlett's contribution as discussant.

14. Louis Cullen on the papers by Sean Connolly and Tom Devine.

15. Although the riots themselves were handled in a traditional manner, subsequent court action suggests that they had in fact provoked very considerable unease.

16. Points emphasised in general discussion by Christopher Smout and David Dickson respectively.

17. However, Mary Daly's paper suggests that this policy may not have persisted into the inter-war period: see below, pp. 288–89.

18. Ron Weir on the papers by Charles Munn and Philip Ollerenshaw.

19. Philip Ollerenshaw pointed out that bank managers frequently acted as agents for insurance companies.

20. A point made by Ron Weir.

21. According to Christopher Harvie.

22. A point emphasised by Christopher Harvie, who acted as discussant in the session which dealt with the papers on the inter-war period.

23. D. S. Johnson, *The Inter War Economy in Ireland*, Studies in Irish Economic and Social History, no.4 (Dundalk, 1985), p. 43.

Part One:

Land, Lordship and the Market Economy

1

LAND AND LORDSHIP IN SIXTEENTH- AND EARLY SEVENTEENTH-CENTURY IRELAND

Mary O'Dowd

One of the main aims of the Tudor governments in Ireland was to modify and ultimately abolish the power of all forms of lordship in Ireland. Many historians would argue that they gradually achieved that aim in the course of the sixteenth century: the departure of the northern earls in 1607 is often depicted as marking the end of Gaelic lordly power. It is the purpose of this paper to examine the main characteristics of lordship in early modern Ireland and to suggest that the replacement of Irish lordships with English forms of government was a much longer process than has been assumed. Lords and lordship remained an important part of government in Ireland down at least to 1641, if not beyond.

One of the principal ways in which Irish lords exerted their power and influence was through the collection of tribute and the imposition of exactions and duties on the inhabitants of the territories within their sphere of influence. These varied from one lord to another but included military service on the lord's behalf, the provision of food and lodging for the lord's mercenary troops for a certain number of days in the year, and labour service on the lord's lands as well as the rendering of agricultural produce to the lord. In the course of the sixteenth century lordly tributes were transformed or commuted into fixed land rents but this did not lead to a general change from payment of rent in kind to payment of rent in cash. A low tenant population meant that labour service was often more valuable to a landlord than cash. For the same reason, receipt of rent in the form of agricultural produce which could be used to feed the landlord and his retainers continued until 1641 to be attractive to new and old landlords. The concept may have changed but the form remained the same.

The main factor which distinguished large Irish lordships from smaller lordships was the ability of the greater lordships to claim the right of overlord over smaller neighbouring lordships. It was the means by which a lord could extend his control and influence. The claim of overlordship manifested itself in several ways. An overlord might demand exactions which were similar to those which a lord received within his own lordship. The overlord might try also to interfere in the political structure of the subordinate territory by imposing his choice as lord (although in many cases the overlord did not interfere) or sometimes he acquired a certain portion of land in the lordships under his control.

The power of some of the largest overlords such as the earl of Desmond, MacCarthy Mor and O'Neill was undermined by the Tudor and Stuart governments in the early modern period, mainly by detaching the subordinate lords from the overlord and encouraging them to make agreements with the crown by which they held their land directly of the crown and not of the overlord. Such agreements were often entered into willingly by the sublords who saw in the crown a potential defender and protector against the impositions of the overlords. English government policy did not, however, destroy the power of all the great lords in Ireland nor did it intend to do so. If a lord succeeded in proving his loyalty to the crown, he might be trusted and in fact have his powers increased. Thus both the earls of Thomond and Clanricard (i.e. the lords of the O'Briens and of the MacWilliam Burke) had their authority enhanced by government policy, a situation recognised at the end of the Tudor regime when they were respectively appointed presidents of Munster and Connacht and entrusted with the administration of the provinces by the central government. Both earls had proved their loyalty as had the earl of Ormond who, uniquely in Ireland, was allowed to retain his palatinate government of Ormond down to 1622.[1] Smaller overlords were also treated favourably by the government; and many succeeded in having their claims as overlords recognised and to a certain extent stabilised by the crown. Thus, for example, in the Composition Book of Connacht, O'Connor Sligo's overlordship was recognised by the fact that he was entitled to collect a rent amounting to more than £250 from the other five lordships in the newly created County Sligo. Similarly, O'Rourke's rights were commuted to an annual rent of nearly £340.[2]

The ability of a lord to exact tribute depended to a large extent on his military strength. Military power was central to the Irish concept of lordship. It enabled a lord to maintain his position within his lordship against rival factions and also to claim overlordship outside the lordship. The military entourage of a lord included men from his own lordship as well as from the sublords (if he controlled any), as well as the mercenary soldiers whom many Irish lords employed. The latter consisted of a mixture of native Irish military families and Scottish men or men of Scottish ancestry, known as gallowglass. Some of the larger lords employed thousands of mercenary soldiers while others had only a small number and some may have had none at all. Despite government disapproval, employment of mercenaries did not decline in the sixteenth century. In fact there was a strong increase in the number of Scottish soldiers employed by Gaelic lords during the century and the number of mercenaries in the country was probably at its highest in the late 1590s.[3] In many instances indeed the employment of mercenaries was authorised and permitted by the government.

In Tudor England one of the methods used to limit the control of the local magnates in the provinces was the prohibition of private retinues. It was not always a successful method and until the end of Elizabeth's reign the government was obliged to license certain nobles to maintain retinues on which the crown at times relied for defence. In Ireland a prohibition on private retinues was even less practical. A poorly financed government needed the free military assistance which loyal Irish lords could provide.

Many Irish lords were licensed to maintain armed soldiers provided they put them at the disposal of the government when requested to do so. The earls of Ormond, Clanricard and Thomond were all licensed to maintain troops which were frequently employed in government service, at the expense of the earls. In the 1570s and 1580s, for example, the earl of Ormond's troops were particularly useful in dealing with the rebellion in Munster.[4] Many of the crown's agreements with other Irish lords referred to the private military support which the lord would give to the crown. Thus in 1585 the earl of Thomond's country agreed to provide 40 horsemen and 300 footmen for provincial hostings in Connacht and 15 horsemen and 50 footmen for the general hostings of the lord deputy. The leading men of County Mayo agreed to provide a similar number of men and Sir Richard Burke (the MacWilliam) also made an agreement with the crown which enabled him to continue to employ as soldiers the Clan Donnells, the traditional gallowglass of the Burkes.[5] Thus most Irish lords in the late sixteenth century had private retinues and many had official government licence for them. The government relied on these private bands to maintain order in the localities.

An important characteristic of lordship in Ireland, as in other countries, was the concept embodied in the English phrase of 'spend me and defend me'.[6] This idea of defence in return for certain privileges emerges clearly in a rare document detailing the arrangement between a lord (Connla Mageoghegan) and a sublord (Breasal Fox) which is dated 20 August 1526. The agreement states that Mageoghegan was to be lord over the Fox and his country and was entitled to a hog for every *gniomh* of land which paid chiefry to the Fox (this amounted to 350 hogs). He was also to be given a *gniomh* of land free from every imposition which Fox demanded from the land within his territory; and to be allowed to redeem land which Fox had mortgaged to any person outside the territory if the Foxes were not able to redeem it. Fox was also required to pay his share of the cess which the king's deputy demanded of Mageoghegan. In return for these and other privileges Mageoghegan undertook to do 'his utmost for the protection and shelter of the Fox and every person in his country, both small and great'. If Mageoghegan failed to do this, the last clause of the agreement stated that he would not have rent, privilege or lordship over the Foxes and every man 'shall be for himself'. This final clause indicates that the Foxes were not permanently subject to the unwarranted demands of the Mageoghegans and could refuse to answer the demands of the overlord if Mageoghegan did not fulfil his side of the bargain.[7] (This was in contrast to the Scottish situation where similar types of agreement tended to be for life.) It was however the ability of the larger lords to offer effective military protection which helped cement a strong and, often in practice, a lifelong bond of loyalty between them and their supporters, a bond which the central government found very difficult to dissolve. Despite the increased impoverishment of many Irish lords in the seventeenth century local loyalties were maintained and were an important factor in the organisation and course of events in different regions in the wars of the 1640s. As late as the 1680s, the Irish army of James II was beset with problems of deserters who refused to continue to serve in the army after their local commander had been killed. Their loyalty to the local leader was still, at that time, stronger than their loyalty to the king.

In many ways, in fact, developments in sixteenth-century Ireland strengthened traditional ideas of lordship. Many Gaelic lords, despite new English titles, retained the traditional loyalty of their followers, and frequently acted as brokers for them in their negotiations or contacts with the English administration. Pardons were often issued to a lord and his followers; lords were often permitted to secure letters patent in their name for land which was owned or held by some of the subordinate families in the lordship. The government, on the whole, found it easier to encourage lords to be responsible for their followers. For example, it was the policy of the first two presidents of Connacht to recognise local power structures in the province but also to try to gradually transform them into more acceptable English political units. Thus lords were knighted and allowed to maintain their traditional power but they usually agreed to pay rents to the crown and in some cases to commute their exactions to a fixed sum of money. Thus in Mayo three successive MacWilliams were knighted and made agreements with the crown. It was hoped to carry the anglicisation process one stage further in the next generation through the education of the sons of the lords in an English environment.[8]

However, in 1586 Sir Richard Bingham, the third president of Connacht, introduced a change in this gradualist approach. On the death of Sir Richard Burke, the MacWilliam, Bingham declared that the position of MacWilliam was abolished and that the lands of the MacWilliam were to be inherited by his son, a young man with no political standing in Mayo. The rebellion of the Burkes in 1586 can initially be attributed largely to Bingham's unwillingness, unlike his predecessors, to recognise the man acknowledged by the Burkes to be the leading member of the family. They might have been willing to accept the abolition of the position of MacWilliam if Bingham had been prepared to knight the recognised head of the family and treat him as their spokesman. Instead Bingham attempted to rule the lordship of the MacWilliam by insisting that no member of the Burke septs should be treated differently from the rest. The Burkes, in fact, explained their second rebellion in 1589 by alleging that they had to have a 'chief man to command the rest' and asserting that there would be no peace until one of them carried the 'authority of the country — they care not by what title or name'.[9] Bingham's policy was a disastrous failure in Mayo, and not surprisingly the administration abandoned it in the 1590s and returned to the former policy of encouraging one member of the family to assume the position of control over the rest. Thus Sir Theobald Burke emerged, with considerable government support, as the leading Burke in the late 1590s. Similarly his brother-in-law, Sir Donagh O'Connor Sligo was returned from London (where he had been banished by Bingham in a comparable attempt to undermine local leadership in Sligo) in 1596 in the hope that he could command loyalty in the north-west of Ireland which the administration could no longer do. This policy undoubtedly strengthened rather than weakened the position of the lord in the localities.[10]

There were also other developments in late sixteenth-century Ireland which strengthened traditional ideas of lordship in some unexpected ways. In 1580 the lord of the Costelloes of County Mayo gave Theobald Dillon 'of free gift a great portion of land' with a castle with the 'consent of all the rest of his kinsmen'.[11]

Dillon was a member of the Anglo-Norman family which settled in the Pale in the early medieval period and the Costelloes, also an Anglo-Norman family, claimed a common ancestry with them. The Costelloes seemed willing to live as tenants to Dillon in return for the defence and protection which he could offer them. Dillon had close family connections with several members of the Dublin administration and so not only had access to the Dublin government but also had the administrative expertise to defend the land rights of the Costelloes and secure pardons and other necessary legal documentation for them from the administration. Bingham, in fact, subsequently accused Dillon and another member of the English administration in Connacht (Francis Berkley) of deliberately encouraging the Burkes to remain in rebellion in 1586 until they (Dillon and Berkley) had an opportunity to talk to the Dublin government in order to secure the dismissal or, at least, the severe reprimanding of Bingham for his behaviour. They also promised to secure pardons for all who took part in the rebellion. Dillon also seems to have taken on some of the duties of an overlord in the Costello lordship by selecting a member of the family to act as lord.[12] Another former Norman family who sought a similar type of protection were the MacEvillys who reverted to their original surname of Staunton in the late sixteenth century, and not 'having amongst themselves so complete a man as might rule or keep them in a loyal course of life when they are oppressed, they have all with one consent chosen for their chief, Captain Thomas Staunton of Wolverton in the County of Warwick. They pray that he may have power to protect them, and they will deliver to him the chief house of their name called Castle Carra'.[13] The proposal came to nothing but it is indicative of the way in which Irish men endeavoured to preserve older concepts of lordship and tried to protect themselves from the worst effects of the introduction of English local government.

At the same time, officials in the English administration also adapted themselves to Irish circumstances and not only took land in return for defending its inhabitants but also lodged soldiers on local inhabitants and demanded exactions such as agricultural produce (allegedly as payment of legal fines or composition charges) in a manner very similar to Irish lords. The complaints levied against members of the local government by the inhabitants of Connacht in 1589 suggest that the officials were making use of local customs to establish themselves in the province. Similarly in Munster in the 1570s and early 1580s, it has been suggested that the president of the province, 'Perrot, like Gilbert [his predecessor] behaved less as an official of royal government than as a superior local war-lord'. Obviously, for English officials in the localities there were practical advantages in dealing with Irish lords on their own terms. But it should also be remembered that notions of lordship were prevalent in sixteenth-century England, particularly in the north. Many Englishmen who came to Ireland in the sixteenth century would therefore have been familiar with the rule of lords and may have made use of such ideas in local government in Ireland.[14]

The strength of lordship in mid-sixteenth-century Ireland is testified by the way in which the restored earl of Kildare quickly re-established the traditional authority of his family in the Kildare area. In the 1550s it was reported that he maintained a private retinue of 200 men for his horses, 40 foot boys to run errands and 160 kern or Irish soldiers, all of whom were lodged on the local inhabitants. Interestingly, however, a report in 1566 alleged that Kildare claimed that he maintained this force for defence but, the report continued, 'though the poor crave his assistance he directs them to the governor saying as he is not governor, he ought not to seek the redress of any such grievances'.[15] In other words, Kildare was no longer prepared to recognise that although as a lord he was entitled to spend his people, he was also obliged to defend them. This may indicate that as the rule of the lord came under attack from the central government it became more exploitative and abandoned its defensive role.

Although strong military backing and a large number of loyal followers were essential for an Irish lord, he also needed to maintain his political power. As in Wales and Scotland, and probably elsewhere, lordship in Ireland demanded a territorial base, and the larger the territory over which a lord held sway, the stronger his political control tended to be.[16] Land was important not just in providing a power base which might be expanded but also as a means of income: lordship could be an expensive business. Little research has been done on the income of Irish lords in the early modern period but it must have varied enormously from the thousands of pounds which the earl of Desmond was entitled to collect to the small amounts of agricultural produce paid to less important lords which when commuted amounted to no more than £30 or £40 annually. The large overlords did, therefore, collect an enormous amount of agricultural produce from their own lands as well as from subordinate lordships. Some of this could have been used to maintain their retinue and household and some may have been used in the sort of exchange system which Dr. Dodghson describes as operating in highland Scotland.[17] Irish lords, however, would also have had access to towns and markets where surplus goods could have been exchanged for wine, salt and other goods not available in rural Ireland. Income, whether in kind or in cash, was needed not just to maintain the lord, his family and followers but also to pay for the mercenary soldiers. In Mayo the payment of the Scottish soldiers was in the form of cattle and corn and may also have included some land. Presumably, the cattle and corn, when they were given to mercenary soldiers for their services, were exchanged for money in an Irish market or town by soldiers who were not permanently resident in Ireland.

We still know relatively little about land usage and customs of inheritance and distribution in Gaelic Ireland and how these changed in the early modern period. A study of land inheritance in County Sligo in the sixteenth and early seventeenth centuries reveals considerable continuity of landownership with the same families holding the same property over several generations. In the neighbouring county of Mayo, however, such continuity cannot be discerned and there seems to have been much more movement in relation to landownership. The reason for this difference is not clear. It may be connected with the quality of the land of the two regions: Sligo has more fertile soil than Mayo and so there may have been more concern there with landownership and maintaining possession. In Mayo, because of the poverty of much of the land, it is possible that there was less interest in defining territories or retaining continuous possession. The difference in landownership and inheritance may also have been related to the political instability in the Mayo region where a number of different Burke septs competed with one another for control of the lordship. By contrast, one branch of the O'Connor Sligo family held the position of lord for several generations.[18]

K. W. Nicholls has found evidence which suggests that some lords worked their own land as well as renting some of it to tenants.[19] A survey for County Sligo dated to the mid-1630s indicates that in Sligo renting most of the estate to tenants was the normal pattern.[20] A small portion of land was kept for the lord's own use on which he lived and built his castle or house; and perhaps did some demesne farming with the assistance of tenant labour service. Some of the smaller Sligo landlords, however, did not rent out their land but worked it all themselves. The survey also gives some indication of the rent which Irish landlords were entitled to collect in the 1630s. Fergal O'Gara, for example, former lord of the small lordship of Coolavin, was entitled to an annual rent of £397. O'Gara appears to have received all his rent in cash. He rented most of the land, keeping only a small townland for his own use. Tadhg O'Hara, the O'Hara Boy, who had roughly the same amount of land as O'Gara, was entitled to £299.3s. as well as 14 meddars of malt, 13 muttons, 36 meddars of butter, 70 meddars of meal, the use of 84 workmen and the fourth sheaf from certain lands. It is impossible to assess the extent to which all this rent was actually collected. Income in any one year may have been considerably lower than the figures indicated by the survey. If such figures are, however, an approximate reflection of the actual income which these men received, then they would compare favourably with the incomes of the middle ranks of the English gentry of about the same time.[21] The amount of land rented by individual tenants ranged from a portion of a townland to 12 or more townlands. The tenants who rented large amounts of land sublet it to other tenants and must have been prosperous men in their own right. The survey notes one such tenant called O Cunegan who rented 13 quarters and sublet them for £71.1s, 26 meddars of butter, 12 muttons, 5 barrels of beer, 38 meddars of meal and the use of 84 workmen.

The absence of detailed studies of land usage and ownership in the Gaelic lordship makes it difficult to assess the extent to which changes took place in the early modern period. The most important change was the increase in primogeniture forms of inheritance. Primogeniture was gradually introduced to all parts of Ireland in the early modern period. It was, however, a very slow process and partible inheritance survived until at least 1641. This was partly because the English administration did not always insist that Irish lords who made agreements with the crown should adopt primogeniture, and the Dublin Chancery court was prepared to recognise the equity of customary laws of inheritance, even after it had been abolished by proclamation in 1605.[22] It might also be pointed out that English landowners in Ireland did not always follow primogeniture forms of inheritance. Partible inheritance had its attractions for Englishmen endeavouring to establish their family as a landowning one. Thus John Crofton who acquired land throughout the west of Ireland left landed estates to all his sons in his will and thus enabled the family name to expand and increase its influence in Connacht, particularly in the north-west.[23] Similarly, in the 1650s many established new English landowning families in Connacht took advantage of the Cromwellian land settlement to acquire landed estates for younger sons and brothers rather than simply extending the landed possessions of the main branch of the family.

Another important change in relation to the land was the increase in the number of English and Scottish landowners in Ireland and the consequent decline in native Irish landowners. The impact of the arrival of new English landowners on society should not, however, be exaggerated. In many cases, particularly in the sixteenth century, they took over waste and uninhabited land and there are few reports of large-scale evictions of native occupiers. Other new landlords remained absentee and sublet their lands to Irish tenants, often the former landlords. The actual occupancy of the land did not, therefore, change. In fact, the O Cunegan referred to above rented his land in County Sligo from a Mr Ridge, a new Englishman resident in County Roscommon. The new landlords were undoubtedly better at exploiting the resources of the land than their Irish predecessors and neighbours. In the 1620s and 1630s many Irish lords lost their lands, largely through financial difficulties which led many of them to sell or mortgage large portions of their lands to new English landowners.

The main emphasis in this paper is on the continuity and, in some areas, strengthening of Irish lordships in the early modern period. But this is not to underestimate the major changes which did take place in the sixteenth and early seventeenth centuries. There is, however, a strong case for arguing that until 1603 government by lords and lordship was still the most effective means of governing Ireland. The reliance of the late Tudor government on the local power of loyal lords such as the earl of Ormond or Sir Theobald Burke in the war of the 1590s and the recognition given to the earl of Tyrone's position in Tyrone in the Treaty of Mellifont supports this argument. The crucial period for the decline of lordly power in Ireland was the reign of James I. The years of peace after 1603 enabled the government to move away from its concentration on military affairs and turn its attention to the introduction of effective local government in the counties. The establishment of the assizes in Connacht and Ulster and the regular visits of the assize judges to all parts of the country ensured that the English local government system began to replace lordly dominance in the localities. The military support of loyal local lords was no longer necessary in the years of peace and the government began to be successful in prohibiting the maintenance of private retinues. Society was gradually demilitarised as the demand for mercenary soldiers, Scottish and Irish, diminished. Irishmen seeking a military career now looked to the continent for employment. The changes which took place occurred slowly and many of the characteristics of Irish lordship remained down to 1641, if not for much longer. As the wars of the second half of the seventeenth century were to prove, local Irish leaders could still at that stage command a loyalty and obedience which the new English landlords could not.[24]

NOTES

1. N. P. Canny, 'Hugh O'Neill, Earl of Tyrone, and the Changing Face of Gaelic Ulster', *Studia Hibernica*, 10 (1979), pp. 7–35; C. Brady, 'Faction and the Origins of the Desmond Rebellion of 1579', *I.H.S.* 88 (Sept. 1981), pp. 289–312; B. Cunningham, Political and Social Change in the Lordships of Clanricard and Thomond, 1569–1641 (unpublished M.A. thesis, University College, Galway, 1979), pp. 79, 82–3, 86.

2. *The Compossicon Booke of Conought*, A. M. Freeman, ed. (Dublin, 1936), pp. 125–139, 143–151.

3. G. C. Hayes-McCoy, *Scots Mercenary Forces in Ireland (1565–1603)* (Dublin, 1937). E. Hogan, *The Description of Ireland and the State thereof as it is at this present in Anno 1598* (Dublin, 1878) gives some indication of the varying military strength of Irish lords.

4. *Calendar of Carew Manuscripts*, 1575–88, p. 164 *passim*.

5. *Compossicon Booke of Conought*, pp. 17, 105; Sir Henry Sidney to Privy Council, 27 Jan. 1577 (*Calendar Carew Mss*, vol. ii); 'Calendar of the Irish Council Book, 1 March 1581 to 1 July 1586', D. B, Quinn, ed. *Anal. Hib.* 24 (1967), pp. 148–150.

6. E. Spencer, *A View of the State of Ireland* (1596) in *Ancient Irish Histories* (2 vols., Dublin, 1809), i, p. 53; *The Social State of the Southern and Eastern Counties of Ireland in the Sixteenth Century* …, H. F. Hore and J. Graves, eds. (Dublin, 1870), p. 160.

7. 'Covenant between Mageoghegan and the Fox …', J. O'Donavan, ed., *The Miscellany of the Irish Archaeological Society*, i (Dublin, 1846), pp. 179–197.

8. See note 5 above; H. T. Knox, *The History of the County of Mayo* (Dublin, 1908), pp. 174–204; Articles between Sir Nicholas Malby and Richard Inyren alias MacWilliam Eughter, 7 March 1580 (P.R.O. S.P. 63/81/15).

9. *C.S.P.I. 1588–92*, p. 300.

10. A. Chambers, *Chieftain to Knight* (Dublin, 1983), pp. 84–102.

11. Sir Nicholas Malby to Sir Francis Walsingham, 10 June 1580 (P.R.O. S.P. 63/73/51); Lord Deputy and Council to Privy Council, 10 Dec. 1581 (P.R.O. S.P. 63/87/33).

12. Sir Henry Wallop to Walsingham, 23 Aug. 1586 (P.R.O. S.P. 63/125/62); Discourse of Sir Richard Bingham c. Sept. 1586 (*C.S.P.I. 1586–88*, p. 178).

13. M. J. Blake, 'Castle Bourke', *Galway Archaeological and Historical Society Journal*, xiv (1928–9), pp. 105–6.

14. Discourse of Sir Richard Bingham, c. Sept. 1586 (*C.S.P.I. 1586–88*, p. 178); Lord Deputy Fitzwilliam to Lord Burghley, 19 June 1589 and enclosures (*C.S.P.I. 1588–92*, pp. 206–7); Declaration of Arthur Clayton, 11 Sept. 1589 (*ibid.* pp. 233–4); C. Brady, 'Faction and the Origins of the Desmond rebellion of 1579', in *I.H.S.* xxi (1981), p. 296. See also Sir Edward Fyton to Sir William Cecil, 8 Feb. 1571 (P.R.O. S.P. 63/31/6).

15. *Social State of the Southern and Eastern Counties*, p. 160.

16. R. R. Davies, *Lordship and Society in the March of Wales 1282–1400* (Oxford, 1978), p. 86; R. A. Dodgshon, *Land and Society in Early Scotland* (Oxford, 1981), p. 106.

17. See below, pp. 27–35.

18. On land inheritance and customs see K. W. Nicholls, *Gaelic and Gaelicised Ireland* (Dublin, 1972); M. O'Dowd, 'Land Inheritance in Early Modern County Sligo', *Ir. Ec. & Soc. Hist.* X (1983), pp. 5–18; P. J. Duffy, 'The Territorial Organisation of Gaelic Landownership and its Transformation in County Monaghan, 1591–1640', *Irish Geography*, xiv (1981), pp. 1–26.

19. *Land, Law and Society in Sixteenth-Century Ireland* (Dublin, 1976).

20. B. L. Harl. MS 2048.

21. G. E. Mingay, *The Gentry: the Rise and Fall of a Ruling Class* (London, 1976), pp. 13–14; J. Youings, *Sixteenth-Century England* (London, 1984), pp. 54–5.

22. K. W. Nicholls, 'Some Documents on Irish Law and Custom in the Sixteenth Century', *Anal. Hib.* 26 (1970), pp. 105–129.

23. H. T. Crofton, *Crofton Memoirs* (York, 1911).

24. The author is grateful to Dr. Donald Woodward and other members of the conference for their comments on this paper.

2

WEST HIGHLAND CHIEFDOMS, 1500-1745: A STUDY IN REDISTRIBUTIVE EXCHANGE

R. A. Dodgshon

The Scottish clan system is hardly a neglected theme. Generations of Scottish historians and clan *seanchaidhean* have left an abundance of literature. Yet whilst there has been much written about how the Scottish clans evolved genealogically and about how they expanded or contracted territorially, there remain important lacunae in our understanding. Above all, there has been no attempt to discuss Scottish clans in terms of their exchange system. Anthropologists have long realised that a form of trade existed before the establishment of marketing. I say a form of trade because this early, pre-market trade could be infused with a meaning that was part religious, social, political and economic. Evolving from the need of early tribal groups to marry out, to establish marriage alliances with other groups, early exchange schemes broadened to embrace supplementary flows of 'gifts' that might include food, axes, items of personal ornament and so on. In effect, early exchange functioned as a form of diplomacy, establishing an equal, symmetrical relationship between tribal groups through a mutual exchange of women and gifts.

With the rise of chiefdoms, exchange systems took on an asymmetrical, centralised form. The process began with the emergence of 'big-men' as tribal bankers, organising the collection and exchange of the tribe's gifts with other tribes. Once 'big-men' exercised this sort of supervisory control over exchange, they could manipulate it to their advantage. In time, what began as a purely neutral role became infused with an instrumental meaning. What they gathered in from kinsmen became tribute, something that signified their superior rank. What they gave out was pure gift, a mark of their liberality. Under pressure from chiefly demands, the whole concept of the tribal economy began to broaden. What kinsmen gave up as tribute was used to maintain the ceremonial feasting of the tribe, feasting in which the chief played a central role: to support a 'tribal' reserve of food under the chief's direct control: and to support the production of 'prestige' goods for the chief's own use or his redistribution. To summarise, then, as chiefdoms emerged, exchange systems became organised around them: the term redistributive exchange is used to describe these movements of exchange into and out of chiefly centres.[1]

The anthropologists Ekholm and Friedman have offered an important extension of such ideas.[2] They argue that the structural character of chiefdoms is capable of undergoing rapid, cyclical adjustment in response to changes in the character of exchange. Where chiefs exercised a monopolistic control over the exchange of goods, especially over prestige items needed for vital ceremonial occasions or display, it tended to generate elaborate social hierarchies. Such prestige items were not essential for subsistence, but they were 'absolutely indispensable for the maintenance of social relations'.[3] For this reason, those who controlled their production were able to forge elaborate hierarchies of power by using them in exchange for wives. The overall effect of the processes involved was for women to gravitate towards chiefly centres, from low-rank to high-rank lineages. Conversely, men tended to marry outwards and downwards, from high- to low-rank lineages.[4]

These elaborate hierarchies collapse in two ways. Dominant groups could lose their monopoly over prestige items, either because their supply dried up or because everyone gained access to them. Alternatively, over-population in dominant political areas could precipitate problems of subsistence. Under such pressures, elaborate social hierarchies tended to break down into flatter, more localised forms, with numerous smaller chiefdoms flaunting their independence and status through feasting and other displays of liberality and asserting their prowess through constant struggles with other petty chiefdoms over the control of land and subsistence. In effect, they were 'fighting with food', each striving to be the centre of a new eruption of power.[5]

By introducing these ideas into a Highland context, I am not suggesting that they can be transposed directly from the New to the old Hebrides without modification. However, if we concentrate on the general processes identified by Ekholm and Friedman — which is what they intended — their work makes it clear that without an analysis of exchange, our understanding of Highland chiefdoms is seriously deficient in a way that may strike at the very heart of their character. In trying to remedy this deficiency, I want, first, to define the nature of Highland exchange systems as we see them during the period 1500–1745, a period which witnessed their final eclipse as systems of chiefly redistribution. Secondly, I want to explore how these systems can be linked to the wider socio-political character of Highland chiefdoms.

By 1500 Highland chiefdoms were organised around landlord-tenant relationships. For this reason we find that the most substantial element within their systems of redistributive exchange was the upward flow of commodities between tenant and landowner. There is, I would stress, no difficulty in seeing such payments in terms of exchange theory. Whilst they had taken on the added meaning of rent, nevertheless they were still imbued with all the meanings that are attached to the commodity flows between kinsmen and their chief. In composition Highland rents were not a simple measure, but appear as a complex amalgam of different dues and obligations. At its core were long-standing obligations which kinsmen owed to their chief. A thirteenth-century charter for Lismore refers to the obligations of cain, ich, conveth, fecht and slagad: these represent the burdens of tribute (cain, ich), hospitality or refection (conveth), expedition (fecht) and hosting (slagad).[6] Although they occur under different terminological guises, such burdens continued down to the period 1500–1745. Those involving the provision of tribute and refection provided the foundation for the extraction of food rents, either as payments to the chief or in the form of hospitality due to him. By the time we can examine such rent bundles in detail, c.1500, they had acquired a cash component, even on the most isolated islands. Although some rentals specify a single cash payment, some suggest that such cash payments could have a compound form, comprising a traditional 'silver mail' plus what some rentals call 'Crown Rent'. Silver mail was undoubtedly the older of the two forms, but precisely how much older we cannot say. Broadly speaking, the proportion of rent paid as cash appears to increase 1500–1745 through the conversion of food rents to cash. Some rentals, though, are ambiguous in the sense that they list food rents plus their conversion value: thus, a 1614 rental for Islay shows that rents in kind amounted to 94% of the value of the total customary rent but that all of it had a stated conversion value that presumably could be taken in lieu.[7]

In content, food formed the principal part of these rent payments in kind, with beer, meal, cheese, butter, hens, geese, sheep and cattle being widely recorded in rentals of the period together with more localised payments of veal, tongue, swine, salmon, ale, and acquavitae.[8] As in chiefdoms in other parts of the world, the major chiefs maintained girnal houses where products like grain and cheese could be stored. The Lord of the Isles, for instance, maintained a girnal house beside Finlaggan Castle in Islay.

Initially such payments in kind would have carried the sole meaning of tribute, a mark of the chief's superiority over his kinsmen. Quite apart from any symbolic purpose of signifying the chief's superior rank and position, they served to maintain the chief and his household, to provide for tribal feastings and chiefly displays of liberality, and to fund exchanges with other tribes. The idea that kinsmen should maintain the chief and his household is conveyed more explicitly by the widespread obligation that tenants owed hospitality to the chief and his household. The obligation to host their chief was known as *cuid-oidhche*. Evidence for its existence is quite widespread. Thus, a sixteenth-century source refers to tenants on Mull and Sleat having to entertain their chiefs with 'sa mekle as thair maister may be able to spend one nicht (albeit he were 600 men in compenie) on ilk merkland'.[9] A bond drawn up in 1549 between John Campbell of Glenurchay and John Menzeis of Rorow agreed that on the matter of 'rychtis meyt' the latter should 'be reddy with mete and drynk and wther necessaris conwenand thairto [for] the said Jhon Campbell his howsald and followaris' when they visit him.[10] Likewise, a 1625 tack for land in Moydart set the land for various payments in kind 'togidder with ane richtis meit or cuddyche to me my houshauld and servandis anes ilk yeir'.[11]

Linked to such hospitality was the obligation that townships had to support the chief's household's men, that is, the various individuals who performed specialised tasks essential to the appearance and status of chiefs, like the *seanchaidhean*, pipers, harpists and armourers, and those who formed the chief's bodyguard, his *uchd tighe*. Naturally, those families which served as *seanchaidhean*, pipers and the like derived some gain from the chief's displays of feasting for they played a symbolic role in these activities. An early description of the inauguration ceremony surrounding the Lord of the Isles talked about how they feasted for a week and how the new Lord 'gave liberally to the monks, poets, bards and musicians'.[12]

Their prime source of maintenance, however, was through holdings granted out to them on a rent-free basis, as 'pure gift'.[13]

The fighting men who surrounded chiefs posed a more complex problem of maintenance. Some, the chief's bodyguard, were almost certainly resident with him, and, as such, were dependent on the food rent which he received or the hospitality which he had right to. However, in some areas, we can identify a different dimension to the problem. Perhaps as a custom deliberately differentiated from the obligation to maintain the chief's household, we find tenants having to maintain the chief's fighting men as members of their own household. In other words, the chief's household appears to have overflowed to become a more direct burden on tenants. According to a sixteenth-century survey of Islay, each merkland had 'to sustein daylie and yierlie ane gentlemen in meit and claith, quhilk dois na labour'.[14] It was, however, a custom that was much abused. The root cause of this abuse lay in its changing social context. The number of sorners involved appears to have increased. At the same time, what probably began as a custom whereby young men from the leading lineages were supported appears to have become open to a wider range of individuals, including non-kinsmen, not all of whom were sanctioned by the chief. Sources, in fact, tend increasingly to link sorning with 'brokin men', men without any kinship affiliations to the clan.[15] We need to see the growing complaints about the custom in relation to these trends. Thus, during the sixteenth century, Glengarry and his followers were said to have sorned not just on the lands of their own tenants, especially the Mathesons of Lochalsh and the Clan Ian Uidhir of Lochcarron, but also on the adjacent Mackenzie lands.[16] Likewise, a petition submitted to the king in 1613 by landholders on Islay complained that 'they ar verie havelie oppreist troublit and wrackit be a nomber of ydili men, vagaboundis and sornaris who lyis upoun thame, consumis thair viveris and spoylis thame of thair goodis at thair pleasour'.[17]

A feature of redistributive systems was that the flows of 'tribute' to chiefs were partly offset by counter-flows from the chief downwards. The idea that Highland chiefs gave as well as received is well-established. Their greater generosity was a mark of their greater status, something to be eulogised by bards.[18] Some downward movements were of a minor nature. For instance, the practice whereby sons from high-rank families were fostered by low-rank families usually involved small token movements or gifts.[19] Particularly significant was the assistance which chiefs were expected to give to kinsmen during subsistence crises.[20] For some, this reciprocal support of kinsmen and chief lies at the heart of chiefdoms. The food renders which kinsmen gave up to their chief were an insurance against risk, a form of social storage, to be drawn upon when need arose. In effect, the chief played the part of system manager, trading surpluses against deficits. One early Irish source actually puts it in such terms.[21] The effect was mutual interdependence between the needs of the chief and those of his kinsmen.

There can be no doubt that feasting also played a major role in Highland exchange systems. This was certainly true of the medieval period[22] and it remained so over the period 1500–1745. 'The gentry,' said a mid-eighteenth-century observer, 'are strong and well bodied men much given to hospitality and drinking.'[23] Quite apart from its functional role in redistributing food, it had an important behavioural function. For a peasant society, particularly one that lived in a marginal environment, the lavishness of chiefly feasts, with their slaughtering of animals and large-scale consumption of grain as drink, would have served to confuse the welfare of chief and kinsmen. Just as some traditions had the chief's welfare as a priority for the clan,[24] so also were his displays of hospitality seen as a measure of the clan's wellbeing and the credit which, through feasting, it was able to store in the wider social system. So successful were they at this mystification of its meaning that the greatness of chiefs was measured no less by displays of hospitality than through the amount of food gathered in. There is a tradition that when a newly-elected chief of the Clanranald, someone who had been tutored by Fraser of Lovat, returned to North Uist for his inauguration, he was concerned at the amount of cattle slaughtered for the occasion. His kinsmen were so affronted that he was discarded in favour of his brother.[25] The quantity of food consumed through feasting can be measured not only through the amount consumed[26] or through the sheer frequency of feasts, but equally, through their length. When Neil Mor MacVuirich visited Dunvegan in the early seventeenth century for the marriage of MacLeod's daughter to the heir of Clanranald, the feasting lasted six days, the participants managing to recall 'we were twenty times drunk every day, to which we had no more objection than he had'.[27]

In addition to the movement of goods between kinsmen and their chief, we can also identify more horizontal movements between chiefs. Strictly speaking, there are two types of flow to be recognised here: those between individuals of equal rank and those between greater and lesser chiefs. In both cases we could be dealing with a variety of different kinds of exchange. A primary form was that bound up with inter-clan marriage agreements. As with other kin-based societies, such agreements were between families, not individuals. Interwoven with them were transfers of property, goods and cash. The property element was given to the prospective wife by her husband's family and usually involved the gift of land, its possession for life or in perpetuity: the intent behind such a gift was to secure her upkeep independently of her husband.[28] Early Scottish legal texts call this sort of exchange a 'morning gift'. It probably originated as a form of bride-price, but it certainly cannot be given this meaning in the context of the sixteenth or seventeenth centuries when it appears as something which, in part, was set against the payment of *tocher-gude*. The latter was a form of bridewealth payment, something paid to the groom's family as a supplement to the value of the wife. I say a form of bridewealth because although it was negotiated by kin groups or families, it had become a payment to the husband. Two kinds of supplement were involved. In some cases, it took the form of cattle, a widely accepted form of storable wealth in tribal societies. When, in 1613, John of Macdonald married Marion, the daughter of Roderick Macleod, her father paid nine score cattle as *tocher-gude* or bridewealth.[29] Likewise, when the son of Allan McInnes of Kockeyltack in Eig married the daughter of John McEan Wic Allan alias Macdonald, the latter gave the former 60 cows as *tocher-gude*.[30]

In some marriage agreements, gifts were made of military equipment and support. Surprisingly, there is no evidence that either the light armour which Highlanders wore — comprising a bascinet, aketon and shoulder mail — or the two-handed claymore figured in exchange systems by the sixteenth century, and certainly no sign of them figuring as bride-price payment.[31] I say surprisingly because their production could not have been in everyone's reach. In all probability it was controlled by the more powerful chiefs, some of whom maintained armourers or smiths on their estate. The cluster of hereditary smiths believed to have lived in Knapdale was possibly an important regional source of such armour and weaponry, presumably servicing the Lordship of the Isles.[32] The armour and weaponry which they produced would have been the sort of items redistributed as prestige goods, items whose exchange could be used to centralise power. This is well shown by the systems of redistributive exchange documented by the *Book of Rights*, an Irish source thought by Binchy to be of eleventh-century date.[33] Amongst the items which it records being exchanged were swords, spears, chariots, shields, corselets, mantles and ships.[34] If such items did once feature in Highland systems of exchange, though, they had lost this function by the sixteenth century. There is, however, at least one example of a galley being given, replete with a crew.[35] In addition to the transfer of such commodities, there also took place straightforward payments of cash as *tocher*.[36]

Filling out these movements of *tocher-gude* were a miscellany of other movements. Some were pure gift or presents. Thus, when the earl of Douglas visited the earl of Ross in Knapdale in 1453, he brought silver, silks and wine, whilst the latter offered, as a counter presentation, mantles and plaid. Angus Mor, Lord of the Isles during the fifteenth century, was said to be a 'great giver of rings', an item that had a place in early Irish exchange schemes.[37] We also need to take into account the fairly complex network of debt that existed between Highland families by the sixteenth and seventeenth centuries. Individuals borrowed freely. Others stood as cautioners for them.[38] The willingness with which individuals lent to each other or acted as cautioner — without adequate security — suggests that operation of this debt network had functions that were diplomatic as much as financial, concerned as much with cementing social dependencies as with rates of return.

I have tried, albeit in a somewhat sweeping fashion, to summarise the direction and content of the various exchange flows that were threaded through Highland society. What I want to do in the remaining section is to ask what such exchange systems tell us about the wider character of Highland chiefdoms.

There are no grounds for thinking that the Highland chiefdoms that we see over the sixteenth century were based on chiefly control over prestige items. This is not to say that chiefdoms of this sort were never present in the Highlands. The *Book of Rights* — which covered some Highland 'tribes' — can be read as documenting complex, chiefly hierarchies of this type. However, there is this major point of difference with those defined by Ekholm and Friedman. Women moved downwards along with prestige items like swords, shields, coats of mail and drinking horns, whilst cattle, oxen, boars, pigs and sheep moved upwards. In effect, control over both prestige items and women was used to accumulate cattle

(=wealth) and the provisions needed for feasting and to maintain a large body of household men. Ekholm has stressed how these complex, hierarchical chiefdoms were permeated by an asymmetrical dualism, one that differentiated between chiefs/commoners, elder/younger, wife-givers/takers and so on. We cannot read such dualism from the *Book of Rights*, but there are certainly traces of such classificatory structures in other sources.[39] Comparable processes may once have operated around the more powerful Highland clans. We can only speculate, though, on what was exchanged against what, and what moved upwards and what moved downwards. In a warring society, yet one in which the basic resources needed to produce the most essential military equipment, timber for boats and iron for armour, were scarce, one would expect those who controlled such resources to have had a strong bargaining position in exchange systems. Similarly, clans blessed with reasonably fertile territories (i.e. Islay) could produce cattle which, in turn, could be used to contract favourable alliances. Macpherson's study of the various *sliochdan* of the Clan Macpherson illustrated how the early stages of clan growth could rely on some high-ranking men marrying out but women always marrying within the clan, the former drawing in new land and allied families, and the latter conserving what was already held.[40] In such circumstances the clan's capacity to contract favourable alliances would have been greatly aided by access to either prestige items or cattle.

A more realistic interpretation of many Highland chiefdoms as they appear by the sixteenth century would be one that emphasises the flatter, more localised and more competitive nature of chiefly power. Following the collapse of the Lordship of the Isles, power in the Hebrides became less coherent. This can be compared with Ekholm and Friedman's cyclical movement of chiefdoms, in which the collapse of highly centralised power structures is followed by more localised systems of 'big-men', each competing for power and status. We cannot attribute the collapse of the Lordship of the Isles in any way to the disruption of its exchange system, but this is not to say that its effects were not comparable with those suggested by Ekholm and Friedman's modelling of chiefdom processes. Their picture of localised chiefdoms competing over subsistence through a mixture of feasting and feuding fits what we know of the Highlands for much of the period 1500–1745, especially down to the early seventeenth century. Mention has already been made of the degree to which Highland clans indulged themselves in feasting. That some clans were notorious for their constant feuding is also well-established. Apart from the ritual slaughter of rival clans and the destruction of their property, either with the support of an official act of fire and sword or without, there was also the booty. Given their role as a form of storable wealth and an instrument of exchange, cattle were a particularly prized trophy and figure in many recorded instances of feuding, such as when the McDonnells of Keppoch raided Strathardle in 1602,[41] or when the Mackenzies of Kintail raided the Macdonalds of Glengarry in the same year.[42] Nor is there any difficulty in documenting the intense inter-clan struggle over the possession of land. The saying that a clan without land was a broken clan just as a man without a clan was a broken man was probably never more apt than when said in the context of the sixteenth and seventeenth centuries.

However, by this point, we are dealing everywhere with land rights based on charter grants. Yet possession of land was still a basis of chiefly power, a source of food and cattle, even though the means of validating one's claim had altered. The problems of trying to maintain clan identity without it are sharply focused by the experience of the MacGregors. Harrassed by neighbouring but hardly neighbourly clans like the Campbells and Buchanans, they struggled hard to keep up appearances.[43] When King James IV visited Inchcalloun in 1506 to see the MacGregor chief, he was feasted for eight days! The King was impressed by both MacGregor's hospitality and the size of his retinue. When MacGregor boasted of Loch Tay being his basin and his plaid being his towel, the King is said to have told him that he was a greater king than he was.[44] Even when their name had been proscribed, and their land base reduced to inhospitable areas like Rannoch, they still expended a fair proportion of their crop on gatherings and feasts[45] although, if we accept the official view, they were forced to maintain themselves through stealing and petty banditry, raiding nearby Lowland farms or Highland droves for cattle and making good their shortfall of grain by raiding the girnal houses of the Buchanans.[46]

The suggestion that some Highland chiefdoms were 'fighting with food' is given support by official perceptions of the Highland problem. During the 1540s, when the Crown still had direct control of areas like Kintyre, it took steps to rid them of what it clearly saw as the basic social problem. It set out to remove 'all thevis, pikaris, and sornaris that oppres the cuntrie and the pure commonys or that takis mete, drink, or ony uthir thing without payment'.[47] Highland chiefs also began taking action. By a bond of manrent in 1586, Duncan Campbell of Glenurchay agreed to keep the lands of William Shaw of Knokhill and Henry Shaw of Cambusmoir in Perthshire 'free from sorning and oppression as he does his own lands'.[48] By the Statutes of Iona in 1609, the government offered a more general solution, suppressing those practices which it saw as vital to the prevailing system of Highland chiefdoms. The size of the chief's household was restricted and sorning outlawed. Finally, noting the 'extraordinar drinking of strong wynis and acquavitie', the Statutes tried to restrict its availability to what was brewed or distilled locally.[49] We can make sense of such legislation only if we accept that some Highland chiefdoms had become a competitive struggle for status through control over subsistence, a struggle that played as much on the surpluses as on the deficiencies of local subsistence. All the signs are that some landowners did acknowledge the force of this legislation. An agreement of 1636 between John and Donald MacLeod reminded the latter how the laws of the kingdom prohibited 'the former abuse of sorneing and cudeachis oppression' and bound them 'to live upon our awen meannes'.[50] By 1610 the captain of Clanranald had accepted that he was 'to forbear the taking of cowdeichies and presents'[51] but his attitude was to prove ambivalent, for by a tack of 1625 he can be found reserving the right of *cuid-oidhche* to the chief of Clanranald or his servants.[52]

Establishing the broad character of Highland chiefdoms, 1500–1745, helps to expose the problems of adjustment which they faced. Once chiefs no longer used food rents to complete for status and prestige, then the whole relationship between production and consumption was transformed. We can see this as a problem of how easily the Highland estate economy adjusted to a strategy of marketing produce. It was not a question of encouraging improvement to realise a surplus: that surplus already existed. The problem was one of diverting it away from local chiefly consumption to markets. The controls eventually imposed on sorning and the decline of feasting as a display of status would have made adjustment in the estate economy almost an imperative. For this reason, we cannot be surprised if some landowners, including some from the Hebrides, were marketing produce, notably cattle, by the early seventeenth century.[53] As in Lowland areas, peasant involvement in marketing began when payments in kind were converted into cash. Logically, we would expect estates along the edge of the Highlands to have made this shift sooner. In fact, the actual pattern is less coherent. Estates like the Robertson of Lude estate,[54] close to the southern edge of the Highlands, had shifted into cash rents by the late seventeenth century, and certainly there were Hebridean estates, like the MacDonald estate on Skye, which still collected some rents in kind in the eighteenth century,[55] but such a neat pattern is disrupted by exceptions: thus, rents on Jura were levied in cash by c.1700[56] whilst the large Breadalbane estate — with its easier access to markets — still saw fit to collect part of its rent in kind.[57] There is, however, an element of ambiguity in rental data, with some rentals specifying a cash rent but accepting a payment in kind and vice-versa.[58]

I have tried in the foregoing discussion to establish two points. First, I have tried to give some shape and character to the system of redistributive exchange that ran through Highland chiefdoms. Secondly, I have tried to draw out the significance which this may have for giving definition to the wider character of Highland chiefdoms. This wider significance needs stating carefully. To stress the importance of redistributive exchange is not just another way of saying that their economy mattered. Like chiefdoms elsewhere, their economy would not have been seen as a differentiated or separate sphere of activity, one possessed of its own 'economic' goals. Instead, its function had to do with status-building goals operating within a kin-based system of ranking, that is, with displays of feasting and hospitality, the production of prestige goods, the ability to contract more favourable marriage alliances, the ability to give gifts and one's capacity to support a large household of servants and fighting men. To study Highland patterns of redistributive exchange is to study how all these different dimensions of its society functioned as a single interlocking system, so much so that changes in the character or form of exchange could mirror changes in the organisational character of the chiefdom.

NOTES

1. M. Sahlins, *Tribesmen* (Englewood Cliffs, 1968), esp. pp. 81–95; G. Dalton, ed., *Primitive, Archaic and Modern Economies: Essays of Karl Polany* (Boston, 1968), pp. 9–15.
2. K. Ekholm, 'External Exchange and the Transformation of Central African Social

Systems', pp. 115–36, in J. Friedman and M. J. Rowlands, eds., *The Evolution of Social Systems* (London, 1977); J. Friedman, 'Catastrophe and Continuity in Social Evolution', pp. 175–96, in C. Renfrew, M. J. Rowlands and B. A. Segraves, eds., *Theory and Explanation in Archaeology* (London, 1982).

3. Ekholm, *op.cit.*, p. 118.

4. *Ibid.*, pp. 118–24; Friedman, *op.cit.*, pp. 184–5.

5. Friedman, *op.cit.*, p. 184.

6. A. A. M. Duncan and A. L. Brown, 'Argyll and the Isles in the Earlier Middle Ages', *Proceedings of the Society of Antiquaries of Scotland*, XC (1956–57), p. 219. Cf. D. Binchy, ed., *Lebor Na Cert: The Book of Rights* (Irish Texts Society, Dublin, 1962), p. 25.

7. C. G. Smith, *The Book of Islay* (Edinburgh, 1895), pp. 487–90.

8. See, for example, *ibid.*, pp. 487–90; A. Macpherson, *Glimpses of Church and Social Life in the Highlands in Olden Times* (Edinburgh, 1893), pp. 503–13; A. Murray, *The True Interest of Great Britain* (London, 1740), table vi; S.R.O. GD112/9/6; GD221/118; BD201/1257/2 and 5.

9. W. F. Skene, ed., *Celtic Scotland* III (Edinburgh, 1880), pp. 432 and 435.

10. *The Black Book of Taymouth* (Bannatyne Club, Edinburgh, 1855), pp. 187–9.

11. A Macdonald and A. Macdonald, *The Clan Donald*, vol.II (Inverness, 1900), p. 773. For further references, see G. Burnett, ed., *The Exchequer Rolls of Scotland*, XII, 1502–1507 (Edinburgh, 1889), pp. 698–700; 'An Old Tiree Rental of the Year 1662', *S.H.R.*, IX (1912), p. 343.

12. J. R. N. Macphail, ed., *Highland Papers*, I (Scottish History Society, Edinburgh, 1914), p. 24.

13. S.R.O. GD201/1257/5; Macdonald and Macdonald, *op.cit.*, III (1904), p. 125; Macphail, ed., *op.cit.*, p. 279.

14. W. F. Skene, ed., *op.cit.*, pp. 438 and 429.

15. See, for example, *R.P.C.S., 1599–1604*, pp. 92, 255 and 336.

16. A. Mackenzie, *History of the Clan Mackenzie* (Inverness, 1879), p. 123.

17. *Collectanea de Rebus Albanicis, Consisting of Original Papers and Documents Relating to the History of the Highlands and Islands*, edited by the Iona Club (Edinburgh, 1847), p. 161.

18. See T. McLauchlan, ed., with introduction by W. F. Skene, *The Dean of Lismore's Book* (Edinburgh, 1862), p. 99; Macdonald and Macdonald, *op.cit.*, I (1896), p. 144; J. Logan, *The Scottish Gael, or Celtic Manners As Preserved Amongst the Highlanders*, first published in Inverness, 1876 (Edinburgh, 1976), p. 195.

19. Mackenzie, *op.cit.*, p. 119; *Black Book of Taymouth*, p. xvii.

20. Instances can be found in S.R.O. GD50/135, p. 602; *Burt's Letters from the North of Scotland*, first published 1754, reprinted with introduction by R. Jamieson (Edinburgh, 1876), 2, p. 158; Macdonald and Macdonald, *op.cit.*, III, pp. 663–4; A. H. Millar, ed., *A Selection of Scottish Forfeited Estates Papers, 1715–1745* (Scottish History Society, Edinburgh, 1909), p. 85; *Black Book of Taymouth*, p. 387.

21. Bincy, ed., *op.cit.*, p. 101 talks of renders 'for storing till the time of need, to be supplied in time of need'.

22. The importance of feasting is well stressed in McLauchlan, ed. *op.cit.*, p. 82.

23. *The Highlands of Scotland in 1750*, with introduction by A. Lang (Edinburgh, 1898), p. 7.

24. The best illustration of this is the story about MacNeill of Barra. After each meal, a servant would climb to the topmost turret in Kisimuil Castle and proclaim that now that Macneill had finished his meal, the rest of the world could start theirs.

25. Logan, *op.cit.*, p. 195.

26. The *Book of Rights*, talks about 60 oxen being sufficient for a week's feasting, Binchy, ed., *op.cit.*, p. 27.

27. Macdonald and Macdonald, *op.cit.*, III, p. 119.

28. For examples, see R. C. MacLeod, ed., *The Book of Dunvegan* (Third Spalding Club, Aberdeen, 1938), I, pp. 51–2, 55 and 57–8.

29. Macleod, *op.cit.*, I, pp. 52–4.
30. S.R.O. GD201/1/81. See also F. J. Shaw, *The Northern and Western Isles: Their Economy and Society in the Seventeenth Century* (Edinburgh, 1980), p. 158.
31. The importance of this armour in building up status is underlined by the extent to which it appears on late medieval funerary sculpture, see K. A. Steer and J. W. M. Bannerman, *Late Medieval Monumental Sculpture in the West Highlands* (Edinburgh, 1977), p. 27.
32. *Ibid.*, pp. 144–5.
33. Binchy, ed., *op.cit.*, p. xii.
34. *Ibid.*, appendix B.
35. MacLeod, ed., *op.cit.*, I, pp. 52–4.
36. S.R.O. GD50/28.
37. D. J. Macdonald, *Clan Donald* (Loanhead, 1978), p. 162.
38. See, for example, Macdonald and Macdonald, *op.cit.*, I, p. 444.
39. R. A. Dodghson, 'Symbolic Classification and the Making of Early Celtic Landscape', *Cosmos*, 1 (1985).
40. A. G. Macpherson, 'An Old Highland Genealogy and the Evolution of a Scottish Clan', *Scottish Studies*, 10 (1966), pp. 18 and 20.
41. *R.P.C.S. 1599–1604*, pp. 500–1.
42. Mackenzie, *op.cit.*, p. 143.
43. Their harassment is emphatically illustrated by the agreement in 1588 whereby Donald and Dougall McTarlichis agreed to 'enter deidlie feid with the Clan gregoure', *Black Book of Taymouth*, pp. 416–7. See also S.R.O. GD50/93.
44. *Ibid.*, p. 41.
45. *O.S.A.*, II (Edinburgh, 1792), p. 457; V. Wills, ed., *Reports of the Annexed Estates, 1755–1769* (Edinburgh, 1973), p. 31.
46. For examples, see *R.P.C.S., 1599–1604*, VI, p. 534; S.R.O. GD50/93, p. 79 and p. 119. Tacks for the Menzies estate were still warning tenants against harbouring 'loose or brokin men' or stolen goods in the 1720s, see S.R.O. GD50/Menzies Book of Tacks 1684–1738.
47. G. Burnett, ed., *The Exchequer Rolls of Scotland*, XII, 1502–1507 (Edinburgh, 1889), pp. 703–4.
48. *Black Book of Taymouth*, pp. 237–9.
49. D. Masson, ed., *R.P.C.S.*, IX, 1610–1613, pp. 26–30.
50. MacLeod, ed., *op.cit.*, p. 183.
51. Macdonald and Macdonald, *op.cit.*, III, pp. 116–7.
52. *Ibid.*, II, p. 773.
53. S.R.O. GD201/1/54; *R.P.C.S.*, 1599–1604, pp. 184 and 459.
54. S.R.O. GD132/541.
55. S.R.O. GD221/118.
56. S.R.O. GD64/1/85.
57. S.R.O. GD112/9/45.
58. W. C. Mackenzie, *History of the Outer Hebrides* (Paisley, 1903), p. 536; Shaw, *op.cit.*, p. 157; G. P. McNeill, ed., *The Exchequer Rolls of Scotland*, XVII, 1537–1542 (Edinburgh, 1897), pp. 602 *et seq.*

3
LANDED SOCIETY AND THE INTERREGNUM IN IRELAND AND SCOTLAND

Raymond Gillespie

Viewed from the perspective of the central administration, the experience of Britain and Ireland in the 1650s was one of increasing uniformity. The London government wished to standardise and simplify complex matters such as the administration of law and to make the Protectorate uniformly taxed, godly and educated. At this administrative level Ireland and Scotland appear to have had a similar fate in the 1650s. There were, for example, strong similarities between the instructions issued to the Commissioners for Scotland in 1652 and their Irish counterparts in 1651. The propagation of the Gospel, regulation of education, justice, and financial matters were all to be managed within a similar framework in both countries, and similar solutions were adopted to local problems.[1] The governors of each country were in contact, as in 1654 when Charles Fleetwood, the Irish lord deputy, wrote to George Monck, his Scottish counterpart, suggesting ways of dealing with the Glencairn rising based on his Irish experience.[2] Contacts between the two countries were not always above suspicion, as Lord Broghill, Munsterman and President of the Scottish Council, noted when a royalist rebellion was feared in 1656: 'possibly Ireland and this place may understand each other better than we could believe'.[3]

Standardisation was not confined to the realms of constitutional theory, such as the Cromwellian Act of Union for Scotland which brought it into line with Ireland's position under the 1541 Act for the Kingly Title. Similar reactions to the Cromwellian regime were evident in both political nations. Both Scots and Irishmen were prominent in the attempt to make Cromwell king, and in initiating the return of Charles II.[4] Moreover the economic history of the 1650s appears to have been similar in both areas. Tales of high taxation, debt, cash shortages, and a collapse of trade abound in the contemporary sources and later writings from both countries.[5]

This appearance of uniformity in the experience of Scotland and Ireland is somewhat illusory. It is a picture drawn from the central government perspective. It is difficult to examine the problem from the local perspective since little estate material survives from the Interregnum in either Scotland or Ireland, and the loss of the Scottish administrative records during the 1650s, and of their Irish counterparts in 1922, hampers study of the relationship between central government and the localities. Thus to compare the experience of the two areas it is necessary to study small regions in detail, within the context of national developments. This essay examines local developments in Ulster and south-west Scotland to see how different were the reactions to the Interregnum.

South-west Scotland and Ulster had strong historical links — most of the Scots settlers in early seventeenth-century Ulster, for example, came from south-west Scotland and much of Ulster's trade was with the ports of Glasgow, Ayr, Irvine and Portpatrick. Most presbyterian ministers in Ulster came from south-west Scotland, and in the 1630s there was a real fear that the Scottish Covenanter disturbances would spread to Ulster. These links were reinforced in the 1640s when the arrival of the Scots army prompted a 'presbyterian revolution' in Ulster. Thus many men in Ulster had ties of kinship, debt, and landownership with Scotland and often responded to developments there.[6]

While we must recognise these historical links, it is important not to overstress them at the expense of contemporary experience. The history of the war in the 1640s, for example, demonstrates contrasts between south-west Scotland and Ulster. While Ulster was badly ravaged by warfare, the fighting in Scotland was largely confined to the east and north, with the south-west escaping relatively lightly.[7] In the same way the experience of landed society in the 1650s was a contrasting one in the two regions despite similarities. From both areas came complaints of increasing debt and poverty. Robert Baillie recorded what he saw as the decay of landed society in south-west Scotland: 'Our noble families are almost gone ... Eglinton and Glencairn are on the brink of breaking; many of our own chief families' estates are cracking'.[8] From Ulster similar complaints emanated. The author of the Hamilton Manuscripts recorded that Lord Clandeboy was 'much straitened in his estate', and because of the compounding for his lands he 'had to contract great debts on his estate by which [the] family [was] brought down in style from his father's time'. His neighbour, Lord Montgomery, also borrowed heavily, and in west Ulster Lord Strabane was described as 'very poor' in the late 1650s.[9] Unfortunately, because of the paucity of family papers, it is not possible to quantify the levels of debt, but by examining the relative levels of income and expenditure in Ulster and Scotland some assessment of the relative scale of indebtedness can be attempted.

The main source of landlord income was rent from land. In Ulster it is clear that the 1650s saw a fall in rental income from the 1630s level. On the Brownlow estate in Co. Armagh, for example, the 1659 rental was about 37 per cent lower than that of 1635. This was not an isolated instance since the income from church land in Ulster in 1658 was between a quarter and a third less than in 1641.[10] Much of the problem stemmed from disruption caused by the war of the 1640s. Many of the early seventeenth-century Ulster settlers had been killed or had returned to Scotland or England leaving their Ulster holdings waste. Comparison of the names on the 1630 muster roll and the hearth money rolls of the 1660s, for example, shows that the percentage of names still extant is consistently less than 50 per cent, often falling as low as 20 per cent.[11] Even allowing for the substantial immigration from the mid-1650s, Ulster land was cheap, but given the unsettled state of the province it was difficult to persuade tenants to take long-term leases and effect improvements, and consequently internal mobility was high. Supply problems meant that tenants had to be tended carefully as Viscount Clandeboy appreciated, stipulating in his will of 1659 that his tenants 'be used with all favour that may be as the occasions of the time will permit'.[12] In this situation the tenant often had the upper hand in bargaining so that, as on the earl of Annandale's estate in Donegal, the rents the tenants were prepared to pay fell far short of what the landlord demanded.[13]

In south-west Scotland the problem was less acute. The money rents in 1655/6 on the Earl of Cassillis's Wigtonshire estate, for example, were substantially higher than the 1640/1 level, although there does not seem to have been any commutation of the food renders, and the same was true of the lands of Kirkhill in the earldom of Carrick.[14] If the upward demographic trend in Scotland is a guide, the availability of tenants there was greater than in Ireland.[15] One indicator is that land values in Scotland were less depressed than in Ulster. In the 1650s, for example, Scottish land could fetch up to 20 years' purchase, and creditors felt they had a good deal at 16 years' purchase, whereas the best their Ulster counterparts could hope for was between 7 and 10 years.[16] In trade also the situation was rather better in Scotland. The port of Glasgow, for example, recovered significantly after 1654 with shipping entries increasing rapidly and the registration of craftsmen and merchant burgesses also rising. Belfast, by contrast, saw little change in the enrolments for freedom, average yearly freemen's and merchants' enrolments remaining the same in the periods 1639–49 and 1650–60.[17] Moreover the Scottish rural economy did not have the Irish problem of a heavily debased coinage affecting both trade and the payment of rents.[18]

On the other side of the landed estate's balance sheet the main charges on estate income were the assessments for the maintenance of the army and the fines for compounding for estates. Both Ulster and south-west Scotland were taxed disproportionately heavily for the army's maintenance in the 1650s. In Ireland the lord deputy, Henry Cromwell, complained in 1658 that the assessment, at a quarter of that for England and Wales, was ten times what it should have been in terms of relative wealth. Monck estimated that while Scotland paid a quarter of the assessment, it had only a sixteenth of the wealth.[19] Such estimates were dubious but reflected a real situation. If anything Ulster was more heavily taxed than south-west Scotland. The 1660 assessment for Ulster, for example, stood at £5,601 when the population was about 250,000, or roughly £22 per 1,000 persons. Assuming a population of one million for Scotland, it is unlikely that the south-west's population was less than 250,000, yet it paid only £2,300 in assessment, or £9 per 1,000 persons.[20]

The same point can be made by relating cess to rent. In Scotland, John Baynes, the Cromwellian Receiver General, estimated that the assessment absorbed about a fifth of the rent. Yet on the Conway estate in Co. Antrim the agent, George Rawdon, estimated that cess could account for anything from all the rent to a third, depending on land quality. On the Earl of Annandale's estate in Donegal the 1658 cess accounted for over 25 per cent of the rental income, including arrears, and on the O'Neill land in Antrim the assessment of 1652 consumed all the rents.[21]

The assessment was a relatively crude tax. County figures were fixed by the central government, so it was difficult to redistribute assessments to reflect change. While this was of limited importance for Scotland, since recent valuations existed on which the distribution could be based, and given apparently little change in population distribution, it was of considerable significance in Ulster. There was no real valuation of all Ulster and so any apportionment of assessment was bound to be haphazard. Even if a valuation had existed it would have had limited relevance since the distribution of population and wealth changed significantly in the 1650s with renewed immigration. Increased internal mobility as new migrants looked westwards for opportunities further complicated the position. As George Rawdon commented in 1657: 'Down and Antrim are much pressed since our people removed with their stocks to the waste countries'; and later, 'cess is so severe that our tenants and stocks leave us yet the cess does not follow them'.[22] Thus Ulster not only bore a higher cess per head of population than south-west Scotland but probably one more inequitably distributed, placing severe burdens on landowners who were ultimately responsible for payment.

The second major charge on landlord incomes was the fine for compounding for delinquency, imposed on those who were on the wrong side at the end of the war. The rules on compounding were radically different in Ulster and Scotland. Political considerations in Scotland meant that the Ordinance for Oblivion was less harsh than the Irish Act of Indemnity.[23] In Ireland, for example, the fine was fixed at twice the annual income of the estate in 1641. While the administration had a limited impact in collecting composition, it had a better than average record in Ulster with most Scottish lords there paying their fines.[24] Robert Adair of Co. Antrim was effectively fined £1,968, Teige O'Hara £614, Lord Clandeboy £9,000 (of which £4,677 was actually paid), Lord Montgomery £3,000 and Henry O'Neill of Killeleagh £1,400.[25] In Scotland fines were lower and were reduced as the decade progressed as the Cromwellian regime attempted to curry favour with the Scottish lords. The Earl of Galloway and Lord Boyd, two landowners in the south-west, had their fines cut from £4,000 and £1,500 to £600 and £500 respectively. However, others remained high, such as Lord Bargany's who actually paid £1,396 of his fine of £4,000.[26] This evidence suggests that while landlords in both countries fell into debt in the 1650s the levels of debt were probably higher in Ulster.

The problems of the 1650s hit both sets of landowners at what was already a difficult time financially. Many of the lords of south-west Scotland had borrowed to contribute to the Covenanter cause in the late 1630s and the Irish campaign of the early 1640s. Changes in political circumstances meant that this debt was no longer recoverable from the administration.[27] Ulster lords had also experienced financial difficulties in the late 1630s due to an economic downturn there. However the two situations were somewhat different in scale. In a 'worst case' situation in Scotland, Sir William Dick, Edinburgh's richest citizen and loyal Covenanter, had public debts of £19,038; but this paled into insignificance compared to the Earl of Antrim's debt of £39,377 even before the war of the 1640s.[28] Even one of the worst indebted landlords of south-west Scotland, Lord Bargany, could muster only £1,900 in debts in 1660, less than two-thirds the average Ulster lord's pre-war debt.[29]

The public debt situation in Ulster was also rather different to that in Scotland.

When the government had borrowed for Ireland through the Adventurers Act of 1642, they had secured the debt by promising grants of Irish land. When these debts fell to be satisified in the 1650s there was chaos. In Ulster more land was required than existed. Inadequate knowledge of the geography of Ulster landholding led to grants being made of land already granted, and the resulting uncertainty caused severe disruption to the Ulster land market and a reduction of landed income which had no Scottish parallel.[30]

The real problem, however, was not the absolute level of debt but the ability to finance it. In any pre-industrial society the normal sources of loans were friends, family, the merchant community (which usually had cash balances on hand to lend), and members of the professional classes such as lawyers or clergy. Scotland was well served with all of these groups who, with the depression of economic activity, saw in money lending as good an investment as was possible, and the courts' strict interpretation of the law on debt gave reasonable security.[31] Lord Boyd, for example, borrowed considerable sums from Edinburgh merchants in the late 1650s while Lord Bargany borrowed extensively from merchants in Edinburgh and Ayr, Edinburgh lawyers, and sundry others such as the chamberlain to the Duke of Hamilton and an Edinburgh apothecary. Many of these bonds were later bought up by Edinburgh lawyers. The Earl of Cassillis borrowed from Ayr merchants and from the minister of Ayr, William Adair, but in the main he was able to borrow from local men. Cassillis was clearly a good risk since in the 1650s his estates usually generated a surplus each year — a fact doubtless well known locally.[32] Ulster, by contrast, had neither a well-established merchant community nor a legal group. Moreover the very fluid land market there meant that the merchants who did arrive in the 1650s had both the means and opportunity to acquire land which conferred both social prestige and economic benefit. Thus, John Corry, a Belfast merchant, purchased within a few years of arriving in Ulster a substantial Fermanagh estate.[33] Within Belfast itself one of the most prominent merchants of the 1650s, George Maccartney, acquired a substantial leasehold estate as one of the head tenants of the Donegall family.[34] Merchants were reluctant to invest in anything other than land and it is not surprising that George Rawdon complained that in developing potash production at Lisburn he could not find a merchant to invest in the project. Likewise it was only with difficulty that he persuaded two Dublin merchants to consider investing in his soap works.[35] Viscount Ards in trying to remain afloat in the 1650s borrowed mainly from clergy families such as the Colvilles, to whom he sold considerable quantities of land, and Rev. Robert Blair of Portpatrick, to whom he sold much of the family's Scottish lands, and other local friends.[36]

The main means by which money was raised in Ulster in the 1650s was through the sale of land. Sales were not always to new men, such as John Corry, and much was sold to pre-1641 settlers who had made their own way in the world. George Rawdon, for example, had come to Ireland in the 1630s as agent on the Conway estate and hence escaped the financial difficulties of landownership in the 1630s. He played an active part in the war of the 1640s, defecting to the Cromwellian forces at an appropriate time, and spent the 1650s acquiring an estate by purchase around Moira in Co. Down. Arthur Hill and Mark Trevor were both younger sons of early settlers who used the fluid land market to build up substantial estates in their own right.[37] The main lines of some early seventeenth-century settlers, such as the Brookes and Caldwells, took advantage of the financial difficulties of other families to acquire land for themselves. Besides the situation created by indebtedness there was also the trade in soldiers' debentures by which a number of Ulster families, including the Warings of Waringstown, and to some extent Rawdon, enlarged their holdings.

The situation contrasts with that in south-west Scotland where only one family seems to have entered the land stakes in any appreciable way: Dalrymple of Stair, who purchased land from the Earl of Cassillis in the 1650s to form the basis of the late seventeenth-century family estate.[38] Examination of the sasines and the records of individual estates confirms this since although there was commonly a significant increase in mortgaging during the 1650s there was usually little outright alienation.

These contrasting patterns were reflected in the distribution of power in the localities. At the higher levels of political status, such as that of M.P., there was a dramatic change in Ulster personnel after the Interregnum. In Fermanagh, Donegal, and Down, none of the early seventeenth-century families which had provided M.P.s was represented in parliament after 1660. In Tyrone and Armagh one family survived, and in Antrim the Clotworthys, supporters of the Cromwellian order, and the Colvilles, who had acquired considerable amounts of land from the Montgomerys in the 1650s, both survived. In Tyrone, the Mervyns had only come to local prominence in the late 1630s.[39] In Scotland, by contrast, there were families who held the office right throughout the century: the Blairs of Ayrshire, the Colquhouns of Dunbartonshire, the Lockharts of Lanarkshire, and the Agnews of Wigtonshire.[40] The same pattern is evident in the office of sheriff. When the heritable jurisdictions were finally abolished in 1747, 20 of the 33 Scottish sheriffs held office through inheritance and many lineages extended back a considerable way, whereas in Ulster there was little common personnel between the sheriffs of the early and later seventeenth century.[41] Ulster J.P.s also experienced an influx of new blood in the 1650s. The Commission of the Peace for Antrim in 1655 comprised two army officers, Lord Chichester, Sir John Clothworthy, Philip Pincheon, George Rawdon and, *ex officio*, the Mayor of Carrickfergus. In County Down, Arthur Hill was a J.P., as were Walter Cope and Thomas Chambers in Armagh. Of these families, only Clotworthy and Chichester can be traced as Justices before the 1650s.[42] In Wigtonshire the Commissioners of Assessment in 1657 (in reality the newly reorganised J.P.s) comprised 32 individuals of whom 23 can be traced on a 1647 rental of the sheriffdom of Wigton, and those 23 accounted for 92 per cent of the landed income of the sheriffdom in 1647.[43]

The experiences of south-west Scotland and Ulster in the 1650s contrasted in many ways. Such contrasts need hardly be surprising since the two societies were fundamentally different. Scottish society in the 1650s was still dominated by its feudal tradition. A landed estate was not primarily a provider of income or an economic unit but rather a mark of social standing; landholding was a sign that a man had reached the pinnacle of the social order. Accounts were still kept in roman numerals and rents collected in kind. The marketing system was little developed, market creations only beginning to expand significantly from the 1660s. In Ulster, by contrast, land itself conferred less social status as it was readily available to all comers: it was a way to wealth rather than a sign that it had been achieved. Ulstermen were often regarded as *nouveaux riches* upstarts. Comments similar to that of Colonel John Jones in 1657, that 'such as have raised themselves from nothing to great estates by the trouble of the times ... many of them minded themselves more than the public interest', were made by many who had contact with Ulster before 1641.[44] As a result, early seventeenth-century Ulster landowners had a different attitude to land, and aspired to manage it as an economic asset. Food rents were quickly commuted to cash with the spread of a market economy and market centres developed rapidly. Land changed hands readily and tenants were not averse to bargaining with landlords for improved terms of tenure. The result was contrasting reactions to the financial problems of the 1650s. In Scotland landed families were determined to hold out against their creditors and succeeded in doing so because of better credit mechanisms, lesser burdens and probably lower interest rates. Thus many landed families in south-west Scotland enjoyed continuity from the early seventeenth into the eighteenth century. In Ulster there was less scruple about alienating lands so that the demise of many early seventeenth-century landed families, such as the Montgomerys and the Hamiltons, can be traced to extensive sales made as a result of debts incurred in the 1650s.

This adaptability of Ulster landowners was important for the province's political history. In Scotland, the Cromwellian regime had little success in its declared policy of reducing the power of the great lords. The heritable jurisdictions, for example, remained intact despite statutory abolition in 1652. In Ulster the power of the greater settlers was effectively curbed in the 1650s so that the resistance to royal authority in the early seventeenth century was not repeated later. A combination of financial difficulties and a central government presence in the localities had effectively clipped the wings of the greater lords.[45]

Adaptability to new circumstances in Ulster also had an economic impact. The 1650s saw the importation of new ideas on agriculture and rural industry. Arthur Hill, for example, invited Robert Child, a member of the Hartlib circle, to his estate. Child was soon reporting an enthusiasm for agricultural innovation. Flax, sainfoin, hops, and woad were all being grown, fruit was being cultivated in some quantities in the Lagan valley area, and zeal for improvement may partially explain the higher yield from Irish crops than their Scottish counterparts.[46] At Lisburn, George Rawdon was making strides in the sphere of rural industry by introducing the manufacture of potash and soap. He also drafted a proposal for establishing jersey stocking knitting and for encouraging tanning. Lead and coal mining were introduced.[47] Some of these projects, such as linen manufacture, flourished in the later seventeenth century; despite the efforts of the landowners concerned, others failed, not least because of the lack of infrastructural development, especially in the west of the province. Thus, the severity of the 1640s and 1650s provided a stimulus for change, and the 1650s saw a restocking of ideas and capital in the Ulster economy and the migration of at least 24,000 Scots and 15,000 English to the province.[48] By contrast the pace of change in south-west Scotland was more gradual but nonetheless effective. While the Covenanters in the 1630s had been advocating economic diversification, their ideas were slow to take root. As Sir William Petty noted in the *Political Anatomy of Ireland*, 'the country about Carrickfergus is far better than that of Scotland opposite'.[49]

In the final analysis, any comparison between Scotland and Ireland in the seventeenth century must reflect the fact that the social arrangements of one country were of considerable antiquity with well-established social patterns, while those of the other were still in the process of formation. As Henry Cromwell noted of Ireland:

> we are but a kind of colony the inhabitants of which places are commonly more compliant with their present governors, more flexible to change . . . such as have tried their fortunes in many places before, used to the tyranny of country governors and always in expectation of change in their superiors makes them such; begetting in them a genius more ingenious indeed but less ingenious than those who reside nearer the seat of empire.[50]

Glasgow was certainly closer to the 'empire' in the sense of maintaining the *status quo* than was Belfast.

NOTES

1. L. M. Smith, Scotland and Cromwell (unpublished D.Phil. thesis, University of Oxford, 1979), pp. 59–61, 85–7, 254–6; Ivan Roots, 'Union and Disunion in the British Isles, 1637–60', in I. Roots, ed., *"Into Another Mould": Aspects of the Interregnum* (Exeter, 1981), pp. 5–19.

2. Thomas Birch, ed., *A Collection of the State Papers of John Thurloe* (1742), II, p. 516 (hereafter *Thurloe S.P.*).

3. *Thurloe S.P.*, IV, pp. 372, 403; B. L. Lansdowne MS 821, f.292; Robert Dunlop, *Ireland Under the Commonwealth* (Manchester, 1913), II, p. 325.

4. C. H. Firth, 'Cromwell and the Crown', *English Historical Review*, XVII (1902), pp. 429–42; XVIII (1903), pp. 52–80; G. Davies, *The Restoration of Charles II* (San Marino, 1955); Smith, Scotland and Cromwell, pp. 100–4.

5. For example, T. Keith, 'The Economic Condition of Scotland Under the Commonwealth and Protectorate', *S.H.R.* V (1908), pp. 273–84; George O'Brien, *The Economic History of Ireland in the Seventeenth Century* (Dublin, 1919), pp. 100–15.

6. Raymond Gillespie, *Colonial Ulster* (Cork, 1985), esp. Ch. 2; also my comments on the army's role, in *Ir. Ec. & Soc. Hist.* IX (1982), pp. 103–4.

7. David Stevenson, *Revolution and Counter-Revolution in Scotland* (1977); *idem, Scots Covenanters and Irish Confederates* (Belfast, 1981).

8. D. Laing, ed., *The Letters and Journals of Robert Baillie* (Bannatyne Club, Edinburgh, 1842), III, p. 387; Rosalind Mitchison, *Lordship to Patronage* (London, 1983), pp. 65–6.

9. T. K. Lowry, ed., *The Hamilton Manuscripts* (Belfast, 1867), pp. 66, 68–9; George Hill, ed., *The Montgomery Manuscripts* (Belfast, 1869), pp. 203–6; P.R.O. SP63/287/16.

10. On Brownlow, P.R.O.N.I. T970; Raymond Gillespie, *Settlement and Survival on an*

Ulster Estate (P.R.O.N.I. Belfast, forthcoming); T. C. Barnard, *Cromwellian Ireland* (Oxford, 1975), pp. 157, 162.

11. W. Macafee and V. Morgan, 'Population in Ulster, 1660–1760', in P. Roebuck, ed., *Plantation to Partition* (Belfast, 1981), p. 47; for continued movement to Scotland in the early 1650s, *C.S.P.I., 1647–60*, p. 793.

12. S.R.O. GD109/2682.

13. S.R.O. GD214/524; generally new lettings in the 1650s were at lower levels than 1641. P.R.O. SP63/260/57 for 1650s; S.R.O. RH15/91/25, 59; *C.S.P.I., 1647–60*, pp. 394–5, 684–5; W. H. Crawford, 'Landlord-Tenant Relations in Ulster 1609–1820', *Ir. Ec. & Soc. Hist.* II (1975), p. 13.

14. S.R.O. GD25/9/47/5; GD27/1/55.

15. M. W. Flinn, *Scottish Population History* (Cambridge, 1977), pp. 150–55.

16. J. D. Marwick, ed., *Extracts from the Records of the Convention of the Royal Burghs of Scotland, 1615–76* (Edinburgh, 1878), pp. 414, 433–59. It was estimated that Glencairn's lands, though heavily indebted, were worth £5,000 sterling in 1656 — considerably more than the much larger Ulster estates in the relatively prosperous 1630s, *Thurloe S.P.*, V. p. 18; Gillespie, *Colonial Ulster*, App. G.

17. T. M. Devine, 'The Cromwellian Union and the Scottish Burghs', in J. Butt & J. T. Ward, eds., *Scottish Themes: Essays in Honour of S. G. E. Lythe* (Edinburgh, 1976), pp. 8–10; R. M. Young, *The Town Book of the Corporation of Belfast* (Belfast, 1892), pp. 246–59.

18. *C.S.P.I., 1647–60*, pp. 620–21, 638, 641, 665; B. L. Lansdowne MS 822, f.118; *Thurloe S.P.* VI, pp. 404, 862; Barnard, *Cromwellian Ireland*, pp. 47–8.

19. *Thurloe S.P.* VII, p. 72; Smith, Scotland and Cromwell, p. 90.

20. C. H. Firth & R. S. Rait, *Acts and Ordinances of the Interregnum* (London, 1911), II, pp. 1359, 1362–3; the Ulster population estimates are based on S. Pender, ed., *A Census of Ireland, c. 1659* (Dublin, 1939); also Macafee and Morgan, 'Population', p. 47. All sums of money in this essay are in sterling.

21. J. Y. Ackerman, ed., *Letters from Roundhead Officers* (Bannatyne Club, Edinburgh, 1856), p. 59; *C.S.P.I., 1647–60*, p. 684; S.R.O. GD214/524; National Library of Wales, Ms.11440 D, f.79.

22. P.R.O. SP3/287/34; SP3/287/47.

23. Smith, Scotland and Cromwell, pp. 64–5, 84, 95–99.

24. *Thurloe, S.P.* IV, p. 668.

25. R. M. Young, *Historical Notices of Old Belfast* (Belfast, 1896), pp. 98, 101; *C.S.P.I., 1647–60*, p. 569; *1660–2*, p. 12; Dunlop, *Ireland Under the Commonwealth*, II, p. 573; *Thurloe S.P.*, IV, p. 673; B.L. Add. MS 34326, ff.2v–3, 21.

26. F. D. Dow, *Cromwellian Scotland* (Edinburgh, 1979), pp. 154–60; *C.S.P. Dom., 1655*, pp. 70–2; S.R.O. GD 109/3886; RH4/57/1/38.

27. Smith, Scotland and Cromwell, pp. 66–7; *Thurloe S.P.* VI, p. 80; David Stevenson, 'The Financing of the Cause of the Covenants, 1638–51', *S.H.R.* LI (1972), pp. 89–123.

28. Smith, Scotland and Cromwell, pp. 129–30; Gillespie, *Colonial Ulster*, pp. 137–8.

29. S.R.O. RH4/57/1/41.

30. K. Bottigheimer, *English Money and Irish Land* (Oxford, 1971), pp. 143–63; *C.S.P.I., 1647–60*, pp. 114–15.

31. Smith, Scotland and Cromwell, pp. 124–32.

32. Based on bonds in S.R.O. GD/775, 800, 807–10 (Boyd); GD109/958–67, 1546–70 (Bargany); GD25/8/336–424; 5/45–6, 71, 88–9 (Cassillis); GD25/9/48–52 (Cassillis accounts).

33. Young, *Old Belfast*, pp. 109–11; for further details, Earl of Belmore, *History of the Corry family of Castlecoole* (London, 1891).

34. P. Roebuck, ed., *Macartney of Lisanoure, 1737–1806* (Belfast, 1983), p. 3.

35. P.R.O. SP63/287/29; *C.S.P.I., 1647–60*, p. 602. Even the Irish government had difficulty in borrowing, Barnard, *Cromwellian Ireland*, p. 17; Nat. Lib. Wales, MS 11440 D, f.266.

36. P.R.O.I. RC6/2, pp. 328, 342; C 3446–7; D15237–40; S.R.O. GD237/174/3; Hill, *Montgomery Manuscripts*, pp. 203–6, 267.

37. M. Beckett, *Sir George Rawdon* (Belfast, 1935); *C.S.P.I., 1647–60*, p. 496; H. O'Sullivan, The Trevors of Rostrevor, (unpublished M.Litt. thesis, Trinity College, Dublin, 1985), pp. 144–63; Gillespie, *Colonial Ulster*, p. 140; *C.S.P.I., 1647–60*, p. 828.

38. Based on P. H. McKerlie, *A History of their Lands and Owners in Galloway* (Edinburgh, 1870–8), 5 vols.

39. R. Lascelles, *Liber Munerum Publicorum Hiberniae* (Dublin, 1852), pt.1, 'Parliamentary Register'.

40. Based on J. Foster, *Members of Parliament, Scotland, 1357–1882* (2nd ed., London, 1882).

41. W. C. Dickinson, ed., *The Sheriff Court Book of Fife* (Edinburgh, 1928), pp. xxv, xxvi; Lascelles, *Liber. Mun. Pub. Hib.* pt.IV, pp. 155–6.

42. Young, *Old Belfast*, p. 100; *Thurloe S.P.* V, p. 336; B. L. Lansdowne MS 822, f.198.

43. Firth & Rait, *Acts and Ordinances*, II, pp. 1147, 1385; A. Agnew, *The Hereditary Sheriffs of Galloway* (Edinburgh, 1893), II, pp. 75–7. For identification of Commissioners of Assessment with J.P.s, *Thurloe S.P.*, IV, p. 342.

44. Nat. Lib. Wales, MS 11440 D, f.198. Gillespie, *Colonial Ulster; idem*, 'The Origins and Development of an Ulster Urban Network', *I.H.S.* XXIV (1984), pp. 15–29; I. D. Whyte, *Agriculture and Society in Seventeenth-Century Scotland* (Edinburgh, 1979).

45. Nat. Lib. Wales, MS 1140 D, f.18; Mitchison, *Lordship to Patronage*, p. 65; Smith, Scotland and Cromwell, pp. 193–5, 204–7; Gillespie, *Colonial Ulster*, ch. 5.

46. Barnard, *Cromwellian Ireland*, pp. 216, 222–3, 235, 239; C. H. Hull, ed., *The Economic Writings of Sir William Petty* (Cambridge, 1899), I, p. 176; Whyte, *Agriculture and Society*, pp. 74–9.

47. *C.S.P.I., 1647–60*, pp. 250, 591, 602, 619–20, 638, 650, 694; R. C. Simmington, *The Civil Survey* (Dublin, 1937), III, p. 265; Dunlop, *Ireland Under the Commonwealth*, II, p. 679.

48. Based on the difference between Scots and English, by surname, *c.* 1630 (B.L. Add. MS 4770) and *c.* 1660 (Hearth Money Rolls, and Pender, *Census*). Given gaps in the data and turnover of about 50 per cent in the pre-1650 population, the immigration was probably nearer 70,000. I am greatly indebted to Mr. W. Macafee for showing me his important unpublished paper, 'The movement of British population into Ulster, 1630–1712'. For differences between east and west Ulster, Gillespie, *Settlement and Survival* (forthcoming).

49. Hull, ed., *Economic Writings*, I, p. 204.

50. *Thurloe S.P.* VII, p. 101.

4
THE EFFECTS OF REVOLUTION AND CONQUEST ON SCOTLAND

David Stevenson

I

There are obvious dangers in looking in late seventeenth-century Scotland for the 'effects' of the mid-century upheavals. Care has to be taken to avoid the temptation of hailing all new developments as resulting from revolution and conquest, just because they come after these events. At the other extreme lies the danger of taking revolution and conquest to mark an interlude of blood and thunder which is dramatic but contributes nothing to the later history of Scotland. This latter interpretation is one that appealed to some in late seventeenth-century Scotland; the events of 1637–60 were seen as a distasteful aberration.

The very fact that some Scots would have liked to pretend that the events of 1637–60 had not taken place is, of course, in itself an indication that these years had been traumatic. The way many Scots perceived their country and their own positions in its society had been changed. Psychologically English conquest in the 1650s, however temporary, had profound and lasting effects. It destroyed overnight one of the strongest national myths of the Scots. They tended to be obsessive in comparing their country with England. On most counts — population, wealth, size — they had to admit the inferiority of their country. But in one respect they claimed to be greatly superior to the English. Scotland was a never-conquered nation. England by contrast had been overrun frequently — by Romans, Saxons, Danes and Normans. All these people had also tried to conquer Scotland, but all had failed, as had the English themselves.[1] Thus the Scots claimed to be superior to the English in courage, fortitude and military skills. From this followed other differences. The English, through repeated conquest, were a slavish, servile people, contemptible in comparison with the never-conquered free-born Scots.[2] The success of Scots armies in 1639–44 in defying Charles I reinforced this myth. But then followed repeated military disasters, culminating in the Cromwellian conquest. The myth of the never-conquered people was shattered for ever. So too was its religious counterpart, the myth which reached its apogee under the Convenanters, of the Scots as the chosen people of God to whom he would bring victory.[3]

The shattering of these myths, by which a small and poor nation had sought to maintain its morale and self-respect, was profoundly important for the future. Scotland had discovered the hard way that in trying to redefine her position under the Union of the Crowns she must ultimately defer to England if this was the only way to avoid a head-on confrontation between the kingdoms; for outright defiance of English interests could lead to conquest. In the 1640s the Scottish Covenanters had sought to impose a settlement on the three kingdoms designed primarily to protect Scotland's interests. But this was the last time in British history that Scotland had the confidence — or arrogance — to take so bold an initiative. In accepting the restoration of monarchy in 1660 and in accepting the revolution of 1688–9, Scotland waited until England had acted — and then followed suit. Attempts to defy English wishes over the constitutional relationship of the two kingdoms in the opening years of the eighteenth century quickly gave way to acceptance of union on basically English terms in 1707 when it became clear that the actions of the Scots had seriously provoked the English. Memories of the devastating Cromwellian conquest half a century before had a significant part in the complex nexus of calculations that led the Scottish parliament to vote itself out of existence. In 1700, as the crisis which was to lead to the new union was developing, men talked in dread of the situation looking like '41 again.[4] The reference was to 1641; the events of that year had represented a triumph for the Scots, for they had extorted a new constitution from Charles I which went a long way towards destroying royal power. But gaining this new freedom had led directly to conflict with England and ultimately to conquest. The Scots wanted at all costs to prevent a recurrence of that pattern.[5] The tail had finally accepted that attempting to wag the dog was impractical.

II

Turning to more general social and political attitudes, some of the influences of revolution and conquest are obvious. Strong reaction in favour of royal power and traditional hierarchy are evident, though some innovation was seen in attempts to strengthen the hold of the landowning classes on society, rather than mere literal reaction to pre-1637 conditions. This explains the seeming paradox of the widening of the parliamentary franchise in a period of political reaction. The old county franchise extended only to those holding land from the king by traditional feudal tenures. The Restoration regime saw this as being archaic, and therefore extended the franchise to some groups of landowners previously excluded. Increasingly what was seen as giving a right to a part in government was the possession of land, effective ownership, rather than feudal technicalities relating to how the land was held.[6]

The reaction of the nobility and other landowners in favour of royal power — since the rebellion against Charles I which they had sponsored had ultimately led to a challenge to their dominance of society — has also been plausibly held to mark an important stage in the transformation of traditional 'lordship' into a 'patronage' system of the type that flourished in the eighteenth century. As Mitchison puts it, Scots nobles might still prove so awkward and unscrupulous in the late seventeenth century as to make stable government difficult; but they were not (on the whole) signing bonds to tie lesser men to them in a quasi-feudal way, or to create alliances with equals; and they were no longer summoning their followers in arms to pursue local feuds or national quarrels.[7] It was now accepted that such activities were archaic and, by undermining the authority of the crown, likely to undermine the social hierarchy.

Moreover, just as the violence of the feud had disappeared, at least from most of Lowland Scotland, by 1660, so had traditional attitudes to justice that had accompanied the feud. The old conventions for settlement of blood-feuds had seen justice as lying primarily in arbitration and compensation to victims or their kin. After 1660 'modern' justice, almost exclusively concerned with retribution and administered by state courts and professional lawyers, finally triumphed. And Wormald has argued that this process was greatly hastened by the legislation and attitudes of the covenanting regime of the 1640s.[8]

Another aspect of the decline of patriarchal or feudal 'lordship' relates to the attitudes of landlords to their tenants, and indeed to their estates in general. With Restoration traditional hierarchical authority in society was re-asserted. But this could not wipe out the fact that it had been defied during the troubles. From the early stages of the troubles many royalist or neutral landlords had found that they had lost the allegiance of their tenants to the covenanters. Others found that even if their tenants wished to continue to obey them, the tenants soon discovered that landlords could not protect them from the demands of the covenanting state for money and men for armies, or the demands of the covenanting kirk for religious conformity. In a great many cases this must have been the first occasion on which the power of the centralising state and church had seemed stronger and more direct to ordinary people than the power of their landlords. The experience of finding that traditional loyalties could no longer be taken for granted, that a lord's tenants might either willingly defy him or be forced to do so by a higher power, must have deeply shocked the landlords concerned. And this experience spread ever more widely in the 1640s as divisions within the covenanting regime led to successive purges. The process culminated in the rule of the kirk party in 1648–50, when the great majority of the nobility were excluded from power. Some, indeed, were forced to do public penance in their parish kirks before the eyes of their own tenants. After such experiences, how could a landlord look on his tenants in the same way as in the past? Or indeed they look at him? To take just one example, in 1645 the earl of Queensberry tried to join the rebellion of the royalist marquis of Montrose; but his own men, instead of following him into battle, arrested him.[9]

Now it is of course true that traditional political wisdom had long insisted that the lower orders were inherently anarchic and needed to be ruled with a firm hand. But the extent of disaffection during the troubles, and the extent to which the covenanters' state could 'rule' tenants directly, without acting through their lords, must have deeply unsettled landlords who had previously taken the loyalty — or at least the obedience — of 'their' men for granted. Moreover covenanting rule was followed by a Cromwellian regime which led a general attack on the power of lords over lesser men. The external feudal and other trappings of lordship might be restored after 1660, but in many cases the old nexus of unquestioned and willing loyalty and duty on the part of tenants, and of 'good lordship' and patriarchal responsibility on the part of landlords, must have been seriously weakened. Does this link up with the slowly accelerating tendency for Scottish landlords to adopt 'commercial' attitudes to their estates? Were they becoming more willing to think about their estates and what they could get out of them in a new way, to think in terms of money rather than men, because they had been freed of their responsibility to their men by the way in which these men had already deserted them by giving obedience to Covenanters or Cromwellians?

The process by which in the eighteenth century clan chiefs converted themselves into commercial landlords has often been described in terms of chiefs deserting their clansmen, abdicating traditional responsibilities and thus destroying lordship. Was it the case that in the Lowlands in many instances the desertion was the other way round; was it tenants, inspired by religious or political ideology, or forced by the imperative demands of revolutionary church and state, who deserted their lords? — with the same ultimate result, the destruction of lordship?

Certainly the experience of the Restoration period lends strong support to the idea that the mid-century troubles had greatly hastened the decline of lordship. The problem of religious dissent which bedevilled the era clearly grew directly from the troubles. But whereas the 1640s had seen many landlords defied by tenants who had the support of a revolutionary church and state, after 1660 there emerged popular defiance of both landlords and the state in many parts of southern Scotland. Admittedly leadership for the dissidents was often provided by ministers expelled from their parishes, and by small landowners; but the dissident movement was nonetheless essentially a popular one. The Restoration period, it has been said, thus contains the first significant political activity in Scottish history not led by the nobility.[10] What comprises 'significant political activity' is of course debatable, but it is arguable that there was in fact one earlier episode of this sort, the popular rising of 1648 (against an attempt at limited counter-revolution) which had been defeated at Mauchline Moor;[11] and this precedent for the 1666 and 1679 rebellions highlights the fact that the Restoration risings grew out of the experiences of the 1640s.

The 1666 and 1679 risings represent the dramatic peaks of religious dissidence, and through their nature as popular risings illustrate the decay of lordship. Less dramatic aspects of the dissidence issue add to the evidence that the problem, inherited from the years of the troubles, was undermining social bonds. In 1674–7 the regime having failed to crush dissent by 'modern' methods — repression by a standing army and militia — turned back to the 'traditional' remedy of making landlords and masters responsible for the behaviour of their own men. Landlords from the south-west, where dissent was strongest, protested indignantly that they could not control 'their' men, and that it was unreasonable to make them responsible for their tenants' actions.[12] Again the question posed earlier arises: did the fact that tenants had thus abandoned the ties of lordship free landlords from traditional restraints on their behaviour in exploiting their estates and tenants? Obviously so far as the later seventeenth century is concerned all that can be detected is the beginning of change in the attitudes of landlords. But even this might not have occurred without the disruption of the old social order brought about by the troubles.

At least where larger landlords were concerned there was another way in which the troubles tended to widen the gap between them and their inferiors — through the anglicisation of landlords. The Union of the Crowns forced, in time, the great landlords of Scotland to choose between two alternatives; becoming anglicised, which cut them off from their countrymen but made them acceptable in English society and court; or remaining 'Scots' and accepting relegation to a provincial nobility to which the court was alien. In the early seventeenth century the majority of the nobility resisted or ignored anglicisation; and it is probable that their resistance to it helps to account for their support for the Covenanters against an anglicising crown. But the disastrous experience of the years that followed forced a rethink. The 'Wars of the Three Kingdoms' showed clearly how intricately the fortunes of the kingdoms and their social elites were linked. Many Scots nobles found themselves working closely with English and Irish counterparts, royalist or parliamentarian — and ultimately sharing the experience of defeat and exile with many of them. All this helped to assimilate the Scottish nobility in manners and attitudes to the English nobility. By 1660 few Scots nobles could have any doubt that the path to power and fortune lay southwards, to England's court. The troubles had proved that Scotland could not dictate to England; and they had also proved that rebellion led to the development of a common threat to the aristocracies of the three kingdoms. Logic therefore suggested making a common front with the English and Irish aristocracies against threats from below in society. But the increasing anglicisation in manners, outlook and culture of the Scottish nobility opened up a new rift between these nobles and their Scottish followers. This in itself could go far to destroy effective lordship. A striking early example of this was the experience of the Marquis of Huntly in the 1640s. When he tried to lead his great 'name' of Gordon into royalist rebellions, most of the Gordon lairds were unwilling to respond, one of their main complaints against Huntly being that he behaved like an English noble, insulting his followers by treating them as servants.[13] Scotland did not experience a major influx of alien landlords, like Ireland in the seventeenth century; instead the 'alienisation' of her native landlords began. This was essentially a long-term result of the Union of the Crowns, but the troubles hastened the process.

It was argued earlier that the Restoration regime in Scotland turned to a traditional solution to disorder (making landlords responsible for their men) only as a last resort. This obviously implies that significant 'modernisation' of attitudes to government was evident by 1660, a theme that has been dealt with by Mitchison. She has noted how land tax based on new valuations rather than on the traditional 'old extent', and the imposition of excise duties, were features of the Restoration period based on precedents set by the covenanting regime in the 1640s. Similarly the Commissioners of Supply of the 1660s were directly copied from the Covenanters' shire committees of war and other local committees, and from the Cromwellian commissioners of the 1650s. Through such bodies there began to emerge in Scotland, late in the day, a weak approximation to the English 'community of the shire', which gave the gentry a sense of corporate identity, through which they often became (in time) dominant in local affairs at the expense of the greater nobility.[14] The emergence of a standing army after 1660 was foreshadowed by the armies of the Covenanters, the first Scotland had seen organised in regiments on 'modern' lines (even though 'feudal' elements remained, some regiments were dominated by followers of particular landlords).[15]

Modernisation and centralisation in government in themselves constituted an attack on lordship, replacing the lord's authority with that of the state. Simultaneously they helped make possible the development of an alternative political system based on patronage. The elaboration of tax collecting (especially customs and excise) systems, the creation of a standing army, and the centrally controlled raising of militias greatly increased the range of patronage available to government. This is a subject that badly needs investigation, but there seems to have been a strong demand from eager landowners for commissions in the militia.

III

In dealing with seventeenth-century Scotland economic historians have shown a strong tendency to avoid the central decades. Lythe has examined the economy up to 1625.[16] Smout has dealt with trade after 1660; Lenman's general economic history also starts at that point,[17] and specialist articles frequently take 1660 as a convenient starting point. Devine has made a very useful pioneering foray into Cromwellian Scotland,[18] but no real attempt has been made to deal with the period of the Covenanters' rule in the 1640s. The justifications for ignoring covenanting Scotland are presumably, firstly, that in these years of confusion, trying to trace the fortunes of the economy is likely to be unrewarding. That is a reasonable point, but the second justification — or assumption — is questionable. This is that the Covenanters had no economic policies (being obsessed with religious fanaticism to the exclusion of all else). In fact, the surviving evidence (though fragmentary) suggests that the Covenanters took a very considerable interest in economic matters, and that their economic policies were in some significant respects innovative, pointing the way to developments later in the century.

From 1640 to 1648 the Covenanters repeatedly tried to obtain free trade with England.[19] They got nowhere, but the fact that they consistently pressed the matter does indicate a sustained interest in Scotland's economic problems. Their legislation supports this suggestion. Most of the Acts of Parliament concerned have been discussed by economic historians, but each Act has tended to be dealt with in isolation, in specialist studies of different aspects of the economy. No-one seems to have drawn attention to the fact that there was a notable grouping of innovative Acts in the 1640s, let alone asked why this was so.

The 1641 Act for encouraging the establishment of manufactories is perhaps the best known — and the most important — of a number of Acts concerning the economy passed in that year. It granted tax privileges, with woollen manufactories particularly in mind, and gave employers extensive powers over their workers by forbidding others to employ them, and envisaged forcing the idle to work in such establishments.[20] The Act has been hailed as marking 'the beginning of a more systematic industrial policy orientated towards solving the fundamental structural problems facing Scots manufacturing, namely, lack of capital, lack of high-quality domestic raw materials, lack of skilled labour, and competition from superior foreign products'.[21] Like all the other Acts of the 1640s it was declared to be null and void after the Restoration;[22] but a new Act based on it was passed in 1661, a clear sign that it was recognised as representing a better policy than the patents and monopolies of the early part of the century (which the Covenanters had attacked).[23]

Evidence as to how the 1641 Manufactories Act came to be passed indicates that it was not merely a well-meaning Act passed in a void of indifference, but reflected a real demand by Scots entrepreneurs for state support. The supplication to Parliament that led to the Act was presented by 'Johne Haistie overman of the clothieris for himself, and in name and behalfe of the erectors, maintainers, favour and remanent maisters of manufactories within this kingdome'.[24] There also survives another supplication, with ten signatures, presented to the Exchequer when it broke the 1641 Act by allowing the export of raw wool, and it was presented in the name of all 'who are favouris of vertue and intertayneris thairof especiallie these who at thair great charges and expenses haiv brought and are daylie bringing in trade of manufactories and using meanes to bring the same to some perfectioune'.[25]

The 1641 Act empowered the Privy Council to appoint a commission for encouragement of the establishment of manufactories. In February 1643 commissioners were duly nominated — and they included a number of those who had been petitioning the exchequer the previous year.[26] Unfortunately all that is known about the work of the commission is that it issued a proclamation the following month — and though it was ratified in 1646 its text has not survived.[27] In these troubled years opportunities to benefit under the 1641 Act were very limited, and in July 1644 sixteen men petitioned parliament for themselves and other clothiers and ropemakers in Scotland, asking that their manufactories should be free of all taxation then being imposed to finance the civil war, and that they, their servants and their apprentices should not be liable to military service. Parliament referred the matter to the Committee of Estates, which issued the orders requested, and followed this up in 1645 with an Act freeing manufactories from taxes, levies and quarterings.[28]

These details, sparse as they are, indicate that there was a real, officially encouraged, manufactories movement under the Covenanters. Even in these chaotic years of war at least three manufactories seem to have been established under the 1641 and 1645 Acts.[29] Moreover, those signing petitions relating to manufactories in the 1640s included merchants from Edinburgh, Glasgow and Aberdeen who had been active in establishing manufactories and/or correction houses with the support of the councils of these burghs in the 1630s.[30] Thus the 'manufactories' movement of the late seventeenth century had its roots in local schemes in the 1630s, which first received national legislative encouragement from the Covenanters in the 1640s.

Turning to agriculture, several Acts show an interest in change and development in the 1640s. The most interesting is the 1647 Act concerning dividing commonties (a topic which had been debated in parliament three years earlier).[31] Though the Act applied only to a few counties, in asserting the right of landowners to insist on a division even if some of the interested parties opposed it, and in granting the court of session jurisdiction, it is an important precursor of the famous 1695 Act, and has been described as 'the first real improving Act in Scotland'.[32] 1641 Acts against destruction of parks and plantings[33] and for draining the Pow of Inchchaffray[34] also suggest an active interest in encouraging rural change. The 1645 proposal to introduce the cultivation of maize to Scotland may have been misguided (and the idea of a foreigner),[35] but it points in the same direction.

The economic legislation of the Covenanters produced virtually none of the results hoped for. Nonetheless, the Acts are important as evidence of changes in attitudes to economic development which were taking place. These changes become visible only through legislation; and that legislation evidently became possible only because a political revolution had brought to power a regime more open to new ideas than its predecessors. The Restoration period saw political reaction — but the new economic policies seen under the Covenanters were not abandoned, but continued and extended. Legislation in favour of manufactories, trading companies and agricultural change takes another major step forward in the 1690s — again in the aftermath of a major political revolution, that of 1688.

It has sometimes been argued that Britain's revolutions of 1688 should be seen as the last act of the great upheavals of the 1640s. Looking at economic policy in Scotland certainly supports this interpretation. One of the implicit themes of this paper has been that studying economic and social change without considering the political background is often distorting and limiting. For example, observing in isolation that the 1647 Commonty Act forms a precedent for that of 1695 is interesting; but the parallel between the two Acts becomes much more interesting when it is noted that the two Acts were passed in the only two periods in the history of Scotland in which her parliament had a decisive voice in policy-making, following political revolutions. Quite what the significance of this is may be obscure. But such 'coincidences' deserve to be noted and investigated.

NOTES

1. Sir Thomas Craig, *De Unione Regnorum Britanniae Tractatus*, ed. C. S. Terry (Scottish History Society, Edinburgh, 1909), p. 464. For the importance of the 'martial heritage' myth in Scotland, see J. Robertson, *The Scottish Enlightenment and the Militia Issue* (Edinburgh, 1985).

2. P. Gordon, *A Short Abridgement of Britaine's Distemper*, ed. J. Dun (Spalding Club, Aberdeen, 1844), pp. 76–7.

3. S. A. Burrell, 'The Apocalyptic Vision of the Early Covenanters', *S.H.R.* XLIII (1964), pp. 1–24.

4. W. Ferguson, *Scotland: 1689 to the Present* (Edinburgh & London, 1968), p. 34.

5. See D. Stevenson, 'The Century of the Three Kingdoms', *History Today*, March 1985, pp. 28–33.

6. R. Mitchison, 'Ireland and Scotland: The Seventeenth-Century Legacies Compared',

in Devine & Dickson, p. 4; R. S. Rait, *The Parliaments of Scotland* (Glasgow, 1924), pp. 211–12.

7. Mitchison, 'Ireland and Scotland', p. 4.

8. J. Wormald, 'Bloodfeud, Kindred and Government in Early Modern Scotland', *Past and Present*, 87 (1980), pp. 92–7.

9. D. Stevenson, *Revolution and Counter-Revolution in Scotland, 1644–51* (London, 1977), p. 36.

10. R. Mitchison, 'Restoration and Revolution', in G. Menzies, ed., *The Scottish Nation* (London, 1972), p. 135.

11. D. Stevenson, 'The Battle of Mauchline Moor, 1648', *Ayrshire Collections*, XI, no.1 (1973), pp. 1–24.

12. W. C. Dickinson & G. Donaldson, eds., *A Source Book of Scottish History*, III (1961), pp. 170, 174–5; G. Donaldson, *Scotland: James V to James VII* (Edinburgh & London, 1965), p. 370.

13. Gordon, *Britaine's Distemper*, pp. 229–30.

14. Mitchison, 'Ireland and Scotland', pp. 5–6; and see D. Stevenson, ed., *The Government of Scotland under the Covenanters, 1637–51* (Scottish History Society, Edinburgh, 1982).

15. See C. S. Terry, ed., *Papers Relating to the Army of the Solemn League and Covenant, 1643–7* (Scottish History Society, Edinburgh, 1917) and D. Stevenson, *Scottish Covenanters and Irish Confederates* (Belfast, 1981), pp. 325–39.

16. S. G. E. Lythe, *The Economy of Scotland in its European Setting, 1550–1625* (Edinburgh & London, 1960).

17. T. C. Smout, *Scottish Trade on the Eve of Union, 1660–1707* (Edinburgh & London, 1963); B. Lenman, *An Economic History of Modern Scotland, 1660–1976* (London, 1977).

18. T. M. Devine, 'The Cromwellian Union and the Scottish Burghs: The Case of Aberdeen and Glasgow, 1652–60', in J. Butt & J. T. Ward, eds., *Scottish Themes: Essays in Honour of Professor S. G. E. Lythe* (Edinburgh, 1976), pp. 1–16.

19. D. Stevenson, *The Scottish Revolution, 1637–44* (Newton Abbot, 1973), pp. 221, 222, 241, 319; Stevenson, *Revolution and Counter-Revolution*, pp. 97, 221.

20. *A.P.S.*, V, pp. 411–12; W. R. Scott, *The Constitution and Finance of English, Scottish and Irish Joint-Stock Companies* (3 vols., Cambridge, 1912), III, p. 125.

21. G. Marshall, *Presbyteries and Profits. Calvinism and the Development of Capitalism in Scotland, 1560–1707* (Oxford, 1980), pp. 131–2; Scott, *Joint Stock Companies*, III, pp. 125–6.

22. *A.P.S.* VII, pp. 86–7.

23. *A.P.S.* VII, pp. 225–6.

24. S.R.O. PA.7/2/107. For an earlier (1639) supplication of undertakers of manufactories, see *A.P.S.*, V, p. 614. John Haistie appears again in a document of 1662 as deacon of the Incorporation of the Clothiers of the Lothians, S.R.O. RD.3/6, Register of Deeds, pp. 255–6.

25. S.R.O. E.4/6, Register of the Exchequer, 1642–7, ff.47r–49v. In response the exchequer banned export of wool, S.R.O. RH.14/1/15.

26. P. H. Brown, ed., *R.P.C.S.* 2nd Series, VII, 1638–43 (Edinburgh, 1906), pp. liv–lv, 308, 391–2, 403, 549.

27. *A.P.S.* VI, i, 608.

28. *A.P.S.* VI, i, 367. See also S.R.O. PA.7/3/101.

29. Scott, *Joint-Stock Companies*, III, pp. 125–6.

30. J. Stuart, ed., *Extracts from the Council Register of the Burgh of Aberdeen, 1625–42* (Scottish Burgh Record Society, Edinburgh, 1871), pp. 108–12; M. Wood, ed., *Extracts from the Records of the Burgh of Edinburgh, 1626 to 1641* (Scottish Burgh Record Society, Edinburgh, 1936), pp. 172–3; J. D. Marwick, ed., *Extracts from the Records of the Burgh of Glasgow, 1573–1642* (Scottish Burgh Record Society, Edinburgh, 1876), pp. 385–6, 388.

31. Sir James Balfour, *Historial Works* (Edinburgh, 1824–5), III, p. 244.

32. *A.P.S.* VI, pt.i, p. 803; I. H. Adams, 'Division of the Commonty of Hassendean', *Miscellany One* (Stair Society, Edinburgh, 1971), p. 172; I. Whyte, *Agriculture and Society in Seventeenth-Century Scotland* (Edinburgh, 1979), pp. 99–100.

33. *A.P.S.* V, p. 420.

34. *A.P.S.* V, p. 552; Whyte, *Agriculture*, pp. 98, 109.

35. Whyte, *Agriculture*, pp. 98–9; *A.P.S.* VI, i, 372–3. 605; S.R.O. PA.11/4, Register of the Committee of Estates, 1645–6, f.40r–v.

5
THE IMPACT OF THE CIVIL WARS AND INTERREGNUM: POLITICAL DISRUPTION AND SOCIAL CHANGE WITHIN SCOTTISH GAELDOM

Allan I. MacInnes

For Scottish Gaeldom the material legacy of civil war and Cromwellian occupation was land devastation, social dislocation, and increasing public and private indebtedness. The unprecedented pressures for ideological conformity, financial supply and military recruitment generated by the Covenanting movement between 1638 and 1651 not only polarised the clans politically, but committed them irrevocably to Scottish as against Gaelic or pan-Celtic politics.[1] Political commitment in turn accelerated the assimilation of chiefs and leading gentry, the *fine* or clan elite, into Scottish landed society. The growing desire of the clan elite to make their mark in Scottish politics and live the lifestyles of Scottish landowners entailed protracted absences from their territories and the accumulation of debts as a persistent feature of estate management. The cost of absenteeism consistently outstripped revenues raised as rents, however expeditious the recovery of estates from land devastation and social dislocation. Thus, the Restoration era was to witness a fundamental shift in the nature and structure of clanship away from traditionalism towards commercialism.

I

The main theatres of war within Scotland were the central and south-western Highlands. The process of land devastation was begun in the summer of 1640 by Archibald Campbell, Marquis (then eighth Earl) of Argyll. Licensed by the Covenanting movement to harry the disaffected in the central Highlands, Argyll laid waste the estates of suspected Royalists in Atholl, the Braes of Angus, Badenoch and Lochaber.[2]

Devastation was to reach an unparalleled intensity following the arrival, in the summer of 1644, of three regiments recruited from the Ulster estates of Randal MacDonnell, Earl of Antrim, commanded by his kinsman, Alasdair MacColla, and sponsored by the Confederacy of Irish Catholics to link up with the Royalist forces of James Graham, Marquis of Montrose, in order to embroil the Covenanters in a Scottish civil war. Argyll and northern Perthshire were ravaged systematically after MacColla had persuaded Montrose to quarter in the south-western Highlands for the winter of 1644. Colonel James MacDonald, an Irish officer accompanying MacColla, recorded contentedly that 'throughout all Argyll we left neither house nor hold unburned, nor corn, nor cattle, that belonged to the whole name of Campbell'.[3] During his second ravaging in the winter of 1645

MacColla concentrated his destructive energies on the Campbell heartlands in the districts of Lorne, mid-Argyll and Cowal. Other contingents of clansmen used the Royalist mantle to despoil the estates of Campbell cadets and their associates in Ardnamurchan, Breadalbane and Lochtayside.[4]

The south-western Highlands were so devastated by Royalist clans that the Covenanting regime was obliged to despatch from the Lowlands to Argyll substantial quantities of malt and meal (at a cost of £18,500 Scots) to provide basic subsistence for displaced and destitute country people at the outset of 1646; to suspend all public dues from that shire in February 1646 pending the award of reparations eleven months later — £180,000 Scots to the Campbell chief and £360,000 to other landowners; and to institute a relief fund for widows and orphans in Breadalbane by January 1647.[5] Because of the inordinate devastation and dislocation in northern Perthshire, the Campbells of Glenorchy, their kinsmen and their Menzies associates were exempted from all levies of troops for the Engagement during 1648. Exemption was granted on the grounds that 'their lands (which have been destroyed these years, bygone) be not laid waste by lack of tenants'.[6]

Townships in the central Highlands were also laid waste by the marching and counter-marching of the armies of Montrose and his Covenanting pursuers from the autumn of 1644 until the Royalist leader's flight into exile two years later. Again, wastage was intensified by clans, previously reluctant to join the Royalist banner, declaring for the cause in order to exact reprisals against Covenanting neighbours. Of the damages totalling £11,727 inflicted by the Royalist forces on the estates of Sir James Campbell of Cawdor in the shires of Inverness, Nairn and Moray, £4,226 was attributable to the plundering of James Grant of Freuchie, his kinsmen and their associates in Strathspey.[7] Damages to the estates held under ward for Hugh, Lord Fraser of Lovat, which were already running in excess of £10,000, were extended to £14,255 by the time of Montrose's unsuccessful siege of Inverness in April 1646, when, according to the Fraser chronicler, 'betwixt the bridge end of Inverness and Gusachan, 26 miles, there was not left in my country a sheep to bleet, or a cock to crow day, nor a house unruffled'.[8]

The problem of keeping land occupied productively in the aftermath of civil war was aggravated by massacres and compounded by plague. In June 1646, 136 clansmen, mainly Lamonts besieged in Cowal, were massacred after surrendering to a contingent of Covenanting irregulars drawn predominantly from and officered exclusively by ClanCampbell. Twelve months later, around 300 clansmen, mainly MacDougalls, were massacred in Kintyre after surrendering to Covenanting forces who carried bubonic plague in their wake.[9] The two-year visitation of this epidemic disease following on from three years' intermittent warfare so devastated townships in Kintyre that Argyll was obliged to commence replenishment of the peninsula's population by drawing heavily on settlers from the western Lowlands; a process the Marquis had already instigated in mid-Argyll, as had Sir James Lamont of Inveryne in Cowal.[10]

The coming together of moderate Covenanters and Royalists in a patriotic accommodation to fend off the Cromwellian occupation of Scotland provided a salutary reminder that martial involvement outwith Gaeldom was no less expensive to reserves of manpower. Of the 1,000 clansmen raised by Sir Hector Maclean of Duart from his estates on the western seaboard, around 700 were to fall with the chief at Inverkeithing in July 1651; a loss which reputedly left insufficient men to till the soil on the islands of Tiree and Mull, and in Morvern on the adjacent mainland. Indeed, these estates had failed to recover fully a generation after the battle. A rental of 1674 disclosed that 32 out of 140 townships on the ClanGillean estates still remained waste.[11] Two months later the clans loyal to Charles II were again to suffer at Worcester. Such was the level of casualties among the 1,000 clansmen recruited from the estates of Rory MacLeod of Dunvegan on the islands of Harris and Skye, and from Glenelg on the mainland, that the ClanLeod was reputedly incapable of mobilising a fighting force for over a generation.[12] The manpower of the clans was further depleted by Cromwell's policy of transporting prisoners to plantations in Virginia and the West Indies. Clansmen counted for a significant proportion — perhaps as much as 40 per cent — of the 1,610 prisoners shipped off after Worcester as indentured labour.[13]

The clans were again the mainstays of the four-year guerilla campaign against the Cromwellian occupation fought predominantly, if sporadically, in Scottish Gaeldom — a campaign which climaxed in the ill-fated Royalist rising led initially by William Cunningham, Earl of Glencairn, then subsequently by Lieutenant-General John Middleton. The spoliation wreaked, as against threatened, by the Royalist forces between the summer of 1653 and the autumn of the following year was minimal. On the opposite side, however, once General George Monck assumed full responsibility for suppressing the rising in the spring of 1654, the Cromwellian forces undertook systematic pillaging and burning from Lochaber to Wester Ross to persuade the clans, collectively and severally, to sue for peace.[14]

Monck's strategy ultimately proved successful. Chiefs and leading gentry of the clans settled separately during 1655.[15] In substance chiefs were obliged to subscribe bonds for the good conduct of themselves, their leading gentry, their followers, dependants and associates. Chiefs were now obliged to find sureties for good conduct scaling down from £6,000 sterling for George Mackenzie, Earl of Seaforth, to £1,000 sterling for Ewen Cameron of Lochiel. In return, chiefs and leading gentry were given indemnity for past engagements against Cromwellian forces, selective help with private debts incurred under the Covenanting movement and partial relief from the monthly maintenance the Cromwellian regime levied on Scotland. Although the Cromwellian occupation continued to be condemned unreservedly by vernacular poets as 'the time of the oppression',[16] Monck's selective favouring of the *fine* undoubtedly took the edge off the widespread resentment among the clans at having to pay not just for the occupying army but also for the series of garrisons littering the Highlands.

Certain chiefs, like Ewen Cameron of Lochiel, prepared to curtail the territorial mobility of their clansmen, and restrict the size of their own and their leading gentry's personal retinues, were also conceded the privilege of bearing arms for defensive purposes. This concession was testimony not to endemic lawlessness but rather to the perennial agrarian problem of masterless or broken men who had all but thrown over the social constraints of clanship.[17] Organised into cateran bands to seek subsistence by banditry, headed usually by landless younger or illegitimate sons of chiefs and leading gentry, they specialised in extorting blackmail for protecting estates on the Lowland peripheries. Their squatting on the territories of clans was rarely welcomed, giving their indiscriminate predatory inclinations.[18]

Political disruption and social dislocation caused the numbers and activities of cateran bands to expand markedly during the 1640s. Following the Cromwellian occupation the Highlands, like the Borders, became the receptacle for mounted marauders known as moss-troopers; a motley assortment of Lowland Scots, Englishmen and Irishmen, led by displaced gentry intent on waging guerilla war. By the break-up of the Royalist rising in 1654, they were pillaging throughout the Highlands at the expense of the clans no less than of the Cromwellian garrisons, their activities serving to exacerbate the difficulties experienced by chiefs in controlling libertine elements among their followers and dependants.[19] Extending the privilege of bearing arms for defensive purposes among trusted clans became a necessity. As a petition from ClanChattan in 1656 affirmed, their current state of defencelessness in Badenoch left them constantly exposed to predatory incursions 'so as we may not subsist, but of necessity must quyt our labouring'.[20]

Moreover, despite the plaudits from Lowland peripheries at the Restoration about the efficacy of the Cromwellian strategy of containment, predatory raiding remained virulent, especially on the north-eastern peripheries.[21] Indeed, freelance raiding by Lochaber clansmen as well as by cateran bands on the Braes of Angus was facilitated by the settlement of Gaels, displaced by the political disturbances of the past two decades in the central Highlands, who were reputedly opposed to the upkeep of the watches, 'loving rather louse libertie than puire and quhitnes'.[22]

II

Despite the inward migration of Lowland settlers, the incursions of non-Gaelic predators and the displacement of clansmen onto the Highland peripheries, the most profound social change resulting from civil war and Cromwellian occupation was in the composition and function of the clan gentry. Whereas leading gentry like their chiefs tended at the outset of the seventeenth century to hold their lands in feu (that is, by charter), the subordinate gentry, particularly among the clans on the western seaboard, were still split traditionally between the tacksman, *fir-tacsa*, responsible for the townships farmed and laboured by the ordinary clansmen, and the military retainers, *buannachan*, billeted on the townships when not employed as mercenaries in Ireland, where they earned notoriety as well as booty as redshanks.[23] As a complement to the plantation of Ulster by James VI and I, Scottish central government was determined to promote the positive redeployment of clansmen's energies on the western seaboard. Hence, chiefs and leading gentry were encouraged to exploit their estates as proprietors rather than their manpower as warlords. Accordingly, as chiefs and leading gentry began to place special emphasis on written leases to define the responsibilities of the tacksman, hitherto entrusted to oral custom, the *buannachan* were made redundant as unproductive burdens on the rest of their clansmen. While the outbreak of civil war in 1644 put a premium on the availability of fighting men within Scottish Gaeldom, the forces despatched from the western seaboard in the wake of MacColla's departure to rejoin the Confederacy of Irish Catholics three years later can be deemed the last campaign of the redshanks,[24] for the work of recovery in the aftermath of land devastation and social dislocation confirmed the redundancy of the *buannachan*. Simultaneously, the growth of indebtedness among chiefs and leading gentry enhanced the role of the subordinate gentry as financial creditors as well as estate managers.

The clan elite undoubtedly experienced financial difficulties prior to the emergence of the Covenanting movement. Chiefs on the western seaboard found particular difficulty in adjusting from Gaelic warlords to Scottish landed proprietors. Annual accountability before central government in Edinburgh not only necessitated periodic absenteeism, but also afforded opportunities for conspicuous expenditure on sophisticated luxuries and on gaming tables; expenditure which largely continued unabated throughout the political disruption of the 1640s and 1650s and which transformed the financial picture on many estates from acute financial embarrassment into chronic insolvency.[25] John MacLeod of Dunvegan inherited debts amounting to £12,172 Scots in 1626. Although he increased the yearly rents on his estates on Harris, Skye and Glenelg from around £6,000 to £15,000 by the outbreak of the civil war, his debts at his death in 1649 totalled £66,700. His son Rory, as well as being fined £30,000 for his opposition to the Cromwellian regime, was 'a prodigal, vitious spendthrift'. Despite augmenting the yearly rent to £18,500, the burden of debts encumbering his estates at his death in 1663 was an extravagant £129,000.[26]

The Restoration served to compound rather than to relax the financial difficulties of the clan elite. Shires throughout Gaeldom were expected to meet in full their complement of the fiscal dues apportioned to Scotland — namely, the excise — to supply the generous annuity of £480,000 awarded for life to Charles II in 1661; the land tax, imposed in 1665 to realise £666,667 over the next five years as Scotland's contribution to England's second Dutch war; and the cess, levied regularly from 1667 to provide £72,000 monthly for the maintenance of the Scottish military establishment. From 1661 the Restoration regime also laid claim to the arrears of monthly maintenance levied on the shires to fend off the Cromwellian occupation between 1648 and 1651 — a claim not relinquished until 1674.[27] The blanket demand of the regime that chiefs and leading gentry throughout Gaeldom, not just from the western seaboard, should be accountable for the conduct of their dependants and followers ensured the clan elite made regular — if not always annual — visits to Edinburgh from 1661. For their part, chiefs and leading gentry were not content to restrict their political ambitions to Edinburgh.[28]

The transmogrification from chief to courtier was best personified by Angus MacDonald of Glengarry who claimed to have encumbered his estates with debts in excess of £148,000 Scots for his involvement in the Royalist cause. Having been rewarded with a peerage at the Restoration, he changed his designation to Aeneas MacDonell, Lord MacDonell and Aros. Over the next twenty years he remained impervious to criticisms from his kinsmen about his adoption of the habits and fashions of a courtier, which were supported by a yearly pension of £3,600. When not resident at court or in Edinburgh, he preferred to dwell near Inverness rather than among his clansmen in Lochaber.[29]

The determination of Sir James MacDonald of Sleat to live conspicuously in the Lowlands, despite having £57,190 apprised from the rents of his estates on the islands of Skye and North Uist in 1666, meant that his son Sir Donald, much to his personal chagrin, was faced with pressing debts in excess of 100,000 merks at his accession in 1678. Because 'the inevitable ruin of the family of the Macdonalds of Sleat' seemed evident, the fourteen leading gentry of the clan, themselves creditors, banded together to protect their chief's patrimony in a document described as 'The Oath of the Friends'. In effect, by accepting joint liability 'to free this family of debt', the clan elite became a mutual assurance society.[30]

The lack of similar remedial action by the ClanGillean left the Maclean of Duart estates exposed to the territorial acquisitiveness of the house of Argyll. Archibald, the Marquis, had deployed both his undoubted prominence within the Covenanting movement and his unrivalled judicial privileges — as heritable justiciar empowered to try all civil and criminal cases (except treason) in Argyll and the Isles — to exploit the growth of public and private indebtedness among successive Maclean chiefs. By 1647 Argyll was confirmed by his own court as the creditor with the foremost claim on the Maclean estates; a decision upheld by the Cromwellian regime in 1658, although the restraining influence of Monck prevented the Marquis annexing Tiree, Mull and Morvern. Despite his forfeiture and execution in 1661, his estranged son, Archibald Campbell, was restored as ninth Earl of Argyll in 1663. When Sir John Maclean succeeded to his estates in 1672, the ninth Earl commemorated the occasion by raising an action for debt in his own court. The sum successfully claimed by Argyll — in excess of £200,000 — represented the accumulated conspicuous expenditure of three generations of Maclean chiefs as well as arrears of public dues since the Restoration. Moreover, since Argyll's court was also accounted a royal court, the armed opposition of the ClanGillean to the partisan judgement ordering their eviction was treated as rebellion against the Crown in 1674. The restored Earl was thus able to secure the backing of central government to mobilise not only his own clan but also the militia of Argyll and three neighbouring shires to effect the expropriation of ClanGillean by 1679.[31]

Although the estates of the clan elite were universally saddled with debt, that only one clan — the Macleans of Duart — should be subject to wholesale expropriation in the Restoration era can be primarily attributed to the revenue generated by the marked expansion of the droving trade in black cattle. While the major expansion of the black cattle trade into England — associated with the phenomenal growth of London, naval and imperial demand for salt beef and embargoes against Irish competition[32] — was dominated initially by droves from Galloway and the Borders, the Highland cattle trade expanded into vacated Lowland markets. Droves of more than 400 beasts occurred regularly during the 1670s. Following the establishment of a market at Falkirk to cater for English demand, droves in excess of 1,000 head of cattle became a noted feature of the Highland economy from the 1680s. As well as enabling the clan elite to pay off pressing creditors, redeem outstanding debts and justify rent increases, the influx of funds from droving was used principally, as clansmen were acutely aware, to underwrite absenteeism and conspicuous expenditure.[33] Thus, despite the marked expansion of the black cattle trade in the Restoration era, the consistent failure of augmented rentals to keep abreast of public and private indebtedness meant that chiefs and leading gentry had increasing recourse to wadsetting — that is, mortgaging portions of their estates to secure ready supplies of credit. The ultimate beneficiaries of this development, which was to fuel a major expansion of proprietorship within Gaeldom comparable to the impact of the secularisation of the kirklands in the Lowlands during the sixteenth century,[34] were the subordinate clan gentry. Lands held customarily under tack were acquired heritably — initially by redeemable wadsets and subsequently, depending on the scale of indebtedness, by irredeemable feu, a conveyance equivalent to an outright sale of property.

The subordinate clan gentry were well placed to take advantage of both the expansion of droving and the financial difficulties of the clan elite on two counts: firstly, because of their more frugal lifestyles and secondly, because of the traditional tendency in estate management of chiefs and leading gentry to favour their own clansmen when granting tacks and wadsets and even when contemplating selling off portions of their property.[35] Conversely, the subordinate gentry's ties of kinship and local association with the *fine* discouraged them from taking legal action to apprise revenues from the estates of heavily indebted chiefs and leading gentry; a process resorted to without compunction by Lowland merchants as major creditors of the elite. Even when lands were sold outright rather than just mortgaged, lesser gentry were content to hold their newly-acquired property within the feudal superiority of the clan elite rather than directly from the Crown, a feature which lent a deceptive degree of stability to the land market within Scottish Gaeldom.[36]

In less than one per cent of 1,615 land transfers in Argyll between 1617 and 1675 was the beneficiary entirely quit of the donor's feudal superiority. Yet, acquisitions by wadset and sale rose from 35 per cent of all land transfers prior to the Covenanting movement to 40 per cent by the end of the Cromwellian occupation, and to 42 per cent in the course of the Restoration era. Although individual wadsets ranged from 200 merks to 38,500 merks, sums mortgaged

Table 1. The Land Market in Argyllshire 1617–75

	Land Transfers	*Wadsets*	*Sales*
1617–38	693	162 (71R, 2A)	83
1638–60	448	132 (27R, 12A)	45
1661–75	474	162 (22R, 26A)	38

(R = redeemed, A = apprised).

normally ranged between 1,000–5,000 merks prior to the Covenanting movement, rising to range between 2,000–5,000 merks by the end of the Cromwellian occupation, and to between 2,000–10,000 merks by the Restoration era. While individual wadsets could last more than 100 years, wadsets prior to 1638 were normally redeemed within ten years. By 1660 the normal period for redeeming wadsets had risen to between 10 and 20 years. During the Restoration era the normal period for redemption dropped to between 5 and 10 years. More significantly, the number of redemptions fell markedly from the outset of the Covenanting movement while sales ran consistently ahead of redemptions between 1617 and 1675. The acquisition of a proprietary interest by lesser gentry became more pronounced in the aftermath of civil war and the Cromwellian occupation. Mortgaging of lands held in tack rose from 6 per cent of all wadsets held prior to the Covenanting movement to 17 per cent by 1660; although the rate fell back to 14 per cent during the Restoration era, this fall was more than compensated by the steady rise in sales of land under tack or wadset — from less than 5 per cent prior to 1638 to 13 per cent by the end of the Cromwellian occupation, and to 23 per cent after the Restoration. The acquisition of a proprietary interest by wadset and sale led to a major expansion in the class of *uachadarain*, or landowners, within Scottish Gaeldom. Thus, the clan elite became an expanding group.

Since 80 per cent of all wadsets and sales in Argyllshire between 1617 and 1675 involved the ClanCampbell and its longstanding associates as beneficiaries, the expansion of the land market serves to demonstrate that the ruthlessly acquisitive policy of the house of Argyll and its leading gentry gave ClanCampbell unrivalled cohesion based upon material success, not just customary affinity or common ancestry. In order to ensure a Campbell presence on lands acquired from other clans either through expropriation or more usually through indebtedness, younger sons of leading gentry were granted wadsets to intrude them as managerial interest over the traditional occupants of estates on their incorporation within Campbell feudal superiority. The Campbells were the main instigators of apprisings to put pressure on clans reluctant to accept their feudal superiority. Within six months of escaping from the massacre of his clansmen in 1646, the Lamont chief was apprised of rents to the value of £9,800 by the Marquis of Argyll. The apprised rents were diverted to promote recovery on the estates of the Campbells of Cawdor on Islay. Although the pronounced rise in apprisings at the Restoration can be attributed to the settling of political scores primarily at the expense of the Campbell elite, the restoration of the ninth Earl saw the successful recovery of apprised revenues from 1665 which could be apportioned among lesser Campbell gentry should leading gentry prefer to live as prodigals. In order to discourage prodigality during the Restoration era, leading gentry passing on the management of their estates to their eldest sons imposed financial restrictions — usually £10,000–£14,000 — on the amount of debt allowed to burden their estates. The imposition of financial limits on debts was subsequently extended to younger sons of Campbell gentry on the conversion of their wadsets into irredeemable feus. The debt burden was usually restricted to 3,000 merks.[37]

III

The Campbells were to the fore not only in seeking to contain indebtedness within their clan, but in promoting a commercial approach to estate management to secure financial recovery from political disruption. Integral to the success of such commercial reorientation was the managerial capacity of the lesser gentry as tacksmen in weaning the ordinary clansmen away from traditional expectations while implementing and supervising the initiatives commanded by chiefs and leading gentry.

When the Campbells of Glenorchy commenced the commercial reorientation of their estates in 1648, they were in dire financial straits. Compounding the damages of £800,000 inflicted by the Royalist clans were apprisings in excess of £90,000 raised by Lowland creditors. The yearly rent had fallen to 2,800 merks. Yet, John Campbell, elder, reduced the burden of debt within six years to 200,000 merks, partly by using reparations promised by the Covenanting regime to forestall legal action by creditors, but principally because 'he did improve ye rent' to 16,000 merks. However, his decision to hand over control of the estates to his eldest son in 1655 set back recovery. John Campbell, younger, because he preferred life in London to the south-western Highlands, contracted fresh wadsets for £40,000 on the Glenorchy estates. Nonetheless, the younger Glenorchy did begin to retrieve the family finances during his English sojourn by contracting a propitious marriage with Mary Rich, daughter of Henry, Earl of Holland, which realised a net profit of £4,500 sterling.[38] By 1659 the younger Glenorchy and his wife had returned to the family seat in north Perthshire where they entertained in a conspicuous but selective manner. Apart from southern visitors, hospitality was restricted to the clan elite, to visiting chiefs and leading gentry (rarely accompanied by more than 12 personal retainers), to tradesmen on contract hire and to ordinary clansmen when directed to assist with landscaping or other work services as part of their rent.[39] Indeed, the general fashion during the Restoration era was for chiefs and leading gentry to restrict lavish hospitality to feast days, hunts, marriages and funerals. Vernacular poets became as accustomed to recollecting past glories as celebrating current festivities in households where chiefs and leading gentry were habitual absentees.[40]

The political ambitions of John Campbell, younger, of Glenorchy, which eventually led to his being created Earl of Breadalbane in 1681, meant that he continued to spend conspicuously as well as to absent himself habitually from his family seat. In order to finance his political ambitions he sought to increase the productive capacity of his estates through sustained investment, by way of steelbow — that is, loans of seed corn, livestock and occasionally money, channelled through the tacksmen to ordinary clansmen to improve arable farming and animal husbandry. Glenorchy was concerned to promote not only agricultural productivity but also commercial diversity on his estates, principally by extending steelbow to equip timber works and by compulsorily directing clansmen to work in sawmills as wood was in steadily growing demand from Lowland towns and the English navy. Indeed, by the time of his ennoblement, Breadalbane was re-investing about two-fifths of the revenue of his estates. As well as facilitating commercial reorientation, steelbow had the added merit of being tax deductible.[41]

Although there is little direct rental — as against testamentary — evidence for the deployment of steelbow elsewhere in Gaeldom,[42] the prevalence of loans to improve productivity from the clan elite to the ordinary clansmen may be inferred from the prevalence of herzelds — death duties which allowed chiefs and leading gentry to recoup a dividend from investing in the labour of their clansmen. Exacted traditionally as the best horse from the deceased clansman's immediate family, the herzeld was being commuted to forty shillings during the Restoration era. At the same time, the Campbell elite demanded a more regular commercial dividend from the townships farmed by the ordinary clansmen — namely, annual, and sometimes bi-annual payments of best agricultural produce under the guise of 'presents'.[42]

Complementing steelbow and 'presents' as indicators of commercial reorientation was the recourse to shorter tacks to monitor the managerial performance of the leading gentry. The Campbell elite were again pioneers in making tacksmen regularly accountable; five-year leases were not uncommon on the Glenorchy estates prior to the Covenanting movement. Short leases became the norm in the Restoration era. Tacksmen, in turn, were prepared to become more mobile to retain their managerial status and to comply with evictions should the ordinary tacksmen fail to fulfil the commercial demands of the clan elite.[43] Elsewhere in Gaeldom, leases tended to remain long, the nineteen-year lease remaining in widespread use in the central Highlands. Nevertheless, there was an acceptance among the lesser gentry of ClanChattan by mid-century that long leases would not inevitably be renewed at their expiry. Even in the western isles, where it was customary to grant tacks to run for several generations, long leases were being reduced to one life or nineteen years in the Restoration era.[44]

Commercial reorientation of estate management undoubtedly contained debt during the Restoration era. Yet, the burden of debt encumbering the estates of the clan elite continued on an upward spiral. Although the rents on the Glenorchy estates had at least doubled from pre-1638 levels, the Earl of Breadalbane consistently ran up annual deficits of between £400 and £1,500 during the 1680s.[45]

Nonetheless, the aftermath of civil war and Cromwellian occupation was to witness a growing realisation within Gaeldom that the containment of debt depended on the commercial solidarity among the clan elite. Partly by refraining from unnecessary absenteeism, and partly by forsaking political ambition, but, above all, by mobilising support from his clan gentry — *uachadarain* as well as *fir-tacsa* — John MacLeod of Dunvegan reduced the burden of debt he inherited in 1664 by £115,000. However, because he was obliged to borrow in excess of £29,000, he left debts of around £41,360 at his death in 1693.[46] Hence, the former poet in residence at Dunvegan was moved to remind Roderick MacLeod, the wastrel successor, to maintain the *fine* on the same footing as himself —

> is na bi'm marbhghean air t'uaislean
> (and so not show indifference to the gentlefolk of your clan).[47]

NOTES

1. A. I. MacInnes, 'Scottish Gaeldom, 1638–51: The Vernacular Response to the Covenanting Dynamic', in J. Dwyer, R. A. Mason and A. Murdoch, eds., *New Perspectives on the Politics and Culture of Early Modern Scotland* (Edinburgh, 1982), pp. 59–94.

2. E. J. Cowan, *Montrose: For Covenant and King* (London, 1977), pp. 94–96; D. Stevenson, *The Scottish Revolution: 1637–1644* (Newton Abbot, 1973), pp. 198–99.

3. G. Hill, *The Macdonnells of Antrim* (Belfast, 1873), pp. 78–81, 90.

4. Cowan, *Montrose*, pp. 176–77; D. Stevenson, *Alasdair MacColla and the Highland Problem in the 17th Century* (Edinburgh, 1980), pp. 260–61.

5. *A.P.S.* VI, pt.1 (1643–47), pp. 498–9, 591–92, 642–43, 702, 713–14. All money in this essay is in pounds Scots unless otherwise stated. The pound Scots was worth a twelfth of the pound sterling; the merk was worth two-thirds of a pound.

6. D. Stevenson, ed., *The Government of Scotland under the Covenanters, 1637–1651* (Edinburgh, 1982), p. 68.

7. S.R.O. P.A.16, section 4/31, Parliamentary Papers, Reports to the Committee on Losses, 1646–47.

8. Ibid. P.A.16, section 4/30; W. Mackay, ed., *Chronicles of the Frasers: The Wardlaw Manuscript* (Scottish History Society, Edinburgh, 1905), pp. 313–15.

9. Stevenson, *Alasdair MacColla*, pp. 214–15, 217, 226.

10. J. Mackechnie, ed., *The Dewar Manuscripts*, I, (Glasgow, 1964), pp. 77–78; D. C. MacTavish, ed., *Minutes of the Synod of Argyll, 1639–61*, 2 vols. (Scottish History Society, Edinburgh, 1943–4), I, pp. 178, 188, 207; II, pp. 45, 72.

11. J. A. Maclean, The Sources, particularly the Celtic Sources, for the History of the Highlands in the Seventeenth Century (unpublished Ph.D. thesis, University of Aberdeen, 1939) (hereafter, Maclean, Celtic Sources), pp. 128–32; J. R. N. Macphail, ed., *Highland Papers*, I (Scottish History Society, Edinburgh, 1914), pp. 277–93.

12. Maclean, Celtic Sources, p. 138.

13. I. C. C. Graham, *Colonists from Scotland* (New York, 1956), pp. 10–11; M. Tepping, ed., *Passengers to America* (Baltimore, 1978), pp. 147–49.

14. F. D. Dow, *Cromwellian Scotland, 1651–1660* (Edinburgh, 1979), pp. 14, 53, 61–160.

15. C. H. Firth, ed., *Scotland and the Protectorate* (Scottish History Society, Edinburgh, 1899), pp. 117–18, 234–37, 269–82, 285–88, 366–81.

16. Maclean, Celtic Sources, pp. 146–48, 150–51.

17. J. Macknight, ed., *Memoirs of Sir Ewen Cameron of Lochiel* (Abbotsford Club, Edinburgh, 1842), pp. 148–50; Stevenson, *Alasdair MacColla*, pp. 275–77.

18. S.R.O. G.D.44, Gordon Castle Muniments, section 27/3; Mackay, ed., *Chronicles of the Frasers*, pp. 224–25.

19. C. H. Firth, ed., *Scotland and the Commonwealth* (Scottish History Society, Edinburgh, 1895), pp. 174–79, 221–22, 231, 266–70.

20. S.R.O. G.D.176, Mackintosh Muniments, section 443.

21. Dow, *Cromwellian Scotland*, pp. 244–45.

22. S.R.O. G.D.16, Airlie Papers, section 41/379.

23. G. A. Hayes-McCoy, *Scottish Mercenary Forces in Ireland* (Dublin, 1937), pp. 12–13, 37–40, 57–58, 61.

24. D. Stevenson, *Scottish Covenanters and Irish Confederates* (Belfast, 1981), p. 18.

25. F. J. Shaw, *The Northern and Western Isles of Scotland* (Edinburgh, 1980), pp. 45–46.

26. R. C. MacLeod, ed., *The Book of Dunvegan, 1340–1700* (Third Spalding Club, Aberdeen, 1938), pp. 85–90, 263–65; Mackay, ed., *Chronicles of the Frasers*, p. 456.

27. *A.P.S.* VII (1661–69), pp. 88–95, 530–35, 540–47; *RPCS*, 3rd series, IV, (1673–76), pp. 164–65.

28. *R.C.P.S.* 3rd series, I (1661–64), I, pp. 24–25; II (1665–69), pp. 599–602, 609–11; III (1668–72), pp. 223–24.

29. *A.P.S.* VII, pp. 181, 274–5, 418–19; A. M. Mackenzie, ed., *Orain Iain Luim* (Scottish Gaelic Text Society, Edinburgh, 1973), pp. 90–91, 26–27, 58–61.

30. Mackay, ed., *Chronicles of the Frasers*, p. 456; L. MacDonald, 'Gleanings from Lord MacDonald's Charter Chest', *Transactions of the Gaelic Society of Inverness*, XIV (1878–88), pp. 65–66.

31. Macphail, ed., *Highland Papers*, I, pp. 245–320; Stevenson, *Alasdair MacColla*, pp. 285–6.

32. D. Woodward, 'A Comparative Study of the Irish and Scottish Livestock Trades in the Seventeenth Century', in Cullen & Smout, pp. 147–64.

33. S.R.O. G.D. 1/2, Breadalbane Muniments, section 21/217; G.D.201, Clanranald Papers, section 1/115 and /128; Mackenzie, ed., *Orain Iain Luim*, pp. 72–73, 158–59.

34. M. H. B. Sanderson, *Scottish Rural Society in the Sixteenth Century* (Edinburgh, 1982), pp. 77–105, 188–90.

35. Mackay, ed., *Chronicles of the Frasers*, pp. 253–55; C. Innes, ed., *The Book of the Thanes of Cawdor, 1236–1742* (Spalding Club, Edinburgh, 1859), pp. 302–03.

36. Shaw, *The Northern and Western Isles*, p. 43.

37. H. Campbell, ed., *The Argyll Sasines*, 2 vols. (Edinburgh, 1933–34), I, the particular registers, II, the general registers.

38. C. Innes, ed., *The Black Book of Taymouth* (Bannatyne Club, Edinburgh, 1885), pp. 99–104; S.R.O. G.D.112, Breadalbane Correspondence, section 39/881 and /905 and /1019.

39. Glasgow University Library, Breadalbane Household Book, 1659–71, MS.Gen. 1032.

40. Mackay, ed., *Chronicles of the Frasers*, pp. 276–77, 475, 481–83, 501; C. O. Baoill, ed., *Bardachd Chloinn Gill-Eathain* (Edinburgh, 1979), pp. 60–67.

41. S.R.O. G.D.112, section 9/3/1 and section 21/215.

42. S.R.O. G.D.124, Mar and Kellie Collection, section 3/38; Shaw, *The Northern and Western Isles*, pp. 56–57. 'Steelbow' is the Scottish term for a form of sharecropping.

43. N.L.S. Register of title deeds produced by landowners in Argyll, late 17th century, Adv. MS. 31, section 2/3; Campbell, ed., *The Argyll Sasines, passim*.

44. Innes, ed., *The Black Book of Taymouth*, pp. 408–27; S.R.O. G.D.112, section 2/202; J. R. N. Macphail, ed., *Highland Papers* IV (Scottish History Society, Edinburgh, 1934), pp. 221–25.

45. S.R.O. G.D.176, Mackintosh Muniments, section 405; Shaw *The Northern and Western Isles*, pp. 50–51.

46. S.R.O. G.D.112, section 9/3/1 and /12 and section 21/71.

47. MacLeod, *The Book of Dunvegan*, pp. 266–67; W. Matheson, ed., *The Blind Harper* (Edinburgh, 1970), pp. 58–73.

6
DEBT AND CREDIT, POVERTY AND PROSPERITY IN A SEVENTEENTH-CENTURY SCOTTISH RURAL COMMUNITY

I. D. Whyte and K. A. Whyte

The tenantry in Scotland before the era of 'improvement' have been viewed as making little contribution to agricultural development. The emphasis has been on landowners as instigators of economic change. Recently there has been some re-assessment of the contribution of tenant farmers to agricultural innovation during the eighteenth century[1] but little attention has been given to their position during the seventeenth century.

The continuation of major subsistence crises until the end of the seventeenth century has been taken as a sign of the inefficiency of agriculture and of the poverty and vulnerability of rural society.[2] Yet Devine has pointed out that the bad years of the later 1690s were an uncharacteristic episode in a century from the 1650s during which agriculture was capable of feeding Scotland's population in most years and providing periodic surpluses for export.[3] This contrasts with the late sixteenth and early seventeenth centuries when subsistence crises recurred with devastating frequency.[4] Does this indicate that agriculture was more prosperous after the mid-seventeenth century? If so, what form did this prosperity take, who benefited, and what effects did it have on rural society? A recent study has indicated that the tenantry in Lowland Scotland were more stratified in socio-economic terms than has been accepted in the past.[5] This implies that contrasts in wealth and in the ability to accumulate capital must have existed. Little attention has been paid to the distribution of wealth within Scottish rural society at this time, possibly because it has been assumed that little significant variation occurred. Central to a study of the distribution of wealth is a consideration of the nature, extent and role of credit. The extent to which credit was available, the forms that it took and the sources from which it came may tell us a great deal about social conditions, indicate whether capital accumulation was occurring, and highlight the economic constraints within which rural society operated. This essay examines the distribution of wealth, patterns of capital accumulation and mechanisms of debt and credit within the context of a detailed case study.

A major body of information on debt and credit exists in the form of Commissary Court testaments, although they have scarcely been exploited.[6] The analysis which follows is based on the detailed study of 200 testaments relating to people living on the Panmure estates in Forfarshire during the seventeenth century. While the sample is too small to allow more than tentative conclusions regarding trends within Scottish society, it was chosen because information from it could be linked to an existing data base on rents, tenure and arrears provided by the unusually detailed and standardised rentals and accounts for these estates.

The testaments in the sample relate to people ranging from the tenants of substantial farms to cottars and farm servants although, as with English probate inventories, there is under-representation of people in the lower social strata.[7] For people engaged in agriculture the testaments list the farming stock, especially animals, growing crops and stored grain, in some detail along with their estimated value. Personal and household possessions are rarely itemised, usually being lumped together in a single valuation. Most testaments include details of the debts which were owing by, as well as to, the deceased. In this respect they are superior to probate inventories which usually list only testators' assets and not their liabilities.[8]

Table 1 shows the proportions of people in different social groups who lent and owed money. The testaments were divided into seven categories. It proved impossible to differentiate tenant farmers according to the size of their holdings as such information was not always forthcoming from rentals; if forthcoming, it was usually expressed only in customary assessments such as ploughgates. Nor was it possible to use the testaments to discover the amount of land which each tenant cultivated, as the size of the area under crop could be estimated only from those inventories which had been drawn up between seedtime and harvest, and which recorded the quantities of seed sown.

A more effective way of differentiating the tenantry would have been by their rents, but even this presented problems of comparability between those farmers who paid rents principally in grain, and those who paid principally in money. Instead, the tenants in the sample were grouped into three broad classes on the basis of the number of plough oxen which they possessed. Given the impossibility of calculating any better measure of holding size which could be used for every tenant, this is probably the best way to categorise them. The acreage which tenants had under crop can be estimated from summer inventories which give the amount

Table 1. Percentage in each Social Group involved in Credit

Category		*Average Cash Assets, £ Scots excluding farm stock and household goods*	*% with Assets*	*Average debts £ Scots*	*% with Debts*
Large Tenants	(20)	785	62	824	92
Medium Tenants	(59)	395	50	200	95
Small Tenants	(39)	79	62	92	100
Cottars, Smallholders	(44)	142	83	15	53
Widows, Single Women	(15)	343	90	7	10
Elderly and Single Men	(17)	472	100	139	18
Servants	(6)	519	100	0	0
Whole Sample	(200)	294	69	307	70

of seed sown. The correlation between numbers of oxen and numbers of acres under crop for this group of 64, R=+0.85, was highly significant statistically, suggesting that for this sample the number of plough oxen is a reasonable predictor of holding size. Tenants who owned 16 oxen or more were notionally capable of working two ploughgates of land. At Panmure this represented upwards of 100 Scots acres (126 English statute acres) under crop in any year. Such farmers were comparatively large-scale operators, and it is among this group that one might expect to find signs of production for the market and capital accumulation. Tenants who owned between 8 and 15 oxen, with between 50 and 100 Scots acres (63–126 statute acres) under crop at any time, would still have needed to be self-sufficient in labour, capital and equipment and are likely to have operated more or less independently even when they leased holdings on multiple-tenant farms. Such farmers might also be expected to have had some commitment to commercial production and some opportunity to accumulate capital. Tenants who owned fewer than 8 oxen would not have been able to furnish their own ploughteam without co-operating with their neighbours. One would expect them to have had little market orientation and to have been closer to the margin of subsistence. If this was so it should have been reflected in the possession of only limited assets and possibly also in a tendency towards proportionally higher levels of debt than the other groups of tenants.

The cottars and smallholders include people who were designated 'cottar' in their testaments or who were described as being 'in' a particular farm but do not appear as tenants on the estate rentals. Smallholders leased an acre or two of arable land but did not own any plough oxen. The category of servants includes both domestic servants at Panmure House and farm servants. Widows and unmarried women formed another distinct group; a final category comprised men who were described as elderly or who were unmarried and who did not fit into any other group.

Table 1 shows the high proportion of people who were involved in credit to some degree: 69% as creditors and 70% as debtors, including people at all levels from tenants to farm servants. The figure for creditors is higher than the 40% found by Holderness for a larger sample of English probate inventories from the late seventeenth and early eighteenth centuries but the representation of various social groups and the social structures undoubtedly differ between the two samples.[9] Clearly there were surplus resources within the rural community and mechanisms for their investment. Only 2% of the people whose testaments were studied were not involved in some aspect of credit. There were, however, variations in patterns of lending and borrowing between different groups. 96% of all tenants had some debts while the figure for cottars and smallholders was only 53%, for widows and single women 10% and for the small group of servants none at all.

The testaments show that various forms of credit existed. Rent arrears and unpaid servants' fees formed a significant part of the debts of most tenants. Money could also be lent on bond or by unsecured loans. Another source of credit was deferred payment for goods, agricultural produce and services. Table 2 gives a

Table 2. Assets and Debts of the Tenants

	Large Tenants	*Medium Tenants*	*Small Tenants*
Average value of Farm Stock, £ Scots	1575	940	408
Average Assets, £ Scots	785	395	79
Average Debts, £ Scots	1230	426	211
Average Debts minus Rents and Fees, £ Scots	824	200	92
Ratio of Assets to Farm Stock	0.5/1	0.3/1	0.2/1
Ratio of Total Debts to Farm Stock plus Assets	0.5/1	0.3/1	0.2/1
Ratio of Debts minus Rents and Fees to Assets	1.0/1	0.8/1	1.2/1
% Tenants with Assets greater than Farm Stock	23	13	11
% Tenants with Debts greater than Assets plus Farm Stock	7	3	12
% Tenants with Debts exceeding Assets	77	80	85
Average % of Debts made up by Current Year's Rents	30	41	50
Average % of Debts made up by Servants' Fees	3	12	6

breakdown of the assets and debts of the tenants. Clearly the mean values for farm stock, assets and debts were in step with holding sizes. The ratios show that the relationship between the level of cash assets and the value of farming stock also varied between the three groups. Mean cash assets amounted to half the average value of farming stock for tenants of larger holdings but to only a third for the middle group and a fifth for small tenants, suggesting that the first group had built up proportionally greater capital reserves. Nearly a quarter of the tenants of large holdings had assets which were greater than the value of their farm stock but this figure fell for the other groups. Tenants of smallholdings were also more likely to have debts which exceeded the value of their farm stock and other assets combined. There was, however, less difference between the three groups in terms of the ratio of total debts to the value of farm stock and assets.

The pattern suggests that many tenants of large holdings were able to accumulate a modest amount of capital and that relatively few tenants, even among those with smaller holdings, were seriously in debt. While larger holdings gave their occupants an edge in profitability, few tenants had accumulated reserves which would have been sufficient to tide them over more than a single bad year. If the value of farm stock is ignored, average debts exceeded average assets for all three groups. 77% of the tenants of larger holdings had debts exceeding assets and the figure rose to 85% for small tenants.

This crude analysis makes the position of the tenants seem worse than it was because it does not distinguish between different types of debt. A major component of debts owing by tenants was rents and servants' fees due for the current year. In most cases these would have been met from the profits of that year's farming activity, and so these debts should be set against the value of farm stock, which included estimates of the likely yield and value of sown crops, and the market price of grain in the barn, rather than against capital assets. Rents due for the current year made up less than a third of the debts owing by the tenants of large holdings, but for the middle group of tenants the figure rose to 41% and for small tenants to 50%. If current rents and servants' fees are subtracted from the total debts, then the average figures for the remaining debts are in balance with the cash assets (excluding farm stock) of large tenants, and slightly better than in balance for the middle group. The tenants of smaller holdings still had debts which exceeded their assets.

This analysis also shows that a greater proportion of the debts of farmers with larger holdings was made up of other kinds of credit than was the case with smaller tenants. These included money borrowed on bond, on unsecured loans, and money due for purchased goods. It is impossible to separate these categories with complete confidence, although an attempt has been made to do this for tenants and cottars, the principal classes of debtor, in Table 3. Money lent on bond is often identified specifically in testaments while in other cases the inclusion of appended sums for annual rents indicates the existence of a bond. It is harder to distinguish between unsecured loans, which were generally smaller than amounts lent on bond, and sums of money due on goods which had been sold or purchased, i.e. credit by deferred payment.

Table 3 shows that tenants of larger holdings were more likely to borrow money on bond, usually in larger sums, than other tenants and that unsecured loans

Table 3. Debts Owed by Tenants and Cottars, excluding Rents and Fees

	Average Debts £ Scots	*% Due by Bond*	*% on Unsecured Loan*	*% Due by Deferred Credit*
Large Tenants	824	33	64	3
Medium Tenants	200	13	82	5
Small Tenants	92	16	70	14
Cottars and Smallholders	15	22	74	4

formed a greater proportion of the debts owed by all other groups. Table 4 shows the origins of the capital borrowed by tenants and cottars. Tenants of larger holdings were able to attract a significant amount of credit from the burghs though this figure may be inflated by money due on unspecified sales of agricultural produce. The importance of the towns as a source of finance declined sharply for tenants in the middle category and was negligible for small tenants and cottars.

Table 4. Origins of Money Owed by Tenants and Cottars

	Burghs %	*Nobility %*	*Gentry %*	*Clergy %*	*Tenantry & Lower %*
Large Tenants	42	7	0	1	50
Medium Tenants	14	3	0	0	83
Small Tenants	5	0	0	0	95
Cottars and Smallholders	3	5	0	0	92

Most of the money which was borrowed by farmers originated within the rural population at the level of the tenantry and below. The lack of finance from the gentry support McFaulds' suggestion that in Angus in the later seventeenth century they were net debtors rather than creditors.[10]

The average assets for each group (Table 1) provide an indication of where finance could be obtained within the rural society. Table 5 amplifies this with a breakdown of the mechanisms by which money was lent.

Table 5. Methods by which Money was Lent within Rural Society

	Average Assets £ Scots	*% Lent on Bond*	*% Lent on Unsecured Loan*	*% Due by Deferred Credit*	** Other*
Large Tenants	785	76	9	2	13
Medium Tenants	395	75	20	1	4
Small Tenants	79	24	71	1	4
Cottars and Smallholders	142	42	57	1	0
Widows, Single Women	343	84	8	8	0
Elderly and Single Men	472	55	44	1	0
Servants	519	76	24	0	0

*Mostly rents due from Subtenants.

Clearly some tenants had sufficient reserves to be able to lend money and the tenants of larger holdings were sophisticated enough to lend most of it on bond. One tenant, James Melville in Camiston, who died in 1640,[11] appears to have been a prominent moneylender with loans totalling £6,738 Scots to over 20 people, including the Earl of Panmure, the Panmure estate factor, and various Dundee merchants. Money lent on bond accounted for three-quarters of the assets of tenants in the two higher-size groups. The potential contribution of individual small tenants to the pool of credit was clearly limited but the large size of this group should not be forgotten. Cottars and smallholders lent a much greater proportion of their assets on bond. The apparent affluence of this group compared with the small tenants may seem surprising until it is remembered that cottars and smallholders had little farm stock and so had proportionally greater liquid assets. Cullen has made the point that in Ireland at this time farmers and artisans might appear to have had comparable lifestyles and to have seemed equal in terms of wealth, but in fact the farmers benefited from security of employment and cheap food and had greater total assets.[12] In Scotland the position of cottars and small tenants may have been closer as both had access to at least some land. Unmarried servants, widows and elderly people must have been major sources of credit within rural society, as in England.[13] They lent a higher proportion of their assets on bond than any other group. Presumably, with their more limited earning power they had, of necessity, to be businesslike. It should be remembered, though, that many of the categories used here are life-cycle stages rather than socio-economic groups. Some farm servants would have been sons and daughters of tenants and might, in addition to any savings from their fees, have obtained capital from their parents by gift or inheritance. Widows of tenants would, under Scots law, have inherited at least a third of the farm stock and other assets belonging to their husbands. Some of the elderly men who had money to lend may have been retired tenants. Thus tenants and their families might have been net recipients of credit at some stages in their lives and net providers of it at others.

Table 6 shows who borrowed money from the various groups within the sample. The overall pattern was that most of the capital which originated within rural

Table 6. Destinations of Loans by Various Groups

	Burghs %	*Nobility* %	*Gentry* %	*Clergy* %	*Tenantry & Lower* %
Large Tenants	1	5	37	0	57
Medium Tenants	12	22	10	0	56
Small Tenants	1	0	0	2	97
Cottars and Smallholders	1	0	15	0	84
Widows, Single Women	3	56	21	0	20
Elderly and Single Men	10	3	28	10	58
Servants	2	0	0	26	72
Whole Sample	7	16	19	1	57

society stayed there. Very little went to the towns and a substantial proportion of money in this category was probably deferred credit on goods rather than loans. On the other hand 35% of the capital went to landowners, ranging from feuars, through lairds, to the Earl of Panmure himself. It was not uncommon for tenants to finance their landlord or neighbouring lairds and there were evidently close links in this respect between large tenants and the gentry, again confirming McFaulds' suggestion that the gentry were net creditors at this period.[14] None of the tenants in the sample appears to have held land on wadset. Proprietors whose lands offered good security attracted relatively large loans from widows. Widows, especially of tenants, may have been particularly attractive to proprietors seeking loans because the social difference between them put the transaction on a more impersonal footing than when credit was obtained from fellow landowners. Borrowing from widows may have been preferable to accepting credit from tenants as the latter occupied land and could use non-payment of rent as a lever if the debt remained unpaid. The fact that landowners did borrow from the tenantry indicates that capital accumulation by farmers was possible, but at the same time it demonstrates that obtaining annual rents on loan was a principal way of putting money to work, and emphasises the tenants' exclusion from the land market.

Table 7 shows the pattern of capital accumulation for tenants over three time periods, 1600–29, 1630–59 and 1660–99, measured by the ratio of their cash assets to the value of their farm stock. The periods were chosen with major price fluctuations in mind. The first thirty years of the seventeenth century were characterised by frequent subsistence crises, notably in 1622–23, while the middle period spanned the disruptions of the Great Rebellion. The period from 1660 to the mid-1690s was characterised by generally low grain prices.[15] Given that rents

Table 7. Capital Accumulation over Time

	Ratio of Assets to Farm Stock		
	Large Tenants	Medium Tenants	Small Tenants
1600–29	Insufficient Data	0.18	0.20
1630–59	0.37	0.20	0.18
1660–95	0.60	0.28	0.20

at Panmure were mostly stable throughout the seventeenth century, it can be suggested that price levels would have been one of the most important influences determining capital accumulation by the tenantry. Bowden has pointed out that in England during the sixteenth and early seventeenth centuries small farmers, with only a limited surplus, found it hard to accumulate capital no matter how prices varied.[16] In years of grain shortage they did not have sufficiently large surpluses to benefit from the high prices, while in years of plenty their small surpluses generated little income due to the low price levels.

It is considered that Panmure tenants would have had more opportunity to accumulate capital during a period of good harvests with low prices than during years of high price when low yields would probably have robbed them of any surplus which they could market. Table 7 supports this argument, showing that the period after 1660 benefited tenants more than the first sixty years of the century. On the other hand the benefit was not spread evenly. Tenants with larger holdings did better than those with smaller ones. There was a distinct improvement in the position of tenants of larger holdings in the later seventeenth century. Tenants with medium-sized holdings also appear to have accumulated more capital during the course of the century though less markedly, while small tenants failed to improve their position at all. If this trend occurred more generally in Lowland Scotland, the implication is that during the later seventeenth century rural society was becoming more stratified in terms of wealth, a trend which would have been reinforced by changes in holding structures, with a tendency towards amalgamation and the creation of larger units.[17] If this trend continued during the eighteenth century, after the recovery from the disastrous 1690s, one can see how tenants with larger farms and greater reserves of capital would have been in a better position to adopt the improvements advocated by enthusiastic landowners than tenants with smaller holdings. Such tenants would have been poised to benefit from rising prices and the increase in output generated by improved farming techniques. The role of agricultural improvement in creating the class of capitalist farmers which had begun to emerge by the end of the eighteenth century has been studied but less attention has been paid to the possibility that long-term trends in capital accumulation and its distribution within rural society might have aided the adoption of such improvements.

This study has demonstrated that, on one estate, far from being uniformly poor, marked contrasts in levels of wealth existed within the tenantry and among the rural population in general. Credit mechanisms were well developed among the inhabitants of the Panmure estates and were utilised almost universally to varying degrees. The kinds of credit which were available, the ways in which they were used, and the sources from which they were derived bear close comparison with England during the same period. On the other hand, the capital reserves, even of the tenants of larger holdings, were relatively modest. It seems likely that most of the available credit was used to weather short-term difficulties rather than to finance long-term expansion. There are indications, however, that capital accumulation increased during the seventeenth century, particularly among the more substantial tenants. This suggests that the combination of better harvests with more stable economic and political conditions during the later seventeenth century generated some modest prosperity for farmers despite influences which worked against the acquisition of wealth, including the disadvantages of low grain prices. Larger tenants, with economies of scale, appear to have been better placed to benefit than those with smaller holdings. On the other hand, the resources of even the larger tenants seem to have been insufficient to allow them to survive more than a single bad year without accumulating serious debts. The disaster of the later 1690s may not have caused widespread starvation and displacement among the Panmure tenantry, but it may still have wiped out the hard-won profits of the preceding favourable years. Nevertheless, it suggests than in the long term agriculture was generating greater profits for larger farmers and that during the seventeenth and early eighteenth centuries rural society may have been becoming more markedly polarised. A tendency towards the creation of larger holdings at this period has been noted.[18] This has usually been attributed to estate policy: the creation of more commercially viable units. Such a process would undoubtedly have increased the contrast between prosperity and poverty within rural society. On the other hand this trend could have been the result of growing inequalities within rural society which allowed a limited number of farmers to take on larger tenancies. Although space does not permit a detailed review of the evidence, there are indications that the distribution of holdings at Panmure was slowly changing during the later seventeenth century, with an increase both in the numbers of large independent holdings and in crofts which were too small to provide a full-time living. At the same time there was a fall in the proportion of middle-range holdings, which required full-time working but were too small to be more than on the margins of profitability. The process was gradual and does not seem to have been due to any concerted policy by the estate. Such structural changes may have been initiated from below by shifts in the distribution of wealth among the tenantry caused by contrasts in the degree to which different groups were able to accumulate capital. If these trends continued during the first half of the eighteenth century, it is probable that the growing polarisation of rural society which has been considered the result of landlord policy may have been generated in part by changes within the farming community itself.

It must be emphasised, however, that only a single case study has been considered here. Before we can evaluate the full significance of the mechanisms of debt and credit which existed, and make estimates of the profitability of agriculture for different social groups and at different periods, more detailed studies are needed. We also need to know more about other elements which affected the accumulation of wealth. These include patterns of inheritance among the tenantry; the role of rural industries, particularly textiles, as generators of income; levels of rent; the extent to which the profitability of tenant farming was reduced by the retention of rents in kind and labour services; and variations in the distribution of holding sizes from estate to estate and region to region. If capital accumulation by farmers did increase during the late seventeenth century, how was the extra profit generated: from arable farming or from a greater involvement in livestock? Although it has not been possible to review here all the authors' findings, it is hoped that enough have been presented to indicate something of the level of detail which is possible for studies of what has often been dismissed in the past as a large but silent majority in Scottish rural society.

NOTES

1. G. Whittington, 'Agriculture and Society in Lowland Scotland 1750–1870', in G. Whittington and I. D. Whyte, eds., *A Historical Geography of Scotland* (London, 1983), pp. 141–164.

2. H. Hamilton, *An Economic History of Scotland in the Eighteenth Century* (Oxford, 1963); J. E. Handley, *Scottish Farming in the Eighteenth Century* (Edinburgh, 1953); J. A. Symon, *Scottish Farming, Past and Present* (Edinburgh, 1959).

3. T. M. Devine, 'The Union of 1707 and Scottish Development', *Sc. Ec. & Soc. Hist.* 5 (1985), p. 25.

4. S. G. E. Lythe, *The Economy of Scotland in its European Setting 1550–1625* (Edinburgh, 1960), pp. 19–23.

5. I. D. and K. A. Whyte, 'Continuity and Change in a Seventeenth-Century Scottish Farming Community', *Agricultural History Review*, XXXII (1984), pp. 159–169 (henceforth 'Continuity and Change').

6. M. H. B. Sanderson, 'The Edinburgh Merchants in Society 1570–1603: The Evidence of Their Testaments', in I. B. Cowan and D. Shaw, eds., *The Renaissance and Reformation in Scotland* (Edinburgh, 1983), pp. 183–99; F. J. Shaw, *The Northern and Western Islands of Scotland: Their Economy and Society in the Seventeenth Century* (Edinburgh, 1980), pp. 7–12; I. D. and K. A. Whyte, 'Regional and Local Variations in Scottish Farming: A Preliminary Survey of the Evidence of Commissary Court Testaments', *Manchester Geographer*, 3 (1983), pp. 49–59.

7. B. A. Holderness, 'Credit in English Rural Society before the Nineteenth Century, with Special Reference to the Period 1650–1720', *Agricultural History Review*, XXIV (1976), p. 102.

8. N. and J. Cox, 'Probate Inventories: The Legal Background', *The Local Historian*, 16 (1984), p. 134.

9. B. A. Holderness, *loc.cit.*

10. J. McFaulds, Forfarshire Landowners and Their Estates 1660–90, (unpublished Ph.D. thesis, University of Glasgow, 1981), p. 95.

11. Brechin Commissary Court, Testament of James Melville, 1640.

12. L. M. Cullen, *The Emergence of Modern Ireland, 1600–1900* (London, 1981), p. 35.

13. B. A. Holderness, *loc.cit.*

14. J. McFaulds, *loc.cit.*

15. R. Mitchison, 'The Movement of Scottish Corn Prices in the Seventeenth and Eighteenth Centuries', *Ec. H.R.* 18 (1965), pp. 278–91.

16. P. Bowden, 'Agricultural Prices, Farm Profits and Rents', in J. Thirsk, ed., *The Agrarian History of England and Wales*, IV, *1500–1640* (Cambridge, 1967), pp. 657–59.

17. I. D. Whyte, *Agriculture and Society in Seventeenth-Century Scotland* (Edinburgh, 1979), pp. 152–55; R. A. Dodgshon, *Land and Society in Early Scotland* (Oxford, 1981), pp. 206–16.

18. *Ibid.*

7

THE ECONOMIC SITUATION AND FUNCTIONS OF SUBSTANTIAL LANDOWNERS 1600–1815: ULSTER AND LOWLAND SCOTLAND COMPARED

Peter Roebuck

> The system of estate management as pursued in Scotland ... is inapplicable to Ireland from the remarkable differences in circumstances which exist in the respective countries. In the former, lands have become more valuable by enlarging the size of farms, from the investment of large capitals, and from agriculture being pursued on scientific principles, under the direction of intelligent persons, whose education entitles them to think and whose confidence in well-tried experiments teaches them to act for themselves. In Ireland the sub-division of lands and other causes have tended to a temporary increase in their value, which increased privations have hitherto in most cases enabled them to pay, but from the want of capital and skill, agriculture has undergone little improvement; bigoted to the errors of their predecessors and from ignorance and prejudice fearful and disinclined to abandon the ever-beaten path of mismanagement.
>
> W. Greig, *General Report on the Gosford Estates in Co. Armagh, 1821*[1]

William Greig's report analyses the ruinous effects of population pressure and associated subdivision on the economy of a single landed estate in Co. Armagh. The situation there in the aftermath of the Napoleonic Wars is also briefly but sharply contrasted with the current, healthy state of the rural economy in Lowland Scotland. Greig was one of very few contemporary observers to compare Scotland and Ireland — perhaps the only one to do so following working experience as a land valuer and surveyor in both countries. Unlike some of his other writings, the report was produced not for public consumption, but on commission from the owner of the estate in question; and the fact that Lord Gosford can scarcely have been expected to welcome Greig's frank conclusions lends credence to the views expressed therein. But what are we to make of the broader implications of the report? How far was Greig's analysis applicable to Ulster as a whole? Were there 'remarkable differences in circumstances' between the two regions which promoted radically dissimilar systems of estate management? If so, when and how did they originate and what was their effect on the pattern of rural economic change?

Two centuries earlier the rural economies of Ulster and Lowland Scotland had certain characteristics in common. Both areas were peripheral, poor and underdeveloped. Much potentially valuable land was not fully utilised; a substantial proportion of the remainder was marginal or waste. In both areas the bulk of the land was organised in large or medium-sized estates, owned by individual proprietors: compared with most parts of England little land belonged to the Crown, to burghs or corporations, or to farmers who occupied their own land. And as long as this situation persisted, the agricultural progress and general economic development of both areas was likely to be strongly influenced by the policies and performance of a relatively small group of substantial landowners. Yet, particularly in this last respect, even at this early stage, common characteristics were overshadowed by significant differences.

Sixteenth-century Scotland had experienced English invasions and periodic internal disturbances. Landowners had continued to cherish their traditional role as protectors and war-leaders of their tenants, and had judged the value of their land by the number of inhabitants, and therefore supporters, it could sustain. However, the old feudal order began to decline in the late sixteenth century, and thereafter gradually gave way to an increasingly powerful central government, and to new and more cohesive structures and attitudes in the localities. The new century witnessed a marked reduction in lawlessness and the growth of internal stability; and although the civil wars provoked a brief re-appearance of disorder, they also demonstrated the inherent weakness of the old-style feudal host in the face of professional military forces. Substantial landowners were both promoters and beneficiaries of these changes. Far from there being any revolution in landownership, proprietors continued to be massively secure in their properties. The estate remained the basic unit of decision-making in the localities and, assisted by a hierarchy of estate officials, landowners presided authoritatively over their property and the local institutions associated with it. From the mid-seventeenth century onwards Lowland proprietors were among 'the most absolute' landowners 'in Britain'.[2]

In Ulster change was revolutionary, not evolutionary. The Gaelic order was overthrown and replaced by an alien system, the main features of which were determined by short-term considerations of political strategy and national security. In scope, speed of implementation and depth of effect, the plantation surpassed what any previous administration had attempted in Ireland. Besides changes in law, religion and local government, there was a rapid transformation in the ownership, organisation and administration of land as well as in virtually every other aspect of economic life. Nevertheless, the plantation was far from an unqualified success. Leading colonists were beset by intractable problems; public aspirations persistently outdistanced private achievements. In contrast to their Scottish Lowland counterparts, Ulster landowners were in a weak position, particularly when bargaining with prospective tenants of their lands.

Unlike the 'indigenous and hereditary elite' which presided in Scotland,[3] Ulster proprietors were a remarkably cosmopolitan group. Harnessing private greed to public gain, the plantation attracted Lowland Scots, Welshmen and individuals from every part of western England; on arrival in Ulster they joined the Irish, the old English, and the old Scots — those (mainly Catholic) Highlanders and Islanders who had settled in the province (particularly in the north-east) from the fourteenth century onwards.[4] Collectively, new proprietors lacked substance and appropriate experience. In principle the plantation scheme catered for uniform amounts of property to be granted to different classes of applicant; in practice (due to ignorance of local topography, inadequate surveying techniques and widespread corruption) many applicants emerged with substantial estates. Although land was cheap, considerable expenditure was required to settle and develop it; there was also the costly 'necessity of building of castles, or stone houses and bawns, if security and peace must be provided for'.[5] With little or no previous experience of discharging such tasks, many grantees soon got into financial difficulties. There was an acute shortage, not merely of capital, but also of recurrent income from property. To encourage them to share the burden of development, proprietors gave their most substantial subordinates fee farm grants or perpetual leases of property, for modest lump sums and low fixed rents — transactions which were virtually equivalent to outright sales. Other colonists obtained very long leases (for lives or terms of years) of sizeable holdings, again in return for small entry fines and low annual rents. Despite these incentives, proprietors were only fitfully successful in persuading others to settle under them. They complained constantly that Ulster was 'unpeopled', that most immigrants were poor, and that immigration was too slow and spasmodic to give the plantation much chance of success. With these complaints in mind the government shelved its original plan to exclude the Irish from the scheme: without them plantation on the scale envisaged would have been insufficiently rewarding for the grantees and, perhaps, totally impracticable.[6] Indeed, a variety of adverse factors (economic, religious and political) persuaded numerous colonists to return to Britain from the mid-1630s and, until the arrival of Monroe's Scottish army in the aftermath of the 1641 rising, the plantation was threatened. By restoring order and establishing the first presbyteries this force created circumstances which encouraged further and much heavier Scottish immigration from the late 1640s. Likewise the presence of Cromwellian forces in the 1650s persuaded nonconformists to migrate from northern England, an inward flow which appears to have increased following the persecution of dissenters in Britain in the early 1660s. There was, therefore, a considerable turnover in the colonial population in the decades after 1635.[7] At the Restoration proprietors were faced with the task of retrieving and consolidating earlier achievements. Following years of political turmoil, many were relieved to have their land patents confirmed by the new government in the 1660s.

In Lowland Scotland circumstances allowed development as well as consolidation. Serious dearths became less frequent: between 1660 and 1700 they occurred only in 1674 and in the mid-1690s. Imports of food declined, grain exports increased, and there was growth in the droving trade. Moreover, the Scottish Parliament passed a series of statutes designed to promote and facilitate agricultural improvement. Lowland proprietors in particular grew more confident of economic prospects and came to regard their estates principally as commercial concerns — as sources of profits which could be increased by careful and systematic management. This shift in attitude would appear to have been structurally well-founded. On Lowland estates many rents were still paid in kind but, more significantly, they were already comparatively high, often amounting to as much as a third of total output. Furthermore, in addition to being remarkably uniform throughout the region, the tenurial system was firmly geared to proprietorial advantage, affording regular opportunities for the adjustment of rents in the light of changing economic circumstances. Tenures ranged from very short terms of around four to six years for the less substantial tenants to maximum terms of around nineteen years for the most substantial, an unusually narrow band of options even, for instance, by the standards of eastern England. For proprietors one advantage of this system was that, while sub-letting was not uncommon, it remained subject to landlord control because of the brevity of tenancies; another, of long-term significance, was that the system facilitated rural depopulation. Immediately below proprietors joint or multiple tenancies enabled farmers to share the risks involved in agriculture but the granting of short tenures prevented inefficient producers from finding indefinite refuge on the land. Successful farmers could expect to enjoy long-term security of tenure; those who failed were obliged to seek their fortune in other rural occupations, in the growing towns or abroad.[8]

Immigrants to Ulster entered a quite different tenurial system which, if it had not positively attracted them, was clearly designed to retain them. In the later seventeenth and early eighteenth centuries the majority of tenants continued to obtain very long leases, for terms of years, or for two or (increasingly) three lives. This had important implications for the role played by landlords and their employees. In one respect the situation was similar to that which obtained under the life leasehold system common in another part of Britain — western (particularly south-western) England. Arrangements there 'set much less of a premium on expertise in husbandry, and ability to deal with tenants on their own level, than did [those on] rack-rented estates'. What was involved 'was a much more strictly administrative task, in which the most important functions were the compilation of a set of records, and keeping them up-to-date ... receiving rents etc.'.[9] However, there were also very significant differences between the use of long leaseholds in Ulster and their use in south-western England which point to an even sharper contrast between Ulster and Lowland Scotland. Firstly, English farmers purchased their tenancies with substantial entry fines, and thereafter paid in annual rents only a fraction of what their land was worth: whereas in Ulster both rents and fines appear to have been of distinctly modest proportions. Secondly, in England tenants were normally (and effectively) forbidden to assign their leases: in Ulster such clauses were absent from leases or were widely ignored; leases became negotiable assets for purposes of mortgage or sale, and by the mid-eighteenth century there was a very active market in unexpired lease terms. Finally, English tenants were strictly forbidden to sub-let their holdings without express permission, which was rarely granted; whereas in pursuit of estate development sub-letting was condoned and sometimes encouraged in Ulster. Thus, in requiring only a low profile of landlords, the system in Ulster provided them with a relatively small income and with minimal control over their tenantry. The latter had considerable bargaining power, a marked degree of legal security, and were liable to little managerial interference or coercion. Two factors in particular were responsible for the entrenchment of this system: although land was relatively cheap and plentiful, there was throughout the seventeenth century a continuing shortage of labour and capital; and until as late as 1750 economic conditions in many areas remained largely adverse.

According to the most recent historian of the plantation, 'if anything, the colonial processes were intensified' during the later seventeenth century.[10] Periods of heavy immigration (the 1660s and 1679–85) alternated with periods of economic distress (the mid-1670s) or political unrest (1686–91), when the flow of migrants was reversed. As a result of the last general famine in Scottish history, however, there was very substantial immigration in the late 1690s: between 1696 and 1701 there was a significant decline in Scotland's total population; conditions were very severe in the southern border areas which hitherto had provided Ulster with many of its colonists. Moreover, to judge from the subsequent establishment of new presbyteries, immigration did not entirely cease at that point.[11] Furthermore, throughout this period there was considerable internal migration, roughly from the north and east of the province to the south and west. Some permanent settlements in peripheral areas were early and well established; other regions, for example Co. Monaghan, did not attract significant numbers of immigrants until very much later.[12] For much of the early eighteenth century, therefore, landlords and tenants in many parts of the province 'were still coming to terms with an underdeveloped countryside'.[13]

In doing so they had to contend with difficult economic conditions. Whereas following the Restoration there was a massive expansion in the number of public markets in Scotland, some of those established earlier in Ulster fell into disuse. In addition to periodic embargoes on exports of grain to Scotland, Ulster was badly hit by the Cattle Acts: while these provided Scotland with fresh opportunities in the droving trade, they deprived Ulster of valuable exports and, because the province was ill-situated for diversification into the provisions trade, disadvantaged Ulster farmers vis-a-vis farmers in parts of southern Ireland. Moreover, despite the stimulus to the further development of the linen industry provided by the abolition in the 1690s of duties on imports to the British market, the ensuing decades were punctuated by economic crises. Spinning and weaving expanded steadily in the linen triangle area; and other regions, such as the port of Derry and its hinterland, sold increasing quantities of yarn to Britain. Nevertheless, the accent elsewhere was firmly on mixed farming and, together with falling exports of beef, butter, hides and tallow, there were regular harvest crises — in 1718–19, the late 1720s, the mid-1730s, 1739–41, and 1745–46.[14]

Although proprietors recognised the need to promote activities, such as the manufacture of linen yarn and cloth, which might supplement farming incomes, they were unable (according to one well-informed contemporary) to provide 'any great help . . . from their purses'.[15] Arthur Brownlow was exceptional in buying up all the linen webs which were brought to the market which he established in Lurgan. Encouragement was generally confined to Brownlow's initial move, the granting of particularly favourable leases to tradesmen. Thereafter the latter's ability to mortgage or sell their leases was of vital importance in the provision of capital for further development. Before long some linen drapers sought and obtained even more favourable terms, viz. the provision of freeholds: these terms, however, further reduced the control of proprietors as well, of course, as their prospective annual incomes. Likewise, landowners were active in promoting urban development, though their chief means of doing so were similar and had identical effects. Besides granting freeholds, for example, the third Earl of Donegall was so straitened financially that he sold life annuities from his estate at ruinously cheap prices; and disregarding a family settlement (and therefore illegally) he renewed certain leases up to the maximum permissible length but well in advance of the expiry of the existing terms. And when his successors reduced permissible terms Belfast decayed until the passage of a private Act of Parliament several decades later allowed the setting of very lengthy building leases. General legislation to cater for such contingencies reached the statute book only in the 1760s.[16]

Nor were efforts in regard to agriculture much less productive of proprietorial unease. Because land was plentiful and rents were low, most Scottish colonists became engaged in farming, where their efforts during much of the seventeenth century were hampered by shortages of draught animals, and of manpower in skilled occupations related to agriculture. In contrast a high proportion of the rural population of Lowland Scotland was already below the tenant class, and craftsmen and tradesmen constituted 'the backbone of rural society'.[17] Moreover, it is clear that Ulster tenant farmers were subject to much less surveillance than their Scottish counterparts. The plantation scheme had promoted the development of a manorial system as a means of supplementing the new structure of local government; and initially individual proprietors used manorial courts in the management of their affairs. However, together with the granting of perpetuities, the policy of setting lengthy determinable leases proved incompatible with the achievement of this objective: where manorial courts persisted beyond the Restoration they met too infrequently and were too formal in their business to be of much effect. In Scotland, on the other hand, while their power was eroded by the spread of forms of central authority, baron courts continued to meet regularly and to perform vital functions, safeguarding property rights, interpreting custom, arbitrating between tenants in dispute, and keeping husbandry running with minimum friction. The very different Scottish system had a further significant feature: most officials employed by landowners — baillies, chamberlains and factors, as well as those appointed to lesser positions — were themselves tenants and working farmers, whereas receivers, agents and stewards in Ulster, however active and conscientious, were almost invariably socially superior to the tenantry, and correspondingly ignorant of the realities of farming life and insensitive to the needs of those in their charge.[18] Furthermore, during the harvest and other crises which punctuated the period down to the mid-1740s the tenurial structure of many estates, particularly in mid- and west Ulster, was seriously threatened and in some instances came near to collapse. Proprietors were confronted by heavy rent arrears and requests for rent abatements; they were required to reduce rents or to re-negotiate leases; and some tenants broke and fled. The incidence of such phenomena was persistently high and some properties remained undertenanted for considerable periods. Owners and officials remained pre-occupied with the need to sustain their tenantry and to achieve a permanent, albeit low and precarious, level of economic activity on their estates. There were few, if any, equivalents in Ulster to the modest but significant new departures made by proprietors in Lowland Scotland — in enclosure, tree planting, convertible husbandry and the selective breeding of livestock; and because tenurial policy was uniformly generous, there was little scope for positive discrimination in favour of the most substantial and successful farmers. Nor as yet did the unfortified house become thoroughly fashionable, as it did in Scotland. A few proprietors built new houses or embellished old ones, but until the second quarter of the eighteenth century the majority continued to live in castles and tower houses or behind bawns which had cost too much and were of too recent vintage to justify substantial alteration or redundancy.[19]

Only from the late 1740s was there a distinct improvement in economic conditions in Ulster, initially in the east of the province and then, a decade or so later, in the west. At home population growth led to a steady extension of the cultivated acreage; abroad it stimulated demand for the province's agricultural exports, especially after the removal in 1759 of the restrictions imposed by the Cattle Acts almost a century earlier. Exports of linen yarn and cloth rose even more dramatically, so that weaving and particularly spinning spread much more widely through the countryside. Following further difficult years in the early 1770s and early 1780s, a long period of hectic growth ensued during the Revolutionary and Napoleonic wars. The province became the world's leading producer of linen, developed a cotton industry and, along with the rest of Ireland, sent huge quantities of food to Britain. By the early nineteenth century Ulster's total population was second only to Munster among the four Irish provinces, and exceeded that of the whole of Scotland. New rents spiralled upwards, particularly from the early 1790s. Influenced by this and by the spirit (and the literature) of improvement emanating from Britain, owners assumed a more active role in estate management. As early as the 1760s it was observed that a proprietor made 'a figure in his country in proportion to the improvements that he makes'.[20]

Substantial landowners were collectively prominent in three types of activity. Firstly, new or elaborately extended country houses proliferated; demesnes were expanded, planted and embellished; and by 1800, with prices rising rapidly, few large properties were without productive home farms and kitchen gardens. A number of families provided themselves with fine town houses and seaside residences; many more built or re-built public utilities such as churches, schools and poor houses; and some of the most substantial proprietors, for example Robinson in Armagh and Donegall in Belfast, were leading participants in a spate of development in the larger urban centres.[21] Secondly, as a means of establishing or developing villages and towns in remoter areas, proprietors were largely responsible for a marked increase in the number, variety and frequency of fairs and markets. They secured new patents and re-activated old ones; some of the capital which they provided (or more frequently borrowed) for building was devoted to commercial premises such as linen and market halls; in addition to discounting bills on fair days and market days, they promulgated more precise regulations for the conduct of business; and they actively promoted growth in coaching, carting and postal services. By 1800 the province had around fifty market centres with populations in excess of 500.[22] Thirdly, proprietors took advantage of a change in the law in 1765 to generate a significant expansion and improvement of the rural road network. Before then the limited finance available to county grand juries had been devoted to the building and repair of bridges, drains and sewers. An Act of that year extended these terms of reference to include roads and, by introducing a levy per acre on all farming households, greatly increased the capital available for investment in this way. Proprietors dominated the juries and vied with one another in securing presentments: previously isolated communities were linked to market centres, major new routeways emerged, and economic activity in the province became steadily more integrated.[23]

Nevertheless, while the scale of these activities was impressive compared with what had gone before, efforts were largely restricted to purely personal concerns or to infrastructural developments. Thus, although landowners supported the Linen Board in regulating and encouraging industry, and while their endeavours in regard to roads, markets and urban development facilitated growth, the forces which promoted an expansion of linen production were fundamentally beyond their control. Similarly, proprietors looked for further opportunities, in mining and quarrying for instance, but confronted by the province's narrow resource base met with little success. A minority became involved with turnpike trusts; the majority deployed public rather than private capital in improving the road system. Only a few great magnates could afford substantial investment in communications. Again there was a sharp contrast with developments in Lowland Scotland. There, involvement in coalmining had originated in the sixteenth century: two centuries later proprietors were closely concerned with the exploitation of new coalfields in the Clyde basin, only leasing mining rights once enterprises were firmly established. Albeit on a smaller scale, a similar pattern emerged in salt-boiling and the production of coal-tar, glass and lime. In the seventeenth century landowners were prominent in harbour construction; later they turned to canal development, holding company directorships and providing much necessary capital. Beyond the mid-eighteenth century they financed the work of turnpike trusts and were major investors in the extension of the private road network. In comparison with Ulster proprietors their participation in all these activities was far more direct; their investments were long-term, sizeable and at times lavish.[24]

One reason for this was that Scottish merchants had been buying their way into substantial landownership over many years, infusing the propertied elite with capital, skill and experience.[25] Conversely, by restricting the market in freehold property, the Ulster tenurial system severely reduced such movement; aspiring Belfast merchants had only occasional opportunities for major land purchases, often in the remoter parts of the province.[26] This was merely a symptom of a deeper malaise. Properties could not be made to yield economic rents until leases fell in, and from the mid-eighteenth century onwards increasing life expectancy boosted the average length of leases. Whatever their background, Ulster proprietors were relatively poor because most rents remained very low and lagged far behind prices.[27] Landownership brought with it political influence and social prestige but, in comparison with other avenues of investment, yielded exceedingly poor dividends. Lord Macartney, for example, was prepared to devote surplus estate income to local improvement in north Antrim, but the bulk of the much greater wealth which he derived from a series of administrative and diplomatic posts was very profitably invested in the London money market. One of his correspondents, hearing that Macartney had embarked on 'an Herculean labour in your farming life', could not believe that he would have 'the time to ruin yourself in tripling the value of your estate': more pertinently, Macartney had neither the ability nor the inclination to do so.[28]

Like other well-intentioned proprietors, his endeavours were hamstrung by policies pursued by predecessors during the economic difficulties of an earlier age. In fact, having been set in 1739 (a decade or so before Macartney's succession), at least one of the lives leases on his estate outlasted him, though he died in 1806; the new rent represented a sixfold increase over its predecessor.[29] Nor is it an inappropriate example: beyond 1750, as separate studies have shown, three-lives leases generally lasted for between fifty and seventy years, if only because the tenant and one of his sons were commonly among the named lives.[30] Moreover, during the early eighteenth century the lease for three lives or thirty-one years (whichever was the longer) became standard for Protestant tenants, while Catholics were usually granted the maximum length permissible under the penal laws (initially twenty-one, and thereafter thirty-one, years). Because covenants against sub-letting were absent or ineffective, population growth in more buoyant economic conditions led to the appearance of tiers of sub-tenancy. Whenever possible, many proprietors strove to by-pass middlemen and to establish a direct tenurial relationship with those who worked their land: of necessity, the process whereby this objective was attained was spasmodic and long-drawn-out. Once it was achieved, proprietors continued to offer leases for three lives and/or thirty-one years until the rapid price inflation of the war years finally dictated otherwise. Even then political considerations cautioned against the complete abandonment of lives leases: for a short period following the enfranchisement of Catholics, terms of one life or twenty-one years became the norm for both religious groups. Only around the turn of the century was there a general transition to a system of tenancies at will. Again, fresh policies could not be implemented until old leases had dropped; a substantial backlog of such leases was ultimately dealt with during the post-war depression.[31]

The consequences of these developments were of long-term significance. At any stage before the nineteenth century large blocks of tenanted property yielded thoroughly uneconomic rents. Ulster proprietors found it difficult, therefore, to resist the temptation to expand their rent rolls by condoning subdivision. Only latterly did they become alarmed by the extent of the diminution in the size of holdings; whereas 'long before 1750 the tendency in the [Scottish] Lowlands was to enlarge the size of individual farms, ruthlessly limit fragmentation ... and increasingly reduce access to land'.[32] Thus, while farm units in Lowland Scotland became larger and economically more viable, their size continued to decline in

Ulster during the early decades of the nineteenth century; and compared with British units the average size remained very low until well into this century. Moreover, Lowland proprietors effectively promoted agricultural improvement schemes, though it is now generally agreed that the success of their personal involvement in farming was for long exaggerated. The key factor in the transformation of the region's rural economy (for which proprietors were largely responsible) was the ability of substantial farmers to carry out such schemes. In Ulster, however, landowners had first of all to rid themselves of a long tradition of aloofness from day-to-day economic activities on their estates; and then to adapt an out-dated tenurial system during a relatively short period of rapid economic change. The first objective was in large measure achieved; the second was beyond their capacity. There were also consequences for industrial development. As a result of fragmentation many tenants had to maintain a dual economy; and in some parts of Ulster, as Greig found in Co. Armagh, domestic producers of linen were able to outbid small farmers in pursuit of tenancies. Yarn and cloth manufacture became entrenched in a densely populated countryside: subsequent competition from factory-based industry at home and abroad produced acute distress and dislocation.[33] In Lowland Scotland on the other hand the linen industry was gradually divorced from farming over a long period. As rural depopulation gathered pace, production became centred in villages and small towns, where ultimately workers were better able to cope with the demands of the industrial revolution.[34]

Finally, the contrasts discussed above are more widely applicable. The lives lease system was widespread throughout Ireland and, under it, other parts of the country, particularly in the west, faced similar problems of adjustment during the more rapid economic development of the period after 1750. Moreover, the Lowlands were not the only region of Scotland to enjoy the benefits of earlier structural change. In the Southern Uplands the farm pattern had filled out completely by the sixteenth century, sheep farming was firmly established by the early seventeenth century, and the reduction of tenant numbers gathered pace from the early eighteenth century. Even in the Highlands the drive for clearance was preceded by decades of experimentation and adjustment in which landlords played, on the whole, a concerned and vigorous role. The collapse of the Highland economy in the early nineteenth century was less an indictment of proprietorial neglect 'than a measure of the objective difficulties which confronted the region'.[35] Such difficulties were also primarily responsible for the contrasting situation and functions of proprietors in the Scottish Lowlands and the north of Ireland.

NOTES

1. Introduced by F. M. L. Thompson and D. Tierney (Belfast, 1976), p. 93.
2. T. C. Smout, 'Scottish Landowners and Economic Growth 1650–1850', *Scottish Journal of Political Economy*, 11 (1964), p. 218 (quotation); *A History of the Scottish People, 1560–1830* (Glasgow, 1972), pp. 107–110, 126, 131; I. Whyte, *Agriculture and Society in 17th-Century Scotland* (Edinburgh, 1979), pp. 7, 31–32, 94, 113–114.

3. T. M. Devine, 'The Union of 1707 and Scottish Development', *Sc. Ec. & Soc. Hist.* V (1985), p. 36.

4. M. Perceval-Maxwell, *The Scottish Migration to Ulster in the Reign of James I* (London, 1973), *passim*; P. Robinson, *The Plantation of Ulster* (Dublin, 1984), *passim*; for the Welsh see H. C. O'Sullivan, The Trevors of Rosetrevor: A British Colonial Family in 17th-Century Ireland (unpublished M.Litt. thesis, Trinity College, Dublin, 1985), pp. 3–4.

5. R. Dudley-Edwards, 'Letter-Book of Sir Arthur Chichester, 1612–1614', *Analecta Hibernica*, VIII (1938), p. 85; P. Roebuck, 'The Making of an Ulster Great Estate: the Chichesters, Barons of Belfast and Viscounts of Carrickfergus, 1599–1648', *Proceedings of the Royal Irish Academy*, 79, C (1979), pp. 1–25.

6. T. W. Moody, 'The Treatment of the Native Population under the Scheme for the Plantation in Ulster', *I.H.S.* I (1939).

7. D. Stevenson, *Scottish Covenanters and Irish Confederates* (Belfast, 1981), *passim*; W. Macafee and V. Morgan, 'Population in Ulster, 1660–1760', in P. Roebuck, ed., *Plantation to Partition* (Belfast, 1981), pp. 52–53; R. Gillespie, East Ulster in the Early 17th Century: A Colonial Economy and Society (unpublished Ph.D. thesis, Trinity College, Dublin, 1982), p. 210.

8. Whyte, *op. cit.*, pp. 33, 50, 109–110, 116, 156, 159, 259; 'Written Leases and their Impact on Scottish Agriculture in the 17th Century', *Agricultural History Review*, XXVII (1979); Smout, *Scottish People*, pp. 108–109, 129; Smout and A. Fenton, 'Scottish Agriculture before the Improvers — An Exploration', *Agricultural History Review*, XIII (1965), pp. 75–81.

9. C. Clay, 'Lifeleasehold in the Western Counties of England 1650–1750', *Agricultural History Review*, XXIX (1981), p. 95 (quotation) and *passim*.

10. Robinson, *Plantation of Ulster*, p. 107.

11. Morgan and Macafee, *op. cit.*, pp. 53–59; Smout, *Scottish People*, pp. 143–145; Whyte, *Agriculture and Society*, pp. 246–251.

12. W. Macafee, 'The Colonisation of the Maghera Region of South Derry during the 17th and 18th Centuries', *Ulster Folklife*, 23 (1977).

13. W. H. Crawford, 'The Evolution of Ulster Towns, 1750–1850', in *Plantation to Partition*, p. 140.

14. Crawford, 'Landlord-Tenant Relations in Ulster 1609–1820', *Ir. Ec. & Soc. Hist.* II (1975), p. 9. I am indebted to Mr. G. Kirkham for information about trade fluctuations and harvest crises.

15. Wm. Molyneux to John Locke in 1696, quoted in Crawford, 'Ulster Landowners and the Linen Industry', in J. T. Ward and R. G. Wilson, eds., *Land and Industry* (Newton Abbot, 1971), p. 119.

16. Ibid., *passim*; Crawford, 'The Origins of the Linen Industry in North Armagh and the Lagan Valley', *Ulster Folklife*, XVII (1971), pp. 42–51; Roebuck, 'The Donegall Family and the Development of Belfast 1600–1850', in P. Butel and L. M. Cullen, eds., *Cities and Merchants: French and Irish Perspectives on Urban Development, 1500–1900* (Dublin, 1986), pp. 125–36.

17. R. Gillespie, *op.cit., passim*; I. D. & K. A. Whyte, 'Some Aspects of the Structure of Rural Society in 17th-Century Lowland Scotland', in Devine & Dickson, p. 37.

18. Crawford, 'Landlord-Tenant Relations', p. 6; Smout, *Scottish People*, pp. 115–118; Whyte, *Agriculture and Society*, pp. 44–45; Roebuck, 'Landlord Indebtedness in Ulster in the 17th and 18th Centuries', in J. M. Goldstrom and L. A. Clarkson, eds., *Irish Population, Economy and Society* (Oxford, 1981), pp. 151–52.

19. Roebuck, 'Landlord Indebtedness', pp. 147–50; Whyte, *Agriculture and Society*, Chapters 5 & 9; Smout, *Scottish People*, p. 109; M. Bence-Jones, *Burke's Guide to Country Houses*, I *Ireland* (London, 1978), *passim*.

20. Quoted in W. H. Crawford and B. Trainor, *Aspects of Irish Social History 1750–1800* (Belfast, 1969), p. 2.

21. Bence-Jones, *op.cit., passim*; L. A. Clarkson, 'An Anatomy of an Irish Town: The Economy of Armagh, 1770', *Ir. Ec. & Soc. Hist*. V (1978); W. A. Maguire, 'Absentees, Architects and Agitators', in K. McNeilly, ed., *Selection from 150 Years of Proceedings, Belfast Natural History and Philosophical Society* (Belfast, 1981).

22. Crawford, 'Ulster Towns', p. 141 and *passim*; 'Markets and Fairs in County Cavan', *Heart of Breifne*, II, 3 (1984), 55-65. For a case-study of market, road and village development, see Roebuck, ed., *Macartney of Lisanoure 1737-1806: Essays in Biography* (Belfast, 1983), Chapter 10.

23. A. McCutcheon, 'Transport, 1820-1914', in L. Kennedy and P. Ollerenshaw, eds., *An Economic History of Ulster, 1820-1939* (Manchester, 1985), pp. 109-11.

24. Smout, 'Scottish Landowners and Economic Growth', pp. 220-28.

25. See e.g. T. M. Devine, 'Glasgow Colonial Merchants and Land, 1770-1815', in Ward and Wilson, eds., *op.cit*., pp. 205-65.

26. E.g. the Warings moved to mid-Down; the Knoxes to Co. Tyrone; and the Macartneys and Montgomerys to north Antrim.

27. Roebuck, 'Rent Movement, Proprietorial Incomes and Agricultural Development, 1730-1830', in *Plantation to Partition*, pp. 82-101.

28. P.R.O.N.I. D.572/2/95, Col. E. Smith to Macartney, 15 Aug. 1772.

29. Roebuck, 'The Lives Lease System and Emigration from Ulster: An Example from Montgomery County, Pennsylvania', *Ulster Genealogical and Historical Guild Newsletter*, I, 7 (1981), pp. 217-19.

30. *Greig's Report*, p. 23; Maguire, *The Downshire Estates in Ireland, 1801-45* (Oxford, 1972), pp. 39-40; Crawford, 'Landlord-Tenant Relations', p. 8; Roebuck, 'Rent Movement', pp. 85, 92.

31. Roebuck, 'Rent Movement', *passim*; see also Dickson, 'Middlemen', in T. J. Bartlett and D. Hayton, eds., *Penal Era and Golden Age* (Belfast, 1979).

32. Devine, 'The Union and Scottish Development', p. 36.

33. See especially B. Collins, 'Proto-Industrialisation and Pre-Famine Emigration', *Social History*, VII, 2 (1981), pp. 127-146.

34. Devine, *loc.cit*.

35. R. A. Dodgshon, 'Agricultural Change and Its Social Consequences in the Southern Uplands of Scotland, 1600-1780', in Devine & Dickson; *idem, Land and Society in Early Scotland* (Oxford, 1981), pp. 205-76; E. Richards, *A History of the Highland Clearances*, I, *Agrarian Transformation and the Evictions, 1746-1886* (London, 1982), pp. 125-26.

Part Two:

Social Adjustment and Economic Transition

8

'TO PAY THE RENT AND LAY UP RICHES': ECONOMIC OPPORTUNITY IN EIGHTEENTH-CENTURY NORTH-WEST ULSTER

G. E. Kirkham

'Though they make a great deal of linen cloth about Derry yet they do not work up into cloth so much as they might do but principally supply Manchester with linen yarn which is exported to Liverpool.'[1] Edward Willes's observation on the linen industry in the Foyle valley in the late 1750s recognised a major difference in the form and pace of economic development between north-west Ulster and other areas of the province. By the mid-eighteenth century linen weaving was widely diffused and played a dominant role in the economy of much of east and south Ulster; in the north-west production was restricted to localised pockets in the Foyle area and its immediate hinterland. Despite expansion of the weaving sector in the region after 1750 a considerable imbalance remained. Market sales of brown linens in counties Donegal, Fermanagh, west Londonderry and west Tyrone more than doubled during the last two decades of the century, totalling £326,000 annually in 1803; even at this peak, however, sales of unbleached cloth in the region as a whole amounted to only three-quarters of the totals for either counties Armagh or Antrim.[2]

As Willes indicated, the predominant form of domestic industry in the north-west was the spinning of linen yarn, primarily for export to the south Lancashire textile industry. Yarn shipments from Derry averaged about 500 cwt. annually in the first two decades of the century, but rose rapidly from the early 1720s to more than 10,000 cwt. per annum during the 1760s.[3] The Linen Board inspector Robert Stephenson noted in 1755 that 'all the yarn made in this tract of country, which takes in most part of Donegal, all Fermanagh, great part of Monaghan, almost all Cavan and Leitrim, and the greatest part of this county [Sligo], which are all great spinning counties, is exported, except some small part the North takes off in its manufactures'.[4] Exports declined slowly from the early 1770s as increasing quantities of yarn were consumed by the growing domestic weaving sector, but only with the rapid development of pure cotton manufacturing in Lancashire, and consequent downturn in export demand for linen yarn, was there a sharp fall in shipments from the region; by 1800 yarn exports were less than a third of the level of forty years previously. Output nevertheless continued to grow; in 1802 production of both yarn and cloth in Donegal was said to be 'every day increasing more and more', and in the same year it was estimated that the acreage under flax in Tyrone had risen by one-third during the preceding decade.[5]

Other elements in the regional economy also underwent considerable expansion during the period. The rearing of beef cattle for the Munster and Leinster markets and the supply of domestic cows to the manufacturing areas of east Ulster grew in importance from the second quarter of the century. Whiskey production, both legal and illicit, was widely established in the north-west before 1750 and became a substantial industry subsequently. Expansion of tillage, while stimulated by demand for flax and barley (for distilling), was more closely bound to subsistence requirements and the progress of demographic change. During the first half of the century the generally depressed agrarian economy, coupled with recurrent harvest crises and high levels of emigration during the 1720s, 1730s and 1740s, effectively limited population growth; in 1749 the number of households in Derry, Donegal, Fermanagh and Tyrone was only marginally greater than the total in 1706, although in the mid-1720s it had been some 15 per cent higher. From mid-century, however, as elsewhere in Ireland, population climbed rapidly, the number of households in these four counties more than doubling between 1753 and 1791, and rising by a further two-thirds by 1821.[6] This rise was accompanied by a major expansion of the area of tillage, primarily through settlement of marginal land. On the Abercorn estate the proportion of arable increased from 31 per cent of land on the property in 1756 to 43 per cent in 1806; late eighteenth-century surveys of the Conolly estate near Limavady showed substantial improvement of waste, and on some holdings the area of 'profitable' land had doubled since the beginning of the century.[7]

The eighteenth century was therefore a period of major expansion in gross output and of specifically market-oriented economic activity in the north-west. Dominant in this process was the rise of domestic industry, particularly spinning, but with an increasing emphasis on weaving towards the end of the period, and these activities provided the primary means of generating household income for a large proportion of the population. This essay seeks to examine three important aspects of the means by which this dominance arose: firstly, the efforts made by landlords to promote the linen industry; secondly, the extent to which specific pressures encouraged participation in and dependence on such activity; and finally, the role of popular attitudes in shaping economic development.

Eighteenth-century Irish landlords have received little praise for their role in economic development. Yet, as Peter Roebuck has pointed out, the ability of many Ulster proprietors to intervene effectively in the rural economy was, by comparison with their English counterparts, subject to considerable restraint. This was primarily a result of the extended tenurial hierarchy and long leases which characterised most estates, but indebtedness and low returns from land must also have reduced the willingness of many landlords to embark upon expensive and often frustrating projects for improvement.[8] Equally, domestic industry offered one of the few possible opportunities for increased levels of economic activity in an otherwise poorly endowed region, and a number of proprietors made specific efforts to encourage its development on their estates. The 6th Earl of Abercorn recalled in 1733 that he had in the period after the Williamite War 'at my own great expense promoted the linen industry in that neighbourhood . . . which has so far succeeded that at Strabane is now the greatest staple of linen yarn in the Kingdom'.[9] The form which his efforts took is unknown, although a linen exhibition and competitions in spinning and weaving held in Strabane in 1700 may have been associated.[10] Encouragement of domestic industry evidently continued as estate policy on the Abercorn property over a considerable period. In the mid-1730s financial assistance was given to a Dublin damask manufacturer and dyer who had been induced to settle on the estate; he undertook to purchase yarn locally to produce 'checquers and tickens; ... it is supposed by many that it will keep money here that now is laid out in Dublin for such goods.'[11] In 1737 flaxseed was offered to new tenants on part of the estate, and during the late 1740s and early 1750s attempts were made to increase yarn production by channelling spinning wheels provided by the Linen Board to male children on the property (spinning was throughout the period a predominantly female occupation).[12] The south Ulster landlord Charles Coote observed to Abercorn in 1748 on the competition between proprietors for equipment provided by the Linen Board: '... we begin to scramble for wheels and reels tomorrow ... if I get a tolerable harvest of wheels and reels I shall go home rejoicing'.[13]

Another early proprietorial project was Sir Gustavus Hume's attempt to develop Church Hill, Co. Fermanagh, as a linen centre. He began to promote the town c. 1714, establishing a market, building an inn and a number of houses 'proper for tradesmen to live in', and offering encouragement to others who would build and settle there. Five years later Hume advertised his intention to 'set up and establish a linen manufactory', providing a bleachyard and financial backing for any undertaker who would use the money in 'carrying on said manufactory and improving the said town'.[14] This attempt to introduce linen manufacture to the remote and largely undeveloped area south of Lower Lough Erne apparently failed, as did George Vaughan's eccentric project in south Inishowen, the 'College of Weavers of Buncrana', established in the mid-1730s.[15] Other urban schemes were more successful. In 1750 Charles Eccles sought to improve the town of Fintona on his Tyrone estate by offering beneficial leases for lives renewable to 'good dealers in the linen and hempen manufactures, and ... other artificers or tradesmen'; a market house was to be built in the town 'in order to promote trade'. New leaseholders in the town during the 1750s included a number of yarn merchants, and Eccles also substantially replaced the former predominantly Catholic tenantry in the immediate area with Protestant leaseholders, whom he presumably thought more likely to involve themselves in domestic industry.[16] Perhaps the most ambitious scheme was that of John Harvey, who claimed in the 1780s to have erected 'at a vast expense the market town of Malin' in north Inishowen, together with a large factory for the manufacture of linen thread and stockings and a bleach green. He employed, he said, some fifty people, 'exclusive of an infinite number of families' engaged in spinning.[17]

At mid-century yarn production was already widespread throughout the north-west. Weaving, however, was confined for the most part to the Foyle valley axis — in 1752 Bishop Pococke found major markets for cloth only at Strabane, Derry and Limavady[18] — and subsequent spatial diffusion of manufacturing was at least in part a consequence of the activities of entrepreneurial proprietors. In the early

1760s, for example, Sir Ralph Gore established the first bleachyard in Fermanagh at Lisbellaw, and enticed an Armagh draper to direct the business. By 1763 bleaching was in progress, weavers had been brought to the area, and a monthly linen market established. Arthur Young, visiting Gore's Belleisle property in 1776, noted that weaving households still made up only 5 per cent of the total in the vicinity, but observed that they 'increase fast; they have doubled their number in 10 years'.[19] At the same time that Gore was launching linen manufacture in Fermanagh, Thomas Conolly was reported to have 'collected a number of weavers together' on his Ballyshannon estate in south Donegal, intending to establish an 'extensive factory' there.[20] A linen market at Letterkenny, set up and provided with premiums by the local proprietor, was described in 1763 as 'grown very considerable ... and the country adjacent is greatly assisted by this market, and weavers encouraged to settle and reside there'.[21] Towards the end of the century flax cultivation, spinning and weaving were encouraged on the remote and barren part of the Conyngham estate around Glenties in west Donegal; through grants of looms and provision of loans for tenants the industry was said in 1802 to have reached 'a very considerable degree of forwardness'.[22]

These examples suggest that during the eighteenth century certain landlords were active, using a variety of strategies, in attempting to promote development of the linen industry on their estates. It is difficult to assess how typical such efforts were or to calculate the cumulative influence of a number of dispersed local projects in encouraging more general adoption of domestic industry; many of these enterprises may have been effective over only a relatively small area. Arguably proprietors as a group may have made a greater overall contribution to the economic vitality of the region by establishing local markets and fairs on their estates and, when sitting in concert as the grand juries for their respective counties, by approving expenditure on roads and bridges, thereby improving the accessibility of underdeveloped areas of the region to trade.[23] One early grand jury decision may have been of more direct consequence for the long-term growth of domestic industry. The 'gentlemen of Donegal' appointed an official inspector of yarn for the county at the beginning of the 1720s, who toured fairs and markets regulating the quality of yarn offered for sale. In 1724 it was claimed that as a result of his attention Donegal yarn had 'grown into such reputation that greater quantities of it than ever are shipped off at Londonderry, and ... two considerable dealers in yarn are come from Drogheda to settle there, for the advantage of the statutable yarn'.[24] The timing of this appointment by the grand jury may have been fortuitous, but it is notable that the growth in trade claimed as its result did begin at precisely this period. Annual shipments from Derry in the four years 1721/22—1724/25 averaged more than twice the level of the preceding four-year period, the beginning of a rapid rise in yarn exports which continued into the 1760s.

Wide popular participation in market-oriented domestic industry was a new phenomenon in the north-west during the eighteenth century. Writing in the early 1750s, Charles O'Hara recorded that the only manufacture known in the contiguous area of Sligo at the beginning of the century was that of woollens;

linens used in the area were imported. According to him, flax cultivation was introduced into the county in the late 1710s by the 'better sort of people [who] made their tenants' wives spin the produce, which they had woven into coarse linens for their own use. This industry descended and the lower sort of people had their linen made at home.' Subsequent expansion in spinning O'Hara attributed to the impact on poorer households of increasing rents in the late 1720s, resulting from rising demand for grazing land. Provision of flax seed and spinning wheels by the Linen Board enabled them to develop 'a branch of industry which they had never before considered but a saving in their own wear ... The English and Northern demands took it [yarn] off and left them money in return which enabled them to pay the advanced rents of their farms ...'[25]

O'Hara's testimony indicates diffusion of spinning engendered by increasing demands on subsistence, in the absence of other ready means of generating income. In the north-west as a whole the poor returns available from agriculture over much of the first half of the century, coupled with recurrent harvest crises and the ready demand from the export market, certainly offer a plausible explanation for a developing reliance on the earnings of domestic industry. In 1736 Alexander Crawford of Drumgun, near Donegal town, informed his landlord that there had been 'such famines for bread in these countries, and great deaths of cattle, and a kind of disease or murrain, that the country is impoverished by it, which is the occasion with rents and tithes to cause the most part of the country to go to America'. He claimed that he would have emigrated himself, and would certainly not have been able to continue to hold his lands, had it not been for a son who had become a yarn dealer in order to support the household. Others in the area, in the face of the depressed agricultural situation, presumably found some maintenance in producing the yarn. Two years later Crawford's neighbour complained, 'there is none can live here by the benefit of farms' (i.e. agriculture), and solicited encouragement for Crawford's son in his business.[26]

Contemporary observers emphasised that much the largest proportion of yarn produced in the north-west was exported (until at least the 1770s), and export data therefore provide some indication of the increase in output. These certainly appear to lend support to the interpretation that agricultural depression and particularly dearth were the major factors in encouraging the diffusion of spinning. Throughout the period from the 'take-off' in yarn shipments at the beginning of the 1720s to the peak in the 1760s the greatest year-on-year increases in export levels were recorded during periods of severe crisis. During the long period of difficulty in the late 1730s, culminating in the dearth of 1740–41, exports of yarn from Derry rose from 5,000 cwt. in 1735/36 to 11,000 cwt. in 1740/41. The disastrous harvest failures of the mid-1740s produced an increase from 9,000 cwt. in 1743/44 to more than 14,000 cwt. in 1746/47. Periods of scarcity in the late 1720s and 1750s produced smaller but substantial upward movements in exports.

To some extent these apparent sudden rises in output may have resulted from retained stocks of yarn coming to market. The agent on the Barrett estate on the Monaghan-Fermanagh border wrote in 1721 that he was unable to obtain linen cloth locally, 'for they have sold all their yarn to help ... this bad winter'.[27]

Equally, however, prices for yarn dropped considerably during most crisis periods, at times by as much as half, and domestic production must have increased in order to sustain a basic level of income. The fact that successive crises produced new peaks in exports also suggests that households on which dependency on spinning had been forced during periods of dearth subsequently maintained their involvement. High cattle mortality during the mid-1730s and in 1745–6 would have left many families in marginal areas with little immediate alternative.

There is little direct evidence from the north-west to support O'Hara's nomination of rents as the specific cause of increased reliance on domestic industry during the first half of the century, and it is perhaps significant that the late 1720s, to which he dated this development in Sligo, were also a period of severe dearth. Upward movements in head rents were generally modest before the 1750s but the lack of quantitative data on rent changes at lower levels of the tenurial hierarchy (to which O'Hara appears to have been referring) must leave the question open for the moment. Rents and tithes were certainly subjects of popular complaint, particularly during periods of distress, but without better information on the actual proportion of incomes they claimed it is difficult to assess the extent to which they were a specific burden on subsistence and thus a direct spur to the development of domestic industry.

From mid-century the upturn in the economy of the region and increasing demographic pressure on land resources prompted much more rapid upward movement in rent levels. In areas where spinning and weaving took a dominant role in the local economy, rents progressively came to reflect not the notional value of land for agricultural exploitation but rather its potential as a base for involvement in domestic industry.[28] Equally, the income available from yarn and cloth production enabled families to maintain themselves on smaller holdings, relying on markets rather than on their own land to provide a proportion of subsistence needs; this dependence on markets also facilitated movement on to marginal, less productive land, which demanded lower rents. Subdivision of holdings between family members, or to sub-tenants or cottiers, divided the effective burden of rent between a number of households, but the reduced subsistence base available for each family also accelerated reliance on income from domestic industry.

For successive generations, therefore, the joint impact of rent and diminishing holding size acted to promote both participation in spinning or weaving and their relative importance as a source of provision for subsistence. Commenting on the growing number of small weaving holdings in the Enniskillen area, Young observed: 'they breed up their sons more and more to weaving, as it increases much, and these people pay their rents by it'.[29] Involvement in domestic industry was possible, if not essential, throughout the lower levels of the social structure, thereby reducing the impact of diminishing opportunities for access to land. On larger holdings female servants were employed to increase the output of yarn from the household; substantial linen manufacturers employed journeymen or apprentice weavers, in addition to male members of the household. At the end of the period McEvoy found weaver-farmers in Tyrone providing cottiers with flax and potato ground, to be paid for, in part at least, by work at the loom. 'Common labourers', he observed, had in recent years taken up weaving in the evenings, after the day's work.[30]

At all levels, therefore, the popular economy was strongly shaped by participation in domestic industry. As noted earlier, areas within the Foyle valley and parts of east Donegal were among the earliest localities to be profoundly influenced in this way. Henry noted of the latter in 1739 that the 'farmer generally contents himself with no more land than is necessary to feed his family, which he diligently tills, and depends on the industry of his wife and daughters to pay by their spinning, the rent, and lay up riches. These small partitions of land contribute vastly to the improvement of the country. It is usual to see 20 or 30 industrious Protestant families living happily together on one farm, called a townland'.[31] The late 1730s were, as has been suggested, a period of considerable difficulty for the rural population of the region, and Henry's description certainly idealises the local situation. Yet in broad terms the emphasis on domestic industry he depicts might be used to represent the household economy of a substantial proportion of the population over much of the subsequent period.

In one crucial aspect, however, Henry's description is seriously misleading. His suggestion that domestic industry enabled families to 'lay up riches', with the implication of a 'rational' profit-maximising view of productive activity, is not borne out by the available evidence. As has been indicated, the course of development of spinning and weaving in the north-west was dictated primarily by coercive pressures, either directly on subsistence or through increasing limitations on access to land; motivation to participate was most strongly exercised through the opportunities for maintaining life at an acceptable level, rather than for amassing wealth in order to transform it. This interpretation is supported by the marked leisure preference which existed within the population. Irregular work patterns and reduced household output in periods of cheap provisions were widespread in eighteenth- and nineteenth-century Ireland, as in other pre-industrial economies.[32] In the north-west the phenomenon was particularly marked within the social group normally at least partly dependent on wages and food obtained by work as farm servants and labourers. The agent on the Abercorn estate declared in 1752 that the local economy had greatly improved in recent years, 'but I really believe the lower people will lose their senses. Many who lately were half starving appear now like gentlemen and cannot be spoke to; servants are hard to be got and day labourers must have double wages; although victualling of all sorts sell pretty dear ... linen cloth and yarn continue to sell high'.[33] Improving economic conditions allowed these individuals, for whom subsistence for themselves and their families had previously been marginal, to elect to maintain themselves within their own households with the income available from domestic industry. This form of economic behaviour argues strongly against any wide distribution of profit-maximising attitudes, but also emphasises the primacy of the family as a dominant feature within economic life. This provides the background to O'Hara's much quoted remark of c. 1760, suggesting that the increased prosperity resulting from domestic industry had given families 'a better bottom than formerly; residence is more assured and families are more numerous as increase of industry keeps them more together'.[34] On farms employing spinners or weavers to increase output, family members nevertheless provided the essential nucleus of the labour force. Attempts to encourage recruitment for the army in the Strabane area in 1759 were largely ineffective; 'the fathers called out that if their sons, who are mostly weavers, or their journey men or apprentices, should leave them, they would not be able to pay their rents'.[35] McEvoy explained that in periods of dearth or recession labour was always cheap, because 'the farmer in order to save provisions endeavours to get through all or part of the labouring work by his own family . . .'[36]

Hutchinson has noted the emphasis on family within Irish culture as a particular limiting factor on individualism and enterprise.[37] However, in a contribution to the recent debate on the popular mentality underlying economic activity in early America, Henretta has suggested that the specifically familial basis of productive activity was in itself a 'crucial determinant' of economic goals within colonial society. The primary goal of enterprise within this culture, he suggests, was the long-term maintenance of the lineal family, each generation in turn endeavouring to provide the succeeding one with a comparable or improved 'subsistence' base.[38] Some element of this mentality can be identified in eighteenth-century north-west Ulster. In 1757 a new lease covenant 'against the tenants bequeathing or leaving to their families their interest' (that is, the customary right to negotiate for renewal) was proposed on the Abercorn estate. The agent warned that this would 'frighten them and make them think that they have no interest in anything; nay, there are people in this country that would not value to tell them they were in a state of vassalage by it. They all now that are able are determined to improve, but if this clause would meet with an ill construction . . . it would do a great deal of hurt'.[39] A substantial tenant and former seneschal on the same estate informed the Earl of Abercorn in 1766 that he had purchased the interest of a large but unimproved farm on the property: 'I have six sons and two daughters and earnestly desire to settle all in my power under your Lordship and convenient to me; on this account I paid Mr Hamilton [the former tenant] considerably beyond the value of the yearly income'.[40] In the early 1780s another Abercorn agent observed of the tenantry that 'they seldom make any other provision for son or daughter than the land'.[41]

In the absence of hard data on inheritance patterns and inter-generational social mobility it is difficult to assess the social distribution or the effectiveness of a strategy of economic activity based on provision for the lineal family. For a large part of the population, of course, the long-term potential of such a strategy was rapidly overtaken by the impact on land resources of rising population and rents; an increasing proportion of the population sank below the level of landholding to become cottiers and labourers. Yet it is clear that for those families who retained a foothold on the land the opportunities provided by domestic industry allowed subdivision between members — creating the base for a subsequent generation — to proceed well beyond the constraints which household economies based solely on agriculture would have imposed. In colonial America the drive to establish each generation played an important role in promoting continuing expansion of the frontier; in the very different circumstances of north-west Ulster a comparable attitude enabled a few generations to maintain themselves against the coercive influences of the wider economy. Ironically, as their range of options narrowed, many households and individuals exchanged the unequal struggle they faced at home for the greater opportunities they perceived on that American frontier.

NOTES

1. Edward Willes to Earl of Warwick, c. 1759, printed in W. H. Crawford & B. Trainor, eds., *Aspects of Irish Social History, 1750–1800* (Belfast, 1969), p. 88.

2. P.R.O.N.I. D.562/6225, John Greer, *Report of the State of the Linen Markets of the Province of Ulster* (Dublin, 1784). This copy is annotated with market data for 1803.

3. P.R.O. CUST 15. All export data in this paper are derived from this source.

4. Robert Stephenson, *An Enquiry into the State and Progress of the Linen Manufacture of Ireland* (Dublin, 1757), pp. 156–7.

5. James McParlan, *A Statistical Survey of the County of Donegal* (Dublin, 1802), p. 91; John McEvoy, *A Statistical Survey of the County of Tyrone* (Dublin, 1802), p. 136.

6. From hearth tax data given in D. Dickson, C. O. Grada and S. Daultrey, 'Hearth Tax, Household Size and Irish Population Change, 1672–1821', *Proceedings of the Royal Irish Academy*, LXXXII C, 6 (1982), pp. 177–8.

7. D. McCourt, 'The Decline of Rundale, 1750–1850', in P. Roebuck, ed., *Plantation to Partition: Essays in Ulster History in Honour of J. L. McCracken* (Belfast, 1981), pp. 123–4; P.R.O.N.I. D.2094/40, 45.

8. P. Roebuck, 'Rent Movement, Proprietorial Incomes and Agricultural Development, 1730–1830', in P. Roebuck, ed., *op.cit., passim; idem*, 'Landlord Indebtedness in Ulster in the Seventeenth and Eighteenth Centuries', in J. M. Goldstrom and L. A. Clarkson, eds., *Irish Population, Economy and Society: Essays in Honour of the Late K. H. Connell* (Oxford, 1981), pp. 149–50.

9. P.R.O.N.I. T.2541/FA1/2/10, Earl of Abercorn to Jas. Nisbitt, 15 January 1733.

10. P.R.O.N.I. D.623/47 (see note in *Irish Economic Documents: A Selection of Irish Economic Documents (1686–1903) from the Public Record Office of Northern Ireland* [Belfast, n.d.], p. 24).

11. P.R.O.N.I. T.2541/IA1/1A/14, John Holden to Lord Abercorn, 8 November 1736.

12. P.R.O.N.I. T.2541/IA1/1A/26, John McClintock to Lord Viscount [Paisley], 25 February 1737; T.2541/IA1/1D/3, same to [Earl of Abercorn], 29 January 1748; T.2541/IA1/2/144, Nathaniel Nisbitt to [same], 10 February 1753.

13. P.R.O.N.I. T.2541/IA1/1D/13, Charles Coote to [Earl of Abercorn], 31 March 1748.

14. *Dublin Gazette*, 1–5 February 1714; *Dublin Courant*, 10 January 1719.

15. *Dublin Evening Post*, 22–26 July 1735; G. T. Stokes, ed., *Pococke's Tour in Ireland in 1752* (Dublin, 1891), p. 46.

16. *Belfast News Letter*, 9 March 1750; P.R.O.N.I. D.526, Eccles estate leases.

17. P.R.O.N.I. D.562/5889, Memorial of the Rev. John Harvey to the Trustees of the Linen Manufacture (n.d. but c. 1780s). I am indebted to Dr. Harry Gribbon for drawing my attention to this document.

18. G. T. Stokes, ed., *op.cit.*, p. 44.

19. Robert Stephenson, *The Reports and Observations of Robert Stephenson made to the Right Hon. and Honourable the Trustees of the Linen Manufacture for the Years 1762 and 1763* (Dublin, 1764) (hereafter, Stephenson, *Reports and Observations*), pp. 26, 76–7; Arthur Young, *A Tour in Ireland 1776–9*, ed. A. W. Hutton (Dublin, 1892), I, p. 198.

20. Stephenson, *Reports and Observations*, p. 76.

21. *Ibid.*, p. 75.

22. McParlan, *op.cit.*, pp. 31, 91.

23. W. H. Crawford, Economy and Society in Eighteenth-Century Ulster (unpublished Ph.D. thesis, Queen's University of Belfast, 1982), Ch.V, *passim*.

24. [James Corry, ed.], *Precedents and Abstracts from the Journals of the Trustees of the Linen Manufactures of Ireland* (Dublin 1784), pp. 68, 85.

25. P.R.O.N.I. T.2812/19/1, Charles O'Hara, [manuscript survey of the economic development of County Sligo, c.1700–c.1755], n.d. but compiled c.1750–75.

26. S.R.O. GD.10/1421/12/489, Alexander Crawford to Alexander Murray, 21 July 1736; GD.10/1421/12/494, Hugh Stephen to same, 1 July 1738.

27. P.O Mordha, 'The Linen Industry in the Clones Area (1600–1840)', *Clogher Record*, X, 1 (1979), p. 144.

28. Edward Willes to Earl of Warwick, c. 1759. Printed in Crawford and Trainor, eds., *op.cit.*, p. 88.

29. Arthur Young, *op.cit.*, I, p. 198.

30. James McEvoy, *op.cit.*, pp. 100, 135.

31. P.R.O.I. MS 2533, Hints Towards a Natural and Topographical History of the Counties of Sligo, Donegal, Fermanagh and Lough Erne (unpublished manuscript, 1739).

32. S. J. Connolly, 'Religion, Work Discipline and Economic Attitudes: The Case of Ireland', in Devine & Dickson, pp. 239–42.

33. P.R.O.N.I. T.2541/IA1/2/122, Jo. Colhoun to [Earl of Abercorn], 10 April 1752.

34. O'Hara, loc.cit.

35. P.R.O.N.I. T.2541/IA1/5/108, James Hamilton to [Earl of Abercorn], 19 August 1759.

36. James McEvoy, *op.cit.*, pp. 144–5. This orientation contrasts strongly with the absence of co-production by family groups which Macfarlane has noted as a major feature of the pre-industrial economy of parts of north-west England: Alan Macfarlane, *The Origins of English Individualism: The Family, Property and Social Transition* (Oxford, 1978), pp. 76–8.

37. Bertram Hutchinson, 'On the Study of Non Economic Factors in Irish Economic Development', *Economic and Social Review*, I, 4 (1970), p. 526.

38. J. A. Henretta, 'Families and Farms: *Mentalité* in Pre-Industrial America', *William and Mary Quarterly*, XXXV (3rd ser.), 1 (1978), pp. 20–26.

39. P.R.O.N.I. T.2541/IA1/4/67, Nathaniel Nisbitt to [Earl of Abercorn], 19 April 1757.

40. P.R.O.N.I. T.2541/IA1/7/52, Tristram Cary to [Earl of Abercorn], 19 December 1766.

41. P.R.O.N.I. T.2541/IA1/14/35, James Hamilton to [Earl of Abercorn], 9 July 1784.

9

WAGES AND COMPARATIVE DEVELOPMENT IN IRELAND AND SCOTLAND, 1565–1780

L. M. Cullen, T. C. Smout and A. Gibson

The origin of this essay lay in a disagreement at the last Irish-Scottish meeting as to whether Ireland or Scotland could be considered the more 'backward', 'underdeveloped' or 'poor' economy in the two centuries before c.1780, when Scotland clearly began to pull ahead. At the first meeting, in 1976, two of the authors agreed that there was an approximate equality of misery in the seventeenth-century economies of the two countries, and that the conundrum was not clearly resolved in Scotland's favour for another three-quarters of a century. At the second meeting, in 1981, one of them revised this opinion by suggesting that throughout the seventeenth and eighteenth centuries Ireland had suffered from such profound structural disadvantages that she could never have been anything other than appreciably poorer than Scotland. Could the problem be resolved by hard data? An investigation into the relative level of real wages in the two countries seemed to be one possible way forward.

It was, however, immediately beset by very substantial problems of a conceptual and methodological nature, not all of which have proved possible to overcome in a convincing way. In both countries wage data are fragmentary, particularly in Ireland, and particularly for the period before the eighteenth century: for the sixteenth and seventeenth centuries they are largely restricted to the building trades in Edinburgh, Aberdeen and Dublin, along with scraps from Glasgow, Kilkenny and Youghal — none provide an unbroken series, and the Irish data in particular are sketchy, though far from unusable. For the eighteenth century, and especially for the second half, rural and provincial data become rather more widely available on both sides, with a particularly useful series from Stirlingshire.

Once a wage rate was obtained, in Irish or Scottish currency, how was it to be compared? One feasible way was to try to reduce both to a common sterling standard, since that was the currency to which both most commonly related themselves. In Scotland the exchange rate progressively deteriorated throughout the sixteenth century: at £4 Scots to £1 sterling in 1559 it fell until 1601 when a par of £12 Scots to £1 sterling was reached. Thereafter the rate remained stable. In 1707 the Scottish currency was abolished — although most of the Scottish sources continued to use Scots money of account until the mid-eighteenth century.

In Ireland from 1561 the par was £1.33 Irish to £1 sterling. This was itself an improvement on the par of £1.50 effective from 1487 to 1552, ahead of a decade of monetary disorder. Apart from the currency experiment of 1600–3 (when the par deteriorated to £3.82), this par reigned into the early decades of the seventeenth century, though the picture became complicated from the 1620s when contemporaries chose frequently to express the purchase of bills of exchange in terms of sterling rather than in Irish money of account. When expressed in money of account, the effective par was still £1.33 to £1 sterling in 1630–32; army monies were converted at that rate in those years. After the proclamation of 1637 Irish prices were required to be expressed in sterling (they had, in any case, been so expressed with increasing frequency from the early seventeenth century). The purpose of this was to do away with the inherent ambiguity of operating prices in either sterling or Irish money of account, a practice which confused contemporaries (often to their loss) as much as later historians. Probably under Cromwell, a one-to-one parity seems to have been finally achieved between the two currencies. A sterling premium of 2 to 4 per cent had emerged again by the early 1660s. Over the 1670s and 1680s its range roughly averaged 7–8 per cent, formalised after 1689 as a par of 8.33 per cent.

If wages in Irish and Scottish money of account are compared, a striking feature is that Scottish wages, like Scottish commodity prices, rose sharply, while Irish wages and prices rose modestly. This in turn is reflected in the fact that the Irish exchange rate with sterling held stable from 1561 to 1600 while the Scottish exchange with sterling progressively deteriorated. Indeed, the state of the Irish currency at the outset of the 1560s was so bad that Ireland seems to have been one of the rare instances where Gresham's law was disproved and good money, pumped into circulation by government military spending, drove out bad. In consequence too, Ireland, like Sweden, is one of the rare countries which seem to have experienced little of the sixteenth-century price revolution.

This situation is reflected in the fact that, if wages in both countries are converted to a common sterling standard, Irish wages actually rose while Scottish wages initially stagnated or even fell. Graph I shows that there was a steady increase in money wages expressed in sterling from the mid-sixteenth century in Dublin, ending around 1615. In Scotland a rise started in the first half of the century, but from 1550 to 1590 there was little change in trend; thereafter, there was renewed acceleration to 1615.

This increase in both countries was followed by a period of stability which, though it lasted little more than two decades in Dublin (where wages were even falling back slightly), continued in Scotland for over a century with little significant change occurring until after 1750. It was only in the third quarter of the eighteenth century that a sudden and rapid increase in wage-rates brought Edinburgh to near parity with Dublin for the first time since the 1630s; an increase was also demonstrated (albeit at a lower level) in rural Stirlingshire. In Dublin, on the other hand, the graph for the seventeenth century shows a distinct improvement of wages in the 1620s and the late 1630s followed by a further step-up of considerable magnitude at some point between 1650 and 1680. Thereafter there was little change until after 1760 when the subsequent movement was small compared to that experienced in Edinburgh.

This graph might, therefore, appear to show that a gap opened up in Ireland's

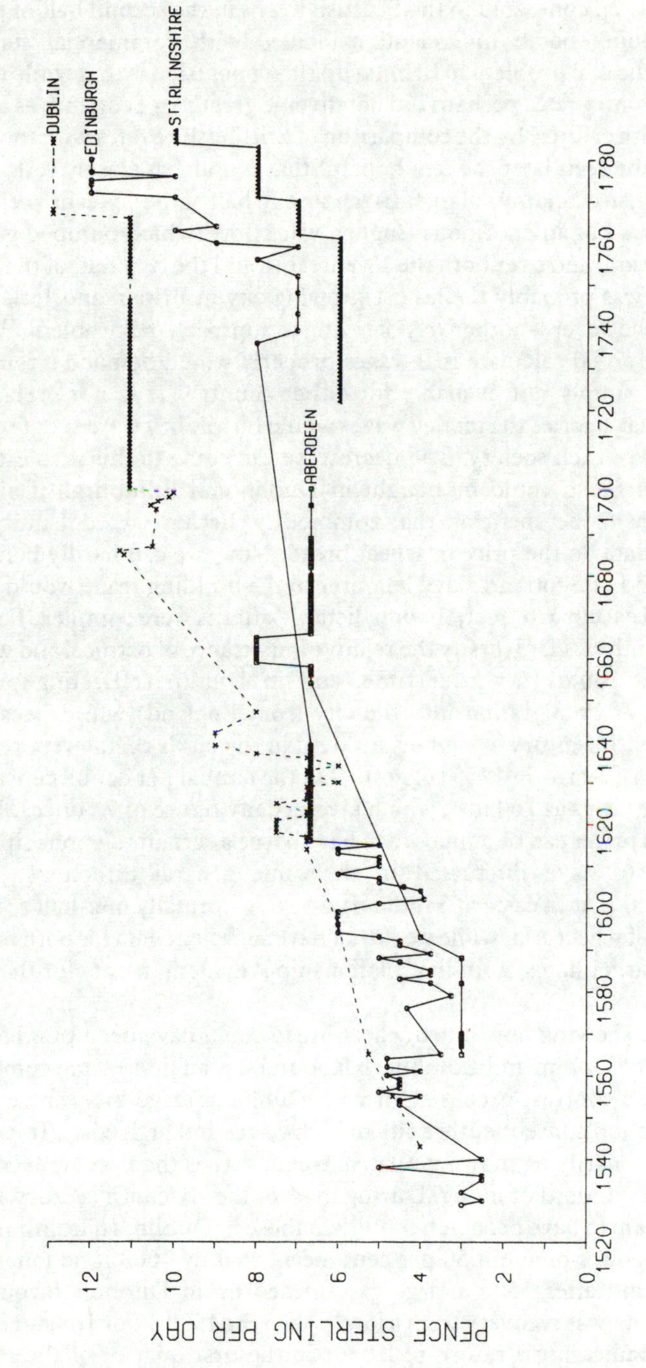
DAY LABOURERS' WAGES IN IRELAND AND SCOTLAND
PENCE STERLING PER DAY
DATE
DUBLIN
EDINBURGH
STIRLINGSHIRE
ABERDEEN
0
2
4
6
8
10
12
1520
1540
1560
1580
1600
1620
1640
1660
1680
1700
1720
1740
1760
1780

favour in the course of the seventeenth century, and that Dublin was doing particularly well compared to the Scottish towns in the second half of the century when a trading boom in Ireland coincided with commercial stagnation in Scotland. The real problem in firming up this conclusion is that while the trend of town and country rates perhaps did not diverge greatly in Scotland, as indicated in the eighteenth century by the comparison of Stirlingshire rates with town rates, we can, as will be seen later, be less hopeful that Dublin so closely reflected trends within the Irish economy at large. In the second half of the sixteenth century it was the bridgehead of an enormous English war effort (which pumped good money into circulation) and over both the seventeenth and the first half of the eighteenth centuries it was probably the fastest-growing city in Britain and Ireland.

There is, however, another way of trying to approach the problem. What would the wage buy? To calculate real wages properly would demand a range of price data that is simply not available for either country. It is not even feasible to calculate what calories the money wages would buy if they were spent solely on the staple foods of each society. The nearest we can come to this is to estimate how much wheat bread could be bought in Dublin and Edinburgh if all the wage available was to be spent on that commodity, because we do, uniquely, have reasonable data on the price of wheat bread. Now, we can hardly believe that in either Ireland or Scotland a day labourer in the building trade would have eaten wheat bread except as a treat, though dietary patterns were complex. For example, even in St Andrews University the relative importance of oatmeal and wheat in the student diet could vary over time, and in Dublin (reflecting perhaps the significance of immigration into the city from England) wheat became by the mid-eighteenth century an important item in the city's diet: a report before the Irish House of Lords in 1755 suggests that the annual per capita consumption of wheat in the city was 160 lbs., which gives a daily figure of 7 ounces. In any case wheat bread prices can be supposed to have borne a certain relationship to oatmeal prices and to have fluctuated in the same general directions. It can be demonstrated that in eastern Scotland oats were normally one-half to two-thirds of the price of wheat and, while we do not have sufficient data for both products for Ireland at earlier dates, a similar relationship is evident in data for the 1740s and 1750s.

Graph II, showing how much wheat bread could have been purchased by the daily wages of Dublin and Edinburgh labourers, is an interesting complement to Graph I. The contrast is consistent with Dublin's image as a centre of English immigration and consequently a city of high wages and high costs. It is of interest, of course, primarily in showing relative trends rather than accurate comparative levels in the standard of living. During most of the sixteenth century Edinburgh labourers seem to have been better off than those in Dublin. In Edinburgh a fall in purchasing power of about 50 per cent meant that by 1600 it no longer held the advantage, and after 1600 a large gap opened up in Dublin's favour. In both countries there was recovery from a low level in the 1590s. For Ireland the rise was very large, indicating a return to labour in the first quarter of the seventeenth century well above what it had been in the sixteenth century. The impression of

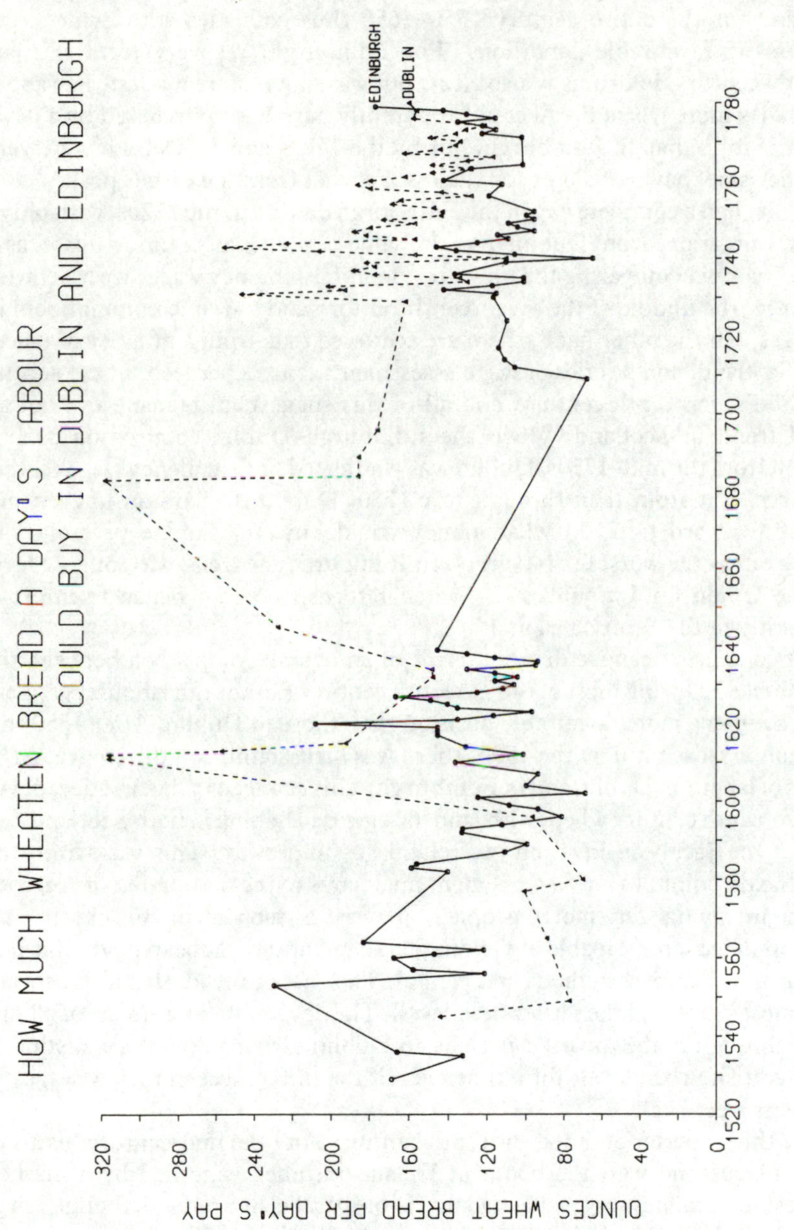
HOW MUCH WHEATEN BREAD A DAY'S LABOUR
COULD BUY IN DUBLIN AND EDINBURGH
EDINBURGH
DUBLIN
OUNCES WHEAT BREAD PER DAY'S PAY
0
40
80
120
160
200
240
280
320
DATE
1520
1540
1560
1580
1600
1620
1640
1660
1680
1700
1720
1740
1760
1780

high real wages at Dublin is substantiated in the 1620s and 1630s at this point by similar evidence in 1611–14 at Youghal and for the Boyle estates at large, at that time a main centre of English immigration. The period of maximum immigration to Ireland for the entire century 1550–1650 thus coincides with evidence of exceptionally favourable conditions. For Edinburgh, recovery from the late sixteenth-century doldrums is also clear, but was much more modest. For about two decades more wheat bread could apparently have been purchased by a day's wage in Dublin than in Edinburgh, but by the 1620s and 1630s both were very much the same, having fallen back again somewhat from the earlier peak.

There is then a complete gap in the Edinburgh data until the 1720s, with only a very few quotations from Dublin over the same period. This is unfortunate, as it prevents us from comparing the upward leap in Irish money wages with Scottish trends after the middle of the seventeenth century and the concomitant boom in real wages. On the other hand, there are scattered data from a number of places within Scotland, and a series of wage assessments from Aberdeen, in the second half of the seventeenth century, and all of this suggests a stagnant and not an upward trend in Scotland. When the Edinburgh–Dublin comparison can be resumed, from the mid-1730s, Dublin was well ahead both in money wages and in real wages. But from then through to c.1780, Dublin displays an uneven but mainly downward trend in what money could buy, the famine year of 1740 standing out as the worst for 140 years. In Edinburgh the trend was roughly level from the Union until around 1770, when returns to labour began to improve significantly in the Scottish capital.

What conclusion can we draw in terms of an overall comparison between the two countries? During most of the sixteenth century Edinburgh labourers appear to have been in a more favourable position than those in Dublin. After 1550 this gap began to close until by the 1590s there was little significant difference in the rewards of labour in Dublin and in Edinburgh. This changed in the first decades of the seventeenth century when, with land-hunger developing in both Scotland and England, the Jacobean invasion of Ireland got underway. This was, from the Anglo-Saxon point of view, a movement analogous to the occupation of America (though involving far more people): it was a movement to cheap and underpopulated land, capable of yielding large quantities of cheap food if farmed by English or Scottish methods and capital. The cost of bread, therefore, stayed low, in most years, and the settlers lived well. The developmental effects of all this worked through to the towns, especially to Dublin, driving real wages distinctly above Scottish urban levels for a time even if the differences in money wages in these years were slight.

In the third quarter of the seventeenth century, after the mid-century hiatus of famine, plague and war, the boom in Ireland resumed, signified by a marked upward shift in money wages that had no visible parallel in Scotland, though it had in England where population was now actually declining. The great growth of external trade made Dublin, and no doubt the remainder of the core immigrant areas, a boom region, highly attractive to migrating artisans and farmers alike. As it was certainly not a period of comparable development in Scotland, the attraction of Ireland to the Scots was doubly enhanced. On the other hand, the Phelps-Brown data for England indicate a modest growth in living standards in the south, which no doubt helps to explain why immigration fell off from England but not from Scotland in the period.

The superior level of Dublin wages to their Scottish equivalents was hardly maintained after the middle of the eighteenth century, when Scotland — including Edinburgh and Glasgow but by no means only the towns — began to enjoy a spurt of enhanced growth which was not shared by Dublin to the same extent. The purchasing power of the Scottish labourer also gradually began to improve, although it was not until the very end of the 1770s that he appeared better-off than his equivalent in Dublin.

So far so good. This interpretation would fit neatly enough with what we were saying in 1976, though giving it somewhat more shape, and more definition in timing. However, Dublin is by no means the whole of Ireland, and it is only when the eighteenth-century data become good enough to examine more of the countryside of both countries that it becomes possible to see the force of the argument of 1981 that structural weaknesses in the Irish economy were much graver than in Scotland. The question of what base to take — the sixteenth century or the seventeenth century — also affects the issue. The prosperity of seventeenth-century Dublin was not an illusion, but it becomes possible to see the manner in which it proved a limited phenomenon.

One way into exploring the problem of the typicality of Dublin, and more generally of investigating structural differences in the two economies, is through examining skill differentials, pursuing the notion that a narrow gap is an indication of relative development. In a poorer country, or region, where skill is rare, it will be relatively highly remunerated; the unskilled, whose productivity will be low by virtue of the area's underdevelopment, will be abundant everywhere and badly paid. In a richer area, more opportunity and more education will encourage a growth of skills, and their relative plenty will narrow the gap in their pay compared to the unskilled, whose productivity will be rising anyway. To take a specific illustration from within nineteenth-century Scotland, the wage rates reported to the 1843 Poor Law enquiry gave agricultural day labourers' rates on Skye and the Outer Hebrides at one-half of those of skilled artisans, but in North Lanarkshire at almost three-quarters: the one was a desperately backward crofting area, the other the heartland of the industrial revolution.

The distance in pay between labourers and craftsmen had tended to vary little over time in major urban centres in both countries, one being roughly half the other until the major shifting up by labourers in Edinburgh in the 1760s. (In England, by contrast, the Phelps-Brown data reveal a remarkably stable two-thirds proportion throughout.) In the later eighteenth-century countryside, however, when it first became possible to measure rural skilled-unskilled differentials, there were significant differences between Ireland and Scotland. How far the contrasts between regions outside the major urban centres were a recent development, and how far a feature of long standing, remains for the moment an open question.

In rural Ireland wages of craftsmen were not far out of line with Dublin rates, but wages of unskilled workers were significantly lower. Thus, according to Arthur Young in the 1770s, the average of carpenters' wages for the country at large was 1s.9d., and 2s.3d. for rural Co. Dublin; for masons it was 1s.9d. and 2s.0d. respectively. The Trinity College rates for both were 2s.6d. On the other hand Young's average for country labourers was 6½d. compared with 10d. for country labourers in Co. Dublin. The rate for building labourers in Trinity College was 1s.2d. The point of his calculations was not lost on Young:

> When it is considered that common labour in Ireland is but little more than a third of what it is in England, it may appear extraordinary that artisans are paid nearly, if not full, as high as in that kingdom.

In Scotland in the 1770s country masons (e.g. in Stirlingshire, Berwickshire and Angus) were being paid about 1s.3d., but labourers 8d. to 10d. — a completely different ratio, suggesting differentials similar to England albeit with lower wages paid all round. Country craft wages could vary enormously of course. In Ireland, below skilled workmen there were 'hedge' workmen whose rates and skills were inferior. On the Flower estate at Durrow, rates of as low as 1s. a day for masons can be found in 1731 and for sawyers as late as 1748. Similarly on the Kenmare estate in Kerry, rates of 1s. for craftsmen can be found in the 1720s. But while employers never seem to have had problems with the rates of the unskilled, disagreeable comments about the wages commanded by the skilled do appear throughout account books. Thus Sir Donat O'Brien in 1707 in Co. Clare thought 1s.4d. a day for masons excessive, and in 1747 Flower grumbled at having to pay 2s. a day for whitewashing and boarding: 'the closet I never desired to be done and the ceiling I think very dear'. Even the hedge workmen could command a good wage in certain circumstances. On the Plunkett estate in Co. Meath in 1749 an agreement was made with a man to let the malt house to him on condition that he did the family malting as well: he was also required to work as a mason if necessary, but the undieted rate was set at 1s.4d.

The gap between rates for skilled and unskilled could become very wide as one moved from town to country. Workers in the iron industry and in the glass industry were paid rates as high as, if not higher, than English rates even in the seventeenth century. Leaving the high technology industries of the age aside, on the Boyle estates in Munster wages for masons were 1s.0d. and 1s.2d. in 1628 and 1629, and for joiners 1s.3d. and 1s.2d., little different from the wages paid in Dublin by Trinity College. On the other hand labourers commanded a mere 6d. At Youghal in 1613 the Corporation fixed maximum wages for craftsmen at 12d. and for labourers at 5d. (averaging summer and winter rates).

In Scotland in the first half of the eighteenth century a very common rural day labourer's wage appears to have been 5d. or 6d., and not to have varied much from late seventeenth-century levels. Adam Smith refers to summer rates of 6d. and winter rates of 5d. for the seventeenth century. 10d. or 1s. often sufficed for a mason or a wright, suggesting a country ratio of 2:1 — similar to that of the town; although country artisans not infrequently got a little above that proportion, it was seldom as much as 3:1. In Ireland Petty, going on a rule of thumb basis, accepted a wage rate for country labour of 4d., and Brewster, familiar with Munster, quoted a wage of 3d. or 4d. with dinner in his *Discourse of Ireland 1698*. Kerry rates were still 5d. a day in the 1720s; and throughout the 1720s, 1730s and 1740s, despite the extensive improvements wrought on the Flower estate, wage rates were almost invariably 5d. Young's calculations suggest a year-round average rising from 4¾d. in 1756 to 6½d. in 1776.

Young's 1776 figures are an important collection of observations from 39 locations and show a range from 5d. to 10d. Wages were 6d. or less, moreover, in no less than 18 of the 39 locations cited. On the other hand his average figures of 1s.9d. for carpenters and masons respectively were ranged more narrowly from 1s.3d. to 2s.3d., and for 46 of the combined 79 observations were 1s.8d. or higher. In other words the craftsmen's rates were skewed towards the top whereas labourers' rates were skewed towards the bottom. This suggests that, at least by then, in rural Ireland the skilled to unskilled ratio was roughly 3:1 or 4:1, substantially above what appears to have been the traditional ratio for pre-industrial rural Scotland. Even more to the point, the ratio was probably not very different between town and countryside in Scotland, even though actual wage levels might have been: but the ratio was distinctly divergent between town and country in Ireland. This reinforces the important suspicion that the development level of Dublin was exceptional in its national context, or to put it another way, that Scotland had a more homogeneous economy than Ireland even at the start of the eighteenth century.

In the early 1790s, a period when Scotland was beyond all possible doubt experiencing rapid agricultural and industrial change of a sort never experienced in eighteenth-century Ireland, the *Statistical Account* provides data that give a very contrasting picture to Young's Ireland, and also to a lesser extent to Scotland itself in the first half of the eighteenth century. It may be analysed as follows:

Labourers' winter wages	28 counties	average 10d.
Labourers' summer wages	28 counties	average 1s. 1d.
Carpenters' wages	17 counties	average 1s. 4d.
Masons' wages	17 counties	average 1s. 6d.

Even with a gap of almost two decades, the craft rates remained significantly and surprisingly below the Irish. On the other hand not only were labourers' rates higher than Irish, but they were much closer together. Adam Smith had not failed to advert to the Scottish situation, commenting on a narrower range in labourers' wages in Lowland Scotland than in England. The summer observations (drawn from 28 counties) for labourers ranged from 7d. to 1s.4d., but all but two were in the range of 1s. to 1s.4d. A consequence was that while skilled rates were often four times labourers' rates in Irish locations, in no case did this happen in the *O.S.A.*, even where lower winter rates were taken. For all but eight counties even the winter rates lay between 10d. and 1s. compared with masons' and carpenters' rates ranging from 1s.2d. to 2s. For the eight deviant counties winter labourer rates of 5d. to 9d. compared with skilled rates of 1s. to 1s.7d. Only Ross and Cromarty seemed to approach the Irish situation, with labourers' rates of 5d. and 7d. winter and summer respectively, compared to carpenters' rates of 1s. and masons' rates of 1s.3d.

In other words the crippling thing about Ireland even at this stage in its history was that it already had a much larger zone of chronic poverty and under-development. Too much of Ireland approximated to the Highlands: what was in Scotland the minority problem was, in Ireland, quite simply the majority problem. There lay the structural difference between the two economies; but price and wages history can take us no further into the problem of exactly when it developed, how it arose or why it persisted.

TECHNICAL NOTE

Ireland

Assize data fixing prices and wages are not plentiful on the Irish side, though they did exist. The records of the city of Dublin, though extensive, do not as a rule appear to contain details of the bread assize, and while building accounts survive, they merely record the total discharged, without details of payments to individual workmen.

Wage data for Ireland are drawn from the building accounts in the Trinity College Muniments; Royal Hospital records in P.R.O.I; Ball building accounts in P.R.O.I. Business Records, Dublin 43; Dublin Corporation Muniments, Treasurer's Accounts, 1543, 1673; N.L.I., Flower estate accounts, MS 11462 and Plunkett estate papers, MS 14232; R. Caulfield, *Council Book of the Corporation of Youghal* (Guildford, 1878), pp. 15, 25; Sir John Ainsworth, 'Corporation Book of the Irishtown of Kilkenny', *Anal. Hib.* no.28 (1978); Sir John Gilbert, ed., *The Inchiquin Manuscripts* (*I.M.C.* 1961), p. 93; E. MacLysaght, ed., *The Kenmare Manuscripts* (*I.M.C.* 1962), pp. 266–84; A. K. Longfield, ed., *The Shapland Carew Papers* (*I.M.C.* 1946); A. Young, *Tour in Ireland* (London, 1780); Sir William Petty, *Political Arithmetic*, in C. H. Hull, ed., *The Economic Writings of Sir William Petty*, Vol. 1 (Cambridge, 1899), p. 210; [Sir Francis Brewster], *A Discourse Concerning Ireland* (London, 1698), p. 20.

We are greatly indebted to Dr Michael McCarthy-Morrogh for a large number of wage quotations from Munster for the first half of the seventeenth century. We are equally indebted to Prof. J. F. Lydon for making available to us the transcript by Mr Michael Ashworth of the remarkable Christ Church Cathedral building accounts of 1564–5. There is an important reference to the demand for masons in Dublin in 1569 in Sir John Gilbert, ed., *Calendar of Ancient Records of Dublin* (19 vols., Dublin, 1889–1944), II, p. 58.

Bread and wheat prices have been abstracted from various sources: the published assize data for Youghal and Kilkenny in the sources quoted above; the Dublin assize for 1683 in Sir J. Gilbert, ed., *Calendar of Ancient Records of Dublin*, V, p. 612; the accounts of the Clerk of the building works at Christ Church Cathedral in 1564–5; and the report on the Gerrard papers in *Anal. Hib.* no.2 (1931), pp. 142–160. Various bread or grain prices have also been drawn from *C.P.S.I. 1592–6*, p. 460; 1625–32, p. 604; 1663–5, p. 695; S. Pender, ed., *Corporation of Waterford Council Books* (*I.M.C.* 1964), p. 52; W. J. Smith, ed. *Herbert Correspondence* (Aberystwyth, 1963), p. 153; E. MacLysaght, ed., *Calendar of Orrery Papers* (*I.M.C.* 1941), p. 63; Sir John Gilbert, ed., *Calendar of Ancient Records of Dublin*, V, pp. 612, 620; *Anal. Hib.* no. 4 (1932); D. R. Hainsworth, 'Christopher Lowther's Canary Adventure: a Merchant Venturer in Dublin 1632–3', *Ir. Ec. & Soc. Hist.* II (1975); Manuscripts Room, Trinity College Library, MS 3961, a merchant's accounts, 1684–5; B. L. Add Ms, 4759, Exports and Imports of Ireland 1683–6; Assize quotations in Dublin newspapers, 1728–1780.

The price data for wheat are of varying provenance and quality. They have been converted into bread prices on the basis of the eighteenth-century assize calculations, allowing 6s. per quarter to the baker. While the peck was widely used as a small and geographically variable measure, the term also had a peculiar use to denote a wheat measure containing 16 gallons statute measure. (See *Anal. Hib.* no.2 (1931), p. 158, and Sir John Gilbert, ed., *Calendar of Ancient Records of Dublin*, II, p. 59.) The absence of adequate price information has meant that some of the sixteenth- and seventeenth-century assize prices and surrogate assize prices calculated from wheat prices have been drawn from Youghal, Kilkenny or Waterford. As wheat prices were generally lower in the provinces than in Dublin, the use of this material may lead to some overestimation of the weight of the Dublin loaf. However, this is to some extent corrected by our assumption that the baker's allowance of 1728 also applied earlier: for of course the allowance must have risen progressively in preceding centuries.

The best introduction to the Irish exchanges in the sixteenth century is in C. E. Challis, 'The Tudor Coinage for Ireland', *British Numismatic Journal*, XL (1971), pp. 98–99. From 1561 the par was £1.33 Irish to £1 sterling, and after various vicissitudes at the end of the 1590s it reverted to this in 1603. The use of the term 'sterling' caused considerable confusion in Ireland where both sterling and 'Irish' coins circulated, as prices were quoted both in sterling and Irish money even in the same document. In many, although by no means all, instances, the term sterling simply implied Irish money of account, as opposed to quoting a price in terms of the popular name of the actual 'Irish' or 'harp' coin, also a common though not consistent practice. The accurate identification and valuation of coins can be difficult, and some price quotations have not been used either because their 'sterling' character is uncertain, or because the valuation of the 'harp' coins in the context of the reference is problematical.

Scotland

Evidence of wages in Scotland has been drawn from six sources:

1. The Edinburgh Town Council Accounts (1553–1780), comprising the Town Treasurer's Accounts, the Dean of Guild Tradesmen's Accounts and the Parliament House Accounts — all held in the City Chambers, Edinburgh.

2. The Master of Works Accounts relative to Edinburgh (1529–1639) printed in the *Accounts of the Master of Works*, I, *1529–1615*, ed. H. M. Paton (Edinburgh, 1957), and II, *1616–1649*, ed. J. Imrie and J. G. Dunbar (Edinburgh, 1982).

3. Glasgow University Building Accounts (1632–1737) held at Glasgow University Library.

4. The Annual Wage Statutes (1565–1701) set by the Town Council of Aberdeen and recorded in the Minutes of the Town Council held in the Town House, Aberdeen.

5. St. Andrews University Building Accounts (1690–1710) held by the University Library.

6. The Farm and Building Accounts (1720–1780) of the Buchanan Estate of West Stirlingshire belonging to the Earl of Montrose (S.R.O. GD 220).

Throughout the period in question the Scottish sources give wages in Scots money. These have been converted to sterling using the ratios determined by R. W. Cochran-Patrick in his *Records of the Coinage of Scotland*, 2 vols. (Edinburgh, 1876).

Thus prior to	1550:	£ 4 Scots to £1 sterling
	1560–1564:	£ 5 Scots to £1 sterling
	1565–1578:	£ 6 Scots to £1 sterling
	1579–1596:	£ 8 Scots to £1 sterling
	1597–1600:	£10 Scots to £1 sterling
	1601 onwards	£12 Scots to £1 sterling

To estimate the purchasing power of labour in Edinburgh the price of wheat bread as set by the Town Council, and then later by the magistrates of Edinburgh, has been compared with actual wage rates. Sixteenth- and seventeenth-century prices are printed in *Extracts from the Records of the Burgh of Edinburgh, 1403–1718* (13 vols., Scottish Burgh Record Society, Edinburgh, 1869–1962), whilst occasional eighteenth-century assize prices can be found in volumes of the *Scots Magazine*. Unfortunately, the eighteenth-century price series is far from complete and for a number of years it has been necessary to estimate the price of wheat bread from the contemporary price of wheat. This is a straightforward process as the assize price was itself established with respect to the price of wheat. The only difficulty arises in that we are forced to use fiars' prices for wheat whilst the magistrates used current market prices. We can only presume that the fiars' price for any crop year did not depart excessively from the market price obtained in the last months of that year.

In comparing the purchasing power of labour in Dublin and Edinburgh two problems have posed particular difficulties: the systems of weight used in the two towns and the quality of the bread referred to in the various assizes. The evidence suggests that prior to 1708 bread in Ireland was weighed by Troy weight (with 12 ounces of 480 Troy grains to the pound) and thereafter by Avoirdupois weight (with 16 ounces of 437½ Troy grains to the pound). In Edinburgh, on the other hand, whilst it is certain that after 1707 Avoirdupois weight was used, there is some doubt about which system of weight was used prior to Scotland's union with England — the claims of Scottish Troy and Tron being equally matched. This awkward and frustrating problem disappears, however, when we take account of the quality of the bread referred to in the various Irish and Scottish assizes. This changed with time and was seldom the same in both countries. In England and eighteenth-century Ireland it was defined (in terms of the extraction rate of the flour from which bread was baked) by various Acts of Parliament, but in sixteenth- and seventeenth-century Scotland it was determined by a series of statutes emanating from the Town Council of Edinburgh which consistently decreed that 140 pounds of bread should be baked from each boll of wheat. If this were 140 pounds Scottish Troy (with 16 ounces of 480 Troy grains to the pound), then each boll of wheat (weighing, on average, 232 lbs. 15 oz. Imperial Avoirdupois) would have provided 2,457½ ounces Avoirdupois of wheat bread with an extraction rate of 52.5%. On the other hand, if this were 140 pounds Scottish Tron (with its much larger pound of 9,600 Troy grains), then each boll of wheat would have provided 3,072 ounces Avoirdupois of wheat bread with an extraction rate of 65.9%. As we must ensure that our figures on the purchasing power of labour in Ireland and Scotland are truly comparable, it is necessary to convert the price per given ounce of local bread into its equivalent price per ounce Avoirdupois of bread of a standard quality. The 'wheaten loaf' made of flour with an extraction rate of 73% used in Dublin prior to 1776 has been used as this standard. When we know the system of weight being used, and the extraction rate of the bread being priced, then this conversion is straightforward; in Scotland prior to 1707 it is only slightly less so. If Scottish Troy weight was used, and the bread was thus of 52.8% extraction, then the given price per ounce must be multiplied by $(437\frac{1}{2} \div 480) \times (52.8 \div 73) = 0.659$ to give the equivalent price per ounce Avoirdupois of bread of 73% extraction rate. If, on the other hand, Scottish Tron weight was used, and the bread was thus of 65.9% extraction rate, then the given price per ounce must be multiplied by $(437\frac{1}{2} \div 595) \times (65.9 \div 73) = 0.6637$ to give the equivalent price per ounce Avoirdupois of bread of 73% extraction rate. That the system of weight used in pre-Union Scotland remains obscure is clearly unsatisfactory, but at least within the context of the present study such ignorance is of little consequence. All figures in Graph II refer to the purchasing power of a day's labour in terms of wheat bread of 73% extraction rate and are expressed in ounces Avoirdupois. The figures should not be taken as an estimate of the maximum amount of bread that a day's labour could buy, as cheaper varieties of bread were available in both countries.

10

ALBION'S FATAL TWIGS: JUSTICE AND LAW IN THE EIGHTEENTH CENTURY

S. J. Connolly

Over the last ten years or so, historians of eighteenth-century England have engaged in lively debate over the workings within that society of the criminal law. Douglas Hay, in a well-known essay published in 1975,[1] focused renewed attention on what had long been recognised as one of the most puzzling features of eighteenth-century English justice: a penal code in which the range of crimes carrying the death sentence was extremely wide, and where the number of capital statutes was repeatedly added to, but in which the number of persons actually executed fell far short of what the laws should have provided for. Hay's suggested explanation of this apparent contradiction — that a bloody penal code allowed a small ruling elite to maintain a careful balance between exemplary use of terror and conspicuous display of leniency and mercy, so strengthening the relationships of authority and deference on which social order depended — has since come under powerful attack. Discretion in the application of the harsh penalties provided by the law — presented by Hay as having been confined to judges acting in collusion with a small, closed circle of large property owners — has been shown to have in fact been exercised by a much wider social group, in their capacity both as potential prosecutors and as members of juries. Its exercise, equally, was governed less by considerations of class than by commonly accepted notions of justice.[2] These arguments undoubtedly modify the original conception of the eighteenth-century criminal law as a direct instrument of class domination. In doing so, however, they only emphasise further the complexity of the real operations of the law. In eighteenth-century England, it seems clear, the maintenance of law depended not on simple repression, but on a harsh penal code applied with what Hay has characterised as 'delicacy and circumspection', so as to retain a fairly widespread legitimacy.

The relevance of all this to any discussion of social relationships in eighteenth-century England is obvious enough. But what of England's subordinate neighbours? What did the rule of law mean in Scotland and Ireland during this period and how was it upheld? This essay will begin by discussing the machinery of law enforcement and criminal justice in eighteenth-century Ireland, and then go on to suggest some comparisons with contemporary Scotland.

I

The formal machinery for the enforcement of law in eighteenth-century Ireland was broadly similar to that of contemporary England. Primary responsibility rested with the landed gentry and the members of urban elites, in their capacity as sheriffs, magistrates and justices of the peace, assisted by a thinly-spread network of lesser officers.[3] In the absence of an effective police, the serious business of law enforcement frequently fell to informally mustered forces. Thus in April 1710 Francis Eustace, wanted for the brutal murder of his wife three weeks before, was apprehended as he tried to leave the city of Dublin by a group consisting of a constable, his father-in-law and three other men. In 1744 Viscount Buttevant set off in pursuit of a group of men who had abducted a woman in Cork city 'accompanied by several gentlemen with a great number of his lordship's servants, well mounted and armed'. In County Kilkenny in 1739 local gentlemen formed an association to track down a band of robbers, over thirty strong, who had been terrorising the surrounding region.[4]

In addition to such informally recruited assistance, magistrates in need of physical backing could of course call on the army. Ireland in the eighteenth century supported what was by contemporary standards a large military establishment of 12,000 men, of which around two-thirds was normally stationed in Ireland itself. The size of this force, however, was not dictated by considerations of domestic order. Instead Ireland was used to house (and pay for) a large standing army of the kind prohibited in Great Britain under the Bill of Rights. At times of crisis, whether arising from foreign war or from domestic threats such as the Jacobite risings of 1715 and 1719, an early move was invariably to withdraw substantial numbers of soldiers from Ireland. While in Ireland, troops could be called on to assist the civil authorities in dealing with particularly serious outbreaks of agrarian or urban disorder. At the same time there were clear limitations on the use of the military for routine law enforcement. In the first place the government was not necessarily willing to make soldiers available in cases where their use did not appear strictly necessary.[5] Secondly, it is clear that many Irish gentlemen shared the reservations of their English counterparts concerning the constitutional implications of using the army to maintain domestic order.[6]

Where the severity or otherwise of the penalties dispensed under the criminal law is concerned, the destruction of virtually all the records of eighteenth-century legal administration makes detailed analysis impossible. Studies of movements of agrarian protest, however, make clear that these, in the period up to 1790 at least, were not normally met with large-scale repression. In Connacht in 1712 the first men convicted of involvement in the hougher outbreak were treated with exemplary severity: six were condemned to death, and three of these were actually executed. Once the disturbances had subsided, however, there appear to have been no further trials or executions, and in early 1713 an amnesty was offered to those who had taken part in the disturbances.[7] The Whiteboy outbreaks of the 1760s and 1780s in Leinster and Munster each gave rise to new coercive statutes, further extending the range of capital offences. But the practical response to the disturbances once again suggests a limited and selective use of judicial terror. Twenty-six agrarian offenders were sentenced to death between 1762 and 1765, and 19 between 1786 and 1788, and the actual number executed in each case was almost certainly considerably lower.[8] Outside periods of major agrarian disturbance, the limited evidence available suggests that death sentences and executions were even less common. Newspaper accounts of the assizes at Cork in spring 1729, in County Westmeath in summer 1744 and in County Waterford in summer 1746 noted that only one man had been sentenced to death in each case.[9] At Kilkenny in 1766 the acquittal of five alleged Whiteboys again left only one man, a coiner, capitally convicted.[10] In County Cork, in the forty years 1767–1806, a total of 130 persons were sentenced to death (24 of these in 1798), and 202 to be transported.[11] Once again it is likely that a substantial proportion of these sentences would not in fact have been carried out.

This relatively low number of capital sentences and executions is clearly linked to another feature of the Irish courts in the eighteenth century, the high proportion of criminal trials which ended in acquittal. The single man sentenced to death at Cork in 1729 had been one of around 200 brought to trial at the assizes. The Crown Book at the same city's assizes in 1789–90, apparently the only record of its kind to have survived for the eighteenth century, suggests that only about one-fifth of all those brought before the court on criminal charges were convicted.[12] Similar high levels of acquittals continued even during the troubled years of the later 1790s. At the Lent and Summer assizes of 1797, in all counties of Ireland, only 24 per cent of those brought before the courts were convicted, while at the Lent assizes of 1798 the figure was 32 per cent. In both cases, the proportion of political offenders convicted was higher than the proportion of those accused of other crimes — in 1798 considerably higher — suggesting that in other times the overall conviction rate would have been lower still.[13]

Three main reasons may be suggested for the failure of such a high proportion of prosecutions. To some contemporaries, the explanation lay mainly in corruption and malpractice. The Rev. Samuel Madden, writing in 1738, blamed the difficulty of executing the laws 'against the plainest crimes, and the most confest thieves and villains' on 'the interest of the landlords, the corruption of prosecutors as well as the villainy and perjury of bribed witnesses'.[14] Arthur Young, forty years later, complained similarly of 'men of fortune' who screened offenders and 'made interest' for their acquittal. Proudly informed in County Fermanagh that there had not been a single person hanged there in the previous twenty-two years, Young commented sourly that in that case 'there had been many a jury who deserved it richly'.[15] At the same time Madden also recognised that the proliferation of capital statutes made juries reluctant to convict, even where the evidence required it. In the same way a correspondent in 1725 argued that to make tobacco smuggling a capital offence would be counterproductive. Juries would be unwilling to convict, 'there would not be an informer in the country', and even revenue officers would be less ready to make discoveries where men's lives were at stake.[16] Finally, rates of conviction appear to have been depressed by an insistence on strict legal procedures. The conduct of criminal cases during the eighteenth century has never been examined in detail, and it is doubtful whether the material for such an examination any longer exists. However, R. B. McDowell, writing of the 1790s, has noted the frequency with which counsel for persons accused of political offences were able to exploit legal technicalities relating to such matters as the precise wording of indictments in order to obstruct and in some cases defeat prosecutions.[17]

A survey of the operation of the criminal law in eighteenth-century Ireland, then, suggests that coercion and legal terror had only a subordinate role in the maintenance of order. The resources available to back up the civil authorities by physical force were at all times limited, while the requirements of legal procedure imposed real limits on the actions of central and local government. To say this is not to suggest that the law was invariably just, much less humane. One incident in particular, the execution of the priest Nicholas Sheehy at Clonmel in 1766, was regarded both by contemporaries and by later writers as blatant judicial murder. However L. M. Cullen has outlined the specific local tensions which lay behind this episode, and its very notoriety marks it out as an exceptional case.[18] A markedly different picture is presented by the official response to the hougher movement in Connacht in 1711–12. Here the Dublin administration, while demanding effective action against the houghers, made clear that this would have to be achieved within the limits of the law. The judges of assize were ordered to enquire into allegations that a gentleman arrested on suspicion of complicity in the disturbances had been ill-treated by his captors, and references to persons against whom a case could not be proved, but whom it was nevertheless desirable to keep confined, make clear that there was no question of anyone being convicted on mere suspicion.[19] In the same way it seems clear that even the harshest penal legislation directed against Catholic clergy and laity was applied with full regard to proper legal procedure, and with the same strict attention to the letter of the law that was seen in other types of case. If the law was harsh in many individual instances, furthermore, it was not by contemporary standards particularly bloodthirsty or cruel. To see this we have only to look at the comments of an Irish medical student visiting France in 1781, to whom the spectacle of criminals being publicly broken on the wheel was something to be reported home with horror.[20]

Such an emphasis on the limited nature of legal repression in eighteenth-century Ireland inevitably becomes impossible to sustain once one reaches the last decade of the century. The harsh and often summary measures by which the Irish government and its local supporters attempted to curb unparalleled levels of popular disaffection in the mid and late 1790s have become notorious. Even here, a recent analysis by R. B. McDowell has qualified traditional accounts of the extent to which legal restraints were thrown off.[21] The essential point, however, is that the undoubtedly brutal measures employed in the 1790s — the burning of houses to compel the surrender of arms, the forced enlistment of suspected but unconvicted men into the navy, the torture of prisoners — marked a dramatic break with traditional methods of law enforcement. It was a break, furthermore, from which the old, decentralised, semi-amateur system never recovered. As in the pattern of popular protest, so too in methods of maintaining order, the 1790s emerge as a crucial decade.[22] Government in the nineteenth century was to develop a new awareness of the need to enforce the laws by methods which did not themselves increase popular disaffection. The task of doing so, however, was now to be entrusted to a professional, centrally controlled and militarised police force of a kind seen nowhere else in the British Isles.

II

The political classes of eighteenth-century Ireland took their constitutional doctrine from contemporary England. A central part of that doctrine was a particular conception of the law, as an abstract force operating within society, the source of a justice detached from particular interests and circumstances. It was to such a conception of law, for example, that the Irish Chief Justice of the Common Pleas appealed when he dismissed a claim that the disturbed condition of County Westmeath in 1795–6 justified the imprisonment of suspects without proper informations having been taken: 'Whether the times be warm or cold, this court feels but one climate'.[23] If such principles were in the 1790s being increasingly modified or abandoned, furthermore, prior to that date they had had a real force. For the greater part of the eighteenth century, as we have seen, the aims of effective punishment and deterrence were firmly subordinated to the need to observe generally accepted principles and rules of procedure. In Ireland, as in England, the rhetoric of the Glorious Revolution was not entirely bogus.

In Scotland the case was slightly different. Scotland had its own system of legal principles and procedures, whose careful preservation at the time of the Union was an important part of the reassurance offered to Scottish sensibilities. Like England and Ireland, it was a society of harsh laws selectively and inefficiently enforced, so that the actual role of legal terror in maintaining social order was more limited than might at first appear. Indeed statistics on transportation to Australia in the late eighteenth and early nineteenth centuries show that Scottish courts made less use of this sanction at least than either their English or their Irish counterparts.[24] At the same time the justice dispensed by Scottish courts appears to have been rather different to what was offered in the other two kingdoms. In particular, there appears to have been a stronger presumption against the accused, so that, although the number of persons brought before the criminal courts was small, the great majority of defendants were convicted of some offence. 'To be brought to court,' Lenman and Parker suggest, 'was, in itself, almost an indication of guilt, a clear sign that the community was convinced that a serious offence had been committed.'[25] The position of defendants may have improved in the second half of the eighteenth century, particularly after the abolition of heritable jurisdictions in 1747. But even in the 1790s the requirements of legal process appear to have offered significantly less protection to Scottish radicals than they did to their English or even their Irish counterparts. This contrast in legal traditions between Scotland and Ireland, it may be suggested, reflected their very different political histories. In Ireland a whole new structure of legal and political institutions was created during the seventeenth century, by a settler population taking its ideological and administrative models from contemporary England. In Scotland indigenous institutions were preserved, even fossilised, by the Act of Union, perpetuating into the eighteenth century the legal practices of a society of small, close-knit communities.

A second major area of contrast between the two societies, on the other hand, reflected differences in current political circumstances. Eighteenth-century Ireland is often thought of as a divided and unstable society, in which a Protestant elite clung to power with the aid of harsh repressive measures. In reality, however, straightforward repression appears to have played a much more prominent part in the government of eighteenth-century Scotland than it did, at least prior to the 1790s, in the government of Ireland. Thus eighteenth-century Ireland had no parallel to the massacre of the Macdonalds at Glencoe, or to the campaign of terror which followed the defeat of the Jacobite army in 1746. If the judicious positioning of military barracks in the early and mid-eighteenth century helped to bring order to some particularly unruly areas of Ireland, similarly, there is nothing to equal the systematic attempts to extend military control over the Highlands in the 1720s and 30s.[26] Nor was there any Irish parallel to the legislative assault on Highland custom and social organisation which followed the rebellion of 1745–6. Even outside the Highlands, the government's reaction to the Glasgow Malt Tax riots of 1725, and to the Porteous riot eleven years later, was far more heavy-handed than anything provoked by the various spectacular demonstrations of which eighteenth-century Dublin proved itself capable. If repression and subjugation by naked force have a more prominent place in Irish memories than in Scottish, this has more to do with the subsequent political history of the two countries than with their actual management in the eighteenth century.

Such a comparison suggests that it might be wise to look again at the way in which problems of popular disaffection and the maintenance of law and order were regarded by the government and the Protestant elite in eighteenth-century Ireland. There is no shortage of comment, throughout the century, on the threat which Catholics and their continental allies posed to the lives and liberties of Irish Protestants. From this, it is easy to build up an impression of chronic insecurity. At the same time it is important to remember, first, that anti-Catholicism was a central element of the political rhetoric of the day, in Britain as well as Ireland, and secondly that the loudest (and most quotable) voices were not necessarily the most representative. In this area even more than in others, actions are more revealing than words. The hougher movement of 1711–12, for example, led some local correspondents to write of French agents moving through the affected areas, masterminding the campaign of attacks on livestock. Such reports, however, were ignored by the Dublin administration, which throughout continued to treat the outbreak as a serious but limited problem, to be dealt with by the normal processes of law.[27] At other times too, official reactions to crises were more subtle than has often been supposed. In 1708 and in 1714, for example, precautions such as the closure of Catholic chapels and the rounding up of known Jacobites were combined with a conscious desire to avoid overreaction. 'We have no more to do,' Archbishop King told a correspondent in 1708, 'than to arm ourselves as well as we can for our defence and disarm our enemies, but in such a manner that we may not provoke them to desperation by harsh and unjust usage whilst they are quiet.'[28]

To understand the official attitude to the maintenance of order in eighteenth-century Ireland, and the contrast it presented with the more heavy-handed methods employed in Scotland during the same period, it is important to recognise that the security of the state was not primarily conceived of, as it later came to be, in terms of the presence or absence of popular disaffection. Sir Richard Cox, writing in 1698, argued that the common Irish

> are a people of so tame and cowardly a disposition, that were they not actuated by their gentry and clergy, and they were in never so great a tumult, did the English but appear to them with their cudgels and scourges only, they would undoubtedly betake themselves to their several labours and employments.[29]

Behind the obvious prejudice lay an accurate enough perception of reality. Observers of eighteenth-century Ireland were agreed on the submissiveness which the common people normally displayed towards their social superiors.[30] In some cases a tradition of strong personal authority was reflected in the continuing influence wielded by descendants of former Gaelic proprietors. Near Ballyshannon in 1752, for example, Bishop Pococke met an O'Donnel, supposedly descended from the earl of Tyrconnel, so that 'though he has only leases, yet he is the head of the Roman Catholics in this country, and has a great interest'.[31] With the exception of one semi-farcical episode in 1786, when the eccentric Roderick O'Connor, 'known as the King of Connaught', raised a force of 400 to 500 men to occupy Ballintober Castle,[32] however, these relics of a former social order had no practical political significance. When two English visitors in the early 1740s observed the 'extraordinary respect' paid to the impoverished descendant of a former proprietor as he rode through the fair at Callan, County Kilkenny, the spectacle struck them only as a pleasing memento of a vanished world.[33]

Here, of course, lay the crucial distinction between eighteenth-century Ireland and eighteenth-century Scotland. Both were societies in which traditions of personal authority and submission to social superiors remained strong. In Scotland, however, it was still possible for that submissiveness to be turned into a weapon against the political establishment. In Ireland, once the Williamite confiscations had completed the seventeenth-century transformation of land ownership, and the Catholic clergy had been cowed into political apathy, no such possibility existed. This was why British governments were able to respond to successive crises in the first half of the eighteenth century by withdrawing substantial numbers of troops from Ireland and sending them, among other places, to Scotland. By the end of the century, however, all this had changed. In Scotland the social organisation which had provided the backbone of the rebellions of 1715 and 1745 was in irreversible decline. In Ireland, on the other hand, popular disaffection was no longer something to be ignored, partly because it had found new leaders among radical elements in the Irish middle and upper classes, partly because popular movements were appearing which were no longer dependent on leadership from above. It was at this point that Ireland replaced Scotland both as the major threat to the security and tranquillity of the British state, and as the theatre for methods of law enforcement radically different to those seen elsewhere in the British Isles. In this as in other respects, the late eighteenth century stands out as having marked a dramatic reversal in the relative position of the two countries.

NOTES

1. 'Property, Authority and the Criminal Law', in Hay *et al*, *Albion's Fatal Tree* (London, 1975), pp. 17-63.

2. J. H. Langbein, 'Albion's Fatal Flaws', *Past & Present*, 98 (1983), pp. 96-120; P. King, 'Decision Makers and Decision Making in the English Criminal Law, 1750-1800', *Historical Journal*, XXVII, 1 (1984), pp. 25-58.

3. J. P. Starr, The Enforcing of Law and Order in Eighteenth-Century Ireland (unpublished Ph.D. thesis, Trinity College, Dublin, 1968); R. B. McDowell, *Ireland in the Age of Imperialism and Revolution 1760-1801* (Oxford, 1979), pp. 63-77.

4. *Dublin Gazette*, 25-28 Mar. 1710, 15-18 Apr. 1710; *Faulkner's Dublin Journal*, 14-18 Feb. 1744; *Dublin Gazette*, 13-16 June 1739.

5. S. J. Connolly, 'Law, Order and Popular Protest in Early Eighteenth-Century Ireland: The Case of the Houghers', in P. J. Corish (ed.), *Radicals, Rebels and Establishments* (Belfast, 1985), pp. 51-68.

6. D. H. Smyth, The Volunteer Movement in Ulster: Background and Development, 1745-85 (unpublished Ph.D. thesis, Queen's University, Belfast, 1974), chap. 3.

7. Connolly, 'Law, Order and Popular Protest', pp. 63-4.

8. J. S. Donnelly, 'The Whiteboy Movement 1761-5', *I.H.S.* XXI, 81 (1978), pp. 46-52; 'The Rightboy Movement, 1785-8', *Studia Hibernica*, 17/18 (1977-8), pp. 193-4.

9. *Dublin Weekly Journal*, 10 May 1729; *Faulkner's Dublin Journal*, 7-10 July 1744; *Pue's Occurrences*, 9-12 Aug. 1746.

10. P.R.O.I. Prim MS, 87, William Colles to Barry Colles, 5 Apr. 1766 (transcript).

11. Thomas Newenham, *A View of the Natural, Political and Commercial Circumstances of Ireland* (London, 1809), appendix, pp. 43-7.

12. P.R.O.I. Crown & Peace Records, Co. Cork.

13. McDowell, *Ireland in the Age of Imperialism and Revolution*, pp. 542, 549-50.

14. *Reflections and Resolutions Proper for the Gentlemen of Ireland* (Dublin 1738), p. 151.

15. Arthur Young, *A Tour of Ireland* (2 vols., London, 1892), II, 154.

16. P.R.O.N.I. D2092/1/3/54, Robert Ward to Michael Ward, 3 Oct. 1725.

17. McDowell, *Ireland in the Age of Imperialism and Revolution*, pp. 543-9, 551, 556-7, 573-4, 655.

18. L. M. Cullen, *The Emergence of Modern Ireland, 1600-1900* (London, 1981), pp. 200-201.

19. Connolly, 'Law, Order and Popular Protest', pp. 62-3.

20. P.R.O.N.I. D906/147, Robert Perceval to William Perceval, 1 Aug. 1781.

21. McDowell, *Ireland in the Age of Imperialism and Revolution*, chap. 16.

22. Thomas Bartlett, 'An End to Moral Economy: The Irish Militia Disturbances of 1793', *Past and Present*, 99 (1983), pp. 41-86.

23. McDowell, *Ireland in the Age of Imperialism and Revolution*, p. 551. For the concept of the rule of law as a central feature in the political life of eighteenth-century England, see E. P. Thompson, *Whigs and Hunters: The Origins of the Black Act* (London, 1975), pp. 258-69.

24. Ian Donnachie, 'Scottish Criminals and Transportation to Australia, 1786-1852', *Scot. Ec. & Soc. Hist.* IV (1984), p. 22.

25. Bruce Lenman and Geoffrey Parker, 'Crime and Control in Scotland 1500-1800', *History Today*, XXX (1984), p. 14. See also S. J. Davies, 'The Courts and the Scottish Legal System, 1600-1747: The Case of Stirlingshire', in V.A.C. Gatrell *et al*, *Crime and the Law: The Social History of Crime in Western Europe since 1500* (London, 1980), p. 149.

26. Rosalind Mitchison, 'The Government and the Highlands 1707-45', in N. T. Phillipson and R. Mitchison, eds., *Scotland in the Age of Improvement* (Edinburgh, 1970), pp. 34-6.

27. Connolly, 'Law, Order and Popular Protest', pp. 65-6.

28. T.C.D. MS 750/3/2, p. 198, King to Bishop of Cloyne, 23 Mar. 1708. See also M. A. Hickson, *Selections from Old Kerry Records* (second series, London, 1874), p. 149.

29. *A Discourse Concerning Ireland and the Several Interests Thereof* (London, 1698), p. 20.

30. Madden, *Reflections and Resolutions*, p. 46; Young, *Tour*, II, pp. 53–4.

31. *Pococke's Tour in Ireland in 1752*, G. T. Stokes (ed.) (Dublin, 1891), pp. 71–2.

32. Historical Manuscripts Commission, Report 14, App. 1, *Rutland Mss* (1894), p. 279. For a brief account, see W. R. Wilde, *Irish Popular Superstitions* (Dublin, 1852), pp. 101–2.

33. [W. R. Chetwood], *A Tour through Ireland in Several Entertaining Letters . . . by two English Gentlemen* (Dublin, 1746), pp. 147–8.

11
UNREST AND STABILITY IN RURAL IRELAND AND SCOTLAND, 1760-1840

T. M. Devine

I

The Agricultural Revolution in Scotland produced profound social effects. In the Lowlands enlarged farms were created as the small farmer class was reduced and the sub-tenant or cottager group eliminated. In the Highlands the consequences of 'improvement' were even more dramatic and notorious. The scale of eviction of peasant communities increased in unprecedented fashion as landlords sought to rationalise estates and respond to the rise in prices for pastoral products. Social dislocation produced popular resistance in varying degrees. The most remarkable response came in the Lowlands. There the old order passed away with little dissent. Apart from the Levellers' Revolt in Galloway in the 1720s, two generations before the main phase of change, and one or two minor incidents thereafter, the consolidation of land proceeded peacefully.[1] There was no folk memory of dispossession and historians even assert that the success of the new farming system was partly due to the positive contribution made to the working of the new agriculture by the Lowland farming and labouring classes.[2] The tranquillity of the Lowland countryside is especially striking when compared with the rise of popular protest in urban Scotland, ranging from the Association of Friends of the People and the United Scotsmen in the 1790s to the major trade union and radical disturbances in the years after the Napoleonic Wars.[3] Protest as such was not uncommon in Lowland society between 1780 and 1840; it was specifically agrarian discontent which was notable by its absence.

The record was significantly different in the Highlands. There eviction or the threat of it did produce disturbances. But even in the north the scale of unrest needs to be kept in perspective. While we can no longer regard the Highlands as a 'pacific fringe', overt protest was still the exception rather than the rule.[4] More common were various forms of passive resistance. A significant number of incidents occurred in certain restricted areas such as Easter Ross and the Sutherland estate, but for vast stretches of the Highlands the record is quiet. The authorities were forced to react vigorously in such years as 1814-16 and 1819-21, but even when resistance did take place it rarely lasted for longer than a few weeks, always collapsed when challenged by military power and, with only a few exceptions, had little enduring impact on landlord strategy. Indeed, even those landlords who feared to provoke peasant reaction were often less concerned with the threat to the success of their policies of 'improvement' than with the public odium their actions might incur outside the Highlands. Until the 1880s, then,

Highland discontent, though indicative of the social misery caused by the clearances, was intermittent, ephemeral and limited in its effects.

Peasant unrest in Ireland offers both points of comparison and contrast with stability in the Scottish Lowlands and sporadic disturbance in the Highlands. As in Scotland, there were few indications of serious agrarian discontent until the second half of the eighteenth century. The Houghers of Connacht in 1711–12 were just as exceptional as the Levellers of Galloway in the 1720s.[5] In Ireland, too, there were pronounced regional variations in the scale of disorder. Though few areas were entirely immune, disturbances tended to concentrate in the west midlands, the south and the south-east of the country.[6] It is possible also to detect certain similarities in the aims of both Irish and Scottish peasant movements. The Whiteboys, Oakboys, and Houghers of rural Ireland, like Highland crofters, sought redress for such grievances as inflated rents, eviction and the conversion of arable land to pasture.[7] The concept of the right to a patch of land for the maintenance of family life was shared by Irish countrymen as well as Highland peasants. Both had traditionalist assumptions, were defensive of existing customary rights and had limited ends. They sought not to change the *status quo* but to preserve it, not to attack or abolish landlordism as such but to force individual landlords, whether they were landowners or employing farmers, to conform to a code which confirmed the customary relationships threatened by new pressures of market expansion and estate rationalisation.

Yet Irish unrest also differed from that of Scotland in certain key respects. Scotland was decidedly more tranquil. While it is vital to remember that only certain areas were prone to agrarian rebellion and that most of the country was quiet at any one time, every decade in Ireland between 1760 and 1840 was punctuated by at least one major outbreak of peasant unrest. Some Irish movements survived for years and in parts of such chronically disturbed areas as Tipperary, Leitrim, Kilkenny and Limerick had a continued existence throughout the first half of the nineteenth century.[8] In the main, Highland protests were desperate reactions to the threat of eviction and were by their nature poorly organised and ill-prepared. But several of the Irish movements had an almost military form of organisation, whose participants wore special dress and were bound together by oaths of secrecy and loyalty. The perceptive contemporary observer, G. C. Lewis, saw them as 'protective unions, coolly, steadily, determinedly and unscrupulously working at their objects but sleeping in apparent apathy so long as their regulations are not violated'.[9] The Irish organisations were indeed forces to be reckoned with; they used intimidation, threats, terrorism and murder against those who transgressed the peasant code and, therefore, had a considerable impact on landlord decisions.[10] Economic historians suggest that the movement towards pastoralism in the central counties of Ireland after 1815 would have occurred more rapidly but for the fear of provoking agrarian outrage and, more generally, that the inward flow of investment capital to Ireland could have been checked by the violent reputation of some districts.[11] On the other hand, not least of the peculiar advantages of the Scottish Lowlands in the development of a more efficient system of farming was the existence of a peaceful and tractable labour force.

In essence, then, Irish peasant movements were better organised, had a longer life and were much more effective in pursuing their aims and objectives than those in Scotland. But unrest in rural Ireland was not limited to 'organised' resistance or even to disputes over the use and occupation of land. There was nothing in Scotland to compare with the vicious rivalries *within* the ranks of the rural poor of some districts which often reached the stage of open, armed conflict between factions, gangs and families.[12] Irish peasant discontent, then, was not simply based on the existence of class tensions between landlords, farmers, cottiers and labourers but also in some areas on the thriving jealousies and insecurities of the rural masses. The remainder of this essay will seek to clarify the social and economic context within which this instability developed and offer an explanation why collective protest was more common in Ireland than Scotland.

II

The capacity of Scottish society south of the Highland line to adjust to profound social change without visible internal conflict was in part at least a reflection of the tightness of social control within the affected communities. Social order in the Scottish Lowlands was supported by a series of influences. The landed class was an hereditary elite whose families had held the same estates over many generations. Before c. 1760 the land market was relatively sluggish and the rapid penetration of newcomers only occurred in the later eighteenth century in some areas close to the larger towns.[13] But the old-established governing classes were also enthusiastic innovators and were able to exploit their inherited authority to gain social acceptance for agrarian change.[14] The influence which flowed from their long tenure of hegemony legitimised reform of estate structure and practice. Their social authority was both symbolised and confirmed by the very late survival of feudal institutions in Scotland. The private courts of the lairds were only formally abandoned in the 1740s, but such practices as thirlage and the provision of labour services survived for much longer even in areas in the vanguard of agrarian progress.[15] Furthermore, Scottish landowners and large farmers were broadly unified in a political, ideological, religious and intellectual sense by the late eighteenth century. There were none of the inter-gentry feuds which characterised some European countries and might have paralysed or severely weakened the structures of civil order and authority.[16] Scottish politics had become a matter of patronage and debate rather than passionate struggle, thanks to the effects of the religious settlement of 1690, the Union of 1707, the final defeat of Jacobitism and the closing of ranks in the face of the twin threats of popular radicalism and French aggression in the 1790s.[17]

The social prerogative of Scottish landowners was also confirmed and reinforced by their relationship with the two national institutions of church and education. They had close links with both, partly through their responsibility as heritors and also through their rights as patrons. It would, of course, be too crude to portray parish ministers and schoolmasters as conscious agents of landed hegemony. The series of eighteenth- and early nineteenth-century disputes over patronage suggests a greater degree of ecclesiastical independence than some critics, whose hold to this view, have allowed.[18] But, equally, both the Kirk and the schools were likely to be significant bastions of social order, professing as they did the value of social harmony and hierarchy. In Ireland, for instance, the vexed issue of the payment of tithes not only incited specific episodes of agrarian discontent but, in a more general sense, stimulated the development of deep tensions between the ecclesiastical and civil orders in society as all landholders, no matter how small, had to share in the tithe burden.[19] In Scotland, however, there was no payment of tithes in kind; they could be valued and, when valued, did not afterwards increase and so this obligation tended to fall in relation to rising land values.[20] An important potential source of stress between secular and religious interests was therefore removed. Indeed, the parish accounts in the *Statistical Account* suggest that the majority of local ministers accepted and supported the ideal of material progress. 'Improvement' was viewed as legitimate in moral terms and most ministers seem to have shared the broad intellectual assumptions of the landed classes in the Age of Enlightenment.

Both the Church of Scotland and the system of parish schools were weakest in the Highlands where social disruption came most violently and rapidly. But there a martial society had survived into the eighteenth century and Highland landlords had a peculiar and personal authority far stronger even than their counterparts in the Lowlands.[21] Vertical loyalties persisted in many areas and these made it difficult to articulate effective strategies of opposition to the plans of improving grandees who had only recently shed the role and function of clan chiefs. Indeed, even after 1760, when the pace of economic change accelerated, several Highland landlords perpetuated the old tribal and military role by seeking to encourage the recruitment of their tenantry to family regiments during the American and Napoleonic Wars.[22] This helped temporarily to disguise the speedy and dramatic shift in the nature of social and economic relationships on some estates, although in the long run it intensified bitterness when evictions finally came about. It is also significant that one of the recurring themes of the waulking songs of the Western Isles was praise of the aristocracy and preoccupation with the exploits of the elite.[23] As late as the 1880s the Napier Commission, during the Crofters' War, could still report authoritatively that 'there is still on the side of the poor much reverence for the owner of the soil'.[24] Such evidence suggests the inability of the Highland peasantry to sever their links with the tribal past; to recognise themselves fully as a social group with powerful interests separate and distinct from those of their landlords. At the same time it is eloquent testimony to the sheer desperation and anxiety of some communities during the Highland clearances that considerable resistance, no matter how fragile and short-lived, did occur.

In Ireland agrarian discontent was more widespread and enduring at least partly because the structures of social control were less effective than in Scotland. It is easy perhaps to discount the popular myth of an historic struggle between Catholic peasant on the one hand and an alien class of heartless and mostly absentee landlords on the other. First, Irish agrarian discontent was not a major recurrent feature of the seventeenth and early eighteenth centuries but only began to reach epidemic proportions *in some areas* after c. 1780.[25] Second, 'none of the perpetrators of outrage are recorded as having appealed to the despoiled rights of a great Gaelic past'.[26] Third, tensions were often as acute between big farmers and labourers of the same denomination as between Protestant landlords and the Catholic rural poor.[27] Fourth, there is no evidence that nationalist or religious affiliation was a significant factor in the selection of victims by the agrarian secret societies.[28]

On the other hand, to deny any link between Irish political and religious history and Irish agrarian disturbances would clearly be naive. It has been suggested that religious loyalty among Catholics, when the Irish state apparatus was dominated by Protestants, may have provided a major source of integration, 'a bond of union', as G. C. Lewis had it, which might have facilitated mobilisation of peasant communities.[29] In Scotland, especially in the Lowlands, Protestantism lent a homogeneity to rural society, an ideology shared by both governors and the governed. In Ireland, on the other hand, the civil administration was carried on by Protestants and the penal system presumed that all Irish Catholics were potentially disaffected to the state. Furthermore, the spirit of defiance of the law manifested in the emergence of such political and sectarian movements as the United Irishmen and the rebellion of 1798 may not actually have caused specifically agrarian disturbances but did contribute to a massive and general weakening of social and political authority within which disorder could flourish. Indeed, recent research suggests that the 1790s were a key decade in the history of governmental authority in Ireland. It is argued that harmony rather than conflict characterised social relations before the 1790s but that this fragile consensus between governors and governed ended abruptly in that decade.[30] The Catholic Relief Acts of 1792 and 1793 fatally destabilised Irish society, leaving Protestants feeling bitter and betrayed while Catholics were initially elated but then disillusioned. These deep tensions came to the surface when the authorities over-reacted to the Militia Riots of 1793. There was always this danger in Ireland as all disturbances, whatever their origin, could be perceived by government as having the final potential for full-blooded Catholic insurrection. Indeed, it could be speculated in a more general sense that the 1790s constituted a sharp break in the character of Irish protest: the appalling experiences of that decade might have had a permanently brutalising effect on Irish society, accustoming all social groups to new levels of violence.[31] The point, nevertheless, needs to be kept in perspective, as areas prone to serious unrest in 1798 were not necessarily those which saw the rise of peasant agrarian movements in the early nineteenth century.

Scotland too had its anti-Militia riots in 1797 but they were rapidly checked by a combination of judicious military action and the speedy conviction of accused persons.[32] These riots occurred after almost a decade of radical reforming activity, but the war with France and the excesses of the French revolutionaries effectively suppressed the cause of political opposition for a generation. The Scottish governing classes emerged from the 1790s with their powers and influence unimpaired and the confidence to maintain their dominant position against renewed political challenge after 1815. There was much greater scope for alienation in Ireland because there the unity of the elites was fissured by religious and political tensions, 'dormant in normal times, but susceptible to manipulation in times of crisis'.[33] As a result, the Irish state, with its draconian legal apparatus, large army and growing police force, had more power to coerce but much less ability to control than its Scottish counterpart.[34]

III

The fundamental causes of unrest and stability lay not in the modes of control available to local and national authorities but in the deep contrasts in the nature of social and economic development in Scotland and Ireland. Irish historians stress that while major outbreaks of discontent had a number of specific, short-term causes, such as protest over tithes, high rents, evictions and encroachment of pastoral farming on arable land, they also reflect the influence of deeper strains and pressures within Irish society. A number of factors can be identified in the literature.[35] First, acute demographic pressure increased as Irish population expanded from less than 2.5 million in 1753 to 6.8 million in 1821. This rate of growth was not only exceptional by European and especially Scottish standards but was paralleled by other developments which combined to ensure the appearance of a vast surplus of labour in the Irish countryside after the Napoleonic Wars. Irish town and industrial growth decelerated over the period 1815 to 1840 after an earlier phase of precocious expansion. In consequence, the great majority of the new generation had to depend on land and land-related employment for survival. There is considerable agreement in the literature that widespread land hunger was a root cause of peasant unrest.[36] Moreover, emigration, a potential safety-valve, was mainly restricted before the Famine to certain areas, such as Ulster and areas adjacent, and to particular groups, such as better-off peasants and redundant workers in declining industries.[37] Second, the Irish rural economy after c.1760 became subject to an intense level of commercialisation with the enormous growth of English demand for grains, beef and pastoral products. Farmers and landlords became more exacting; the easier-going relationships of earlier days were replaced by more vigorous methods reflected in rent increases and encroachments of dairy and beef cattle on commonage. The resulting social pressures contributed to the first main wave of agrarian unrest associated with Whiteboys, Oakboys, Rightboys and Houghers of the last quarter of the eighteenth century.[38] Third, after 1815 there was an incentive to shift from tillage to pasture in response to price movements in Ireland's major external markets. Again, this provoked bitter resistance in parts of the central and south-east regions from cottiers and labourers who saw their source of subsistence threatened.[39] Fourth, the social structure of several areas outside the eastern zone was decidedly fluid.[40] For small farmers and cottiers both upward and downward mobility was possible and this tended to deepen anxieties in a society which lacked a Poor Law until 1837 and where insecurities were aggravated by the twin evils of unemployment and seasonal underemployment after the Napoleonic Wars.

This short précis of some of the underlying causes of peasant discontent suggests both parallels and contrasts with patterns in Scotland. In the Highlands the social and economic pressures were similar and, if anything, the scale of eviction was significantly greater than anything experienced in Ireland. Ironically, however, resistance was subdued, at least when compared to the chronic discontent of parts of the Irish countryside. Partly this may be explained by the social influences already described earlier in this essay. One detects, for instance, a longer tradition of protest on the fringes of the Highlands, in Easter Ross and some of the eastern parishes of Sutherland where clanship might have been weaker than in the central Highlands and the western isles.[41] Again, clearances affected different communities in widely contrasting ways and so provoked different responses. In some cases tenants were evicted without compunction or alternative accommodation; in others efforts were made to establish evicted communities on the coast and to encourage employment in fishing, kelping or textile manufacture. It is possible also that migration was either easier or more attractive for the Highlander than for many small farmers and cottiers in Ireland.[42] There was much 'group' emigration to the United States and Canada from all parts of the region, assisted no doubt by the traditional links of Highland communities with the transatlantic military settlements and the tacksmen-led parties of the later eighteenth century.[43] In Skye in the early nineteenth century, for instance, crofters on some estates used the threat of emigration to compel landlords to rescind or alter plans for improvement.[44] Throughout the period, too, there was a heavy haemorrhage of population from the southern and eastern Highlands to the industrialising and urbanising centres of the central Lowlands.[45]

But one can also argue that the partial quiescence of Highland society, even in the wake of profound social dislocation, was analogous to the social experience of the extreme west of Ireland. It, the poorest region in Ireland, was also one of the quietest.[46] Eric Wolf's well-known observation — that the poorest communities rarely protest because peasants require a certain degree of tactical power or leverage to give them sufficient independence to engage in collective action — may be as apposite to certain parts of the Highlands as to the poverty-stricken west of Ireland.[47] Furthermore, both in the north of Scotland and in the west of Ireland, it was still possible for the peasant family to maintain a foothold on the land, practise sub-division among kinfolk and employ young adults in temporary migration because much of the land itself was so poor that landlords were not always concerned to control access to it in rigorous fashion. Even clearances in the Highlands did not break the hold of the crofting class on the land; often eviction simply meant movement to the coast or resettlement on even poorer plots where families could still eke out a living before the 1840s by a combination of potato cultivation and seasonal migration.[48] Significantly peasant unrest in Ireland was most intense and violent in those midland and south-eastern counties where the population was not quite as deprived as in the far west, and where the deeper penetration of commercial pressures and the higher value of land made farmers and landowners more determined to resist sub-division of peasant holdings.[49] Here conflicts of interest between social groups existed in acute form.

IV

In the Scottish Lowlands consolidation of tenancies and the elimination of sub-tenancies failed to produce widespread resistance because the mode and context of economic change were conducive to peaceful adjustment. The process of tenant reduction was evolutionary and was already occurring on a considerable scale in the seventeenth and early eighteenth centuries in the Borders and eastern counties.[50] Recent work suggests that the ranks of full tenants in some areas were thinned as part of the normal process for reletting of farms.[51] There seems to have been little of the systematic eviction of entire communities so common in the Highlands. Sub-tenancy was crushed more dramatically but loss of land was not as serious a threat to survival as in some parts of Ireland. Demand for all forms of agricultural labour was buoyant in Lowland Scotland between 1770 and 1815 when sub-tenancy was destroyed, because of the expansion of labour-intensive rotation systems and the elaboration of the infrastructure of the new rural economy.[52] Average agricultural money wages in the central Lowlands more than doubled between the 1750s and the 1790s as farmers competed with industrial and urban employers for assured supplies of labour.[53]

It is also vital to keep the disappearance of sub-tenancy in perspective. It was not necessarily a wholly radical upheaval for the rural population. There were important continuities between the old and new worlds, recognition of which can help to explain why no folk tradition of dispossession gathered round the 'Lowland clearances'. There were indeed differences between the sub-tenant system in which land was given for labour, and the new age where landless employees were engaged in return for payments in money and kind. Sub-tenants and cottagers seemed to possess a greater degree of 'independence' and security because of their access to land, whereas the 'landless' servant was more dependent on the employer class and hence more vulnerable to unemployment. But sub-tenants held the merest fragments of land and had little option but to work on adjacent larger farms to gain a full subsistence. Grinding poverty before 1750 was the lot of many sub-tenant families and there is considerable contemporary comment about the miserable conditions in which they often lived because of the chronic seasonal underemployment which characterised Lowland agriculture before the adoption of the new rotations.[54]

On the other hand, the married farm servants of the new order were hired by the year, were paid entirely in kind and allowed ground for planting potatoes and the keep of a cow. Single servants did not hold land in the manner of sub-tenants but were paid in cash, employed on six-monthly contracts and received food and accommodation as an integral part of the total wage reward. Employment, though more difficult to come by after 1815, was widely available for most grades of farm labour during the Napoleonic Wars and real wages rose during the phase of greatest disruption.[55] There was an obvious contrast with the experience of the Irish rural population. As one historian of Ireland has put it: 'In a period of rising prices, the value of payments in kind such as Scottish labourers received tended to rise, whereas the Irish labourer was caught in the scissors-like effect of nominal money wages which were depressed by competition for employment and rising rents for land as inflated produce prices pushed upwards farmers' valuations of land let to labourers'.[56]

By the early nineteenth century, then, a number of significant differences had emerged between Lowland Scotland and those districts in central and southern Ireland most prone to agrarian disturbance. First, though both countries had experienced urban and industrial expansion after c.1760, town development and manufacturing growth were already more pronounced throughout the Lowlands than in any area of Ireland, with the possible exception of Ulster. Both societies were still mainly ruralised but the alternatives to agricultural employment were already more fully developed in Scotland.[57] Second, the Lowlands had become a highly stratified society with landlords, farmers and labourers clearly demarcated and little possibility of movement between these social groups except where a smallholding structure survived, as in the north-east, or in areas such as the western dairying counties where family farms of limited size predominated.[58] There was therefore less risk of the proliferation of the social anxieties which characterised the more fluid social system common in whole areas of rural Ireland.[59] Third, the majority of the agricultural population in the Lowlands had become landless employees by 1815. This break with the land facilitated the very heavy rates of local migration which characterised nineteenth-century Scotland and served to reduce demographic pressure in country areas.[60] Much of Ireland, however, was still a peasant society where access to land remained vital. As numbers rose, many districts began to suffer the linked evils of chronic subdivision of land and relative population immobility which produced the intense social strains within which rural disorder could thrive.

Furthermore, the transition from a sub-tenancy structure to one where landless employees were engaged in return for payment was sustained in Scotland by the maintenance of the farm servant system. This functioned to preserve social order at a number of levels.[61] The yearly and six-monthly contracts gave security of employment over extended periods. Payment in kind insulated farm servants from the market price for food and married ploughmen gained in periods of high prices because they were accustomed to selling a proportion of their 'in kind' earnings back to farmers, to day labourers wholly paid in cash, or in local markets.[62] The young male and female servants were boarded in the steading and were constantly under the eye of the master, a custom which helped to maintain the hierarchical relationship of the old days. But the farm servant system also allowed for a delicate balance of relationships between farmers and workers rather than the complete subservience of one group to the other. The hiring fair or feeing markets were an 'institutional alternative to strikes . . . wages had to be re-negotiated each year'.[63] When the labour market was tight, as it was in most years during the Napoleonic Wars, farmers had to maintain 'a good name' in order to ensure a supply of efficient servants who could (and often did) move at the end of the term if wages or conditions were not to their taste.[64] In Ireland, however, living-in servants were much less common and cottagers of considerably greater significance.[65] The latter often paid by their labour for the land they occupied, a system prone to gross exploitation when the numbers eager for land rose swiftly from the second half of the eighteenth century.[66] Once again there existed potential for acute conflict between masters and men.

These contrasts became even sharper after the Napoleonic Wars. Rural Scotland like rural Ireland was affected by the downward trend in grain prices during the years of economic deflation. There was unemployment among farm workers in 1817–18, 1821 and 1827 but it is important to stress that there is no evidence of the emergence of a vast labour surplus of the type which was the main underlying cause of violent protest in Ireland.[67] Rural unemployment in Lowland Scotland was cyclical rather than structural and had begun to diminish by the early 1830s.[68] Social stability was maintained even in the decades after 1815 because a rough balance was achieved in most years between the number of workers on the land and the range of employments open to them. This equilibrium in turn depended on a variety of factors. Scottish population growth accelerated from a rate of 0.6 per cent per annum in the later eighteenth century to 1.2 per cent between 1801 and 1811 and rose again to 1.6 per cent from 1811 to 1821. But this increased rate of expansion was still significantly lower than that of Ireland. Scottish population grew from 1,265,000 in the 1750s to just over 2 million in 1821; Ireland's from 2.5 million in the 1750s to 6.8 million in 1821. While Irish town and industrial development stagnated between 1815 and 1840, the Scottish industrial economy, despite cyclical fluctuations and slow expansion between 1815 and 1830, grew apace thereafter. By the early 1830s Scotland was entering the second phase of industrialisation as investment quickened in coal, iron and engineering production. Scotland, therefore, had the burgeoning alternative employment opportunities outside agriculture which Ireland lacked. By the 1840s no Lowland Scottish county had a majority of householders engaged in farming.[69] To this key advantage Scotland could add a highly mobile work force. Migration increased significantly over late eighteenth-century levels and was facilitated not simply because of rural proximity to urban employment but because of pressures making for movement within the fabric of the agricultural communities.[70]

Finally, the adaptation of the agrarian economy after 1815 did not threaten to reduce employment opportunities to the same extent as did the tendency towards pastoralism in Ireland. Scottish agriculture was less export-orientated than Ireland's and so was less exposed to the violent oscillations in demand in external markets. To this advantage was added the fact that the Scottish system of mixed farming allowed for adjustment to the new price structure. There was a more intensive cultivation of those crops, such as potatoes and barley, least affected by price falls.[71] The north-east Lowlands became a cattle-fattening rather than simply cattle-rearing area and the south-east, where grain farming had always been central, moved towards a more closely integrated regime of arable production and stock-fattening.[72] Flexibility of response rather than radical alteration was the favoured policy and there was therefore little significant shedding of labour in most years.[73]

Urban Scotland, like several rural districts in Ireland, experienced considerable unrest after the Napoleonic Wars. But the Lowland countryside was quiet. A social and economic structure had evolved which promoted stability rather than conflict and ensured the further development of advanced and internationally renowned systems of husbandry. In Ireland, on the other hand, the social pressures already emerging in the later eighteenth century became even more acute after 1815 and provoked the successive agrarian rebellions which in some districts at least aggravated the nation's economic weaknesses.

NOTES

1. T. M. Devine, 'Social Stability in the Eastern Lowlands of Scotland during the Agricultural Revolution', in T. M. Devine, ed., *Lairds and Improvement in the Scotland of the Enlightenment* (Dundee, 1979), pp. 59–70. I wish to acknowledge with thanks the assistance of Dr. Sean Connolly, University of Ulster, who read this paper in draft form and provided me with several useful comments. I also benefited from discussions with L. M. Cullen and David Dickson. The preparation of the material was aided by a generous grant from the Carnegie Trust for the Universities of Scotland.

2. Rosalind Mitchison, 'The Highland Clearances', *Sc. Ec. & Soc. Hist.*, I (1981), 4–20.

3. K. J. Logue, *Popular Disturbances in Scotland, 1780–1815* (Edinburgh, 1979); M. I. Thomis and P. Holt, *Threats of Revolution in Britain, 1789–1848* (London, 1977), pp. 5–28, 62–84.

4. E. Richards, 'Patterns of Highland Discontent, 1790–1860', in J. Stevenson and R. Quinault, eds., *Popular Protest and Public Order* (London, 1974), pp. 75–114; *idem, A History of the Highland Clearances*, I (London, 1982), pp. 249–283; R. Walker, The Insurrection of 1792 in Easter Ross and the Adjacent Parishes of Sutherland (unpublished B.A. dissertation, Department of History, University of Strathclyde, 1983); J. Hunter, *The Making of the Crofting Community* (Edinburgh, 1976), pp. 89–106.

5. S. Connolly, 'The Houghers: Agrarian Protest in Early Eighteenth-Century Connacht', Paper read at the Irish Conference of Historians, 1983. I am grateful to Dr. Connolly for providing me with a copy of his paper.

6. J. Lee, 'Patterns of Rural Unrest in Nineteenth-Century Ireland: a Preliminary Survey', in L. M. Cullen and F. Furet, eds., *Ireland and France, 17th to 20th Centuries* (Paris, 1980), pp. 221–237; S. Clark and J. S. Donnelly Jr., eds., *Irish Peasants, Violence and Political Unrest, 1780–1914* (Manchester, 1983), p. 25; J. Hurst, 'Disturbed Tipperary, 1831–60', *Eire Ireland*, IX, 3 (1974).

7. Connolly, 'The Houghers'; Lee, 'Patterns of Rural Unrest', pp. 228–9; K. B. Nowlan, 'Agrarian Unrest in Ireland, 1800–45', *University Review*, II, 6 (1959); M. R. Beames, 'Peasant Movements: Ireland, 1785–95', *Journal of Peasant Studies*, II, 4 (1975), pp. 502–6; *idem, Peasants and Power: The Whiteboy Movements and Their Control in Pre-Famine Ireland* (London, 1983); G. E. Christianson, 'Secret Societies and Agrarian Violence in Ireland, 1790–1840', *Agricultural History*, XLVI, 4 (1972); J. S. Donnelly Jr., 'The Whiteboy Movement, 1761–5', *I.H.S.*, XXI, 81 (1978), pp. 20–54; *idem*, 'The Rightboy Movement, 1785–8', *Studia Hibernica*, 17 and 18 (1977–8), pp. 120–202; 'Hearts of Oak, Hearts of Steel', *Studia Hibernica*, xxi (1981), pp. 7–73; 'Irish Agrarian Rebellion: the Whiteboys of 1769–76', *Proceedings of the Royal Irish Academy*, LXXXIII, C, 12, pp. 293–331; T. D. Williams, ed., *Secret Societies in Ireland* (Dublin, 1973), pp. 13–35; J. W. O'Neill, 'A Look at Captain Rock: Agrarian Rebellion in Ireland, 1815–45', *Eire Ireland*, XVII, 3 (1982).

8. Clark and Donnelly, eds., *Irish Peasants, Violence and Political Unrest*, pp. 25–35.

9. G. C. Lewis, *On Local Disturbances in Ireland and on the Irish Church Question* (London, 1836), p. 124.

10. *Ibid., passim* and works listed in n. 7 above.

11. L. M. Cullen, *An Economic History of Ireland since 1660* (London, 1972), p. 114; J. Mokyr, *Why Ireland Starved: A Quantitative and Analytical History of the Irish Economy* (London, 1983).

12. Lewis, *Local Disturbances*, pp. 280–294; D. Fitzpatrick, 'Class, Family and Rural Unrest in Nineteenth-Century Ireland', in P. J. Drudy, ed., *Ireland: Land, Politics and People* (Cambridge, 1982), pp. 37–76.

13. L. Timperley, 'The Pattern of Landholding in Eighteenth-Century Scotland', in M. L. Parry and T. R. Slater, eds., *The Making of the Scottish Countryside* (London, 1980), pp. 137–176.

14. T. M. Devine, 'The Union of 1707 and Scottish Development', *Sc. Ec. & Soc. Hist.*, 5 (1985), pp. 23–40.

15. I. Whyte, *Agriculture and Society in Seventeenth-Century Scotland* (Edinburgh, 1979), pp. 35–6, 45–6; Timperley, 'Pattern of Landholding', p. 138; E. Gauldie, *The Scottish Country Miller, 1700–1900* (Edinburgh, 1981), pp. 43–63; L. M. Cullen, 'Incomes, Social Classes and Economic Growth in Ireland and Scotland, 1600–1900', in Devine & Dickson, p. 257.

16. A. Murdoch, *The People Above: Politics and Administration in Mid-Eighteenth-Century Scotland* (Edinburgh, 1980), pp. 1–22.

17. W. Ferguson, *Scotland: 1689 to the Present* (Edinburgh, 1968).

18. See, for example, T. Dickson, ed., *Scottish Capitalism* (London, 1980), p. 117.

19. Donnelly, 'Rightboy Movement', pp. 120–202; P. O'Donoghue, 'Causes of the Opposition to Tithes, 1830–38', *Studia Hibernica*, 5 (1965), pp. 7–28; *idem*, 'Opposition to Payment of Tithes in 1830–1', *Studia Hibernica*, 6 (1966), pp. 69–98; M. J. Bric, 'Priests, Parsons and Politics: The Rightboy Protest in County Cork, 1785–88', *Past and Present*, 100 (1983), pp. 100–122.

20. A. A. Cormack, *Tithes and Agriculture: A Historical Survey* (Oxford, 1930).

21. E. Burt, *Letters from a Gentleman in the North of Scotland* (London, 1754), pp. 261–2.

22. Richards, *Highland Clearances*, pp. 147–154; J. Prebble, *Mutiny* (London, 1975); B. Lenman, *The Jacobite Clans of the Great Glen* (London, 1984), pp. 177–220.

23. T. J. Byres, 'Scottish Peasants and their Song', *Journal of Peasant Studies*, 3 (2) (1976), p. 240.

24. *Report of the Commissioners of Inquiry into the Condition of the Crofters and Cotters in the Highlands and Islands of Scotland* (Napier Commission), (P.P. 1884, XXXII, 36); see also S. Maclean, 'The Poetry of the Clearances', *Trans. of the Gaelic Society of Inverness*, XXXVIII (1939), p. 319.

25. M. Wall, 'The Whiteboys', in Williams, ed., *Secret Societies*, pp. 13–25; Connolly, 'The Houghers'.

26. Lee, 'Patterns of Unrest', p. 228.

27. J. Lee, 'The Ribbonmen', in Williams, ed., *Secret Societies*, pp. 26–35; Cullen, *Economic History*, p. 114; G. O Tuathaigh, *Ireland before the Famine, 1798–1848* (Dublin, 1972), p. 138.

28. Lewis, *Local Disturbances*, pp. 124–139; M. R. Beames, 'Rural Conflict in Pre-Famine Ireland: Peasant Assassinations in Tipperary, 1837-47', *Past and Present*, 81 (1978), pp. 75-91; Hurst, 'Disturbed Tipperary'.

29. Lewis, *Local Disturbances*, p. 155.

30. T. Bartlett, 'An End to Moral Economy: the Irish Militia Disturbances of 1793', *Past and Present*, 99 (1983), pp. 41–64.

31. I am most grateful to Dr. Sean Connolly for suggesting this point to me.

32. Logue, *Popular Disturbances in Scotland*, pp. 75–115.

33. M. Elliott, 'The Origins and Transformation of Early Irish Republicanism', *International Review of Social History*, XXIII (1978), p. 406; *idem, Partners in Revolution: the United Irishmen and France* (New Haven, 1982); J. S. Donnelly, Jr., 'Pastorini and Captain Rock', in Clark and Donnelly, eds., *Irish Peasants, Violence and Unrest*, pp. 102–141.

34. Galen Broeker, *Rural Disorder and Police Reform in Ireland, 1812–1836* (London, 1970), p. 235.

35. These are conveniently summarised in Clark and Donnelly, eds., *Irish Peasants, Violence and Unrest*, pp. 26–35.

36. Mokyr, *Why Ireland Starved*, p. 128; Fitzpatrick, 'Class, Family and Rural Unrest', pp. 43–4.

37. S. H. Cousens, 'The Regional Variation in Emigration from Ireland between 1821 and 1841', *Institute of British Geographers, Transactions and Papers*, 37 (1965), pp. 15–30; C. O Grada, 'Across the Briny Ocean: Some Thoughts on Irish Emigration to America, 1800–1850', in Devine & Dickson, pp. 118–130.

38. Donnelly, 'The Whiteboy Movement', pp. 65–104; *idem*, 'Hearts of Oak', pp. 7–73; W. A. Maguire, 'Lord Donegall and the Hearts of Steel', *Irish Historical Studies*, XXI (1979), pp. 374–75.

39. Mokyr, *Why Ireland Starved*, pp. 130–1.

40. Cullen, 'Incomes, Social Classes and Economic Growth', p. 258; Beames, 'Rural Conflict', p. 58.

41. A. Charlesworth, ed., *An Atlas of Rural Protest in Britain, 1548–1900* (London, 1983), p. 25.

42. T. M. Devine, 'Highland Migration to Lowland Scotland, 1760–1860', *S.H.R.*, LXII (1983), pp. 137–149.

43. J. M. Bumsted, *The People's Clearance, 1770–1815: Highland Emigration to British North America* (Edinburgh, 1982), pp. 55–107; I. Levitt and C. Smout, *The State of the Scottish Working Class in 1843* (Edinburgh, 1979), pp. 236–258.

44. R. A. Berry, The Role of Hebridean Landlords in early Nineteenth-Century Emigration (unpublished B.A. dissertation, Department of History, University of Strathclyde, 1979).

45. Devine, 'Highland Migration', pp. 137–149.

46. Lee, 'Ribbonmen', pp. 28–29; Lewis, *Local Disturbances*, p. 90.

47. E. Wolf, *Peasant Wars of the Twentieth Century* (New York, 1969), pp. 290–293.

48. Devine, 'Highland Migration', p. 142; *idem*, 'Temporary Migration and the Scottish Highlands in the Nineteenth Century', *Ec.H.R.*, XXXII (1979), pp. 344–59.

49. Cullen, *Economic History*, p. 113; O Tuathaigh, *Ireland before the Famine*, p. 138; Lee; 'Patterns of Unrest', p. 225.

50. Whyte, *Agriculture and Society*, pp. 137–172; R. A. Dodgshon, *Land and Society in Early Scotland* (Oxford, 1981), pp. 205–76.

51. R. A. Dodgshon, 'The Removal of Runrig in Roxburghshire and Berwickshire, 1680–1766', *Scottish Studies*, XVI (1972), pp. 121–7.

52. Devine, 'Social Stability', pp. 60–2.

53. V. Morgan, 'Agricultural Wage Rates in late Eighteenth-Century Scotland', *Ec.H.R.*, XXIV (1971), pp. 181–201.

54. P. Graham, *Agricultural Survey of Clackmannanshire* (Edinburgh, 1814), p. 332; *O.S.A.*, VIII, p. 610; I. Carter, *Farm Life in Northeast Scotland, 1840–1914* (Edinburgh, 1979), pp. 16–17.

55. M. E. Goldie, The Standard of Living of Scottish Farm Labourers in Selected Areas at the time of the first Two Statistical Accounts, 1790–1845 (unpublished M.Phil. thesis, University of Edinburgh, 1970).

56. Cullen, 'Incomes, Social Classes and Economic Growth', p. 257.

57. L. M. Cullen and T. C. Smout, 'Economic Growth in Scotland and Ireland', in Cullen & Smout, p. 5.

58. T. M. Devine, ed., *Farm Servants and Labour in Lowland Scotland, 1770–1914* (Edinburgh, 1984), pp. 107–8.

59. T. M. Devine and D. Dickson, 'In Pursuit of Comparative Aspects of Irish and Scottish Development', in Devine & Dickson, p. 263; Fitzpatrick, 'Class, Family and Rural Unrest', pp. 54–68.

60. M. Gray, 'Migration in the Rural Lowlands of Scotland, 1750–1850', in Devine & Dickson, pp. 104–117.

61. T. M. Devine, 'Scottish Farm Service in the Agricultural Revolution', in Devine, ed., *Farm Servants and Labour*, pp. 1–8.

62. R. Somerville, *General View of the Agriculture of East Lothian* (London, 1805), p. 210.

63. J. P. D. Dunbabin, *Rural Discontent in Nineteenth-Century Britain* (London, 1974), p. 132.

64. Carter, *Farm Life in Northeast Scotland*, pp. 113–118; *idem*, 'The Peasantry of Northeast Scotland', *Journal of Peasant Studies*, 3 (1976), pp. 178–9.

65. O Tuathaigh, *Ireland before the Famine*, p. 133.

66. Lewis, *Local Disturbances*, pp. 311–13; M. Beames, 'Cottiers and Conacre in Pre-Famine Ireland', *Journal of Peasant Studies*, 2 (1975), pp. 352–3; Lee, 'Patterns of Rural Unrest', pp. 228–9; J. S. Donnelly, *The Land and People of Nineteenth-Century Cork* (London, 1975), pp. 16–19. Of course, once again, the force of these pressures varied according to the general economic and social context of particular districts. 254 outrages were committed in Tipperary in 1844 compared to only 32 in the much more populous county of Cork. Donnelly argues that the central difference between the two areas may have been the much greater difficulty faced by labourers and cottiers in obtaining adequate potato ground and conacre at reasonable rents in the grazing county of Tipperary. See Donnelly, *Land and People*, p. 54.

67. *Farmer's Magazine*, 'Quarterly Intelligence Reports', 1811–25; *Farmer's Register and Monthly Magazine*, 1827–8; *Report from Select Committee on the Present State of Agriculture*, (P.P. 1833, V), pp. 30, 56, 132; G. Houston, 'Farm Wages in Central Scotland from 1814 to 1870', *Journal of the Royal Statistical Society*', Ser.A (1955), pp. 118, 224–7; T. M. Devine, 'Social Stability and Agrarian Change in the Eastern Lowlands of Scotland, 1810–1840', *Social History*, 3 (1978), pp. 338–346.

68. I. Levitt and C. Smout, 'Farm Workers' Incomes in 1843', in Devine, ed., *Farm Servants and Labour*, pp. 167–8.

69. Devine & Dickson, 'In Pursuit of Comparative Aspects of Irish and Scottish Development', p. 269.

70. Gray, 'Migration in the Rural Lowlands', pp. 108–110; Devine, 'Farm Service in the Agricultural Revolution', p. 6.

71. *N.S.A.* (Edinburgh, 1845), IV, pp. 205, 304, 956; J. Dickson, 'The Agriculture of Perthshire', *Trans. of the Highland and Agricultural Society*, II (1868–9), pp. 167–8; *First Report from Select Committee on Agricultural Distress* (P.P. 1836, VIII), QQ.11170, 10352, 10651–60, 11840.

72. *N.S.A.*, XI, pp. 140, 202, 684; G. Channon, 'The Aberdeenshire Beef Trade and London: A Study in Steamship and Railway Competition, 1850–1869', *Transport History*, 2 (1969), pp. 1–23.

73. *Report from Select Committee on Agricultural Distress*, 1836, Q.13640; *Farmer's Magazine*, XVIII (1817), p. 101; IXX (1818), p. 106; *Farmer's Register and Monthly Magazine*, II (1828), pp. 229, 231; Houston, 'Farm Wages', pp. 324–7; T. M. Devine, 'The Demand for Agricultural Labour in East Lothian after the Napoleonic Wars', *Trans. East Lothian Antiquarian and Field Naturalist Society*, 16 (1979), pp. 49–61.

12

WHO WERE THE POOR IN SCOTLAND, 1690–1830?

Rosalind Mitchison

In normal times 'the poor' formed two groups: those in no way contributing to the local economy and unlikely to do so for some time, and those marginal to it, whose contribution, often interrupted, was not commensurate with their needs. The first group contained those with major handicaps: the cumulative infirmities of old age, or some serious defect such as blindness or insanity. It also included orphans, foundlings and vagrants, though some vagrants might be travelling in the hope of finding work. In the latter group came people whose personal or family handicaps, ill-health, or the need to care for young children, prevented them from being fully self-supporting. In Scotland this group could include considerable numbers of disabled: I have found a man with only one arm described as 'able'.[1]

Besides these main groups there were two other types of poor who might appear in times of stress, the unemployed and those peasants or craftsmen who found themselves at risk of starvation. The unemployed were not usually specifically labelled as such. A person lacking work would either claim from his own parish as totally destitute or take to the road and become a vagrant until he fetched up where there was work. In times of a crisis in food supply these categories would become blended, and together amount to a large proportion of the local population. Their interaction is revealed in a discipline case in Crichton parish in the famine year of 1699: John Spevine was arraigned before the kirk session for immoral or indecent behaviour, because he was sharing a single bed with his wife and their two grown-up children, a son and a daughter. Spevine declared that this unseemly arrangement 'did not proceed from any wilfulness in him but only from his poverty': 'if any would take any of the bairns to service they should have them for their meat in this strait time'. He could not place his children in service, even when prepared to forego a fee. Later in that year the heritors (the main landowners) of Crichton declared that children of the poor under the age of fifteen should be handed over to any tenant or tradesman willing to take them in return for food and clothes, generalising the personal decision made by Spevine.[2] Another instance of recognition that harvest failure could lead to unemployment is shown by the action of the kirk session of Bolton in October 1695, and in later years of the famine, when it offered payments of a few pounds Scots to various 'poor' to enable them to pay their 'shearers' (harvest workers).[3] In the course of this famine the kirk session of Yester parish, with a population in 1755 of 1,100, had over 120 families getting help, approximately a third of the total population.[4]

These surges in the number of the poor show failure of the labour market. The decision of Crichton would suggest that it was only cottars, not tenants or tradesmen, who were at risk in famine. But to accept this would be simplistic. The repeated crop failures of the 1690s could have thrown others into destitution, as comments by landowners expecting to have land 'vacant' show. In 1780 the poorhouse at Inveresk was admitting craftsmen; and even millers, the skilled workers with most in the way of resources, can be found on poor rolls. Ineffective wrights might be provided with occasional work by the privilege of making pauper coffins, so reducing the frequency of other support. Similarly the making of clothes for orphans going into service would be given as paid work to ageing spinsters barely able to support themselves.

But there is some evidence that in normal times tenants and craftsmen did not need parish help. By a lucky chance we have a full list of the households of Dairsie in Fife in 1747, with their economic status, in the recording by the Commission of the General Assembly of opinion over a disputed Call, and this can be compared with various surviving lists of the poor. There were 34 householders labelled tenant or craftsmen, and 51 labelled cottar. Poor relief in the 1740s and '50s was in practice confined to those on the cottar lists, or their dependants.[5]

The wages of women, though they approached those of men in harvest time, were markedly lower at other times. This fact, and the slightly longer expectation of life, probably form the basis of the much larger share taken by women in the rolls, the lists of those needing regular support. In some (randomly chosen) 30 parishes in the 1690s for which the pauper figures for the two sexes are given, single women added up to twice as many as single men: there were also usually widows with children on the roll, and more of these than fathers with children.

The social burdens of the famine of the 1690s, following shortly after a major political and religious upheaval, produced not only an unusually high number of orphans on rolls, but also occasionally travelling beggars described in the register as gentlemen or gentlewomen. The famine did much of its killing through associated epidemics; and because of the impact of these as a chance element they often removed adults while sparing dependent children. The gentry component, which continued as late as 1710, came from the drastic expulsion of ministers who had accepted episcopacy.

In the eighteenth century harvest deficiencies, followed by drastic price rises, led various parishes to respond to the emergencies by a system of food subsidy. In 1740 the landowners of Midlothian raised £2,000, and used it for the purchase of grain abroad. The grain was put on offer at lower than cost to the parishes. The parish of Currie can be seen buying from this store, adding its own subsidy and making the grain available to all householders at a price somewhere at the upper end of normal fluctuations. All on the roll had their pensions doubled, so that they could afford to buy the grain.[6] The policy can be seen as a forerunner of the English Speenhamland system, the aiding of those with earning power by relief money. There is also evidence of real unemployment in the crisis produced by the hard winter of 1739–40.

In the harvest failure of 1800 the use of Poor Law funds to aid those with an earned income became common. It has been found in parishes in Stirlingshire, East Lothian and Berwickshire,[7] and will probably, if looked for, be found elsewhere too. It led, in Duns, an assessed parish, to the famous legal process of

Pollock versus Darling . In East Linton the scale of subsidy for purchase of grains, which varied according to the wage level of the recipient, was published in a newspaper as an example to others.[8] Given this widespread use of poor relief funds to supplement wages, it is somewhat surprising that the practice should soon after have been stated to be unknown in Scotland by a large and apparently authoritative work on the Scottish Poor Law.[9]

These wage-subsidy activities, though they show that in times of stress a large part of the working population came under the head of 'poor' usually called 'the industrious poor', do not show whether there was not also a rise in unemployment. In 1800 this may not have occurred on a big scale, though the bad harvest sent up the numbers on the rolls: the manpower demands of the war period would have reduced the normal slack in the economy. The unemployed would have been classified as 'occasional poor', and any taken onto the rolls were probably already infirm as well as unemployed.

The normal practice of parishes in the eighteenth century was to make up a 'roll', containing the names of those who needed total or near total support, and who were unlikely (ever or for a considerable time) to cease to have such need. These were often called the 'ordinary' or the 'regular' poor. These people would get a pension, and might also receive extra occasional help. The remarkably stable nature of parish rolls shows that small payments could keep these people alive for many years. Such money as the parish had after providing for these might go in occasional payments to them, or to other short-term needs — aid to a nursing mother, to a father needing to hire a wet nurse, a surgeon's fee, or in stray payments to vagrants. If the number on the roll made it inescapably clear that the parish's voluntary funds (church collections, legacies, fines and mortcloth fees) could not cope, the parish would have to call on the heritors to accept assessment. The heritors and tenants could share support of those on the roll, and the session would have to hand over half the collections to them. The rest of the voluntary funds would meet minor parish needs, such as new equipment for communion, the salary of the parish officer etc. What was left was available for the 'occasional' poor. The system meant that the support of those who had become temporarily unemployed was separated from the 'regular' poor, and often not clearly labelled. It is therefore not possible to quantify the unemployed's share of relief. Much of it may have gone to 'vagrants'. 'Unemployment' was not a contemporary word and parishes, while supporting those whose destitution came from it, were always more interested in the actual need of people rather than in their economic category.

Need from lack of work can also be identified in various other ways. A session might help a man to buy essential equipment: animals for instance 'because through death of his beasts he is disabled to work for his livelihood'.[10] David Loch in the 1770s could comment on 'the many hundred inhabitants in our streets without shoes and stockings . . . actually starving for want of employment',[11] and that was after the expansion of the linen industry had done much to widen the work opportunities. The fall in linen sales in 1755–6, when the bounty on export stopped, sent many men in eastern Scotland into the army, the most despised of occupations.[12] In peacetime a similar depression would mean unemployment. Unemployment may have inspired an outbreak of county schemes for controlling vagrants and supporting the poor in numerous counties in 1772–3. These schemes acknowledged that those in need included many who 'in a normal year would be able to support themselves'. There are frequent comments on vagrants in Justice of the Peace records implying that these people had wilfully separated themselves off from the rest of society and should be forced to work. This image had been conveyed by Andrew Fletcher of Saltoun in the late seventeenth century, but we have no good evidence that such a group existed, and certainly if it normally numbered 100,000, as he alleged, we would expect to find signs of it. In the Stewartry of Kirkcudbright, which took a tough line with vagrants, the handful arrested and forced to promise to leave the country and not return can be found signing such promises, which is an argument against outcast status.[13] In Dunbartonshire and Wigtonshire the Justices of the Peace threatened to fine those fit for service who did not take it up, but this seems simply to have been an attempt to prevent cottars' children keeping themselves from low-paid work to be available for better-priced hire in harvest time.[14]

That we today can recognise unemployment as a source of destitution and low wages in the eighteenth century does not mean that it was generally accepted as a reality by contemporary upper-class observers. In 1740 the Earl of Selkirk, donating 20 bolls of oatmeal to the parish of Cramond for the poor, insisted that none of it should go to 'the idle'.[15] Parishes took care that those who had no visible means of support should not settle there, and this was clearly aimed at the unemployed. The separation of 'regular' from 'occasional' poor in the source of their supply in assessed parishes, and the rapid increase in the number of such parishes in the second half of the eighteenth century, made it easy for the heritors, who carried much of the administration for the 'regular' poor, to ignore the existence of these others. Heritors could assert that the entire burden of relief lay upon themselves, on the assumption that any money owed by their tenants came indirectly from the landowner, and in so doing they stressed the significance of the parish roll, ignoring the occasional poor. Out of these beliefs and prejudices came the view, first expressed by a gentleman farmer in Aberdeenshire in 1780, that the Scottish Poor Law gave no right to those 'merely destitute'.[16]

In the 1780s there started, in Scotland as well as in England, anti-Poor Law publications, one reason perhaps why there is no consistent evidence of a rising demand for relief in the eighteenth century. If we compare the number of paupers and their annual cost in the 1780s with what it had been in the early 1700s, in those parishes already fulfilling their duties of relief at the earlier date, there is no upward trend. But it had become much harder by the 1780s for a parish to ignore this duty. Pressure by sheriffs and Justices of the Peace, in a recurring series of county schemes, had been placed on parishes where the kirk session was negligent or where the landowners had resisted assessment. As a result there was more money flowing regularly through the relief system at the end of the eighteenth century than at the start.

The economic developments after 1740, particularly the expansion of domestic industry, might be expected to have reduced the share of relief going to single women. Women's wages rose in the second half of the century, though at a markedly slower rate than men's.[17] The agricultural reorganisation which began in the 1770s, and later the establishment of the early spinning factories, might have resulted in either a higher or a lower proportion of women needing support. As domestic industry waned the more fully capitalised economy might have led to a demand only for full-time and well-muscled labour. On the other hand the widening of the pay differential between the sexes may have made female labour attractive. After 1750 the change in status of the subordinate farm population from cottars to day labourers or servants may have made more apparent the shortage of winter work in some areas. It was stated in 1815 in Bendochy, Perthshire, that the reduction in tenant numbers and the demolition of cottar houses had increased the numbers of the poor.[18] But in the new set-up, the development of the farm servant's obligation to provide a woman for work in harvest may have been of more help to the working family than had been the benefits of domestic industry.

After 1790 sharper fluctuations of the economy may have thrown many wage-earning families into temporary bouts of hardship. But it is also possible that the mixed employment pattern of the early modern period, in which many could find some work commensurate with their capacity, continued well into the early industrial age: we know very well that only a small part of the labour force was working in factories in the early nineteenth century. The reply by the minister of Lanark to the questionnaire on Poor Law expenditure of 1815 is relevant here. 'All the persons on poor's lists except six may be called industrious poor as they depend in some degree on their own exertions', he wrote.[19] Similar remarks came in from other parishes, Aberdour, Cramond, Cargill and Coupar Angus.

In the early nineteenth century the new system of more intensive farming used long-term hire of farm servants for six months or a year, which resulted in their being little surplus labour in country areas.[20] Many such areas in lowland Scotland were not more than one or two days' walking from an expanding town. Highlanders had since the mid-eighteenth century a pattern of seasonal migration for harvest work. These features meant that though rural unemployment certainly existed, particularly in winter for women, most of the slack in the use of labour was passed to the towns.

This is shown clearly in an inquiry made at the moment when nervousness about the scale of pauperism was building up to a major alarm in England and influencing Scottish opinion. From 1815 to the early 1820s there was a continuous concern in both countries that the burden of poor relief was getting out of hand.[21] Bills were introduced into Parliament to reduce the scope of the Poor Laws, or to make some part of them voluntary in the financial base. T. F. Kennedy, the Scottish Member of Parliament who was to be responsible for two of these, gave special attention to the topic of the Poor Law and in 1815 launched a questionnaire to all parishes through the sheriffs, asking among other questions about the annual cost of poor relief since 1790, the share in it of assessment, the number of poor on the roll and the number of 'industrious poor'. About 200 replies to this exist, mostly partial.[22] The full replies come from rural parishes and small towns and make it possible to measure the change in the burden of relief and in the numbers of regular poor. In money terms the average cost of relief to these parishes rose by 98% between 1780 and 1814, but adjusted by the cost of living this rise is reduced to 18%.[23] The numbers on the roll had peaked in 1800, suggesting that some of the unemployed or other marginal poor were being included on the roll, but in 1814 stood at only 94% of the figure for 1790.

These figures show that contemporary complaints about the rising cost of poor relief are misleading. The landowning class who voiced them, and the clergy who acquiesced in them, had profited by the rise in grain prices. In the case of landowners there was also the advantage gained by the enhanced productivity of reformed farming. The complaints were probably based on a fear of a fall in prices and rents in the peace. That the cost of relief had risen in real terms by 1814, though numbers had fallen, may indicate a slight rise in rural unemployment. We can take these figures further for the same parishes in 1820, from a Church of Scotland report,[24] which shows a rise in real cost of 20% since 1790. This report also gives the ratio of the sexes on relief; as in the 1690s, this was almost exactly two women for each man. The long-term changes had led to no alteration in the relative likelihood of destitution between the sexes.

Given the severity of the qualification for being on the roll, limited change should not surprise. In the industrial areas the main volume of requests for relief would have been from the 'occasional' poor. There was uncertainty in law whether three or seven years' residence was necessary for the establishment of settlement in a parish. Under either definition, the growing towns contained many in need with no entitlement. The view that only the disabled had a legal claim to relief was gaining ground. The new urban population in the growing towns, and the anonymity that it produced, made relief for the 'occasional' poor by voluntary funds unlikely to be effective.

In 1819 Kennedy introduced a Bill into Parliament aimed at preventing appeals to any court from the decisions of the kirk session of a parish on poor relief matters. His argument was that it was best to have these decisions wholly in the hands of those who would have to pay for any expense involved. He stated that there was now to be found 'a new class of person as poor . . . denominated "the industrial poor"'.[25] He was claiming either that unemployment was a new phenomenon, or that aid to it from the Poor Law was new.

Neither of these claims was true. Unemployment had existed, and sometimes gained relief, in the eighteenth century. But behind his misstatements lay a very real point, that unemployment was now creating concentrations of severe poverty on a new scale. We know too that the problem of urban destitution caught the eye of the Reverend Thomas Chalmers in 1819, when he launched his 'experiment' to show that it could be coped with by private charity. In the same year there came to the Court of Session an appeal by the parish of Paisley against a sheriff court decision ordering it to pay relief to nearly 1,000 unemployed textile workers. The Court of Session did most of the work of Kennedy's unsuccessful Bill and announced, in the teeth of precedents, that no poor relief appeal could lie to any court but itself.[26] The lawyers then went on to write into the text-books explicitly that the unemployed were not entitled to poor relief.

In the end this manipulation of the law by the landed and legal establishment was shown to be an unwise and extreme action. Further destitution in the depression of 1841–3 in Paisley was to force the government to bring forward a reform of the Scottish Poor Law in a form which, though it did not acknowledge any right of relief to the unemployed, instantly forced a large number of parishes into assessment.[27]

What the events and pressures of the early nineteenth century show is the success of the Scottish farming system in tailoring the rural population to its labour needs, so that the slack was passed to the towns. Such figures as we can collect do not suggest that this was merely a forcing out of the infirm. By the 1830s and '40s, the time of the *New Statistical Account* and the Poor Law *Report* of 1844, it was indeed a common complaint from the towns that the old were landed on them by the rural areas. Generally the fairly even spread of the level of those entitled to relief, approximately 2.5% of the population in the *New Statistical Account*, is a strong indication that this had not happened. There seem by the early nineteenth century to have been fewer orphans to be supported on poor relief than in the early eighteenth century, and no begging gentry, but otherwise there was not much change in the kind of people needing help. The failure of numbers on the roll to rise in the later years of the Napoleonic struggle suggests that, whatever new reasons had come into existence for destitution, these were compensated for by improved health, working capacity and opportunity.

There is still a major, unresolved puzzle about the extent of poverty, and its definitions, in the fact that by the second decade of the nineteenth century the average expenditure of poor relief per head of the population in Aberdeenshire and the Mearns stood at a fifth of the level in the Lothians and Border counties. Some part of this difference was one of accounting: faced with a likely heavy burden, for instance a family or settlement which had suffered a major disaster, the parishes, instead of funding the need directly, would appeal to the whole presbytery or synod, and the money collected would not count as Poor Law supply. A further process of keeping expenditure down had resulted from a long-standing hostility to any system of assessment among the landowners. This attitude had led a Mr Burnett to bequeath his estate, worth some £3,000, into trust with the interest on it to be used in sporadic donations to local parishes which had never been assessed. The chance of receiving such a donation inspired landowners to do all they could to keep down Poor Law expenditure, and to rely on private initiative and generosity. The region in any case was not conspicuous for the industrial developments in which unemployment tended to manifest itself, and surplus population had been leaving. Even so, there was poverty in the north-east, unrecognised and unaided, even in times of prosperity.

This essay shows that in many areas the decentralised and patchwork administration of the Scottish Poor Law developed, during the eighteenth century, the capacity to cope with the needs of those who could not make an economic contribution. At intervals harvest failure brought other sections of society to need which they could not meet for themselves, and a system of charitable gift and special aid was set up for a while to deal with this problem. With the new scale of concentration of the workforce in towns, and the fluctuations of the business cycle, the amateur nature of the emergency procedure not only was inadequate to cope, but also, by its peripheral nature, prevented the recognition of unemployment as a reality. The propertied classes had learned to cope with natural disaster, and urban crisis,[28] and this failure arose to a considerable degree from the structure of the system of relief and the definitions that it produced.

NOTES

1. S.R.O. CH2/357/19, Tranent KSR (Kirk Session Register), March 1745.
2. S.R.O. CH2/71/1, Crichton KSR, May 1697 and October 1699.
3. S.R.O. CH2/3/3, Bolton KSR.
4. Rosalind Mitchison, 'A Parish and its Poor', *Transactions of the East Lothian Antiquarian and Field Naturalist Society*, XIV (1974).
5. S.R.O. CH1/2/87, f.169 and CH2/427/2.
6. J. M. Gray, ed., *Memoirs of the Life of Sir John Clerk of Penicuik* (Scottish History Society, Edinburgh, 1892), p. 159; S.R.O. CH2/83/3, Currie KSR.
7. G. M. Birnie, Tradition and Transition, the Scottish Poor Law, Harvest Failure and the Industrious Poor (unpublished M.A. thesis, Department of Economic and Social History, Edinburgh University, 1976), ch.5.
8. *Caledonian Mercury*, 5 December 1800.
9. Rev. Robert Burns, *Historical Dissertation on the Law and Practice of Great Britain and Particularly of Scotland with Regard to the Poor* (Edinburgh, 1819), p. 62.
10. S.R.O. CH2/377/2, Yester KSR, 1663.
11. David Loch, *Essays on the Trade, Commerce, Manufactures and Fisheries of Scotland* (Edinburgh, 1778), vol.1, p. 136.
12. A. J. Durie, The Scottish Linen Industry, 1707–15, with particular reference to the early history of the British Linen Company (unpublished Ph.D. thesis, Edinburgh University, 1972), p. 72.
13. E.g. S.R.O. JP2/2/1 and 2; Andrew Fletcher of Saltoun, *Second Discourse concerning the Affairs of Scotland* (Edinburgh, 1698), p. 24; S.R.O. JP1/2/1.
14. E.g. S.R.O. JP6/2/1, June 1751 and JP17/2/1, March 1748.
15. S.R.O. CH2/426/8, Cramond KSR, June 1740.
16. James Anderson of Monkshill to Jeremy Bentham, in I. R. Christie, ed., *The Correspondence of Jeremy Bentham* (London, 1971), III, pp. 18–39.
17. Valerie Morgan, 'Agricultural Wage Rates in late Eighteenth-Century Scotland', *Ec. H. R.*, XXIV (1971).
18. See Tulliebole MSS, note 22 below.
19. Ibid.
20. T. M. Devine, 'Scottish Farm Service in the Agricultural Revolution', in T. M. Devine, ed., *Farm Servants and Labour in Lowland Scotland, 1770–1914* (Edinburgh, 1984).
21. J. R. Poynter, *Society and Pauperism* (London, 1969).
22. These are at Tulliebole Castle, Kinross-shire, in the possession of Lord Moncrieff of Tulliebole, who has kindly allowed me to work on them.
23. I have used as cost-of-living index base the middle fiar for oats, East Lothian, of the crop of the year before.
24. *Report on the Management of the Poor in Scotland* (P.P. 1820, VII).
25. *Hansard* (Commons) XXXIX, 1264.

26. *Faculty Decisions*, 29 November 1821, *Richmond and others v. the Heritors and Kirk Session of the Abbey Church of Paisley*.

27. T. C. Smout, 'The Strange Intervention of Edward Twistleton: Paisley in Depression, 1841–3', in T. C. Smout, ed., *The Search for Wealth and Stability* (London, 1979).

28. T. C. Smout, 'Famine and Famine-Relief in Scotland', in Cullen & Smout.

13
IN SEARCH OF THE OLD IRISH POOR LAW

David Dickson

One of the more obvious contrasts between Scotland and Ireland in the early nineteenth century was the operation in the former of a tolerably efficient system of parish-organised welfare for the impotent poor and an absence in the latter of any statutory safety-net for those in distress. The origins of Scotland's Poor Law can be traced in sixteenth-century legislation that had been directly inspired by English statutes against vagrancy; ironically, the same legislative precedents had been established in Ireland. The first major statute relating to the Irish poor (33 Hen VIII c.15) was a mere re-iteration of the English vagrancy act of eleven years previously; it empowered magistrates and constables to register the impotent poor of a town or parish to beg within its bounds, to punish them if they wandered, and to detain able-bodied beggars in the stocks; there was no reference to the possibility of temporary destitution among the able-bodied. Sixteenth-century Scottish legislation was similar, but significantly there were some modifications of Westminster statutes. In neither country was there any consistent use made of this legislation until the harvest crises of the 1620s.[1]

The vigour of the Dublin government in that decade was, by later standards, impressive. In addition to reminding the major urban corporations of the Henrician law (adding that the *bona fide* beggars should be issued with identification seals), the government borrowed from England some of the crisis-management techniques developed over the previous half-century, which were embodied in the various 'Books of Orders' issued to English J.P.s, and in several years it also embargoed the export of grain.[2]

For the remainder of the seventeenth century there was a series of legislative, political and administrative developments in the general area of provision for the poor in both countries, modest in themselves but in Scotland's case of great long-term significance; in Ireland's case less fruitful. Prof. Mitchison has established the evolutionary pattern for Scotland; here we give a brief summary of Irish developments.

In the troubled Dublin parliament of 1634–5 another English penal act against vagrancy, that of 1610, obliging each county to construct a house of correction for 'setting to work rogues, vagabonds, sturdy beggars ...' slipped into Irish law (10 and 11 Car. I. c.4) virtually unchanged. There had in fact been a Dublin 'bridewell' since 1602/3, but not until the Protectorate in the 1650s were there any attempts to construct such institutions in the provinces. These were short-lived, but the novel Commonwealth interest in confronting the idle poor survived the Restoration: in the first parliamentary session the Commons petitioned government to initiate legislation 'for the relief of the poor and putting out poor children apprentices', but nothing came of this tantalising initiative, except that in 1665 a clause was inserted into a more general ecclesiastical statute enabling the Church of Ireland vestry of St. Andrew's parish in Dublin — a growing upper-class suburb — to assess its inhabitants for, among other things, 'the relief of the poor'.[3] Then in 1669 the particular problem of rural vagrants 'infesting' the capital led the government to push Dublin Corporation into establishing a 'hospital' to care for the local 'poor and aged' and to educate the orphaned children 'such as this city is bound to provide for', thereby making the banishment of strange beggars the more easy. The corporation pursued the matter immediately, but had lost sight of the commitment to care for the impotent adult poor by the time the 'King's Hospital' was opened as a free school in 1675.[4] The unresolved issue of controlling the poor in Dublin was tackled afresh by the Jacobite government in 1687: the Viceroy, Lord Tyrconnell, possibly with Gallic models in mind, secured an extensive site on the city's edge for a 'workhouse' and enlarged house of correction, and the city corporation was preparing the site when the coming of war froze the project. Despite subsequent confusion over the title to the site, interest in the place remained alive through the 1690s.[5]

Elsewhere, rapid urban growth in the main ports during the Restoration period led to the more regular use of parts of the Henrician vagrancy law, such as the detention or expulsion of non-local beggars, coupled with the registration of the indigenous poor. In addition it seems that most Church of Ireland clergy within the major towns were already operating regular poor collections in their churches and distributing the proceeds. It was at the instigation of a number of Dublin city parishes in 1695 that the Irish Commons debated and approved the heads of a general bill which would have enabled any parish in the country to assess its inhabitants for *inter alia* the relief of its poor. The 'heads' never reached the English Privy Council and a similar proposal suffered no better fate in 1697. A third draft in 1698 was accepted by the Lord Justices but was also not forwarded to London. The political background to this curious set of disappointments is obscure, but it was not co-incidental that some of the promoters of an Irish Poor Law were the same M.P.s behind the abortive linen bills of 1695 and 1697, which had been intended to create county corporations for employing poor children in spinning and weaving linen.[6]

It was only in the restricted sphere of Dublin itself that legislative progress was actually made: in 1703/4 the corporation managed to secure sufficient parliamentary support to carry its bill 'for employing and maintaining the poor of the city and county of Dublin' into (albeit emasculated) statute law. The prestigious new workhouse, erected over the next three years at a cost of nearly £9,000, was by its very scale something of a national institution, although its current revenue came from a tax on city householders. Its initial function was to keep city streets clear of beggars, and when its doors opened in 1706, 124 vagrants were promptly marched in; a year later the city's church wardens brought in their 'parish poor' — presumably the impotent poor and older orphans registered by the vestries or magistrates — thereby adding some 200 to the workhouse population and broadening its welfare functions.[7]

This metropolitan showpiece was less than successful, even in the short run. Its formative period came when the city was growing very rapidly, and after a few years it was unable to receive the numbers being referred to it; for this and other reasons city parishes delayed handing over their assessment of the poor tax, and resentment at the spatial distribution of the costs and benefits of the new scheme built up. As early as 1723 further penal legislation was passed to keep beggars off Dublin's streets, and in 1728 the workhouse's constitution was recast, its finances improved, and its role as a repository for foundling children first explicitly stated.[8] Swift, a governor of the workhouse for many years, wrote a typically swingeing attack in 1737, criticising the way the house was being subverted by having to accept out-of-town beggars and to take in foundlings and orphans sent from the countryside. His recipe was a sterner application of parish badging, inside and outside Dublin, for 'by the old laws of England still in force, and presumably by those in Ireland, every parish is bound to maintain its own poor'.[9]

Swift's presumption as to parochial responsibility was of course wrong. The precedent for a fully-fledged parish Poor Law had been created in the 1665 legislation for St. Andrew's parish, but despite the development of welfare activity akin to Scottish practice in some Church of Ireland parishes, there was still no statutory authority for this. Given the very small number of early vestry books extant, it is not clear when rural parishes began to keep poor lists and to assume welfare functions embracing the whole parochial community. Shankill (Co. Armagh) in the 1670s seems to be the earliest documented case of a mainly rural parish maintaining a poor list, but parishes which are known (from numismatic evidence) to have introduced systematic badging of their legitimate poor were presumably also distributing alms to those they badged and licensed to beg. At least six parishes or parish groups in Ulster were operating a badging scheme between 1699 and 1709 (2 in Armagh, 3 in Down, 1 in Antrim). And in 1707 the Antrim County Grand Jury, because of the 'great increase of vagrant persons and idle beggars', directed all clergy and parish officers to list and badge persons 'whom they esteem objects of charity and fit to be relieved'; they were also to search and arrest all other beggars who were to be whipped or exposed in the stocks, and then despatched to their parish of birth or of three years' residence (an echo of the Scottish laws of 1667 and 1672). This directive still rested on the Henrician legislation — although considerably extending its application.[10] The strong east Ulster pattern of parish action is striking: was it a response to a particular regional problem of itinerant beggars, possibly from Scotland in the wake of the 'ill years', or the influence of Scottish parish conventions in areas of greatest Scottish settlement? Whatever may have prompted this initiative, east (with south) Ulster was later to develop the most advanced institutional responses to poverty within Ireland, and this reflected the uniquely large Protestant congregations of the region.

Outside east Ulster the role of Church of Ireland vestries in the eighteenth century is less clear. In the major cities, where congregations were generally substantial, vestry involvement in communal welfare was common practice. In

Dublin parishes at least, multi-denominational poor lists were maintained, financed by weekly collections, charity sermons and bequests. Parochial taxation to cover the cost of maintaining foundlings became the norm (receiving legal backing in 1728). But the overall number of citizens touched by parish charity remained limited.[11] As for the situation elsewhere, it seems to have been assumed that Sunday collections for the poor at large were common in Church of Ireland and Dissenter churches. It is evident from a small sample of eighteenth-century Church of Ireland registers so far examined that provision for the poor varied at least as much as in contemporary Scotland. No Irish parish seems to have approached the comprehensive support given to the impotent poor in many parts of the Scottish Lowlands, but the sums allocated to the registered poor in some Ulster parishes were probably well above those given in more parsimonious parishes in northern Scotland.[12] Those on Irish lists (the number ranged from a handful to several dozen adults) received small cash allocations several times a year, rarely exceeding £1.00 p. a. The parish poor both in Ireland and Scotland were primarily the old and the infirm (disproportionately older widows). In Irish practice there was some bias towards Protestant poor but Catholic names were usually present, sometimes forming a clear majority; in Scotland the position of poor Dissenters seems to have been at least as ambiguous as that of the non-Anglican poor in Ireland.

The restricted coverage of the Irish parish lists is obvious by their generally short length. The amount of public alms available in a parish depended on the size of the regular Anglican congregation, but the alms budget could be greatly augmented where there was an energetic and socially well-connected minister able to raise money by charity sermons and voluntary subscriptions, and quite a few parishes received small bequests or annual donations for the poor from local landlords. In Scotland, parish funds for the disabled poor where alms collections were inadequate could be topped up, even in the seventeenth century, by the kirk session levying a stint or assessment, i.e. poor tax, on landowners and tenants. Enabling legislation to facilitate this development in Ireland seems to have been the aim of the Poor Law promoters in the 1690s: as long as the established church commanded the loyalty of only a minority of the population — albeit a disproportionately wealthy one — there was a strong case for extending parish cess to cover the maintenance of the impotent poor. The failure to grant vestries such powers did not, however, prevent some parishes from assigning part of the general cess collected to maintaining the registered parish poor.

The Church of Ireland parish also came to play a role in coping with crisis poverty. The early displays of government intervention at times of harvest failure in the 1620s were not followed up in the later seventeenth century: for example, the bad harvests of the early 1670s and 1683–4 do not appear to have led to government action. Ireland, unlike Scotland, escaped major food scarcities in the 1690s but the grain shortages of 1708/9 were severe, and while they led to thousands taking to the roads they did not provoke any obvious government response. By contrast the run of harvest failures between 1726 and 1729 did lead to limited action and marked something of a turning point. The worst of the crisis in the winter of 1728/9 came during the Viceroy's absence, and the most active Lord Justice was the recently appointed English Archbishop of Armagh, Hugh Boulter; his double authority, secular and ecclesiastical, enabled him to organise emergency importations on government account, to lead public subscriptions for relief, to use clerical networks for food distribution (it was claimed) to every parish in Ulster, and to direct part of his own episcopal rents to local charity funds.[13] The fact that the worst affected areas included much of his archdiocese helps explain his energy, but a precedent was set. The corporations of Derry, Coleraine and probably other towns imported and distributed grain below cost. Yet despite such decisive public responses the harvest failure still caused a jump in the death rate in some of the inland areas of Ulster. The scarcity in Dublin itself was the worst in memory, and the problems of municipal provision led to a new Tillage Act (of no real consequence) and, more importantly, triggered the sudden enthusiasm for establishing turnpike roads radiating from Dublin in the 1730s. But the real significance of the emergency was in the precedent established by raising large numbers of subscriptions to finance food purchases for the poor and the complementary actions of government in food procurement.[14]

The distinctly southern complexion of the 1739/41 crisis posed great difficulties for government, given the grave international scarcity and the less developed state of parochial administration than in Ulster.[15] Dublin Castle did attempt to revive Book-of-Orders-type instructions to J.P.s (grain surveys were undertaken in Louth, Dublin Co. and Wexford); markets were vigorously policed, and port corporations were encouraged to import grain for distribution to charitable committees. In response, corporations from Drogheda round the coast to Kinsale undertook grain imports on public account, but the fact that no city except Cork had a municipal granary made the task of price control very difficult. The one-and-a-half years of extreme food shortages and famine fevers during 1740–41 in Munster and parts of the other two southern provinces led to a large if quite unquantifiable response by the resident upper classes: agents, clergy and landowners became involved both in raising subscriptions for food purchase, and in food distributions from urban or estate centres. The impact of this may, however, have made little dent on what was the worst trauma for the poor during the century, relief being very uneven in geographical distribution and disproportionately urban. The motivation behind the propertied classes' reaction to the crisis was largely prudential: that mass malnutrition and vagrancy went hand in hand and that beggars spread fluxes and fevers which recognised no class barriers were conventional wisdoms in Munster by 1741.

John Post's recent survey of the 1740–1 crisis across Europe[16] provides an excellent demonstration of the growing responsiveness of most *ancien régime* states to major food crises. The comparative performance of the Irish executive in these years turns out to have been not particulary impressive, and the exceptionally high mortality in Ireland (and Norway) is blamed by Post on administrative and institutional failure, both in defective anticipation of famine and in inadequate reaction to the actual crisis. By contrast the relatively modest impact of the crisis in Scotland is attributed to the scale of kirk and voluntary relief programmes, together with swift organisation of public grain imports. Certainly if the voluntary response in Ireland was feeble, it was a rural not an urban failure; for example, when the Edinburgh house of correction was having to cope with the maintenance of 500 beggars, the Dublin workhouse was feeding over 8,000 poor.[17] But even in the Irish countryside the level of élite charity given to the poor was probably unprecedented. Thus, although Post's indictment is not necessarily unfair, it was probably the convergence of several disasters afflicting Ireland in these years — grain failures, potato failures, cattle losses, maritime trade embargoes — that explains why Irish mortality was so unusually high. And insofar as there was a welfare failure it arose more from the underdeveloped state of rural institutions at county and parish level than from the quality of compassion.

No major policy innovation resulted from the 1740–1 crisis, but the return of severe grain shortages and distress in 1755–7 prompted two major urban developments: a permanent subsidy on the transport of domestic grain products to Dublin (which banished the fear of food riots in the capital), and the introduction of a comprehensive urban Poor Law in Belfast, a year after the unprecedented food riots of 1756; the scheme involved a tax on all householders and the provision of fortnightly outdoor relief for, to begin with, some 500 'objects'; it functioned, without statutory authority, until a lottery-financed poorhouse opened in 1774.[18]

The social dislocation caused by intermittent grain and potato failures after the 1750s was lessening but still severe. The incidence of communal vagrancy was falling, and a rise in smallholder incomes seems to have taken the sting out of local supply shortages. But the problem of endemic vagrancy in Dublin was if anything worsening; the workhouse had become almost exclusively a foundling hospital — despite occasional appeals to the governors to remember their original functions. With the attenuation of Protestant congregations in the old city, provision for the poor based on collections and bequests was quite inadequate; only compulsory assessment for the poor might have re-invested vitality in parochial institutions.

The last great initiative to establish a general Poor Law in Ireland, which came in the 1770s, should therefore not be related to a specific crisis, but to the context of a slightly wealthier society concerned to tackle an unsavoury aspect of life: regular uncontrolled begging, both by the infirm and the sturdy, most evident in the capital. Dean Richard Woodward provided the catalyst: in 1766 he published under the auspices of the Dublin Society a revived proposal for the construction of county workhouses, to be established under the direction of the grand juries and to be funded by miscellaneous taxes; their function would be to provide facilities for the aged and the sick, and indoor supervised employment for vagrant beggars.[19] Apparently independent of this, legislation (5 Geo. III c.20) was passed in the same year enabling county infirmaries to be established under the trusteeship of the Church of Ireland but funded by county presentment; already six counties in the south had such institutions, and in the ten years after the Act another sixteen modest county infirmaries catering for the sick poor were constructed.[20]

Woodward developed a philosophical base for his general proposals on provision for the poor in his more famous essay of 1768 in which he grafted onto the old utilitarian argument, that the public maintenance of the poor would increase national wealth and diffuse industriousness, a fresher natural-right argument: 'it is the indispensable duty of the rich to provide a competent maintenance for the poor'.[21] And although he suggested that some compulsory law be enacted, the legislation directly inspired by Woodward, the act for 'badging the poor' (11 & 12 Geo. III c.30) was an enabling statute only. It repealed the ancient vagrancy laws, and authorised the setting up of county corporations which were to arrange for the badging of all 'the helpless poor', and to raise subscriptions and county grants for the establishment of county houses of industry. It was a rather archaic piece of legislation; for instance in its explicit distinction between the disabled — who could still be allowed to beg — and the able-bodied who were to be institutionalised if they persisted. But the Act did bear some immediate fruit. Badging was introduced or revived in a number of parishes — again overwhelmingly in east Ulster with a few southern outliers.[22] But as a means of controlling vagrancy, badging 'impotent' poor was a highly dubious procedure in an Irish context; the volume of begging, at least in the bad years, was too great, and in any case it was very unpopular: only half the 225 licensed beggars in Queen's Co. in 1773–4 wished to be even issued with badges,[23] and there was a similar reaction in Dublin. The mendicant sub-culture, so highly developed by the 1830s, was probably well-formed even in the 1770s; control by the parish officers in town and countryside can rarely have been welcome and was easily evaded. More basically, the peripatetic character of begging was deep-rooted — partly for the reasons advanced by the parish priest of Lower Creggan, Co. Armagh in 1833: 'my people, from a sense of shame, go to other parts, whilst strangers, actuated by a similar feeling, come here'.[24]

As for the houses of industry, county subscriptions were raised in Cork, Waterford, Limerick, Clare, Queen's Co., Wexford and Dublin itself. The Belfast poorhouse and Poor Law schemes, and those for Coleraine and Lisburn, were quickly brought within the ambit of the Act. The functions of the much larger Dublin house of industry were very similar to the original aims of the 1704 workhouse, except that it had greater capacity, had no proselytising element, and excluded young children. After the doors of the house were opened to voluntary admissions of both able-bodied and infirm beggars in 1773, city begging was markedly reduced. But by the 1780s it seemed as bad as ever, despite the growing intake at the house: initially equipped with 300 beds, the institution took in nearly 4,600 people in the hard year of 1783, with stays averaging about four months, and over 8,000 in the even worse year of 1800.[25] The majority in bad years were voluntary admissions, probably referred by the parishes, but a sizeable minority of beggars and street-walkers were being detained as well. During the depression and food shortages of 1783–4 the house of industry became a centre for the distribution of emergency food rations financed by private subscriptions: some 5,500 were being fed in February 1784, and individual parishes in the poorer quarters were also raising funds for food hand-outs, appealing not to their own small and probably indigent congregations, but to wealthier citizens through the newspapers. In 1800, under Castle orders, the governors of the house set up three large soup kitchens across the city and for a period fed more than 20,000 people.[26]

The reliance on voluntary subscriptions, which was a central feature of the 1771–2 Act, worked out tolerably successfully where and when the problems of the poor were visible to the wealthier classes: in the larger towns and in the bad years. Income for the Dublin house of industry sagged after the initial enthusiasm, and from 1777 there was continuous parliamentary support. After 1800 the house was forced through pressure of demand and government policy into concentrating on its narrower medical functions, providing a growing range of facilities for the sick, the aged, the orphaned and the 'lunatic' poor, so that employment of the vagrant poor became a marginal concern. This expansion was only possible because the house, like the capital's other public charities and utilities, was cosseted by parliament (the grant by 1814 was little short of £50,000 p. a.), whereas the provincial houses of industry were maintained by county presentments and public subscriptions, and remained as token gestures against urban vagrancy.

Such institutions could not cope with the new dimensions of distress caused by economic recession and food shortages in 1816–18. The crisis produced a new wave of voluntary action in the form of mendicity associations: the Dublin Society sought to give productive employment to all city applicants, providing some with shelter and some with daytime employment only; by the mid-1830s it was helping between 3,000 and 4,000 cases p.a.[27] Other charities, medical, moral, educational, financial, Protestant, Catholic and even non-denominational, had proliferated in the city since the mid-eighteenth century. Their very number gave rise to some self-congratulation, but in fact Dublin's growing social inequality and industrial decline in the early nineteenth century demanded far more fundamental welfare provision.

From the time of the Union central government became more prominent as initiator and coordinator of emergency relief: the almost passive behaviour of a stumbling executive during the 1783–4 crisis was in contrast both to government action in the Scottish Highlands in those years and to the anxious monitoring of Cornwallis and Castlereagh in Ireland in 1800–1. In addition to stirring up voluntary action in the capital, they financed large imports of rice and maize from America and used the army commissariat structure to reduce regional scarcities. Exchequer funds were provided in 1801 to augment by 50 per cent all local voluntary subscriptions. But the government's primary concern, it would appear, was 'the populous towns as being the places most liable to tumult'.[28] In the post-war crises of 1816–18 and 1822–3 the government continued to widen its role: in 1817 introducing outdoor public works schemes, importing seed grain and subsequently establishing local and national boards of health; in 1822 assessing more critically the relief needs of particular areas and using employment schemes more effectively.[29] Public works schemes in times of crisis were a novel departure only in an Irish context — but their exclusively rural character distinguished them from European precedents.

The role of county-financed institutions in providing regular medical aid was transformed in the post-Union period: by 1830 there were at least 38 county infirmaries, 52 fever hospitals, 10 asylums and nearly 400 public dispensaries, financed by subscriptions and by county cess.[30] These county facilities and the local organisation of emergency relief arrangements were ultimately dependent on the willingness of the wealthier classes to become involved and make substantial recurring contributions. But with the growth of state involvement, the souring of social relations in the countryside in the 1820s and 1830s and the growing challenge of endemic poverty, the vulnerability of voluntarism was exposed. Part of the problem by the 1830s was simply regional imbalance: public alms-giving and emergency subscriptions were proportionately far larger in the bigger towns and the eastern counties, whereas the worst of the pre-Famine food crises were in the western counties — areas where parish and institutional provision had evolved least.

There had therefore been an old Irish Poor Law of sorts — a *'lex non scripta'* operating at parish level in which the Church of Ireland vestry had been an active or potentially active welfare body, both in channelling alms to the endemically poor and in organising local charitable committees in the really hard years. Its failure to be as effective or as widespread as the old Poor Law in Scotland directly resulted from the continuing minority status of the established church in Ireland (although it was only in the nineteenth century that the parish vestry became an exclusive denominational body). No aspect of local government at parochial level functioned well where the Anglican community was below a critical minimum size, perhaps 15–20 per cent of the local population. And in addition to the religious demography factor was the lack of political will within the old Irish parliament to deliver legislation that would have given vestries the statutory authority to levy a cess for the poor. The dismal record of parliament, especially in the eighteenth century, reflected the gentry's horror of the English Poor Law, and the even more burdensome form it might take if applied to Ireland. The one eighteenth-century interest group with political muscle which had intermittently sought reform was the Church of Ireland itself, and individuals within its ranks — Swift, Boulter, Berkeley, Woodward, Skelton, down to Whateley, Chairman of the Poor Inquiry itself — stand out for their public commitment to alleviating permanent impoverishment. But the Church's limited impact on legislation and actual practice is further evidence of where real power lay in pre-Union Ireland. Only after 1800, with the gradual emancipation of Dublin Castle from a gentry-dominated view of Irish society, was there a prospect of Irish property being forced to support Irish poverty.[31]

NOTES

1. For a survey of pre-Union Irish Poor Law legislation, see [F. S. Flood], 'Report upon Vagrancy ... in ... Dublin', in *Poor Inquiry (Ireland),* Appendix C, part ii (P.P. 1836, XXX), pp. 1a*–19a*; for a survey of Scottish Poor Law over the same period, see Rosalind Mitchison, 'The Making of the Old Scottish Poor Law', *Past & Present*, 63 (1974).

2. For a general survey, see Raymond Gillespie, 'Harvest Crises in Early Seventeenth-Century Ireland', *Ir. Ec. & Soc. Hist.,* XI (1984) pp. 11–15.

3. [Flood], 'Report', p. 6a*; T. C. Barnard, *Cromwellian Ireland* . . . (Oxford, 1975), pp. 74–5.

4. J. T. Gilbert, ed., *Calendar of the Ancient Records of Dublin* (19 vols., Dublin, 1889–1944), IV, pp. 459–61; Lesley Whiteside, *A History of the King's Hospital* (Dublin, 1975), pp. 7–9.

5. Gilbert, *op.cit.*, V, pp. 418, 458, 477, 498; VI, pp. 179, 218.

6. For two aspects of this debate, see Sir Francis Brewster, *New Essays on Trade* (London, 1702), p. 122, and 'Memorandum on Linen', in *Report on the MSS of the Duke of Buccleuch and Queensberry,* II (Historical Manuscripts Commission, 1903), pp. 742–4.

7. Marsh's Library, Dublin, MS. Z.3.1(1), pp. cxlvi, cliii; [Flood], 'Report', pp. 7a*–8a*.

8. 1 Geo. II c.27; see also 3 Geo. II c.17 and 5 Geo. II c.14. The Cork city 'workhouse', when it opened in 1747, operated exclusively as a foundling hospital.

9. [Jonathan Swift], *A Proposal for Giving Badges to the Beggars in All the Parishes of Dublin* (London, 1737).

10. T. G. F. Patterson, 'A Co. Armagh Mendicant Badge, Inscribed Shankill Poor, 1669', *Ulster Journal of Archaeology*, 3rd ser. X (1947), p. 113; W. A. Seaby, 'Ulster Beggars' Badges', *Ulster Journal of Archaeology*, 3rd ser. XXIII (1970), pp. 101–6; W. N. C. Barr and W. C. Kerr, eds., *The Oldest Register of the Parish of Derriaghy, County Antrim . . . 1696*–1772 (Derriaghy, 1981), pp. 91–2.

11. See for example W. E. O'Brien, St. Michan's Parish 1725–75 . . . (unpublished B.A. dissertation, Dept. of Modern History, Trinity College Dublin, 1983), pp. 69–78.

12. R. A. Cage, *The Scottish Poor Law 1745–1845* (Edinburgh, 1981), pp. 35–6.

13. Marmaduke Coghill, Dublin to [?], 5 Nov. 1728, Huntington Library, San Marino, MS HM/28678; Account Book of Archbishop Boulter 1724–41, T. C. D. MS 6399; *Daily Journal* (London), 21 Dec. 1728; *Universal Spectator and Weekly Journal* (London), 9 Aug. 1729; *Letters Written by His Excellency Hugh Boulter* . . . (Dublin, 1770), i, pp. 151, 178, 181–2, 202, 228–31, 237.

14. There seems to have been a similar turning point in the public response to harvest crisis in Scotland in 1740–1: T. C. Smout, 'Famine and Famine-Relief in Scotland', in Cullen & Smout, pp. 25–6.

15. For a general account of the crisis, see Michael Drake, 'The Irish Demographic Crisis of 1740–41', *Historical Studies VI,* ed. T. W. Moody (London, 1968).

16. J. D. Post, *Food Shortage, Climatic Variability and Epidemic Disease in Pre-Industrial Europe: the Mortality Peak in the Early 1740s* (London, 1985).

17. *Ibid.*, pp. 145–52, 174–8.

18. George Benn, *A History of the Town of Belfast* . . . (London, 1877), pp. 511–14. 593–8; David Dickson, 'The Place of Dublin in the Eighteenth-Century Irish Economy', in Devine & Dickson, p. 187.

19. [Richard Woodward], *A Scheme for Establishing County Poor-Houses in the Kingdom of Ireland* (Dublin, 1766).

20. K. H. Connell, *The Population of Ireland, 1750*–1845 (Oxford, 1950), pp. 201, 274–5.

21. Woodward, *An Argument in Support of the Right of the Poor . . . to a National Provision* (Dublin, 1768), p. 25.

22. See parish list in Seaby, *loc.cit.*, pp. 101–6.

23. Edward Ledwich, *First Annual Report of the Corporation Instituted for the Relief of the Poor . . . in Queen's County* . . . (Kilkenny, 1776), p. 6.

24. *Poor Inquiry (Ireland),* Appendix A (P.P. 1835 XXXII), Supplement, p. 298.

25. *Watson's Treble Almanac* (Dublin, 1778–1788); *An Account of the Proceedings of the Governors of the House of Industry in Dublin* (Dublin, 1801), esp. pp. 23, 44.

26. House of Industry Minutes, 1772–1839, Royal College of Surgeons of Ireland Library; *Account of the Proceedings*, pp. 57–9.

27. *Letter to the Public from the Association for the Suppression of Mendicity in Dublin* (Dublin, 1818), *passim*; [Flood], 'Statistical Report on the . . . Institutions in the City of Dublin Not Receiving Parliamentary Aid', in *Poor Inquiry (Ireland),* Appendix C, part ii, p. 9a.

28. State Paper Office, Dublin, OP/115/15, Mr Geale, Cork to Under Secretary, 15 Jan. 1801. See also State Paper Office, Dublin, OP/100/3.

29. Timothy O'Neill, The State, Poverty and Distress in Ireland 1815–45 (unpublished Ph.D. dissertation, National University of Ireland (U.C.D.), 1971), *passim.*

30. *Appendix to the Third Report of the Select Committee on the State of the Poor in Ireland*, (P.P. 1830 VII), pp. 836–916.

31. Cf. Oliver MacDonagh, *Ireland* (Englewood Cliffs, N. J., 1968), pp. 23–30.

14

A QUESTION OF ATTITUDE: RESPONSES TO THE NEW POOR LAW IN IRELAND AND SCOTLAND

Gerard O'Brien

The New Poor Law was introduced to the British Isles in three stages: England and Wales in 1834, Ireland in 1838, and finally Scotland in 1845. Specialists of the poor law's administration have usually noted this fact in passing. But they have overlooked the possibility that the administrative procedures of the Irish and Scottish poor laws may have been framed not only with regard to the different regional environments but also with a view to improving the adaptability of the institution to its new popular audience. In short the poor law between 1834 and 1845 may have *evolved* in response to its experiences, successes and mistakes. The importance of such a comparative approach lies partly in the fact that the poor law, rooted in a paternalistic concept of society, has frequently been the victim of a not-dissimilar paternalist approach by its historians. With rare exceptions[1] the poor law has been treated as a solution imposed by the higher strata of society upon those below them. Consequently it is the values, motives, attitudes and politics of the imposers which have come to form the bulk of the poor law's historiography. Little consideration has been given to the likelihood that those upon whom the institution was imposed had at least as much formative influence on the poor law as it had upon them.

This comparative treatment is not concerned with the English poor law; however useful such an inclusion might be, the relatively short gap between its implementation and the introduction of the poor law to Ireland would render conclusiveness uncommonly difficult. But by 1845 virtually all of Ireland's 130 workhouses were in operation, and it should be possible by examining the structures and experiences of the Irish and Scottish poor law administrations to suggest the extent to which the latter system had been designed to reflect the successes and counteract the shortcomings of the former.

Curiously, the old Scottish relief system had featured, albeit briefly, in the controversial Third Report of the Irish Poor Inquiry Commission of 1833–6. The Commission had divided unevenly on the issue of who was to provide the financial support for the proposed new system. A minority of the members held out for a system of support by assessment, partly national, partly local. But the bulk of the Commission was in favour of a national rate supplemented by 'voluntary associations' or privately-administered institutions supported by public subscriptions. In part the majority view represented the cautious practical attitude of men who feared the possible failure of one or other of the twin systems and so took refuge in a combination of both. Against their colleagues who deplored the ineffectiveness of existing Irish relief funds and asylums it was pointed out that the voluntary system in Scotland was 'eminently successful'.

But of even greater interest is the implicit suggestion in the majority Report that the continuation of voluntary relief on a more organised footing might act as a sop to popular expectations and so facilitate the integration of the newer structures of poor law commissioners and national poor rates. They conceded that assessment would be a faster means of raising funds but feared that 'it would every day become more difficult to manage, and tend to bring the country into a worse state than our inquiry has found it'. More explicitly they argued that a properly-organised voluntary system, gradually applied, would 'tend to bring the population into a sound state with respect to the poor . . . and probably supersede in many places, as the Scottish system does so extensively, the necessity of a compulsory rate'.[2]

George Nicholls'[3] rejection of the Scottish system was founded less on its unsuitability to Irish conditions than on the more fundamental point that recipients of such relief came to regard it as a right rather than as a gift. The disparity in attitude between Englishmen and Scotsmen as to the pauper problem may have been partly determined, as one specialist has suggested, 'because of differences of scale and stages of development'.[4] But some allowance would perhaps be made for the personnel and immediate circumstances connected with the poor law's introduction to each region. Royal Commissions staffed by natives of the respective regions preceded poor relief measures in all cases, and in England and Scotland the measures were based largely upon the recommendations of those Commissions. In Ireland the Whateley Commission's recommendations were set aside. The Irish poor relief measure of 1838 was founded upon the proposals of George Nicholls, an Englishman unacquainted with Ireland and whose close connections with the origins and practice of the New Poor Law rendered him a less-than-impartial investigator.[5]

The resistance to the poor law in the north of England had its origins in the temporarily abnormal economic climate which coincided with its introduction. But the essence of the resistance included local rejection of centralised control and popular rejection of the unfamiliar workhouse test.[6] In Scotland the poor law encountered no such resistance, and this has been attributed 'to the different methods of treating the controversial issues'.[7] In Ireland resistance to the poor law cut across class divisions and local boundaries; it was perhaps the first Irish agitation that was both national *and* spontaneous, its occurrence and extent being determined almost solely by the progress of the poor law's introduction.

The belief amongst Scottish commentators that Scotland's acceptance of the New Poor Law was based upon the lessons of northern England[8] begs the question as to the role played by the Irish experience in formulating the Scottish Act of 1845. In Ireland, unlike northern England, there could be no suggestion that a good system was being replaced by an unproven one, for there had never before been an Irish poor law.[9] For the 130 Irish boards of guardians formed under the provisions of the 1838 Act[10] the poor law regulations were personified by the assistant commissioners whose duties included the formation of townlands into unions and preventing local boards from bending or straying from the commissioners' regulations. The element of coercion made the assistant commissioner almost invariably an unpopular personality. The boards, composed of landowners and their agents, accustomed to unchallenged local hegemony, and of middlemen concerned with personal and party advancement, bitterly resented the interference of a 'government' official whose raison-d'être was the enforcement of meddlesome regulations.

By 1841 the Cork Board 'anticipated no difficulty that could possibly arise, which the guardians were not fully competent to overcome, without the aid of the assistant-commissioner, whose hoity-toity feelings would not permit him to step from his mansion at Villa Nova [near Bandon], to honour them with his august presence'.[11] This personal attack on the busy and well-intentioned William Voules had originated in the sharp conflicts which had taken place in the preceding years between several boards of guardians and the commissioners on the question of whether or not press reporters should be admitted to board meetings. In Cork Voules's initially friendly attempts to enforce the rule which provided for the exclusion of press reporters from board meetings were met with frigidity, protest, and finally with open defiance from the guardians for whom the issue was apparently one of great importance. Ostensibly the guardians' position on the matter was that publicity was essential if public confidence in the boards was to be maintained, and that the ratepayers had a right to see how their money was being spent.[12] It was a position from which the guardians could not be driven by either the guile or the wrath of the commissioners.

In the early stages of the struggle when Voules himself defended the commissioners' right to order the exclusion of the press, the guardians first threatened to arrange the election of a press reporter to the office of guardian, and later insisted that as elected representatives their power derived from the people and not from the commissioners.[13] Even during the period when Voules succeeded in enforcing the commissioners' edicts, detailed accounts of board meetings continued to appear in the press by courtesy of 'the friends of publicity'.[14] Only in 1841 when it became clear that continued pressure would 'endanger the peaceful and orderly establishment of the law' did the commissioners drop their opposition. The commissioners were understandably bitter about the affair and later claimed that the behaviour of the Cork Board had led boards in other areas astray.[15] Thereafter, anybody who wished to condemn or ridicule the poor law or any of its officers was assured of at least one inch of newsprint.

In Scotland the press appeared less concerned with the proceedings of the local boards, perhaps due to the admittedly strong similarities between them and those of the pre-poor law period.[16] The week-by-week (and sometimes blow-by-blow) adventures of the Irish local boards had no counterpart in the Scottish press, and the rules which ordered the conduct of the Board of Supervision made no mention of journalists.[17] But the formulators of the 1845 Act did attempt to ameliorate the frosty relationship between the central authorities and the local boards. Whereas in Ireland assistant-commissioners were 'entitled to attend' local board meetings as of right, officers of the Scottish central authority could only attend locally with written permission from above.[18]

The Scottish press was, however, prepared to interest itself in the anomalies which occasionally marred the introduction of the law. One such incident was the barely-cordial collision between the magistrates and town council of Glasgow, and the Directors of the Town's Hospital as to which body (or both) should form the new parochial board. Notably the issue arose less from local or personal rivalries than from an instruction from the Board of Supervision to a non-existent parochial board to appoint an Inspector of the Poor. The Board, it was indignantly opined, 'had acted in an extraordinary manner, by issuing instructions . . . before the parochial boards were formed'.[19]

The cold impact of official instructions upon men unaccustomed to being addressed as erring civil servants played its part in alienating the Irish boards of guardians also. In response to the commissioners' attitude to their choice of a rate collector the South Dublin guardians complained that 'the commissioners' letter of the 8th June is written in a tone not calculated to invite that cordial co-operation from the board without which it is vain to hope to carry into proper execution the provisions of the poor law act'.[20] If the assistant commissioners were intended to act as liaison officers in such situations, these efforts failed miserably. Despite the commissioners' pious assertions in 1841 that 'perfect cordiality' prevailed between the assistant commissioner Richard Hall and the Dublin Boards, a strong attempt was made at the first meeting of the newly-elected North Dublin Board for 1842 to table a motion for his dismissal. In February 1841 the Cork Board publicly plotted the removal of Voules, and the clerk of the Kanturk Union resigned 'in consequence of Mr. Voules being opposed to his retaining his office'. In 1843 the Dungarvan Guardians suggested unkindly that their assistant commissioner John O'Donoghue 'go out with the collector to collect the rate, as the board were quite competent to do their business without him'[21] Ugly scenes such as the assistant commissioner's threat to make the master of the Sligo Workhouse personally responsible for the difference in expense should board persist in opposing the commissioners' ban on an improved diet were unlikely to endear George Nicholls and his minions to Irish guardians.[22] A similar judgement may be passed on Voules's tactics in threatening individual journalists with prosecution or in peremptorily ordering them from the room during the press conflict at Cork.[23] Joseph Burke's necessary request that the Tuam Board cease to bestow on him time-consuming votes of thanks was a rare experience in the life of an assistant commissioner.[24]

One of the more peculiar characteristics of the Irish poor law's chain of command was that the workhouse staff were bound to obey the orders of the commissioners no less than those of the board of guardians, and the commissioners could overrule the board. The commissioners naturally were sensitive to the indelicacy of forcing an officer to act in conflict with the board by whose good offices he had been elected, but the potential advantage of such power was never fully forgotten by the central office. This issue came to a head in the autumn of 1844 when the Limerick Board objected to an article of the revised regulations issued the previous year. The offending article removed from the boards the power to suspend their clerks. Following a vain effort to keep the clerk from attending a board meeting in mid-October the guardians withdrew from the board, and within days their example had been followed by neighbouring boards.[25] Simultaneously a number of the usually well-behaved Ulster boards passed resolutions condemning the article in question. Later the commissioners admitted publicly that 'a large majority of the unions' had expressed similar views. Although the legal advice received by the commissioners was contradictory, they proceeded to seek a mandamus against the Limerick and Rathkeale Boards under the relevant section of the 1838 Act for disobeying the orders of the central authority.[26] The gentlemen of the Queen's Bench, aghast at the prospect of Limerick's merchant barons propelling a treadmill, refused to issue the writs and recommended to the commissioners the lesser expedient of dissolving the two boards. At a stroke the commissioners had been revealed as powerless to impose their will on boards of guardians, other than by the unpalatable threat of dissolution.[27]

All these incidents contrast unfavourably with the conduct of the Scottish Board of Supervision which 'preferred to settle matters without threats and tried to achieve local co-operation without force'.[28] It would have been scarcely conceivable, for instance, for any Irish board to have succeeded, as did the Edinburgh City Board, in operating an illegal emigration fund for a quarter of a century.[29] Scottish local boards, while reserving a degree of independence, were rarely prepared to risk the kind of legal collision provoked by the Limerick and Rathkeale Boards.[30]

A considerable proportion of the friction between the commissioners and the Irish boards, and one which evidently had no Scottish counterpart, arose out of the various attempts by guardians to use their boards as instruments of party propaganda. In a published report on the Dublin Unions in 1842 the South Dublin Union was referred to as having a 'small preponderance' of Liberals, but it was stated that in the North Dublin Board 'the Conservative Party has a majority'. It was pointed out, however, that these boards were composed of 'men of all parties'.[31] It was the 'third' party of the day — the Repealers — which had most to gain from the publicity allocated to board meetings that gave the greatest cause for concern.

In Scotland the attention paid to the new law by hostile politicians was short-lived and apparently confined to the Chartists. Although their attitude to the poor law was never other than a minor element in the development of the Chartist movement in Scotland,[32] some of the terms in which this hostility was expressed held peculiar echoes of the law's Irish experience. While the bill was being pushed through Parliament a public meeting in Glasgow heard Dr. Willis[33] criticise the provision that the poor of each area should be supported by their own community as 'unjust to the large cities, by throwing the support of a great number of the destitute upon the densely-populated districts'. Willis's point was that 'wealthy landlords' were escaping their full share of the burden, and he suggested the establishment of a central fund to be supported by a national (rather than local) assessment.[34] The settlement provisions of the 1845 Act proved both expensive and difficult to administer and the worst of the burden fell naturally upon the larger urban areas. This in turn led to coolness between urban and rural boards as the latter frustrated the former's attempts to ascertain the origins of individual paupers.[35] But in Ireland where no law of settlement had accompanied the new relief system the coolness was transferred to the boardrooms of individual unions. The dispute revolved around the disparity in the numbers of paupers whose true place of residence could not be accurately ascertained and the cost of whose upkeep was therefore divided amongst all the electoral divisions of the union. The collision arose from the accusation of the guardians from rural electoral divisions that their districts were being exorbitantly charged for paupers who were the responsibility of the urban ratepayers, and the failure of the urban guardians to rebutt that accusation.[36] This coolness extended even beyond national boundaries as Irish boards offered little co-operation to Scottish inspectors in the latter's efforts to re-settle Irish paupers.[37]

The prevalence of a degree of religious animosity at some Scottish local boards bespoke the inability of the 1845 Act's designers to cope with the type of entrenched attitude also experienced in Ireland. The Board of Supervision frowned on the behaviour of the Edinburgh City Board in fostering Catholic children with Protestant families. Despite the City Board's excuses the Board of Supervision believed this to have been a deliberately sectarian gesture.[38] In Ireland the two Dublin Boards had been sharply divided along religious lines throughout the early 1840s. Innumerable board meetings in Dublin were marred by rancorous disputes, spurred on by the enrivalled chaplains, in which Catholic guardians accused Protestant guardians (and vice-versa) of encouraging proselytism. The inability of the South Dublin Board in 1842 to agree on an application from Catholic nuns to add religious instruction to their task of visiting sick inmates led ultimately to the exclusion of all such groups.[39] This affair had scarcely ended when a more bitter conflict occurred over a complaint that Catholic paupers were forced to remain in the room while the Protestant chaplain read prayers to 'his' inmates. This charge called forth countercharges that no distinction had been made between Catholic and Protestant paupers when planning the Lenten non-meat diet, and that Protestant paupers had been given the benefit of the Catholic holiday Easter Monday.[40]

But the animosity at Irish boards was directed by those who helped to administer the poor law against particular aspects of the regulations. A rejection of the law which approached totality occurred amongst the ratepayers. Unlike Scotland where a rating system, however unequal, had traditionally existed, the Irish poor had always been supported by voluntary contributions. The determination of the law's designers that the unfamiliar tax should apply right to the depths of the almost bottomless Irish social scale was a monumental error. As early as October 1840 the collector for Cork City electoral division reported that 145 civil bills had been served on defaulters in the city alone.[41] The Dungarvan Board's plans to purchase supplies for its newly-built (but unopened) workhouse were frustrated when the ratepayers refused to contribute towards the support of an apparently incalculable number of paupers.[42] As a means of extracting unpaid rates from defaulters the civil bill was soon found to be an uneconomic expedient. At the Cork quarter sessions in 1842 'the court considered it an exceedingly afflicting circumstance to find 140 or 150 degrees granted for sums so low as three, four and five shillings, the cost upon which amounted to 6s 6d'.[43] Distraint, a process which could at best prove profitable and at worst inexpensive, was used to counteract defaulters whenever possible. The limits of the collector's powers of distraint were ill-defined. The Commissioners believed that 'the collector cannot force open outer doors, but if he can get into a house ... without force he may break open inner doors'.[44] To such efforts the ratepayers reacted predictably. At Skibbereen a collector fled from a mob that desired to deprive him of his ears. A Galway collector in attempting to distrain two horses was set upon by a crowd 'who assaulted me violently with stones and threatened to deprive me of my life'.[45] In Tipperary a woman was killed in a scuffle with collectors who were attempting to levy a distress in lieu of a 4d assessment.[46] Police, accompanied not infrequently by troops, were summoned to the aid of collectors on 185 occasions in 21 unions during 1843.[47] The cost of such expeditions, particularly in view of the fact that very little was collected on these occasions, was the subject of angry comment in the Commons.[48] Further up the social scale gentlemen ratepayers showed themselves to be less violent but no less reluctant to pay.[49]

Part of the problem in Ireland stemmed from the slow and unsteady impact of the law upon mendicancy in the early years and the accompanying conviction amongst ratepayers that they were paying for an inefficient system as well as being importuned on the streets.[50] In Scotland the relief system had operated, though with decreasing effectiveness, until the Disruption of 1843 which split the distribution of church poor funds and brought about a critical situation.[51]

Many of the more serious problems which had attended the introduction of the poor law to Ireland were related to the basic unfamiliarity of the institution.[52] It was to this difficulty that the framers of the Scottish Act of 1845 were to address themselves. In a notable departure from the practice in England and Ireland no serious attempt was made by the Scottish Royal Commission to ferret out the mainsprings of poverty in the region.[53] Clearly by 1844 the decision had already been taken not to reform the Scottish relief system primarily in relation to social and environmental needs but rather to complete the extension of the centrally controlled New Poor Law to the remaining areas of the British Isles. In England the new system had been roughly grafted onto the social fabric, replacing the existing relief mechanisms. In Ireland, which was without experience of institutional relief, it had settled like an invading army. But in regard to Scotland James Graham, who had been Home Secretary during the worst of the Irish anti-rate campaign, was determined 'to adhere as much as possible to the ancient law ... with respect to the poor'.[54]

In the institutional sense the key distinction between the Scottish Board of Supervision and the poor law commissioners as they operated in England and Ireland *seems* to have resided in the passivity of the former as compared to the activity of the latter. The powers exercised by the commissioners in Ireland were sweeping. The administration of the 1838 Act was to be entirely 'subject to the direction and control of the commissioners'; this included dictatorial power in relation to all personnel (including guardians) involved in any capacity whatsoever under the provisions of the Act.[55] The only sphere in which the commissioners could exercise no direct control was in the appointment of guardians, who had to be elected by the ratepayers. In the event of the electoral system failing to produce a competent guardian the commissioners were empowered to 'appoint any person whom they may deem fit' to temporarily fill the gap.[56] The power of forming unions and of altering the boundaries of those unions was held exclusively by the commissioners.[57] The Scottish Act of 1845 contained no such sweeping declarations. Most of those early sections which relate to the Board of Supervision are concerned with the Board's powers to regulate its own proceedings and to make enquiries. No reference is made to the relationship between the central authority and the parochial boards until the section allowing the attendance of Board of Supervision clerks at local meetings.[58] Parishes were to be combined for poor law administration purposes at the discretion of parochial boards.[59] The 'whole administration' of the Act was placed 'under the direction and control' of the parochial boards.[60]

These features had led commentators on the 1845 Act to emphasise the essential dissimilarity between it and the poor law elsewhere. The *advisory* character of the Board of Supervision and the absence of compulsion in the provisions of the Act have been stressed. It has been accepted that James Graham's intention to adhere to the ancient law of Scotland was sincere and that the relative success of the Scottish relief experiment was a direct result of this policy.[61] The Scottish poor law has been seen even as fitting into a recent historiographical trend which emphasises the continuity between old and new poor relief systems in the nineteenth century.[62] On the surface therefore, the differing experiences of relief administrators in the two regions and in particular the relatively untroubled introduction of the Scottish poor law would seem to support the hypothesis that the government and the commissioners had learned their lesson in Ireland and accordingly had adopted a 'softer' approach when planning the 1845 Act. But a closer look at the legislation as well as at the experiences of some Scottish local boards suggests that the differences between the two Acts lie less in their content than in their appearance. While it is true that combination of particular parishes in Scotland had to wait upon application from the parochial boards themselves, the Board of Supervision did reserve to itself the power to foist additional parishes upon an existing combination on application from the parishes concerned, and 'if they see fit'.[63] As in Ireland, the central authority retained a firm hold on election procedures.[64] Similarly the manner of imposing the assessment could not be implemented without the approval of the Board of Supervision.[65] While it is true that the power of appointing the Inspector of the Poor lay with each local board, he was then responsible to both levels of the authority but could be removed only by the Board of Supervision.[66] While it was true that the parochial boards were allowed to draw up their own regulations for the management of poorhouses, no poorhouses could be built or in any way structurally altered nor could any regulations be put into practise without the approval of the central authority.[67] While the provision whereby a pauper could complain directly to the central authority of inadequate treatment by the local board may have constituted one of the more truly enlightened aspects of the 1845 Act, it also represented the ultimate type of interference by the Board of Supervision in parochial affairs.[68] A study of the Edinburgh City Board has revealed that 'a certain amount' of unwanted attention 'was forced upon' the Board by the central authority, 'both through complaints and subsequent investigation' and via the inspectors.[69]

In all these most important respects the control and direction of the poor law in Scotland was retained, as in Ireland, in the hands of the central authority. What had been learned from the Irish experience was not that smooth administration should be rooted in devolution but rather that a greater degree of subtlety was required. The essence of the relationship between central authority and local management had not changed between 1838 and 1845. What had altered was the attitude of the government and perhaps also of the central authority at Somerset House towards that relationship. This change reflected a new awareness that the efficient and productive administration of the poor law depended not only on the administrators but also on the attitudes of those on whom the system was being imposed.

NOTES

1. For instance M. A. Crowther, *The Workhouse System, 1834–1929* (London, 1981).
2. Quoted in Sir G. Nicholls, *A History of the Irish Poor Law* (London, 1856).
3. Sir George Nicholls (1781–1865), poor-law reformer who advocated abolition of outdoor relief and reliance solely upon the workhouse test; one of the first poor law commissioners appointed under the Amendment Act of 1834; resident poor law commissioner in Ireland 1839–42.
4. R. A. Cage, The Scottish Poor Law, 1745–1845 (unpublished Ph.D. thesis, University of Glasgow, 1974, p. 194.
5. Nicholls left for Ireland in mid-August 1836 and presented the first of three reports on the feasibility of the New Poor Law in an Irish setting on 15 November 1836.
6. N. C. Edsall, *The Anti-Poor Law Movement, 1834–44* (Manchester, 1971), *passim.*
7. A. Paterson, A Study of Poor Relief Administration in Edinburgh City Parish, between 1845–1894 (unpublished Ph.D. thesis, University of Edinburgh, 1974), pp. 12–13.
8. Ibid., p. 12.
9. Edsall, p. 46.
10. 1 & 2 Vic., cap. 56.
11. *The Constitution*, 23 Feb. 1841.
12. B. Inglis, *The Freedom of the Press in Ireland, 1784–1841* (London, 1954), pp. 219–20; R. B. McDowell, *The Irish Administration, 1801–1914* (London, 1964), p. 178.
13. *The Constitution*, 29 June, 26 Sept. 1839.
14. *The Constitution*, 16 July 1839; *Tuam Herald*, 18 Apr. 1840.
15. *7th Annual Report of the Poor Law Commissioners* (London, 1841), pp. 89–90.
16. D. E. Gladstone, The Administration and Reform of Poor Relief in Scotland 1790–1850 with especial reference to Stirlingshire (unpublished M.Litt. thesis, University of Stirling, 1973), p. 228.
17. *1st Annual Report of the Board of Supervision*, (P.P. 1847, XXVIII), appendix B, p. 27.
18. 1 & 2 Vic., cap. 56, sec. 27; 8 & 9 Vic., cap. 83, sec. 15.

19. *Glasgow Herald*, 3, 31 Oct. 1845.
20. *Freeman's Journal*, 25 June 1842.
21. *Freeman's Journal*, 7 Apr. 1842; *The Constitution*, 16 Feb, 2 Jan. 1841; *Tipperary Constitution*, 3 Feb. 1843.
22. *Freeman's Journal*, 5 Feb. 1842.
23. *The Constitution*, 26 Sept. 1839, 25 Aug. 1840.
24. *Tuam Herald*, 22 Feb. 1840.
25. Commissioners to Limerick Board, 24 Sept. 1844, P.R.O.I. Poor Law Commissioners' Paper, 1A/50/21, vol. 6; *Londonderry Journal*, 15 Oct. 1844.
26. *Londonderry Journal*, 26 Nov. 1844. At this time the guardians had not actually resigned because the commissioners had not accepted their resignations.
27. Commissioners to J. Burke, 17 Oct. 1844 as in 1st reference, note 25; *Londonderry Journal*, 19, 26 Nov. 1844; *11th Annual Report* (1845), p. 38.
28. Paterson, p. 89; Gladstone, pp. 236–7.
29. Paterson, pp. 87–8.
30. Ibid., p. 89.
31. *8th Annual Report* (1842), pp. 288–9.
32. L. C. Wright, *Scottish Chartism* (Edinburgh, 1953), p. 15.
33. Robert Willis (1799–1878), surgeon and medical writer.
34. *Glasgow Herald*, 11 July 1845.
35. Paterson, pp. 175–6.
36. G. O'Brien, 'The New Poor Law in Pre-Famine Ireland: A Case History', *Ir. Ec. & Soc. Hist.* XII (1985); G. O'Brien, The Administration of the Poor Law in Ireland, 1838–1853 (unpublished M.A. thesis, University College, Cork, 1980), pp. 117–19.
37. Paterson, p. 177.
38. Ibid., pp. 236–7.
39. *Freeman's Journal*, 18 Feb., 5 Mar. 1842.
40. *Ibid.*, 25 Mar., 8 Apr. 1842.
41. *The Constitution*, 6 Oct. 1840.
42. *Tipperary Constitution*, 12 May 1843.
43. *Cork Examiner*, 6 Apr. 1842.
44. State Paper Office of Ireland, Chief Secretary's Office, 2nd div. Reg. Papers, 1843, A/118.
45. Ibid.
46. *Tipperary Constitution*, 18 Aug. 1843.
47. *Returns of the Dates on which and the Places where the Military or police have been employed in enforcing the Collection of Poor Rates in Ireland* . . ., (P.P. 1844, XL), 2-5.
48. *Londonderry Journal*, 2 Apr. 1844.
49. *Cork Examiner*, 3 Aug. 1842; Miles Walsh (rate collector) to Ballinrobe Board, 15 Aug. 1843 (State Paper Office of Ireland, Chief Secretary's Office, 2nd Div. Reg. Papers, 1843, 0/11668).
50. O'Brien thesis, pp. 128–30.
51. Paterson, p. 11.
52. G. O'Brien, 'The Establishment of Poor Law Unions in Ireland, 1838–43', *I.H.S.* XVIII (1982), pp. 97–120.
53. Paterson, p. 6.
54. Quoted in Paterson, p. 204.
55. 1 & 2 vic., cap. 56, sec. 3.
56. Sec. 25.
57. Sec. 15 & 16.
58. 8 & 9 Vic., cap. 83, sec. 15.
59. Sec. 16.
60. Sec. 17.

61. Paterson, pp. 12–14.
62. Gladstone, pp. 228–30, 246–7.
63. 8 & 9 Vic., cap. 83, sec. 16.
64. Sec. 18, 19, 20.
65. Sec. 24 & 25.
66. Sec. 55 & 56.
67. Sec. 63 & 64.
68. Sec. 74.
69. Paterson, p. 88.

15

DIETARY DIRECTIONS: A TOPOGRAPHICAL SURVEY OF IRISH DIET, 1836

L. A. Clarkson and E. Margaret Crawford

This essay examines food consumption patterns among the bottom one-third of the population, focusing specifically on the evidence contained in the report of the Poor Inquiry, 1836, and drawing also on an investigation into diets carried out by the Poor Law authorities in 1839.[1] Our first objective is to establish the broad eating patterns among the labouring classes across the country. The second is to show how the basic pattern varied regionally. Related to this is a third objective, of discerning dietary differences within the labouring classes who are often treated as as lumpen a mass as the potatoes they consumed. Finally we attempt to put pre-Famine Irish diets into perspective by comparing them with diets in Scotland at roughly the same time, and also with labouring diets in Ireland in the second half of the nineteenth century.

Before going further we must consider whether the Poor Inquiry report provides a reliable picture of Irish diets. The commissioners dispatched lengthy questionnaires to prominent residents of the 2,500 or so parishes in Ireland. One question asked was: 'what is the ordinary diet . . . of the labouring classes of your parish?' It was straightforward save for the use of the adjective 'ordinary' and was answered by most respondents although a few replied with useless statements such as 'the diet is very low'. Discarding these, we are left with 1,569 usable answers; 61 witnesses came from urban areas and the rest from the countryside. Many answers referred to groups of two, three or four parishes. Against this there were 241 parishes or groups for which there was more than one respondent. All told, we have information from about 65 per cent of the parishes in Ireland. Table 1 shows the provincial distribution.

Ulster and Leinster were over-represented, Munster slightly under-represented and Connacht considerably so. The main consequence of the biased distribution is to skew the national picture towards the two eastern — and better-off — provinces.[2]

Table 1. Poor Inquiry, 1836: Food Respondents by Province

Province	*Number*	*Percentage*	*Population Share 1841*
Ulster	525	33.6	29.2
Leinster	445	28.4	24.1
Munster	428	27.3	29.2
Connacht	171	10.9	17.4

Since the commissioners did not interrogate the poor directly but sought information from their social superiors, the results may be coloured by the prejudices of the observers. There were four categories of witnesses: Church of Ireland clergy, Catholic priests, Presbyterian ministers, and the 'gentry' (landlords, land agents, J.P.s, peers, esquires, plus the occasional police superintendent and manufacturer). The gentry were exclusively Protestant, so effectively we have a Protestant-Catholic split among the testimonies. Table 2 shows that over three-quarters of the reports came from Protestants in a country that was over three-quarters Catholic. Even in Ulster, Catholics were under-represented, as were Presbyterians in a province where they formed 26 per cent of the population.[3]

Table 2. Proportion of Witnesses to the Poor Inquiry by Socio-Religious Status

Province	*R.C.*	*C. of I.*	*Gentry*	*Presb.*
Ulster	18.7	42.2	21.5	17.4
Leinster	24.4	39.7	35.3	0.6
Munster	21.1	43.0	35.1	0.8
Connacht	29.8	32.3	37.3	0.6
Ireland	22.1	40.9	30.7	6.4

Does it matter? After all, secular as opposed to spiritual succour is not a matter of profound doctrinal dispute. To test whether the testimonies of witnesses varied according to religion or status, the answers coming from parishes or groups of parishes supplying more than one response have been examined. These places produced a total of 568 answers and there was general agreement among witnesses. All stressed the dominance of potatoes and the unimportance of other foods. Nevertheless, there were interesting differences in the numbers of foods noted (see Table 3). Catholic priests had a narrower vision than other witnesses, with those of the south and west taking a particularly restricted view. There were also other subtle differences. Priests, for example, were much more likely to distinguish between buttermilk and whole milk; being close to their parishioners they knew that labourers were rarely able to afford whole milk. Few priests in Ulster remarked on the consumption of oatmeal, presumably because their flocks rarely

Table 3. Total Number of Foods Mentioned by Witnesses

Province	*R.C.* N=87	*C. of I.* N=215	*Gentry* N=205	*Presb.* N=61
Ulster	11	18	15	14
Leinster	10	15	17	—
Munster	8	11	14	—
Connacht	8	10	13	—

ate it, unlike Presbyterian and Episcopalian labourers. But outside Ulster there were relatively few Protestant labourers and all witnesses were observing similar sections of society.

The gentry, it might be thought, were socially remote from the poor. Nevertheless, they had a good idea of how their labourers lived. Elizabeth Smith, for example, wife of a County Wicklow landowner in the 1840s and '50s, focused a sharp and unsympathetic eye on them. A charity shilling, she believed, would be spent on tea and snuff even when they were starving. But she also knew that a man with a wife and children consumed over 40 pounds of potatoes a day.[4]

More important than the status of the witnesses was the interpretation put upon the words 'ordinary diet'. 'Potatoes are the usual diet of the labouring classes in these parishes', wrote the parish priest of Kilmurray and Kilfarboy, County Clare, behaving as a good examination candidate in answering the question set. On the other hand, another County Clare witness wandered from the question by replying: 'potatoes chiefly, with occasionally milk, herrings, and cheap meat'.[5] The differences introduce a slight distortion into the testimony; in reality, diets were probably a little more varied than the Inquiry suggests.

Related to this problem is the failure of witnesses to mention the glaringly obvious. The parish priest of Ardnugeehy, County Cork, asserted that the poor in his parish subsisted on 'potatoes and water', but according to a neighbour they lived on 'potatoes only'. Although rarely mentioned, water must have been drunk by labourers everywhere. Indeed, in 1839 it was explicitly described as 'the only beverage' of the poor when the milk supply failed.[6] The same line of reasoning suggests that berries, wild fruit, nettles, rabbits, hedgehogs and game were eaten more often than the Inquiry suggests.

None of these reservations undermines the value of the Poor Inquiry. The answers it contains have been coded for computer analysis according to the frequency of consumption as shown in Table 4.[7] The coded data have been used in

Table 4. Frequency Scoring of Food Consumption

Daily	5
Weekly	4
Monthly	3
Sometimes, seldom, occasionally	2
Seasonal, festival, etc.	1

two ways. First, the number of times a food was mentioned, regardless of frequency, has been counted and the percentage of observations mapped, county by county. Second, the percentage of observations has been combined with the frequency code to calculate an *intensity index*. For example every respondent from County Mayo reported that potatoes were eaten daily; the index therefore is 500. It is possible for a value to be produced in more than one way (100 per cent $\times$ 4, and 80 per cent $\times$ 5, for example). Nevertheless, the *intensity index* is a useful method of combining information about the geographical distribution of consumption with information about the regularity of consumption.

Table 5 and maps 1–11 summarise consumption patterns for the eleven foods most commonly mentioned in the Inquiry. Milk has been treated as a single item but we have retained the distinction between herrings and other fish made by many witnesses. There were some other foods mentioned — sugar, flour, pork, poultry, cabbage, onions, seaweed — but very infrequently and they are therefore omitted. There were many references to salt in the Report but we have not treated it as a food.

A notable omission is alcohol which most witnesses ignored. But there was a separate question asking about the number of public houses and illicit stills, and one or two respondents linked their answers to this to their responses on diet. One witness from Clonmel, for instance, exclaimed 'how much more their [i.e. the poor] want of food and raiment is increased by the use of ardent spirits . . .' In 1839 a Poor Law official reported a decline in the 'pernicious custom of whiskey-drinking', which he attributed to the temperance movement and an increased consumption of tea, coffee and bread. This was being wildly optimistic; it was poverty, not temperance, that restricted whiskey and beer-drinking to the occasional binge.[8]

The foods have been listed according to the value of the coefficient of variation. This is a convenient way to indicate whether consumption was widespread or regionally concentrated. The maps contain similar information with the added advantage of showing consumption county by county. Potatoes were clearly a class apart with only milk in its various forms coming at all close to them. Three-quarters of all witnesses reported its consumption, with little variation in the

Table 5. National food consumption patterns, 1836

(1)	*(2)*	*(3)*	*(4)*	*(5)*
Potatoes	32	100.0	—	—
Milk	32	74.4	13.6	.18
Herrings	32	25.8	12.1	.47
Beef	31	14.0	7.9	.56
Oatmeal	31	28.4	21.2	.75
Butter	30	10.1	7.8	.77
Eggs	23	6.0	6.5	1.08
Fish	21	6.9	7.9	1.14
Bread	25	7.6	9.3	1.24
Tea	14	2.3	3.1	1.35
Bacon	23	4.0	5.7	1.44

(1) Food
(2) Number of counties reporting consumption
(3) Percentages of parishes in Ireland naming certain foods
(4) Standard deviation of county percentages from national averages in (3)
(5) Coefficient of variation.

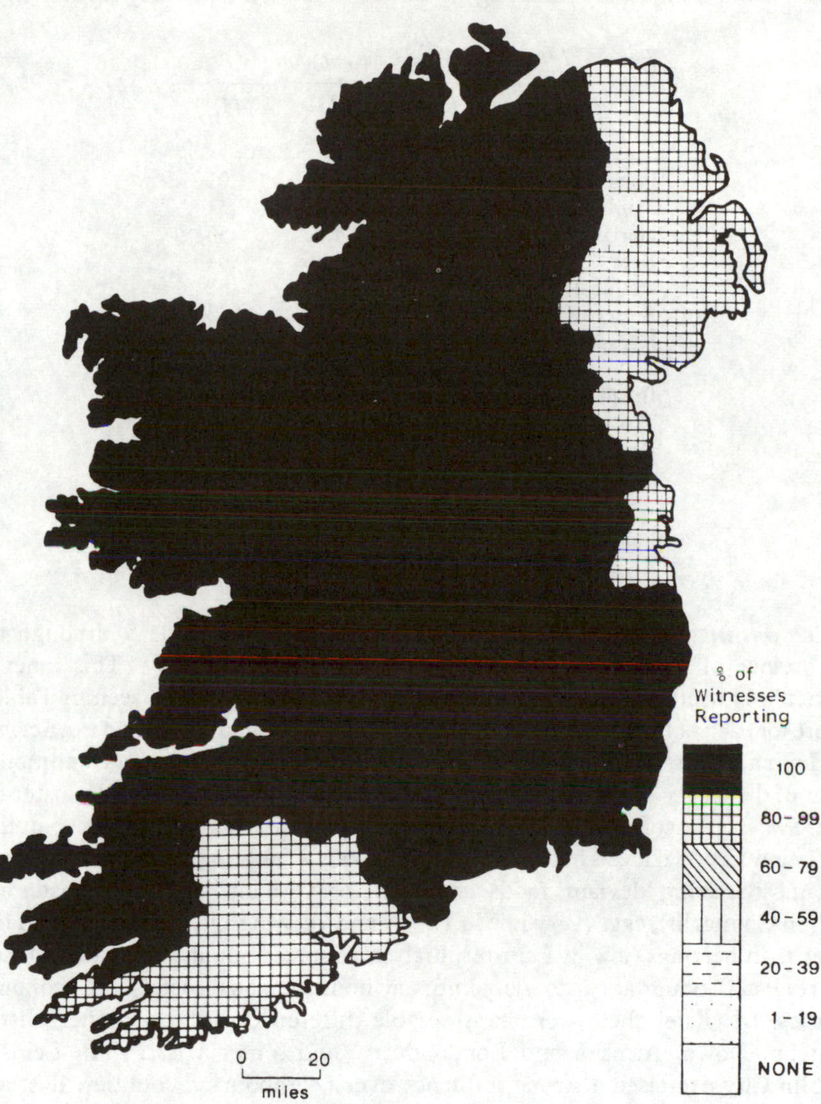

proportion from county to county. However, the *intensity index* (see Table 6) of milk was less than half that of potatoes. Roughly a quarter of witnesses reported the consumption of herrings and oatmeal but the regional distribution of the two was different. Herrings were eaten throughout Ireland, although less extensively in the midland counties; the consumption of oatmeal, on the other hand, was skewed towards the northern and eastern counties. Beef and butter consumption were noted in most counties, beef, surprisingly, more frequently than butter. However, both the numbers of witnesses involved and the frequency of use were very low. The consumption of the remaining foods was small and regionally restricted.

Table 6. Intensity of Food Consumption, 1836

(1)	*(2)* (max=500)	*(3)*	*(4)*
Potatoes	496	7.3	.01
Milk	242	73.8	.31
Herrings	82	45.2	.55
Beef	33	21.0	.64
Oatmeal	104	85.4	.82
Butter	37	30.8	.83
Eggs	23	26.1	1.13
Fish	22	26.0	1.18
Bread	28	39.3	1.38
Tea	8	11.8	1.48
Bacon	11	16.1	1.44

(1) Food
(2) Intensity index, average of 32 counties
(3) Standard deviation of (2)
(4) Coefficient of variation.

The *intensity index* (Table 6) confirms the pattern in Table 5 although the importance of potatoes and milk emerges even more strongly. This index is particularly useful in demonstrating regional patterns as can be seen in Table 7 where for each of the four provinces its value has been calculated as a percentage of the Irish average. A marked east-west pattern emerges. In Ulster consumption of eight of the eleven foods was at or above the national average and in Leinster the figure was ten out of eleven. In Munster and Connacht, by contrast, consumption was below national levels in the case of seven foods — although not the same seven. The most striking 'deviant' foods were butter (a very low value in Munster and high in Connacht), eggs (very low in Ulster and very high in Connacht), and fish other than herrings (low in Leinster, high in Munster but absent in Connacht).

Provincial boundaries do not embrace homogeneous social and economic entities. In Ulster there were considerable differences between 'inner Ulster' (Antrim, Down, Armagh and Londonderry) and 'outer Ulster'.[9] In Leinster Dublin City exercised a strong influence over neighbouring counties. East and west Munster were economically different worlds; whilst in Connacht Leitrim was aberrant in matters of diet and possibly other things as well. To reveal intra-provincial differences we have resorted to one last statistical device. Simply by adding the eleven intensity indices for each county we have created a *variety index* shown in Table 8. Theoretically it could take any value between zero and 5,500; in practice the range was much narrower, between 800 (reflecting a potato and milk diet) and 1,600 (potatoes and milk plus a liberal scatter of other items). The index generally confirms the impression of more varied diets in the east than in the west. But it also reveals two bands of particularly poor diets: one running westwards

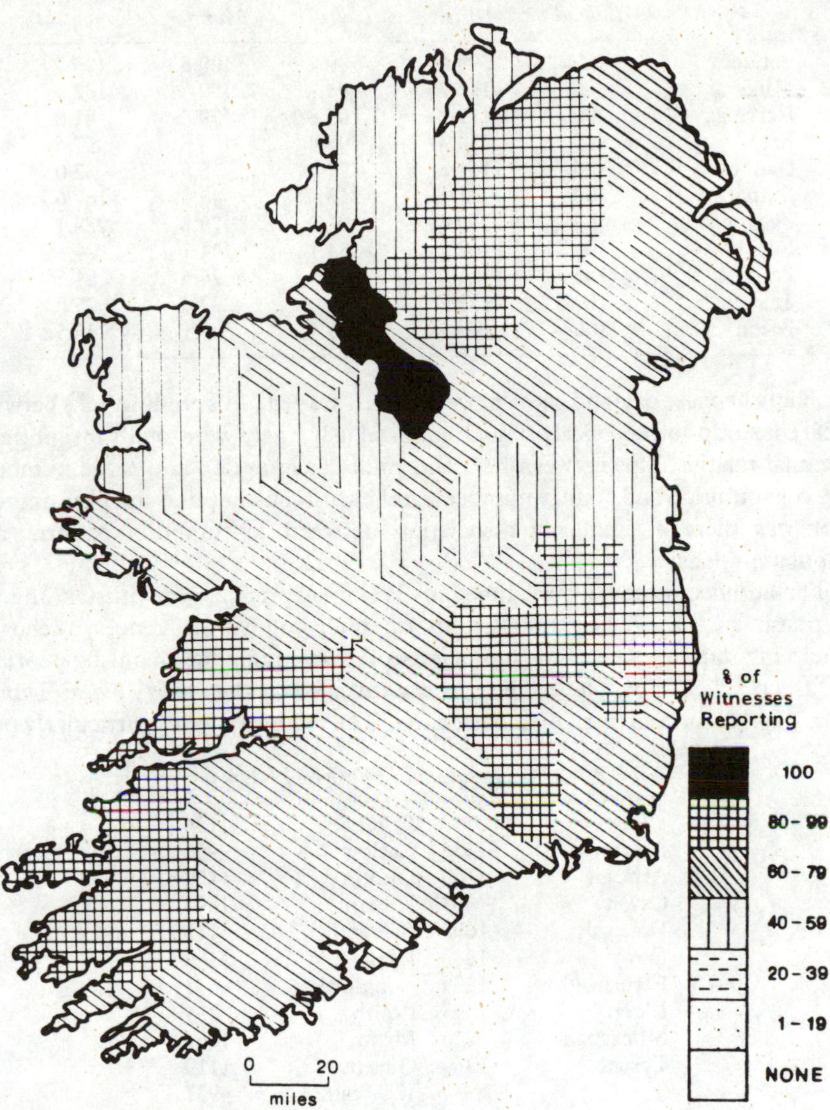

from north-east Leinster through south Ulster into Connacht; and a second in the south stretching westwards from Waterford to Limerick (see Map 12).

Attempts to relate consumption and regional production patterns do not get us very far except in the most obvious way. Mokyr has shown that in 1841 the potato acreage ranged between 7 and 29 per cent of the cultivated acreage of the individual counties; whether or not a county was at the lower or upper level was immaterial to consumption.[10] Correlating oatmeal consumption with the proportion of cultivated land under oats produces a low r^2 statistic of 0.19,

Table 7. Intensity Index by Province

Food	*Ireland*	*Ulster*	*Leinster*	*Munster*	*Connacht*
Potatoes	100	99.6	99.2	100.6	100.4
Milk	100	113.2	98.3	100.8	102.9
Herrings	100	119.7	103.8	79.4	81.8
Beef	100	139.4	97.0	75.6	57.6
Oatmeal	100	161.8	121.4	8.5	32.0
Butter	100	81.1	113.5	48.6	167.6
Eggs	100	39.6	101.3	79.3	229.1
Fish	100	112.2	54.1	144.1	—
Bread	100	81.0	183.1	24.6	31.7
Tea	100	112.5	150.0	37.5	25.0
Bacon	100	118.2	154.5	9.1	45.5

probably because oats and oatmeal were widely traded, thus eroding links between local consumption and local production. Similarly, there were totally insignificant regional relationships between beef and milk consumption and cattle numbers, egg consumption and poultry numbers, and bacon consumption and pig numbers. Nor was there a significant association between consumption patterns and population density.[11]

The absence of obvious relationships is not surprising. Notwithstanding the emphasis in the previous paragraphs on inter-county differences, the overwhelming impression is of the uniformity of diets among the labouring poor; the differences were tiny. Nevertheless those revealed by the *variety index* (Table 8 and Map 12) raise an intriguing possibility. The western zone of particularly poor

Table 8. Variety Index by Province and County

Ulster	1189	*Leinster*	1134
Antrim	1384	Carlow	950
Armagh	1149	Dublin	1450
Cavan	863	Kildare	1593
Donegal	1098	Kilkenny	1115
Down	1343	Kings	1148
Fermanagh	1239	Longford	811
L'derry	1395	Louth	834
Monaghan	1026	Meath	1061
Tyrone	1239	Queens	1119
		W'Meath	957
		Wexford	1286
		Wicklow	1288
Munster	921	*Connacht*	1029
Clare	1016	Galway	1032
Cork	969	Leitrim	1230
Kerry	911	Mayo	1024
Limerick	861	Roscommon	806
Tipperary	956	Sligo	1052
Waterford	812		

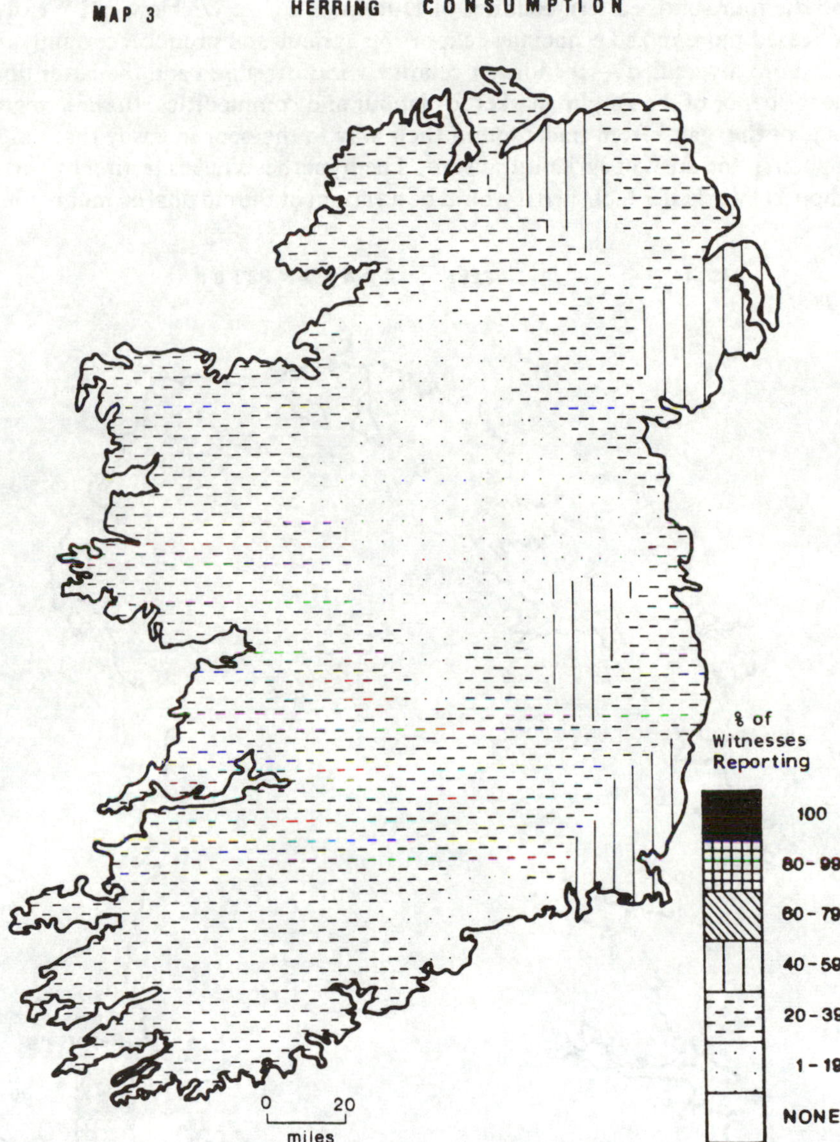

diets from Mayo to West Cork can plausibly be explained by poor agricultural conditions and a low level of commercialisation, but what of the two bands running roughly east-west in the north and south of the country? The former was a region of agricultural production serviced by the Boyne-Blackwater and upper-Shannon river systems; the latter by the Suir-Nore and lower-Shannon systems. These regions exported their agricultural surpluses, leaving the poor to live on commodities such as potatoes and buttermilk for which there was little external market. By contrast, counties with relatively good diets, particularly 'inner Ulster' and the four south-eastern counties of Dublin, Kildare, Wicklow and Wexford, possessed more mixed economies, exporting agricultural produce, certainly, but also more diversified — the former relatively industrialised and the latter under the influence of the Dublin market for labour and commodities. In these regions some of the 'gains from trade' found their way to the poor in a way that did not happen in the areas of agricultural vent. The hypothesis needs testing by further empirical work; if established it would be a variant of the old dual economy thesis.

MAP 4 BEEF CONSUMPTION

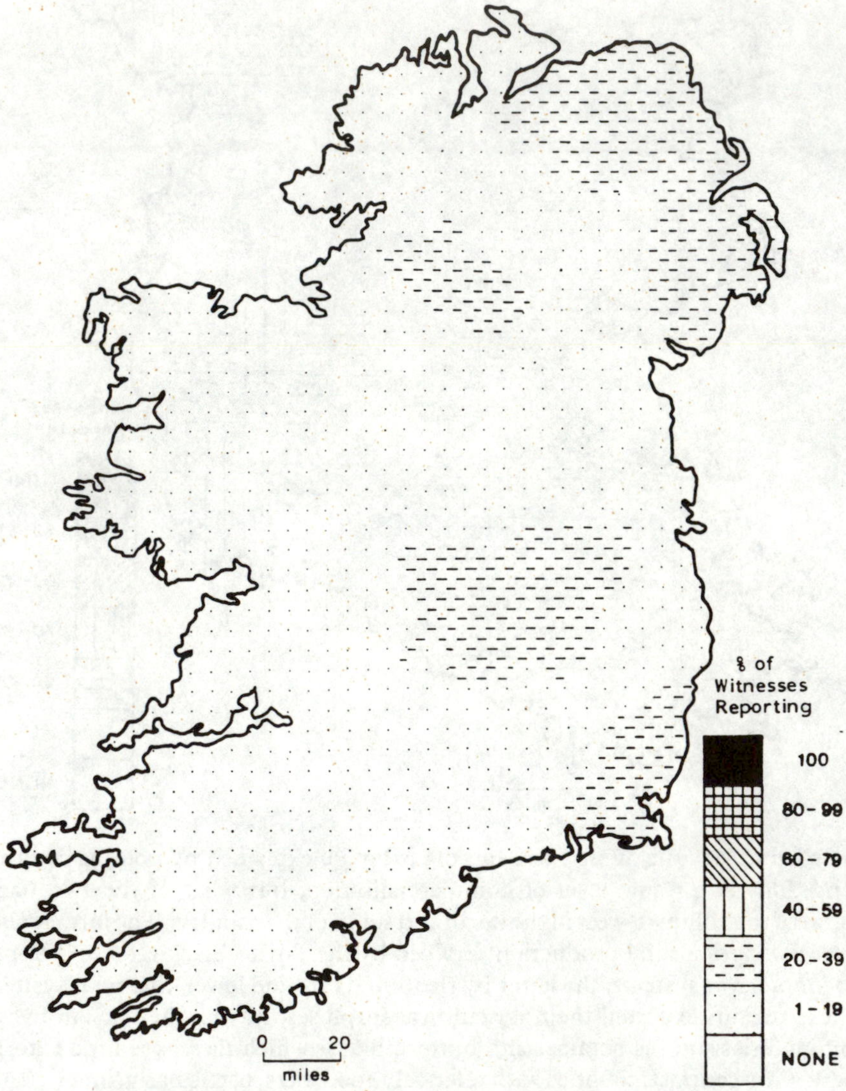

% of Witnesses Reporting

100
80-99
60-79
40-59
20-39
1-19
NONE

0 20
miles

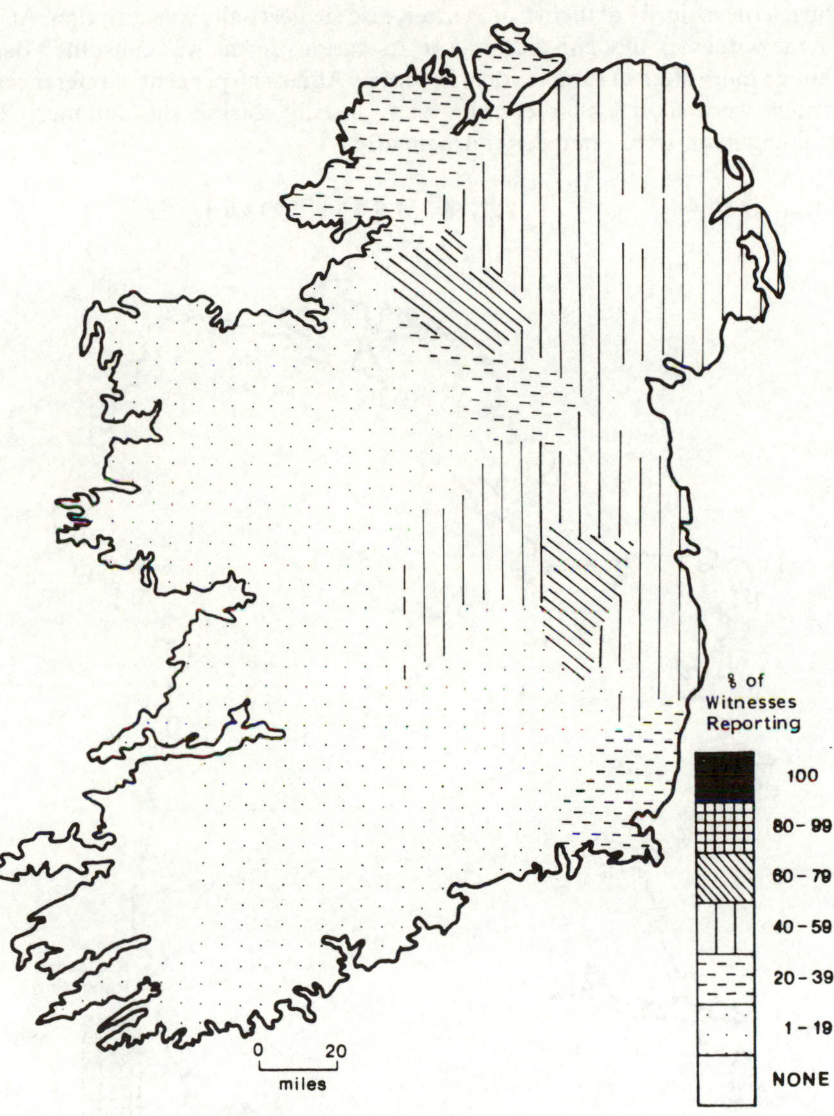

Turning from regional to seasonal differences in diet, in 1839 the Assistant Poor Law Commissioner, W. H. T. Hawley, remarked that 'the potato is eaten at every meal and throughout all seasons of the year'. Even the 'meal months' had diminished as the extensive cultivation of the prolific 'lumpers' and 'whites' enabled supplies to be stretched out for most of the year. For just a few weeks in the summer other foods such as 'oatmeal, eggs, butter, lard, dripping, and herrings [were] ... partially, though sparingly, substituted for [the potato]'.[12] Hawley's opinion was amply supported by the 1836 Inquiry where references stated or implied that the potato was eaten every day. Nearly two-thirds of the references to oatmeal, the majority of them from Ulster, also suggest daily consumption. About half the witnesses thought that milk in its various forms was consumed daily, although more often in summer than in winter. Almost 60 per cent of references to herrings were to irregular consumption, usually during the summer. The remaining items were eaten very infrequently.

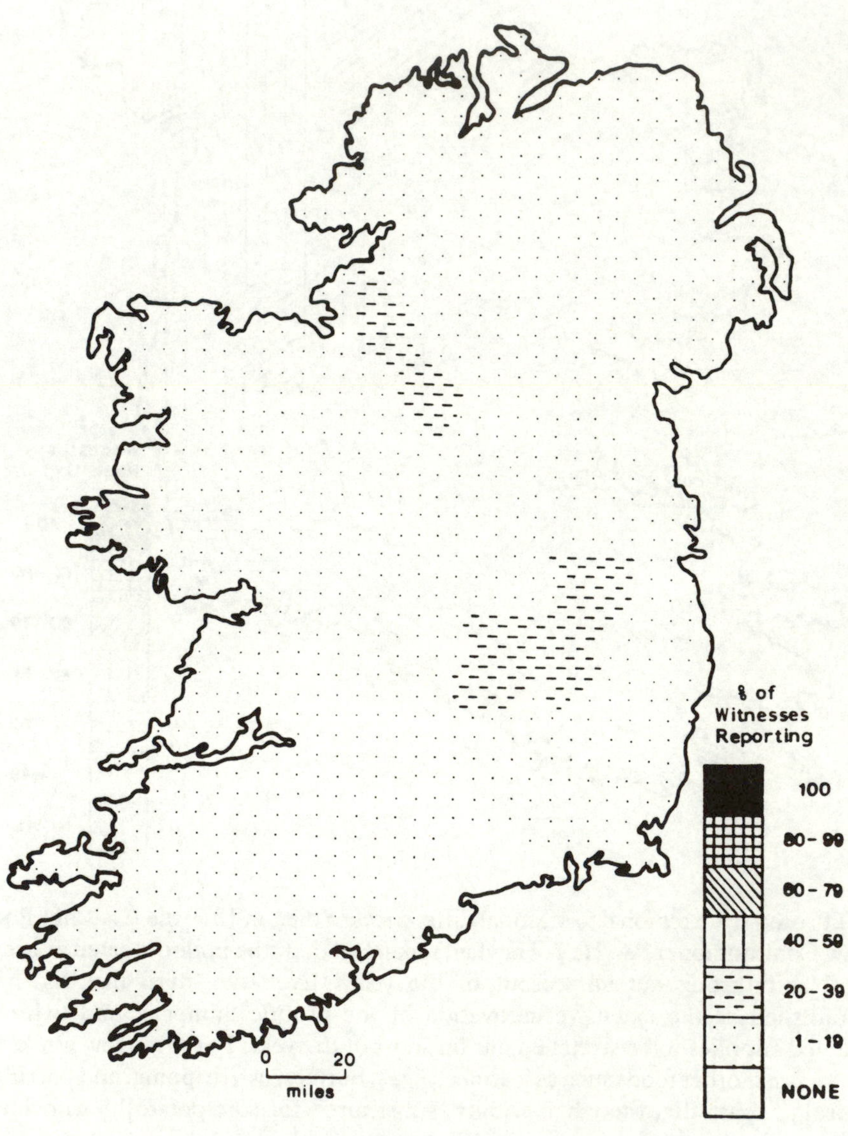

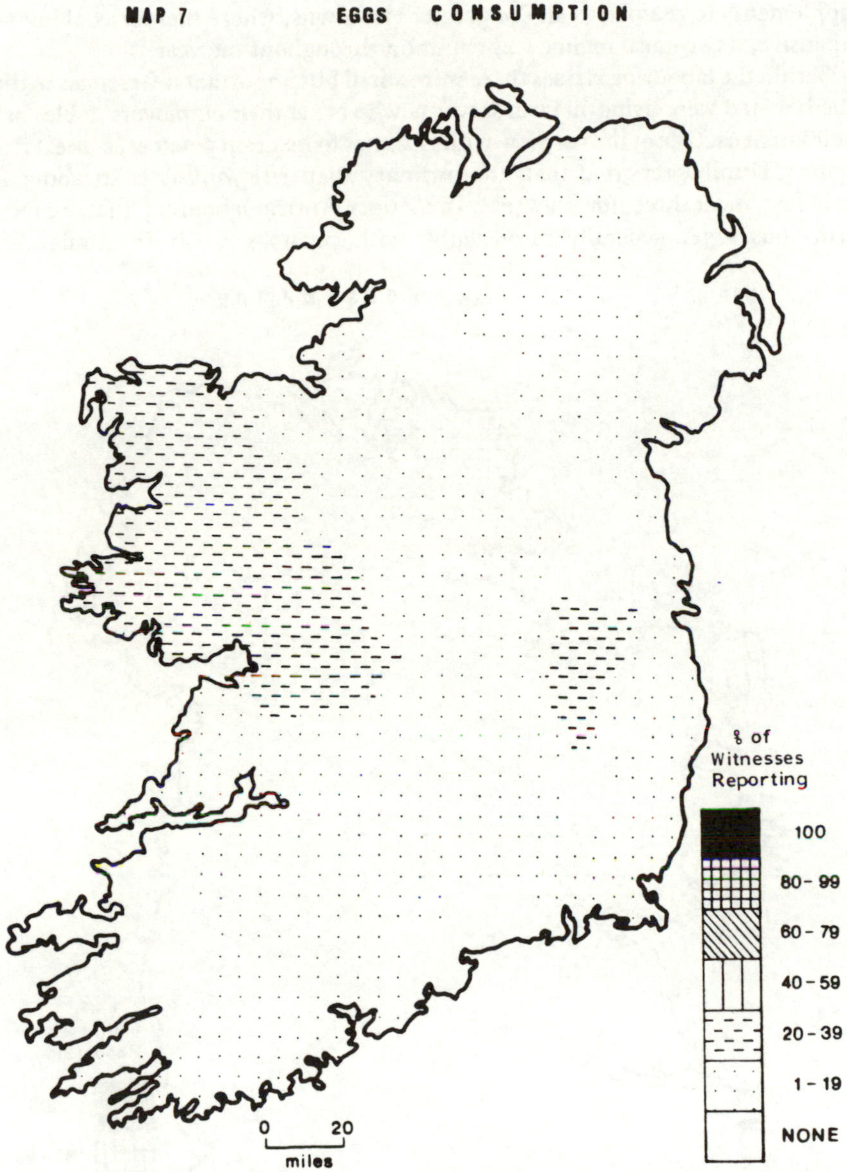

MAP 7 EGGS CONSUMPTION

% of Witnesses Reporting

100

80-99

60-79

40-59

20-39

1-19

NONE

0 20 miles

The greatest seasonal variation occurred not in the range of foods consumed but in the number of meals eaten during the day. In November, December and January when the days were short and 'when turf is scarce and dear, the supply of potatoes falling short, and employment scarce, supper is frequently omitted; but at other times, and under different circumstances, particularly where hard labour has to be performed, a third meal is partaken of.' The need to nourish physical exertion in the spring and summer with three daily meals made the demand for supplements to the potato all the greater. In towns, where fuel for cooking was expensive, a two-meal regime was common throughout the year.[13]

Within the labouring classes there were small but important differences in diet. The best-fed were living-in farm servants who ate at their employers' tables or in their kitchens. One of the very few witnesses not to mention potatoes, a priest from County Dublin, reported that 'the ordinary diet *with farmers* is stirabout for breakfast, meat three times a week'. In County Antrim labourers 'that are fed in farm-houses get generally meat daily, with potatoes ...'[14] In similar vein

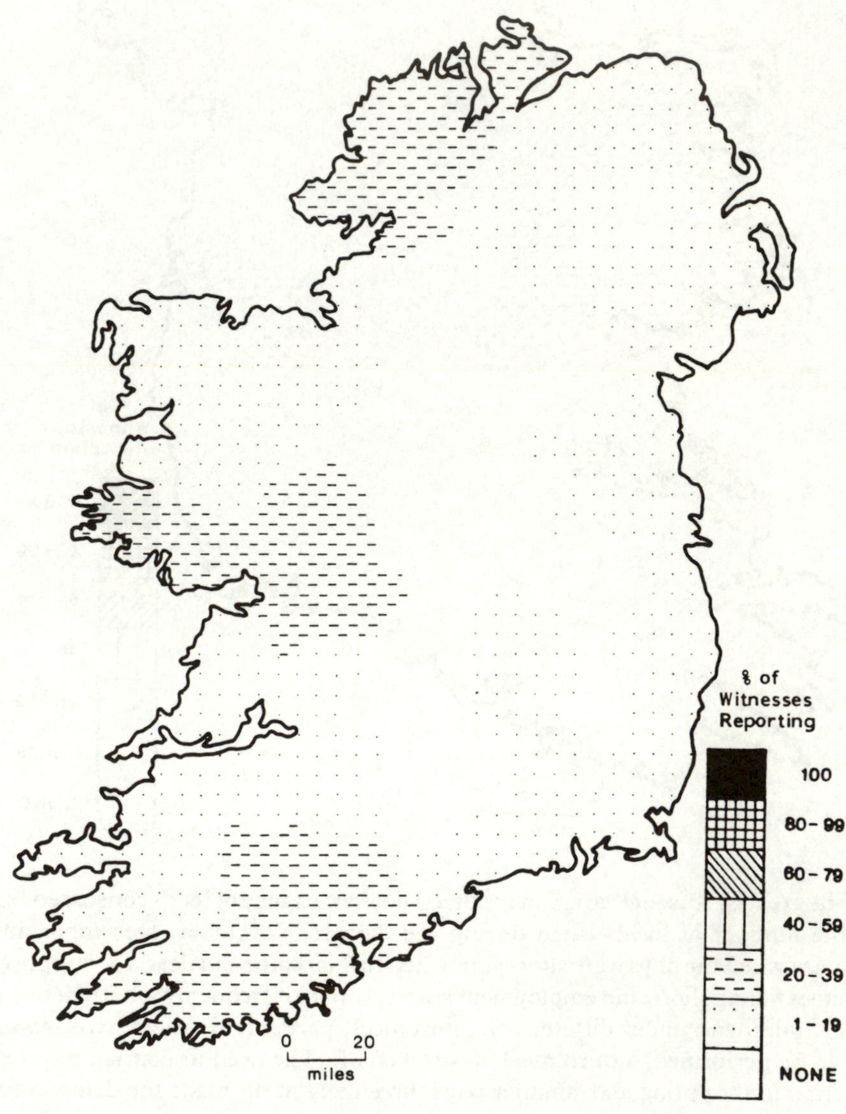

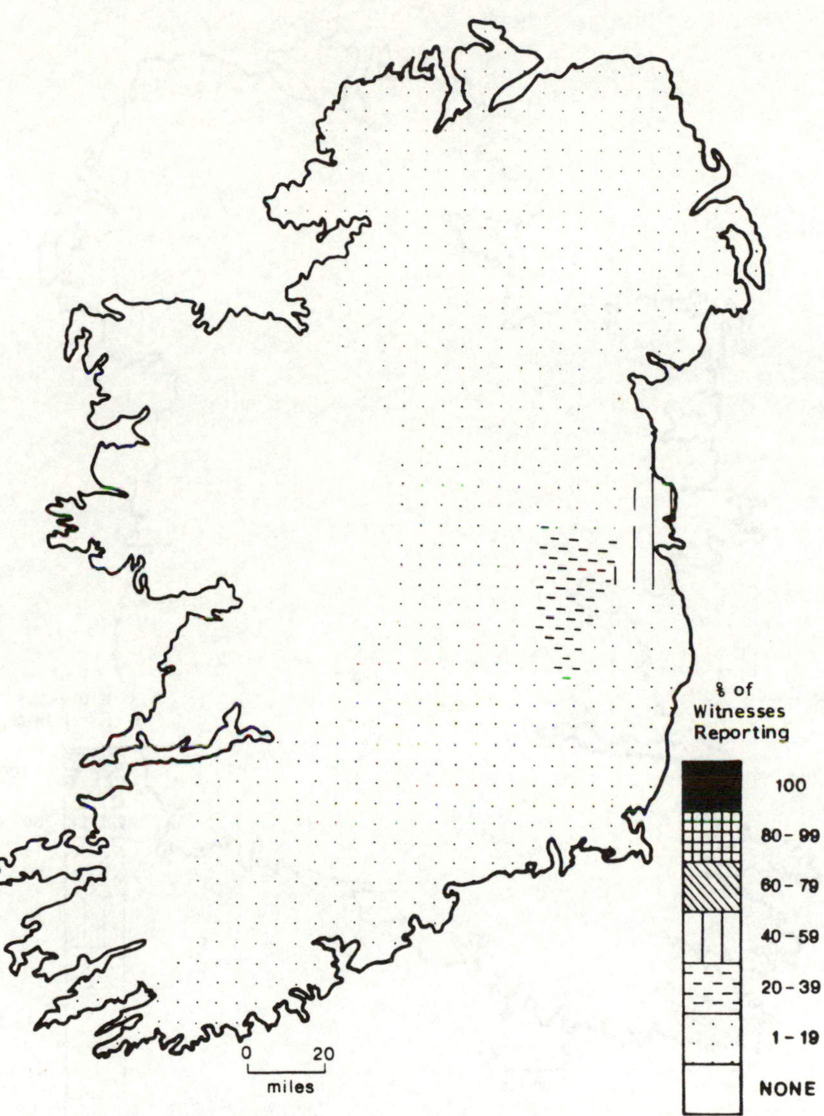

Elizabeth Smith recorded in her diary in September 1841 her abortive attempt to find a kitchen maid for a neighbour.

> ... fancy I shall fail, the progress of civilisation indisposing any girl who has a hope of doing better to take a situation where the women servants sleep on a shakedown in the *kitchen* , three together, bring all the water from the river, wash all the potatoes for man and beast, have low wages, meat but twice a week cut into rations in the parlour and sent out in portions; they would bear this well in a farmer's house and be glad to get the place but when with low degree in kitchen there is the utmost profusion in

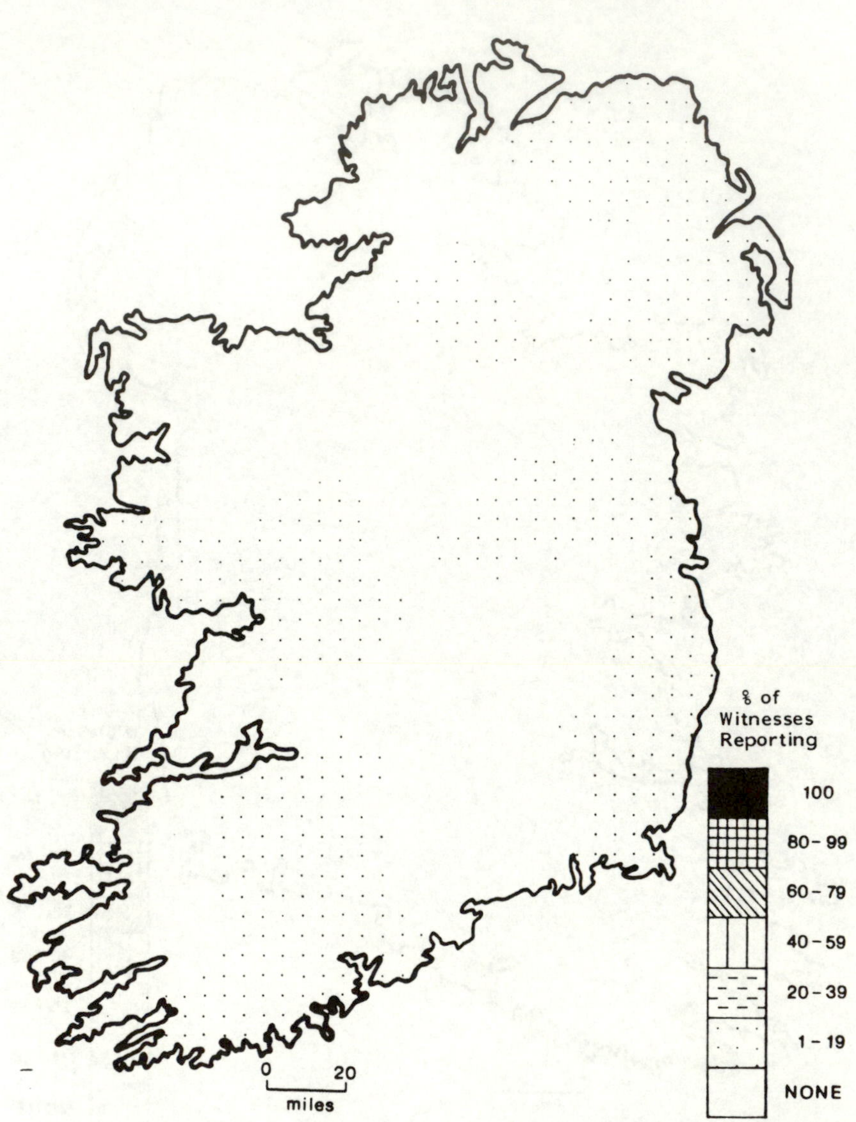

hall . . . they who practise such contradictions must be content with the refuse of the serving class . . .[15]

Apart from living-in servants, the most secure in their diets were rural labourers, who rented a cabin and land from farmers in return for labour, for they were assured of their potatoes. But because they existed in a semi-monetised state their ability to buy other foods was extremely limited. As a witness from County Limerick explained: 'the farmers prefer sending their milk to the next market town, though a distance of five miles Irish, to selling it to the labourer, who cannot

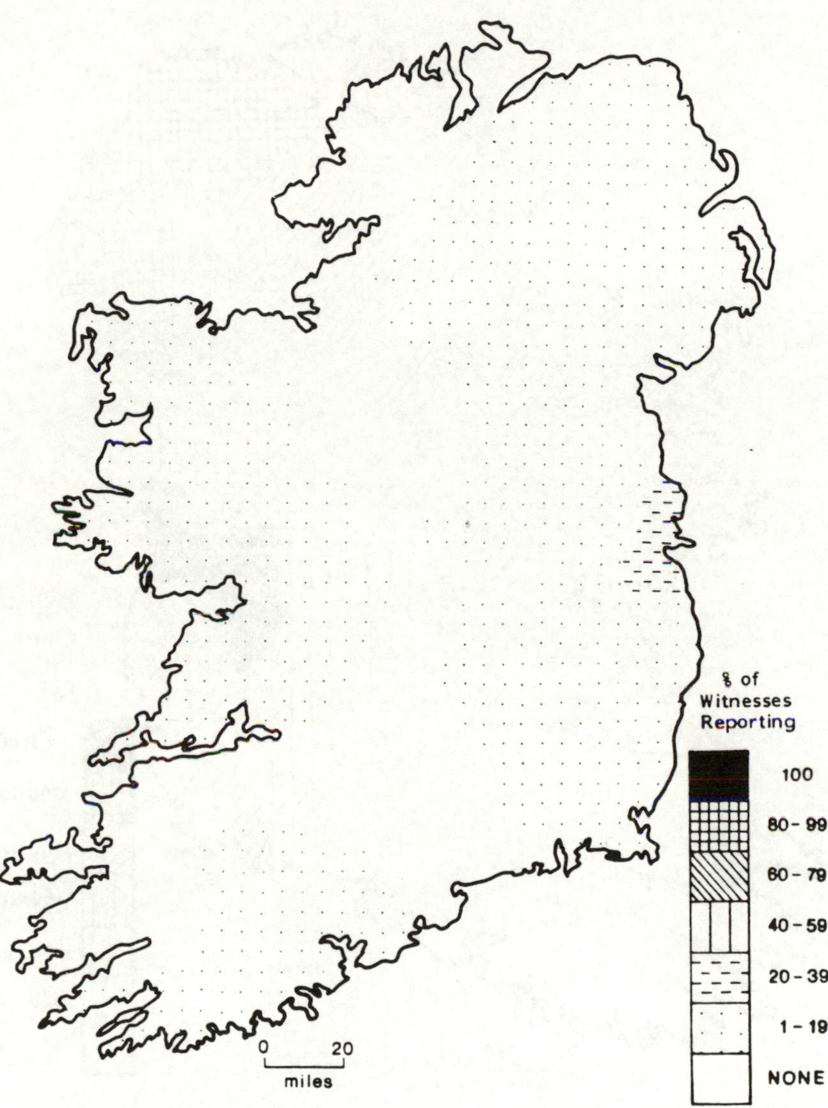

be a constant ready-money customer'. Unless they kept a cow, their best chance of securing milk was 'when they receive it from the generosity of the considerate farmer'.[16]

The most precarious section of the rural population were cabin dwellers working for money wages — when they worked at all — and who rented potato land on conacre, often at high rents. A Tipperary clergyman contrasted the condition of the better-off labourers renting a cabin and an acre or two of land with

MAP 12 FOOD VARIETY INDEX

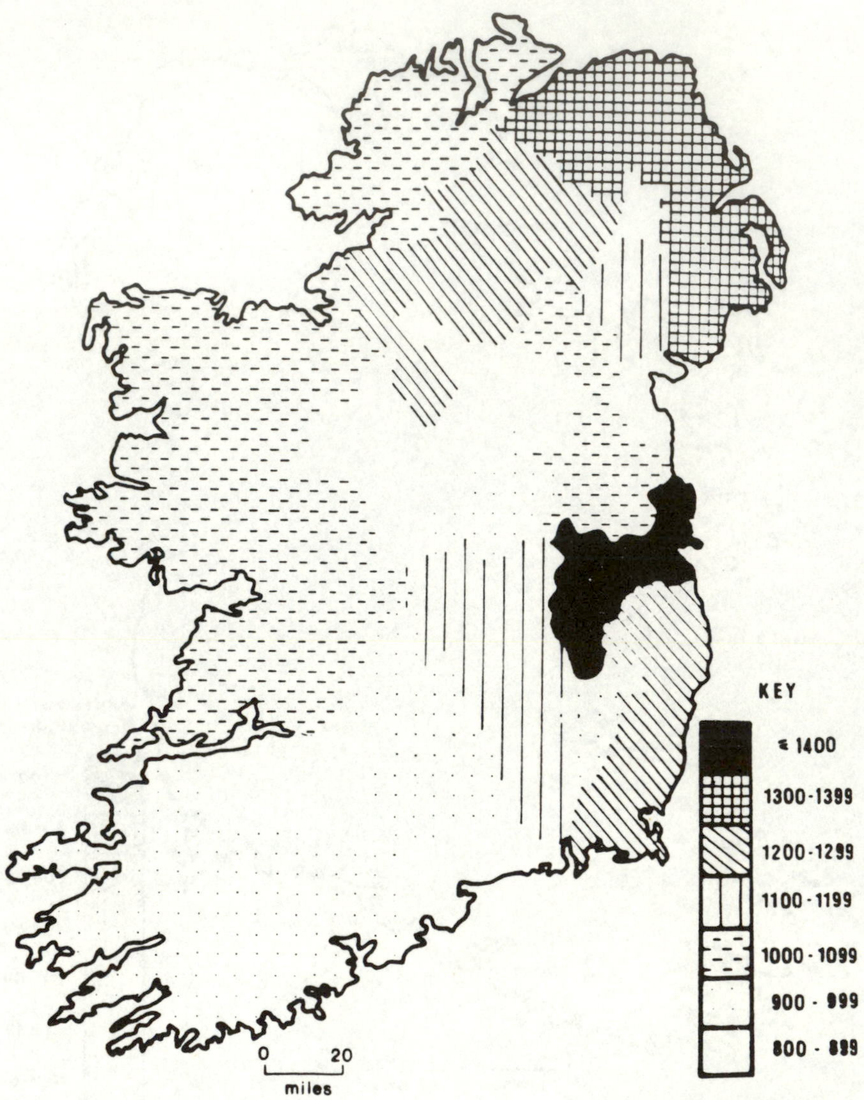

that of those possessing only a cabin. The former had potatoes and perhaps also milk, butter and bacon; 'the condition of the latter, especially when there is a family, and not sufficiently grown to labour, is generally very wretched'.[17] When unemployed, their survival was a mystery:

> When out of employment it has puzzled me to know how they subsist [confided the Resident Magistrate at Cashel], but I believe it is principally by scraping together heaps of manure from the streets and roads; and when the season comes, procuring what they call a free crop for potatoes; on this free crop they subsist for three-fourths

of the year; some of them subsist solely on potatoes, but others, when they get employment, are enabled to purchase sour milk ...[18]

The diets of urban labourers varied according to the level of wages and the state of local food markets. In Waterford City the principal food was potatoes, but 'within these few years past the consumption of wheaten bread has increased considerably'. As a by-product of the provisioning trade 'pork offal can be purchased at very low rates; and not unfrequently fish, such as hake, herrings, sprats, etc, are selling at prices sufficiently low as to be within their [i.e. labourers'] reach'.[19] In Monkstown, Dublin, labourers generally ate 'potatoes, herrings, bacon, oatmeal, butter, and ... invariably strong tea'.[20] On the other hand urban labourers without land were even more vulnerable to destitution than their rural counterparts. 'There is no general or public method of maintaining unemployed labourers,' reported the rector of St. Mary's Clonmel; 'they live the best way they can, and often are indeed victims of wretchedness, being compelled, by dire necessity, to restrict themselves to *two* and not unfrequently, I understand, even to *one* meal of potatoes and salt, or sour milk, during the 24 hours.'[21]

Witnesses to the 1836 Inquiry all agreed that the diet of the labouring poor in Ireland was wretched, but how did it compare with diet elsewhere? The report of the Scottish Poor Law Commission in 1844 provides data to set beside the Irish material. The results are presented in Table 9.

Table 9. Percentages of Parishes Naming Certain Foods, 1836 Ireland, 1843 Scotland[22]

Food	*Ireland*	*Scotland*	*Scotland excl. central Lowlands*
Potatoes	100	95	95
Milk	74	48	51
Herrings	26	—	—
Beef	14	3	2
(All meat)	—	48	41
Oatmeal	28	95	92
Butter	10	6	4
Eggs	6	—	—
Fish	7	35	42
Bread	8	11	5
Tea	2	10	8
Bacon (pig meat)	4	27	22

The Scottish figures are given for the whole country, and also with the central Lowlands excluded in order to remove the bulk of the industrialised counties. Both show Scottish diet to have been more varied than that in Ireland, an impression that is strengthened when it is remembered that items such as barley meal, vegetables, cheese and mutton figure in the Scottish survey but scarcely at all in the Irish Inquiry. Only with potatoes, milk, butter and — surprisingly — beef — was consumption more widespread in Ireland than in Scotland. To judge merely from the number of foods consumed, Ireland was a poorer country than Scotland in the 1830s.

A country with a third or more of its population living almost exclusively on two or three foods may reasonably be thought of as poor, whether we use conventional definitions of poverty stressing lack of income or Mokyr's more recent formulation of the likelihood of lapsing into starvation.[23] Nevertheless, the numbers of foods consumed is not the whole story.

Many nineteenth-century observers debated whether the Irish diet was adequate for health and physical labour. A survey of eating patterns carried out in 1839 among about 14 per cent of the rural population revealed that the adult labourer ate almost 13 lbs. of potatoes a day and drank about three pints of buttermilk. Inquiries into labouring diets exist also for 1859 and 1903–4; they demonstrate much-reduced levels of potato consumption but increased consumption of tea, sugar, bread and meat. Nutritional analysis clearly demonstrates the superiority of the 1839 diet.

Table 10. Nutritional Content of Labourers' Diets, 1839–1904[24]

	*1839**	*1859*	*1903–4*
Protein (g)	135	110	82
Fat (g)	4	40	87
Carbohydrate (g)	1099	760	590
Energy (kcal)	4720	3682	3370
Calcium (mg)	2398	1348	650
Iron (mg)	25	23	20

*The nutritional analysis of the 1839 diet is based on a menu of potatoes and buttermilk; hence the very low fat content.

The pre-Famine diet exhibits exceptionally high values of protein, carbohydrates, energy value (calories) and minerals. The vitamin C score (not shown) was also high, although the diet was somewhat deficient in vitamins A and D. All nutrient values declined after 1839 with the sole exception of fat. As the nutritional quality of diet declined, so the poorer classes became more prone to certain infectious diseases, particularly tuberculosis. Ireland was not unique — something similar happened in Scotland — but nutritional decline was more severe in Ireland than elsewhere. The paradox of Irish poverty was that economic hardship forced a large section of the population to subsist on a single foodstuff which was, fortuitously, extremely nourishing.

Once the potato had become firmly established in diets it possessed three great virtues. It yielded abundantly; it could be eaten in large quantities — up to 10 or 12 lbs. a day — unlike foods such as rice or Indian meal which swelled in cooking to a volume beyond the capacity of the human stomach; and it provided most of the nutrients necessary for health and physical exertion. Over thirty years ago Connell pointed to the healthfulness of the potato-based diets and linked potato consumption with population growth. The subsequent debate about the diet-population connexion has obscured the fact that diets in the 1830s were excellent, not merely when measured by the 'recommended daily intake' of the nutritionist, but also when set against the historical reality of the later nineteenth century. The Famine temporarily drove the Irish labourer away from the potato, and growing wealth in the later nineteenth century made possible much more varied eating habits. But not until the twentieth century were the poorer classes in Ireland as well nourished as they had been in the decades when their destitution made them an object of pity throughout western Europe.

NOTES

1. *Third Report of Commissioners for Inquiring into the Condition of the Poorer Classes in Ireland (Poor Inquiry (Ireland))*, (P.P. 1836 (36) XXXI), Appendix (D); *Sixth Annual Report of the Poor Law Commissioners*, (P.P. 1840 (245) XVII), Appendix (D), No. 21.
2. J. Mokyr, *Why Ireland Starved: A Quantitative and Analytical History of the Irish Economy, 1800–1850* (London, 1983), p. 10.
3. W. E. Vaughan and A. J. Fitzpatrick, *Irish Historical Statistics: Population 1821–1971* (Dublin, 1978), p. 53. (The figure cited in the text refers to the year 1861).
4. D. Thomson and Moyra McGusty, eds., *The Irish Journals of Elizabeth Smith, 1840–1850* (Oxford, 1980), pp. 24–5, 90.
5. *Poor Inquiry (Ireland), op. cit.*, p. 155.
6. *Sixth Annual Report, op. cit.*, p. 243.
7. These codes give an impression of tidiness that the answers do not possess and we have adopted a number of conventions to overcome ambiguities. These are best demonstrated by example. Thus, from Ahern, County Cork it was reported the 'the ordinary diet is potatoes and milk for about three-fourths of the year, and potatoes only, or potatoes and salt or herrings, for one fourth'. This has been coded as potatoes (5), milk (2), herrings (2). From Kilbonane in the same county the entry reads 'potatoes and milk, sometimes salt fish, and seldom a relish of pork'. The codes are 5,5,2,2.
8. *Poor Inquiry (Ireland)*, p. 236.
9. The phrase is borrowed from L. Kennedy, 'The Rural Economy, 1820–1914', in L. Kennedy and P. Ollerenshaw, eds., *An Economic History of Ulster, 1820–1939* (Manchester, 1985), p. 34.
10. J. Mokyr, 'Irish History with the Potato', *Ir. Ec. & Soc. Hist.* VIII (1981), p. 29.
11. Data for livestock production come from the *Census of Ireland for the Year 1841* (P.P. 1843 (504) XXIV), pp. 454–7; see P. M. A. Bourke, 'The Agricultural Statistics of the 1841 Census of Ireland. A Critical Review', *Ec. H. R.* XVIII (1965), pp. 376–9.
12. *Sixth Annual Report*, p. 243.
13. *Ibid.*
14. *Poor Inquiry (Ireland)*, p. 262.
15. Thomson and McGusty, p. 37.
16. *Poor Inquiry (Ireland)*, p. 223.
17. *Ibid.*, p. 235.
18. *Ibid.*, p. 245.
19. *Ibid.*, p. 252.
20. *Ibid.*, p. 57.
21. *Ibid.*, p. 238.

22. I. Levitt and T. C. Smout, *The State of the Scottish Working Class in 1843* (Edinburgh, 1979), p. 37.

23. Mokyr, *Why Ireland Starved*, pp. 15–16.

24. E. Margaret Crawford, 'Dearth, Diet and Disease in Ireland, 1850: a Case Study of Nutritional Deficiency', *Medical History*, 28 (1984), pp. 151–161; *idem*, Aspects of Irish Diet, 1839–1904 (unpublished Ph.D. thesis, University of London, 1985).

16

REGIONAL IMBALANCE AND POVERTY IN EARLY NINETEENTH-CENTURY BRITAIN

Eric Richards

I

Any map of poverty in the British Isles in the early nineteenth century would show severe regional disparities. Over the period of rapid industrialisation and population growth these variations in living standards may have become more pronounced. We are not well endowed with explanations of poverty and its particular shape during the industrial revolution. In the spirit of comparative economic history it may be productive to consider some simple basic propositions about the geographical distribution of poverty and some of its general sources.

The venerable debate about the standard of living in the Industrial Revolution offers some recognition of deviations from the national average — though sometimes only to the extent of excluding Ireland altogether. Too little is known about the regional configuration of poverty and the disproportional trends in social welfare. Yet it is likely that a relationship exists between regional poverty and the structure of economic change on a national scale. Indeed it may be the case that some of the causes of economic growth (for example, inter-regional specialisation) were simultaneously the causes of much regional poverty. It is probable that the broad determinants of economic growth also shaped the regional distribution of national income.

It is obvious, especially but not only in Ireland and Scotland, that certain regions fared much more prosperously than others in the long period of industrialisation. There were some regions in which per capita growth lagged far behind the national average, and others in which the new wealth was distributed in such ways as to bring little advantage to the majority of the people residing in these regions. Much of the great movement of people within Britain and Ireland was a clear expression of that differential experience. It is evident that, at least in the short run, some regions gained little from industrialisation. The perennial difficulty of defining 'regions' should not obscure this simple reality.

One dimension of this general process was the survival and exacerbation of pre-industrial varieties of poverty in the remoter areas of Britain. Some of this poverty, in the nineteenth century, was expressed in congestion, 'overpopulation', vulnerability to food shortage, poor diet, and eventually, emigration. The evidence of such poverty is not hard to find, although the long-term trends are less easily identified. But it is possible to argue that regional poverty not only survived but was re-affirmed by industrialisation: that the regional disparity of incomes was reinforced by the process of industrialisation itself. This is a serious allegation to be laid against the Industrial Revolution and it is not, of course, the first time it has been made. Verification is extraordinarily difficult. The ostensibly extreme case of the Scottish Highlands provides some of the elements in the *prima facie* case. Barbara Solow has spoken of 'Scotland's fairly smooth adjustment from a traditional agricultural society to a modern agricultural and industrial one';[1] yet this is a travesty of several parts of the Scottish and, especially, of the Highland experience. Indeed there were enough similarities in the circumstances of disadvantaged regions in Britain and Ireland to suggest the possibility of a systematic relationship between zones of poverty and the process of economic development.

Explanations of differential regional development tend to fall back on ideas about geographical advantage, economies of scale and externalities, capital availability and transport costs. It has been suggested, however, that 'the prevailing distribution of real income in the world ... is largely to be explained, not by "natural" factors, but by the unequal incidence of development in industrial activities'.[2] In effect current doctrine tends to emphasise principles of cumulative causation — that comparative success and comparative failure are, once begun, self-reinforcing tendencies. How it begins is profoundly mysterious and the literature on divergence and convergence is generally regarded as inadequate and inconclusive. But for regions which experienced relative or absolute retardation, the consequences in terms of poverty and deprivation were catastrophic. As Rosalind Mitchison has said, 'it is high time we thought long and hard about the intractable subject of economic growth in outlying areas that are set in their ways'.[3]

Joel Mokyr suggests that the Irish experience serves as 'a grim reminder of the cost of failing to industrialise'.[4] Beckett says that 'for the lowest classes of [Irish] society ... the development of the national economy brought little or no benefit', that real incomes fell, and that an increasing proportion of the population lived on the edge of destitution.[5] In other regions the costs were not so grim, but certainly bad enough for those, such as the Scottish Highlanders, who lived in the squalor of famine-prone crofting. The problem, however, was more than a simple failure to participate in the process of industrialisation: economic growth produced negative consequences for certain types of region. This proposition, of course, is associated with the modern critique of capitalist development which denies that the system is self-equilibrating. Indeed the stubbornness of regional problems in the modern economy has led some commentators to stress the phenomenon of cumulative imbalance. Stuart Holland contends that 'the neo-classical theory of location became increasingly unreal as unbalanced capitalist development left a trail of wrecked regions and problem areas which, according to theory, should never have occurred'.[6]

Consequently, while the question of inter-regional relationships stands at the centre of explanations of successful industrialisation, it is also vital to any understanding of the concomitant failure in those regions which suffered disproportionate poverty. Such an emphasis does not require us to lose sight of other causes of differential poverty. Arguments about geographical disadvantage now usually assume less importance than the idea that retarded regions suffered from unfavourable institutional structures. For instance landlordism, by way of sub-division or eviction, may have impeded the development of agricultural output. This factor often merges into debates about the actual distribution (as opposed to the aggregate size) of a region's income. Much of the discussion of Irish, Scottish Highland and Welsh agrarian history revolves around the contention that the landlords appropriated a large and increasing proportion of the region's wealth and thereby exacerbated the poverty of the rest of the society. But the most fundamental explanation is that rooted in the very low productivity of certain types of economic activity in the retarded regions — in industrial activity and various types of agriculture. It is not controversial to say that the most basic cause of Celtic poverty in the nineteenth century was excessive population, a low productivity in tradeable goods, and the vulnerability of subsistence output. The low productivity factor is often expounded in tandem with residual arguments about native indolence, low 'animal spirits', backward-sloping supply curves of labour, and various indeterminate elements in the peasant psyche.

Without either excluding or diminishing the relevance of these explanations, it is also useful to press the claims of external factors bearing upon the plight of retarded regions. There is, of course, a certain reluctance in using explanations of poverty which invoke exogenous elements — to explain even a part of Highland destitution, or the poverty of agricultural labourers in Wiltshire, or Irish mortality, in terms of external and ungovernable factors, is tantamount to diminishing the liability of the landlord class. Yet it would be difficult to deny that the economic pressures bearing on, for instance, the Scottish Highlands, which forced the regional economy into sheepfarming, kelping, and crofting, and caused the loss of industry, were externally generated and arguably irreversible. They were pressures inherent in the process of industrialisation, and possessed a status similar to T. S. Eliot's 'blind forces of nature' or S. B. Saul's 'objective environmental conditions'. In each of these phrases there is a danger of determinism since they may appear to divest the region and its owners of any sense of agency or responsibility. W. A. Maguire expressed a more cautious version when he described the context of the Downshire estates: 'serious economic and social problems existed of a sort that landowners were not primarily responsible for creating, and with which even the most sympathetic of them could not adequately deal'.[7]

Without doubt, the causes of poverty in the unsuccessful regions were manifold, inter-connected and mutually exacerbating. It is unnecessary to discount landlord oppression or inactivity, or geographical disadvantage, the Poor Law, or capital deficiency, to give a fuller account of the wider set of inter-regional forces which created much of the framework of economic activity in regions.

II

The weaker regions commonly experienced two types of economic depressant (usually in a context of rapid population growth) which ultimately resulted in low levels of social welfare. The first adverse influence normally took the form of structural change which radically undermined the level of local demand for the abundant supply of labour. The second was the severe reduction in the level of industrial and handicraft production within the region. The depressants were administered by the mechanism of regional differentiation. As Sidney Pollard says, 'one of the significant features of the industrial revolution in Britain was its complex inter-relationships'. And regional specialisation is often regarded as a dynamic element in industrialisation, as the indispensable requirement for cumulative economic growth. Pollard regards it as the engine of economic development: the free operation of regional trade, and the resultant specialisation of output, 'far from being harmful as so often alleged, was vital for ensuring a fast and healthy development' of the national and the European economy, even when it involved the connection of 'regions at different stages of development'.[8] In effect there was a dynamic reciprocation between regions with differing technologies and wage/cost structures, and this operated in such a fashion as to encourage economic integration by means of 'a certain internal economic logic'. Pollard's idea of the benefits of trade fits most conventional explanations of British industrialisation: 'from the local exchange between village and market town, it became intra-regional, then a trade between neighbouring regions, and ultimately between each region and the world'. But the process is invested with a Panglossian air — Pollard likens such growth to a beneficial 'infection' by which every part of the reciprocating mechanism is advantaged: 'ultimately the whole of Britain became modernised and industrialised'.[9]

Naturally, not all regions benefited immediately or to the same degree, and Pollard acknowledges the initial unevenness of development. But it is obvious that some regions did not industrialise at all, and that the pressures of rural specialisation thrust their economies into new structures of production which, in some cases, reinforced their commitment to agriculture or commodity production, including mining. Some districts, such as northern Shropshire, found themselves responding to the food demands of the new towns in Lancashire and the Midlands: arable and dairying production were directly stimulated into forms of new investment, more efficient labour usage, and rising living standards for most of the people who remained in the region. Other zones were less fortunate in the sense that the stimuli from industrialisation did not match the existing disposition of the human resources of the region affected. In the Scottish Highlands the derived demands of industrialisation were complicated but generally cataclysmic upon a society already in the throes of population upheaval. Kelp, cattle, linen manufacture and fishing were all activated by inter-regional demands identifiable in the late eighteenth century — indeed, between them, they offered the promise of rapid economic growth and the prompt absorption of spare labour resources. They even gave the prospect of rising living standards at a time of population growth. In the long run, by 1820, they rapidly lost impetus: the industrial demand for kelp supply collapsed; the production of linen became centralised in southern Scotland and in Ulster; fishing, though more successful, was incapable of supporting the great accumulation of population. Of all the derived demands of the new industrial economy as it affected the Highlands, only wool was sustained through this period. The Highlands became committed to sheep farming on a scale which left a large proportion of the human population redundant. Here, indeed, was a classic instance in which industrialisation in the south had altered factor rewards on the periphery, and imposed on the region massive structural change which brought little or no benefit to the majority of the people of the region. The exogenous forces at work were virtually irresistible and almost entirely negative: a rapidly expanding peasant population was left redundant by the sudden surge in demand for the raw materials of the woollen mills. To the production of wool, the majority of the people of the Highlands had practically nothing to contribute.

The structural change imposed on the Highlands was especially severe but nevertheless symptomatic of the regional imperative of the age. The diversity of the regional experience during industrialisation was long ago emphasised by D. C. Coleman.[10] There were some regions, certainly in the west of Ireland, where there appeared to be no augmentation of income-generating opportunities while the peasant population simply expanded within the old frameworks of life. But mostly, as John Langton has argued recently, 'national economic cohesion brought greater regional specialisation in the short and medium terms' (and reinforced regional identities for many decades).[11] The configuration of these regional effects has yet to be established, but it is clear that the impact on human welfare was highly variable and complex. And, while Pollard stresses the indispensability of regional specialisation for the purposes of national economic growth, some regions bore the brunt of the required adjustment in a manner both painful and enduring. In Stuart Holland's more contentious formulation, the process of national development necessarily entailed regional inequality: 'regional inequality is intrinsic to capitalist economic growth'.[12] The structural adjustment of the British economy imposed differential costs across the regions, a process which in many zones required almost a century to run its course.

The dictates of structural change contain only part of the story. For many regions the negative consequences were powerfully reinforced by the decline of local industry. The centripetal tendencies of industrialisation are well charted: the concentration of textiles in Belfast, Glasgow, Lancashire and the West Riding, metal trades in Central Scotland, Sheffield and the Black Country, and so on. Yet large tracts of Britain were entirely bypassed by industrialisation. Moreover, the success of Manchester, Dundee, Birmingham and other great centres was bought at the cost of other regions which, in the process, were savagely denuded of their traditional (and so-called proto-) industries. This phenomenon is well enough established in the literature. Pollard states it clearly: 'regional specialisation associated with modernisation, for example in pottery, in cutlery, and toolmaking, or in woollen textiles, was tantamount to de-industrialisation elsewhere'.[13] Nor was it confined to Britain and Ireland. Francois Crouzet has described the effects of British industrialisation on the rest of Europe — he coins the phrase 'pastoralisation' which fits well the circumstances of the Scottish Highlands and North Wales: 'By 1800 Continental Europe was threatened by pastoralism and the fate of India in the 19th century. In fact countries like Spain, Portugal and Sweden which fell into the economic orbit of England during the wars suffered a crisis or a collapse of their traditional industries without any compensating rise of new ones'. Some missed the boat altogether and never industrialised: competition from parts of Britain was, in some cases, lethal.[14]

Within Britain the catalogue of regional casualties is long and uneven. Sometimes the process of de-industrialisation was two-phased. In the first phase there may have been considerable expansion within the rural base of industry — for instance the rapid expansion of linen production in rural Ireland and parts of Scotland (including the Highlands) in the late eighteenth century, before its concentration in Belfast and Dundee.[15] There were many well-known examples of such rural development in the years 1760–1810, and Cyril Erlich has suggested the phrase 'fragile industrialisation' since, very often, the development turned out to be superficial and transitory. It does not particularly help to call the phenomenon proto-industrialisation since much of it was rapidly extinguished in the second phase of specialisation.[16]

It is evident that the subsequent destruction of rural industry was not exclusive to outlying regions — indeed it was common to practically all agricultural zones after about 1830. In some places, for example in the East Riding, the decay was somewhat protracted and relatively well accommodated by the local economic framework. The social and economic consequences of rural decay depended particularly on the proximity of urban industrialisation and the absorptive capacity of local agriculture. Cullen has rightly emphasised the decay of English rural industry in parallel with that of parts of Ireland.[17] In East Anglia rural textile activity which had employed 'many thousands over the countryside' fell into severe decline by the 1830s and 1840s and caused greater poverty than could be found in the factory towns.[18] Sometimes the dissolution of local handicrafts — e.g. lace-making, domestic manufacture of straw plait, gloves, buttons, pins and so on — damaged female employment disproportionately, and depressed family incomes which, on the margin, were reduced to a critical minimum.[19] It was the story of handloom weavers writ widely across the rural world.

In some localities the impact of industrial competition was expressed in the form of frustrated hopes for development. For instance, in the Highlands in the late eighteenth century, government, corporate and landlord agencies all attempted to reverse the process of industrial decline (and also combat adverse population conditions). Yet they produced a long record (even until the enterprise of Lord Leverhulme) of almost comprehensive failure.[20] Similarly A. H. Dodd records that North Wales thought itself on the verge of imminent industrialisation in the 1830s:

> There were still those who believed, on the eve of the repeal of the coal tax in 1831, that, with this obstacle removed, the industries of the North Wales coal field could hold their own with the Black Country; others, as late as the middle of the century ... thought that only a railway was needed to complete the triumph of the Montgomeryshire woollens.[21]

In the event it was all illusion, and the coming of the railways merely increased the exposure of north Welsh industry.

While East Anglia was de-industrialised to the advantage of the West Riding, whole areas of west Wales, rural Derbyshire and Cornwall were divested of their domestic industries — from textiles to chairmaking to paper-manufacture — low productivity industries which had no way of resisting the competition of modern factory production. Houston and Snell[22] have prepared a long list of regions on both sides of the North Sea which suffered this fate, often zones which had hosted development in the 'proto-industrial' form. Galloway and North Wales and many parts of Ireland suffered the same fate. But de-industrialisation was not confined to regions that failed: alterations in the pattern of economic output were inherent within the shifting matrix of structural change in practically all regions. A radical re-adjustment of economic activity was, as Pollard properly emphasises, integral to economic advance. It is not at all difficult to regard the industrial revolution as a vast exercise in Schumpeterian 'creative destruction'. The problem was that the destruction was regionally concentrated — some regions were left with no industrial structure whatsoever, and were consequently saddled with an economy which had little use for their increased populations, and from which migration was often inadequate and too slow. The more distant from the centres of positive industrialisation, the more intractable the problem — it led to continuing poverty or worse; it certainly created adverse effects on social welfare which were impossible to compensate from the internal resources of the region. It could cause cumulative retrogression in the local economy, a dependence on an increasingly precarious economic structure. It was expressed in East Anglia and other parts of England most visibly in low wage levels, endemic underemployment, and the burden of the poor rates.[23] As is well known, regions which were entrenched in agriculture without industry tended to be restricted to relatively very low incomes, the more so if engaged in low productivity agriculture.[24]

For Ireland Joel Mokyr and Cormac O'Grada have given realistic prominence to rapid de-industrialisation as a source of poverty, and suggest that 'a part of the demographic adjustment in Ireland in the decades before the famine can be attributed to the decline of rural industry'.[25] The roll-call of casualties of regional Irish domestic industries was appalling: cotton weaving, stocking production, hand knitting, homespun tweed, embroidery, Wicklow flannel, Kilkenny woollens, muslin, boots and shoes. Where Ireland had been self-sufficient in woollen textiles in 1800, it produced only one-seventh of its requirements by 1838.[26] As Cullen points out, much of the general decline pre-dated the end of duties,[27] and it seems unlikely that any amount of protection could have saved manufacturing in south and west Ireland. But the decline of domestic industries was neither smooth nor unilinear. W. H. Crawford cites the temporary resurgence of domestic linen production in 1847 when Scots and English manufacturers sent yarn to a village in Co. Londonderry to take advantage of the extremely low rates of pay of female labour, competition which momentarily out-competed the machinery.[28] It was a minor, insignificant exception to E. H. Hunt's proposition that 'low wages and abundant small town and village labour was no longer attracting capital because low wage labour was no longer cheap'.[29]

The re-orientation of industry in Scotland at the end of the eighteenth century[30] requires little emphasis, but the extent of the decline of domestic enterprise is less well known. Its previous ubiquity and its importance as a source of income and employment for both men and women are suggested by the great number of packmen in operation in Scotland at the time of the Union.[31] The ultimate elimination of rural industries was, in most places, a relatively slow process stretching over seventy years; most of the slack thereby created was absorbed in the new economy of the Lowlands. But in the Highlands the social and economic consequences were more pronounced and more severe. The *Old* and the *New Statistical Accounts* were full of repeated statements about the erosion and elimination of local production. It affected two forms of domestic production both of which were important for the operation of the peasant economy. A certain degree of domestic production was commercial and showed varying degrees of concentration within the Highland economy — linen spinning and weaving, but also some cotton output, were quite widespread before 1760, and both served a broad market. But there was also another level of output, almost totally obscured, which hardly surfaced in any form of market transaction. Here our best guide is Dr I. F. Grant.[32] Her close analysis of Dunachton 1769–1782 reveals the fine structure of a local exchange economy in which much of the economic activity of the community was self-contained, one in which most transactions were encompassed within the district, village or family. Meal was itself employed as a medium of exchange, of calculating debts and storing wealth, as well as functioning as a means of subsistence. Within this framework there was a substantial low-level division of function, a stratum of local craftsmen and workers, usually operating on a part-time basis — they were smiths, weavers, tailors, bagmakers, carpenters, fox killers, wrights, masons, fiddlers, bark peelers, spinners and so on — whose standards were 'fit only for the coarsest work' and whose primitive degree of specialisation could not satisfy Adam Smith. Much of the payment was in kind and the key to the primitive system was 'the parochial scope of most of the transactions' Dr. Grant characterised it thus:

> The workers' markets were at their very doors, for they were producing goods for the use of folk of their own class and living in their own district . . . The old fashioned system of agriculture, with its seasons of business and slackness, tended to foster the carrying on of subsidiary trades, and the isolation from industrial centres ensured a regular local demand.[33]

These layers of rural manufacture were gradually swept away by the competition of the new industrial economy. For instance, the collapse of linen spinning and weaving in Aberdeenshire was virtually complete by 1843; the knitted stocking industry was also finished. Local manufacture of cloth had almost disappeared by the 1840s; even shoes were being imported. Imports of cheap manufactured textiles, even in the abysmally poor north-west, destroyed local crafts. Imports proved irresistible even in districts frequently on the margins of subsistence. Imported coal increasingly replaced peat; iron ploughs replaced locally produced wooden tools; imported lumber, hemp, sailcloth, slates and bricks all made incursions against local products.

The loss of industry exerted a debilitating effect across the local economy. It was a process which ate into the lowest levels of economic activity within the home, and it rendered more redundant the labour of all members of the family household. Moreover it was doubly disadvantageous in terms of regional income: it reduced activity within the region by the loss of production; equally, however, it increased regional imports of manufactured goods. One of the most astonishing aspects of the economic history of the nineteenth-century Highlands was the rapid increase in the propensity to consume imported products, especially, but not only, textiles. This was well documented even in the poorest districts and even where levels of social welfare were deteriorating. The consumption behaviour of the Highlanders was as perplexing as their reproductive behaviour.[34]

The erosion of peasant household manufacturing — primitive though that was (the words 'industry' and 'de-industrialisation' do not properly apply in this context) — had serious effects. It reduced labour demands, increased disguised unemployment, diminished its surpluses for rent and food, and for small-scale capital accumulation. Most of all it reduced the region's ability to pay for food supplies during periods of harvest shortage. It increased the region's dependency since it had smaller cash reserves for subsistence crises: it was a cause of poverty which crept gradually across the local economy and generated little outcry, but its influence was superimposed heavily upon the other depressants of the Highland economy. In the 1838 report on Highland poverty Fullarton and Baird demonstrated the almost total lack of any type of manufacturing in the region, and a decade later the MacNeill report provided a vivid demonstration of the extraordinarily constricted foundations of life in the west Highlands.[35] For the Scottish Highlands the industrialisation of Britain had re-affirmed its pre-industrial rural character and narrowed its sources of income. There was a desperate asymmetry between the scale and distribution of population growth and the character of economic change in regions such as the Highlands.

III

In his account of the costs of economic development, Martin Bronferbrenner remarked that 'where native arts and crafts and religious observances and ethical obligations are incompatible with high productivity in a machine age, they will shrivel and wither and sometimes disappear altogether'.[36] Of course, to make such claims about the causes of poverty and about the consequences of de-industrialisation and regional divergence in nineteenth-century Britain raises monumental problems of measurement and verification, well beyond the speculations of this paper. Of nineteenth-century Ireland, Mokyr says that 'the data appear consistent with an economy in which at least half of the transactions between labourer and farmer involved barter deals'.[37] In the Highlands there were relatively few wage earners, many were still subject to labour services and victual rents, many rents continued to be paid through middlemen, much consumption was internal to the family economy, and much of its poverty was relieved by mechanisms of communal support which left little trace in any statistics. Indeed, during the phase of 'modernisation' many landlords believed they were reducing rents by eliminating the tacksmen. Difficulties of comparison over time are compounded by shifts in the bases of economic life — towards, for instance, greater dependence on potatoes and on seasonal day-labour. They create problems analogous to those exposed by Polly Hill in her study of the socio-economic standards of the present-day rural tropics.[38]

Any claim that conditions in regions such as the Highlands deteriorated under the influence of 'regional divergence' has to negotiate the reality that circumstances in the eighteenth century were so poor that there was little scope for much subsequent worsening.[39] Living standards over the period 1780–1860 are extraordinarily difficult to establish. It is possible to construct price indices of some of the main products of the crofting economy but we have little knowledge about levels of output. Moreover a large part of the Highland diet comprised potatoes and meal which were not much marketed, and for much of the 'internal' crofting economy we are entirely in the dark. Consequently most of the clues about living standards must be deduced from the relationship between prices and rents.[40]

Standards of life in the late eighteenth century depended primarily on productivity and cash income (from cattle, kelp, linen, fish, oatmeal and wages) in relation to the demands of rent and the cost of exchange items and imports. An increasing proportion of the population seems to have been drawn into the market economy — in kelping, fishing, and in the new villages, for instance — at a time when (especially after 1813) the sources of cash income became more unreliable. The low level of key prices until the 1840s depressed living standards — and probably caused a retreat towards greater dependence on inadequate crofts and on seasonal migration. The precise consequences are obscured to some degree by the changing economic status of many Highlanders (e.g. from landholders to wage-earning villagers) and diminished access to land.

As in certain parts of Ireland, it is likely that the potato output of the smallholders held up reasonably well for most of the time, and that potatoes (extremely efficient in yield per acre and per capita) were an increasing proportion of the diet. Needless to say the problem of the potato was not its productivity but its reliability as a subsistence crop for a densely packed population.[41] In their relation with the market the crofters were poorly placed — in tradeable goods their marginal productivity of labour was very low, and the exchange value of their marketable surpluses was declining. This affected seriously their capacity to pay rents and buy meal imports during crises. The available evidence suggests that between 1813 and 1848 conditions were adverse; compared with the relatively good times of the French Wars, living standards fell. The main depressants were a fall of prices greater and in advance of the diminution of rents, reinforced by the elimination of by-employments, a reduced access to land, and the intermittent failure of the potato.

Poverty in the Highlands seems to have been worst in the least-cleared districts, and emigration was greatest from the most favoured parts. Poverty probably reduced the ability to emigrate, and it is not unreasonable to regard the low living standards as a prolongation of pre-industrial conditions, as was the continuing vulnerability to the effects of the weather. Comparisons of these standards with trends in the south are vitiated by wide differences in conventions about diet, housing and general consumption preferences: it may be more fruitful to think of Highland trends in terms of the relative command over food resources and food imports, and of economic security. On this definition the Highlands probably retrogressed in the first half of the nineteenth century.

After 1850 — until about 1880 — the trends appear to reverse. And though famine conditions threatened in several years, there were many signs of an improvement from an admittedly very low base. In this, as before, the Highland evidence appears to parallel that of recent Irish studies.[42] Prices were more favourable, and in this phase the rents of small tenants lagged behind the trend. It seems likely, in essence, that there was a distribution of income from the landlords back towards the crofters at a time when regional income was rising and its population falling.

The experience after 1850 did not necessarily constitute a narrowing of the gap between the retarded and the advanced regions of the British economy: living standards were moving ahead across the country. Nor did it end the rural squalor of so much crofter life. But it marked a new trend in the Highlands, and elsewhere among the less favoured regions. It may cast some doubts on the notion of cumulative imbalance over historical time as posited in the Myrdalian and the Perrouxist models.[43]

IV

There is no clear evidence that the long-term improvement of living standards in the Highlands (and in comparable regions in Britain) constituted a process of 'convergence' in the national economy; nor does it, of itself, demonstrate that an effective mechanism of regional equilibration had been set in motion.[44] Nevertheless local living standards rose and it is evident that some form of adjustment was in progress. Better prices for cattle, wool, fish and labour may (or may not) represent the transmission of benefits from industrialisation to areas remote from the centres of industry. But the reduction in poverty was accomplished, as in Ireland, partly by the reduction of population after 1851 — by means of net migration and reduced marriage and reproduction rates — which recent anthropologists have called 'the multi-component system that is human adaptation' to 'ecological stress'.[45]

To a degree the loss of population was a substitute for development.[46] Seasonal migration was also strengthened, helping to prolong the crofting system, while emigration remained relatively sluggish from the poorest districts. Indeed there was considerable communal resistance to the requirements of regional adjustment which seemed to dictate that the region should shed population and concentrate its reduced labour and capital into the production of wool, fish and sporting facilities. This adaptation was resisted for decade after decade until it was actually sanctioned by the Crofters Act and its successors.

In 1822 William Cobbett had proclaimed that 'one part of the nation had been depopulated to increase the population of the other part',[47] and over the very long run this was the main basis for regional convergence. In the Scottish Highlands (and elsewhere) there were other components of local improvement, which included various forms of cross-subsidisation within the region (by way of differential rent policies which favoured small tenants),[48] and subsidisation from outside the region (usually through landlords' capital imports). The adjustment at the crofting level was in the form of slow migration, and of a stoic acceptance of very poor conditions of crofting life. None of this was incompatible with slowly rising living standards, nor with relative deprivation and continuing poverty. In the 1860s the Highlands, mid-Wales and the West Country remained the lowest wage regions in Britain, though they rose relative to the national average in the following thirty years.[49]

In theory — that is, in a system of automatic adjustment in a free market economy — there should have been more positive development.[50] Regions such as the Highlands (*ceteris paribus*) should have attracted capital and enterprise to take advantage of the prevailing low levels of wages and living costs. After about 1820 there was virtually no such investment: indeed most of the adaptation was negative, a running down of labour-intensive activity throughout the economy. As E. R. R. Green said of Ireland in the nineteenth century, there was 'a failure of either theory or policy to grasp the central human problem of providing for a surplus population and of giving security to the cultivator of the soil'.[51]

The processes of economic adjustment in outlying regions were generally hesitant and not necessarily mutually consistent. They were undoubtedly affected by poor relief policies, differential migration, land productivity, social attitudes to the land, and the erratic behaviour of landlords. Painful and sluggish, the broad adjustments to industrialisation were effective only in the 'very long run'.[52] Moreover, as this essay has argued, these were common elements in the structural causes of poverty, and it is likely that there was some concurrence in the timing and the form of their economic rectification. Relative failure during industrialisation, like success, is probably best tackled by means of comparative analysis.

NOTES

1. Barbara Solow, review of Devine & Dickson, *Journal of Economic History*, XLIV (1984), p. 852.
2. N. Kaldor, 'The Case for Regional Policies', *Scottish Journal of Political Economy*, 17 (1970), pp. 339 *et seq.*
3. Rosalind Mitchison, 'Rough Highland History', *New Statesman*, 29 June 1973.
4. J. Mokyr, *Why Ireland Starved* (London, 1983), p. 281.
5. J. C. Beckett, *The Making of Modern Ireland, 1603–1923* (London, 1966), pp. 243ff.
6. Stuart Holland, *Capital Versus the Regions* (London, 1976), p. 36. On the unsatisfactory character of core-periphery arguments, see J. Mokyr, 'Industrialisation and Poverty in Ireland and the Netherlands', *Journal of Interdisciplinary History*, 10 (1980), p. 450, and Percy Selwyn in D. Seers, Bernard Schaffer and M. L. Kiljunen, eds., *Underdeveloped Europe* (London, 1979), esp. pp. 35–6.

7. W. A. Maguire, *The Downshire Estates in Ireland, 1801–1845* (Oxford, 1972), p. 247.

8. Sidney Pollard, *The Integration of the European Economy since 1815* (London, 1981), p. 38.

9. S. Pollard, 'Industrialisation and the European Economy', *Ec.H.R.*, XXVI (1973); see also his *European Economic Integration* (London, 1974), esp. pp. 36–9. A similar view is taken by Alec Nove who says that 'specialisation based on trade is a necessary and universal phenomenon', but emphasises the incidental regional problems that often accompany the process. 'On Reading Andre Gunnar Frank', *Journal of Development Studies*, 10 (1973–4), pp. 445–55.

10. D. C. Coleman, 'Growth and Decay during the Industrial Revolution: the case of East Anglia', *Scandinavian Economic History Review*, X (1962).

11. John Langton, 'The Industrial Revolution and the Regional Geography of England', *Transactions, Institute of British Geographers*, 9 (1984), p. 164.

12. Stuart Holland, *op.cit.*, p. 53.

13. Pollard, 'Industrialisation and the European Economy', *loc.cit.*, p. 638.

14. F. Crouzet, 'Wars, Blockade and Economic Change in Europe 1792–1815', *Journal of Economic History*, XXIV (1964), pp. 577 *et seq.*

15. See A. Durie, 'The Market for Scottish Linen, 1730–1775' in *S.H.R.*., 41 (1973), 'Linen-spinning in the North of Scotland', *Northern Scotland* (1974–5), and *The Scottish Linen Industry in the Eighteenth Century* (Edinburgh, 1979); W. H. K. Turner, 'Flax Weaving in Scotland in the early Nineteenth Century', *Scottish Geographical Magazine*, 99 (1983); J. P. Shaw, 'The New Rural Industry: Water Power and Textiles', in M. L. Parry and T. R. Slater, eds., *The Making of the Scottish Countryside* (London, 1980), pp. 291–318; H. D. Watts, 'Agricultural Industries: The Decline of the Small Business', *Business History*, IX (1967); W. H. Crawford, *Domestic Industry in Ireland* (Dublin, 1972); David Dickson, 'Aspects of the Rise and Decline of the Irish Cotton Industry', in Cullen & Smout; Dennis R. Mills, *English Rural Communities. The Impact of a Specialised Economy* (London, 1973), pp. 15 *et seq.*

16. C. Erlich, in a seminar at Queen's University, Belfast in 1975; the relationship between this type of industrial growth and subsequent industrialisation (in addition to the demographic effects) is explored by Eric L. Almquist, 'Pre-Famine Ireland and the Theory of European Proto-Industrialisation: Evidence from the 1841 Census', *Journal of Economic History*, XXXIX (1979).

17. See L. M. Cullen, ed., *The Formation of the Irish Economy* (Cork, 1969), p. 113, and *An Economic History of Ireland since 1660* (London, 1972), p. 107.

18. Coleman, *loc.cit.*, p. 127.

19. The impact on female employment and poverty was probably disproportionate, as charted by Rowntree and Kendall's investigation of rural poverty in 1911, quoted in E. H. Hunt, *British Labour History, 1815–1914* (London, 1981), p. 23.

20. An exception must be made of some of the new villages on the eastern margins of the region.

21. A. H. Dodd, *Industrial Revolution in North Wales* (Cardiff, 1951), p. viii.

22. R. Houston and K. D. M. Snell, 'Proto-Industrialisation? Cottage Industry, Social Change and Industrial Revolution', *Historical Journal*, 27 (1984), esp. pp. 490–1. See also A. H. John, *The Industrial Development of South Wales, 1750–1850* (Cardiff, 1950); John Saville, *Rural Depopulation in England and Wales, 1851–1951* (London, 1957), chapter 3.

23. Coleman, *loc.cit.*, p. 125; Hunt, *British Labour History*, p. 71.

24. See D. Lucey and D. R. Kaldor, *Rural Industrialisation* (London, 1969), p. 23. There is an excellent discussion of the decline of the outer zones in E. J. T. Collins, 'The Economy of Upland Britain, 1750–1850', in R. B. Tranter, ed., *The Future of Upland Britain* (2 vols., Reading, 1978), pp. 586–649.

25. Joel Mokyr and Cormac O'Grada, 'New Developments in Irish Population History', *Ec.H.R.*, XXXVII (1984), p. 482; see also Mokyr, *Why Ireland Starved*, p. 281.

26. The process is tracked by Brenda Collins, 'Proto-Industrialisation and Pre-Famine Emigration', *Social History*, 7, no.2 (1982); also, in 'Irish Emigration to Dundee and Paisley during the first half of the nineteenth century', in J. M. Goldstrom and L. A. Clarkson, eds., *Irish Population, Economy and Society* (Oxford, 1981); T. W. Freeman, *Pre-Famine Ireland* (Manchester, 1957); James Meenan, *The Irish Economy since 1922* (Liverpool, 1970), p. 203.

27. L. M. Cullen, *Economic History*, p. 106.

28. W. H. Crawford, *op.cit.*, p. 54.

29. E. H. Hunt, *op. cit.*, p. 28.

30. The limited extent of the change by 1776 is stressed by T. C. Smout, 'Where had the Scottish Economy got to by 1776?', in Istvan Hunt and Michael Ignatieff, eds., *Wealth and Virtue* (Cambridge, 1983), p. 63.

31. I. F. Grant, 'Highland Rural Industries', *Edinburgh Review*, 241 (1925), pp. 167–184. The origin and accuracy of Dr. Grant's estimate of packmen numbers in 1707 deserve re-consideration.

32. I. F. Grant, *Everyday Life on an Old Highland Farm, 1769–1782* (London, 1924), and *Highland Folk Ways* (London, 1961).

33. *Old Highland Farm*, pp. 37–8.

34. See T. C. Smout, review of Devine & Dickson, *Agricultural History Review*, 32 (1984), p. 104, and on peasant consumption behaviour during the onset of development, see H. Myint, *The Economics of Developing Countries* (London, 1967), pp. 41–2.

35. Allan Fullarton and Charles R. Baird, *Remarks on the Evils at Present Affecting the Highlands and Islands* (Glasgow, 1838), and *Report to the Board of Supervision by Sir John McNeill, G.C.B. on the Western Highlands and Islands* (Edinburgh, 1851), especially the evidence of Kenneth McCaskill of Carron, in Appendix A.

36. Martin Bronferbrenner, 'The High Costs of Economic Development', *Land Economics* (1953).

37. J. Mokyr, *Why Ireland Starved*, p. 15.

38. See Polly Hill, 'The Poor Quality of Official Socio-Economic Statistics Relating to the Rural Tropical World: with special reference to South India', *Modern Asian Studies*, 18 (1984), pp. 491–514.

39. See Eric Richards, *A History of the Highland Clearances, vol.I: Agrarian Transformation and the Evictions* (London, 1982), chapters 2 and 3; R. A. Dodgshon, *Land and Society in Early Scotland* (Oxford, 1981), chapter 8. Rosier pictures abound, a recent example being D. Watson, *Caledonia Australis* (Sydney, 1984), chapter 1.

40. Evidence about the incidence and intensity of 'famine' is hard to gauge. In virtually every decade from 1770 to 1870 there were serious shortages which observers called 'famine', and this may indeed indicate that the gap between the Highlands and the modernised parts of the economy had widened. But it is not clear that famines actually worsened in these years, though it is likely that relief measures became more efficient.

41. Cf. L. A. Clarkson in J. M. Goldstrom and L. A. Clarkson, eds., *op.cit.*, p. 31.

42. See W. E. Vaughan, 'Landlord and Tenant Relations in Ireland between the Famine and the Land War, 1850–1878', in Cullen & Smout, and 'An Assessment of the Economic Performance of the Irish Landlords, 1815–1869', in F. S. L. Lyons and A. A. J. Hawkins, eds., *Ireland Under the Union* (Oxford, 1980), and Barbara Solow, *The Land Question and the Irish Economy, 1870–1903* (Cambridge, Mass. 1971). For price and rent indices in the Highlands, see Eric Richards, *A History of the Highland Clearances, vol.2: Emigration, Protest, Reasons* (London, 1985), Appendix.

43. See Stuart Holland, *The Regional Problem* (London, 1976), chapter 1.

44. The question is touched on by E. H. Hunt, *Regional Wage Variations in Britain, 1850–1914* (Oxford, 1973), Introduction, and in I. Levitt and T. C. Smout, *The State of the Scottish Working Class in 1843* (Edinburgh, 1979), pp. 10, 262–3, and especially T. C. Smout, 'Scotland and England', *Review*, III (1980), pp. 601–30.

45. See John W. Sheets, 'Economic and Demographic Consequences of Population Decline — Colonsay and Jura, 1841–1891', *Northern Scotland*, 6 (1984), and E. J. Clegg, 'Some Factors Associated with Island Depopulation: The Example of St. Kilda', *ibid.*

46. Cf. Barbara Solow, review, *loc. cit.*, p. 852. J. Mokyr, 'Industrialisation and Poverty', *loc. cit.*, p. 458, and R. D. C. Black, 'The Irish Experience in relation to the Theory and Practice of Economic Development', in A. J. Youngson, ed., *Economic Development in the Long Run* (London, 1972), p. 203.

47. Quoted in A. Redford, *Labour Migration in England, 1800–1850* (Manchester, 1964 ed.), p. 67.

48. See Eric Richards, 'An Anatomy of the Sutherland Fortune', *Business History*, XXI (1979).

49. E. H. Hunt, *Regional Wage Variations*, p. 59.

50. See P. N. Rosenstein-Rodan quoted in Lucey and Kaldor, *op. cit.*, p. 19. Cf. Richard Ned Lebow, *J. S. Mill and the Irish Land Question* (Philadelphia, 1979), *passim.*

51. E. R. R. Green, review of R. D. C. Black, *Economic Thought and the Irish Question*, in *Victorian Studies*, 4 (1960–1), p. 359.

52. Cf. A. W. Coats, 'The Classical Economists, Industrialisation and Poverty', in *The Long Debate on Poverty* (IEA, London, 1972), pp. 164–6; and Joel Mokyr, 'Industrialisation and Poverty in Ireland and the Netherlands', *Journal of Interdisciplinary History*, X (1980), p. 431.

Part Three:

Private Enterprise and Public Policy

17

THE SCOTTISH AND IRISH LINEN INDUSTRIES COMPARED, 1780–1860

Alastair Durie and Peter Solar

The spectacular rise of the linen manufacture in Ireland and Scotland in the later eighteenth century has long attracted interest. The early growth of these industries was promoted by a number of common factors, including the growth of demand at home and abroad, access to the English and colonial markets, government support and protection. Yet if the 'take-off' has been studied in depth, rather less attention has been paid to the subsequent progress of linen manufacture in either country, particularly from the 1820s onwards, and very little has even been attempted of a comparative nature.[1] This essay, therefore, breaks new ground: it will take up some, and only some, of the parallels and contrasts which may be found in the Irish and Scottish experience with linen. Its starting point is c. 1780, when linen was without doubt the leading industry in both societies. The closing date is c. 1860, by which time linen was still a significant activity in Scotland, but no longer pre-eminent. In Ireland, however, it remained the dominant industry.

I

In 1780 in both Scotland and Ireland linen dominated the textile scene, with wool and silk taking subordinate positions and cotton about to make a spectacular entrance. It appears that the Irish linen industry was considerably larger than its Scottish counterpart, with a much higher output by value. Scottish output of cloth, yarn and thread can be put at just under £1m, whereas the corresponding Irish figure was double that, at £2m, according to Gill.[2] The actual manufacture of linen was widely dispersed in both countries, particularly the spinning. All of the main stages of production, other than finishing, involved the commitment of large quantities of male and female labour, mostly on a domestic basis. The Irish industry was able to draw on a population two-and-a-half to three times larger than that of Scotland.

Scotland, despite all the efforts of the Board of Trustees, was becoming more and more dependent on imported flax, whereas Ireland was virtually self-sufficient, except in flaxseed which was imported from Holland, Russia and America. Though the degree of inter-regional trade within Ireland in flax and yarn should not be underestimated, Irish linen workers tended more than their Scottish counterparts to hold land on which to grow both their food and the raw material for their work. The relationship between agriculture and the linen industry in Scotland was becoming more attenuated, except at harvest time.

Both countries produced a wide range of fabrics, some fine, some medium and others of a coarse nature, and in certain lines Scottish and Irish linens competed with each other. In the West of Scotland, in and around Glasgow, the fine linen industry was so well established that it was able to make substantial exports of kentings and lawns to Ireland, the textile equivalent of sending coals to Newcastle, because even by 1780 Ulster was beginning to dominate the supply of fine linen to the British and colonial markets. Equally, Dundee had already risen to a position of some strength in the manufacture of coarser cloth. Both the Scottish and Irish linen industries were highly export-oriented, if England is taken to be a 'foreign' market: 55–60 per cent of Irish linen was sold outside Ireland, and the Scottish figure was perhaps not far short of this.

By 1860 things had changed for both industries, with the degree of change in some respects greater in Scotland than in Ireland. Mechanisation of spinning had become total in Scotland, and the power loom was appearing in increasing numbers. Scottish production was overwhelmingly an urban or small-town activity. Irish production was also becoming more mechanised and more urban, though there were still fairly large numbers of rural handloom weavers in Ulster. In Scotland the cultivation of flax was virtually extinct, but Irish farmers still produced most of the raw material used by the local industry, even if flax-growing had become divorced from spinning and weaving. Some Irish flax was exported, perhaps up to a quarter of total output on occasion. Ireland also imported high-quality Continental flax, drawing its supplies mainly from Holland and Belgium. Scottish manufacturers took some Irish flax, but relied principally on imports from Russia and the Baltic. As in other Scottish textile industries, dependence on imported raw materials had become total.

Two of the changes since the 1780s to which this essay will draw particular attention were the increased specialisation of each industry's product mix and the spatial concentration of production in east Ulster and in Angus. By the 1850s their product ranges showed little overlap, so that instead of competing, they pursued activities that were essentially complementary. Ireland's linen production had become concentrated in the fine and medium ranges, Scotland's in the coarse fabrics. This complementarity was not total. If Irish spinners were putting pressure on English spinners of fine yarn in the 1850s, they were also beginning to encroach on the province of Scottish spinners at the lower counts. And production of table linens at Dunfermline ensured that Irish control of the finer fabrics was not complete. But the broad picture is one of complementarity, of the Scots giving up the manufacture of fine linen and of thread to the Irish and taking total control of the coarse range of cloth, much of which was destined for industrial use.

Well before the 1850s linen had given way to cotton as the leading employer of textile workers in Scotland. The 1861 census showed less than one-third of Scotland's textile employment in the linen manufacture, whereas in Ulster (and Ireland as a whole) cotton was decisively in second place to linen as an employer.[3] The growth of the cotton industry had a major influence on the development of the linen industries of Scotland and Ireland. These industries had always operated in a competitive world, from which they were only partially shielded by protection and subsidy. The French and the Flemish, for example, could offer formidable competition in fine linen, the Germans in medium, and the Russians in coarse sheeting and sacking. Nonetheless, cotton greatly increased the pressure of competition. Cottons were close substitutes for linen in certain uses, and the raw material proved more amenable to mechanisation than did flax. Moreover, supplies of cotton were quickly expanded as cultivation spread across the American South. One result of cotton's attractions was the rapid transfer of textile activity in the West of Scotland from fine linen to cotton, a movement that may have benefited the Irish industry by removing some of the competition in fine linen. What the Irish may have gained in linen, however, was to some degree offset by the competition of cotton.

II

The world of linen was competitive in the later eighteenth century and became more so with the arrival, first, of cotton and, later, of jute. Moreover, the framework of government support for Scottish and Irish producers, which had existed since the early eighteenth century, was summarily dismantled in the 1820s. We shall take up two elements in this episode of deregulation: the demise of cloth inspection and the abolition of export subsidies.

The writing was on the wall for both Linen Boards by the early 1820s. After the Union of 1801 the Irish Board, like the Scottish, had been brought under the control of Westminster. Increasingly their position came under attack from within and without the industry, particularly from the advocates of laissez-faire.[4] In both countries, the Boards' powers of regulation and inspection provided the targets for criticism: the sealing system in Ireland (especially after the reforms from 1816) and the stampmaster network in Scotland. Dundee and Aberdeen manufacturers were in the van of the agitation in Scotland for repeal of the linen laws, arguing with some justice that they did not need the stamping system; were not their name and reputation sufficient? In defence, the Scottish Board's strongest argument was the need to protect the position of the small manufacturer and independent weaver. In 1820, for example, a meeting at Dundee concluded that

> to change the present system of stamping would infallibly ruin the lesser manufacturers who compose the great bulk of the Trade . . . the Linen Trade will fall entirely into the hands of the Capitalist, the lesser manufacturers will disappear and be reduced to the Condition of Workmen in the employ of the more wealthy, and become dependent on them.[5]

Similar sentiments were expressed throughout the debate. There seems to have been a quite genuine belief that the stamping system was an objective guarantee of quality which buyers could trust.[6] Some London linen merchants did testify that buyers would not be prepared to risk purchase of linens without a stamp, and that the abolition would confine the trade to the large manufacturers, but for all the evidence of the social value of perpetuating the Board's system, it was a lost cause, which the Board itself fairly quickly realised.[7] While they would have preferred things to continue and many of their officials publicly associated themselves with the anti-repeal movement, privately they settled for securing the best compensation possible for their officials, a move in which they were very successful. The alliance against reform had wide support, and the argument that abolition would accelerate the movement of the industry into factories, 'large establishments alike prejudicial to the health and morals of those employed in them', played on current concerns.[8] But Huskisson and his colleagues could not be moved, and the system came to an end in 1823.

The Irish Board was now very vulnerable to a parallel reduction in its powers and met its fate with a resignation similar to that of the Scottish Board. As James Corry, the Secretary, conceded: 'there is a popular opinion now abroad in which I feel I participate, that after a certain point of prosperity has been attained, the less any manufacture is encumbered with legislative regulations the better'.[9] The assault took only a short time to materialise, and after a House of Commons enquiry, the inspection of white cloth was ended in Ireland on 1 July 1825. Effectively both Boards had run their course, although a few residual functions remained.

But did the virtual abolition of the Boards make any real difference to the subsequent development of the linen industries of Scotland and Ireland? The general view, which we accept, is that their passing made no odds; and Gill's conclusion that the Board was no longer needed, though it had been useful in the early days, would have been totally acceptable to Warden, the historian of the Scottish industry. Yet there is more than a suspicion that the abolition of compulsory stamping in Scotland did accelerate the movement of the industry into the hands of the larger manufacturers, just as the anti-repeal school had anticipated. It must be emphasised that such a movement was already underway; more and more of the manufacturing was organised on a large scale through the giving-out system or in the new power-loom factories; less and less of the marketing was taking place at the traditional open fairs and markets. This process was also evident in Ireland, particularly in Co. Down, but was more advanced in Scotland, as the Secretary of the Scottish Board explained to his Irish counterpart:

> It appears that [at Dundee] they have no public markets on stated days . . . nor is there any public linen market in any of the contiguous manufacturing counties. In Dundee . . . the great part is sold in the Warehouses of the Manufacturers, and the Buyers are in the habit of going to these warehouses. On one day a week the smaller manufacturers (or Hawkers as they are called) bring linens from the distant manufacturing villages where they reside, and sell them in warehouses of their own.[10]

The abolition of public stamping accelerated an existing trend, and the voluntary system which was tried in Scotland proved no substitute. In Ireland, where the seal-stamping had never been as total or as efficient, the loss of the system had less effect.

The ending of the export subsidies on linens followed the demise of inspection. The subsidy on Irish exports was progressively reduced from 1825 until 1830 when it was abolished entirely; the British subsidy lasted two years longer, ending on 5 January 1832 amidst scenes of frenzy as exporters shipped twelve million yards of cloth from Dundee in the last quarter of 1831, a quantity vastly in excess of the normal.[11] As in the case of the linen regulations, there was a general view that the industry needed no special treatment, and to add to the ideological objections, the cost of the export subsidy was substantial: in the last year of full subsidy the amount paid on British linens was over £200,000, of which Dundee merchants received a third, and Irish exports collected some £87,000.[12] The Scottish Board privately conceded the loss of the bounty long before it actually happened, despite their official line that it was essential. In January 1817 the Secretary wrote to one Fife manufacturer who had optimistically suggested an attempt to extend the scope of the bounty to Northern Europe:

> It has been a matter of astonishment to me that the present bounties have been so long continued: it is surely a very questionable policy to bolster up the manufacturers at such a very great expense, though we in this office are every year in the practice of *eulogising* it in our annual report to the King as absolutely *necessary* ...[13]

The loss of the bounty was more serious to Scottish manufacturers than to the Irish, given that the manufacturing strength of the East of Scotland was so orientated to the production of coarse to medium linens, a high proportion of which went for export, either directly or by way of London, to the West Indies or North America. Yet there seems little evidence to suggest that the withdrawal of the subsidy held back Scottish exports after 1832. In fact, they pursued the rapid growth which had begun in the late 1810s. Exports at Dundee increased from 44 million yards in 1831 to 79 million yards in 1845.[14] Given the rate at which the Scottish trade grew, it seems likely that the bounties simply boosted profits rather than significantly widened markets. When the bounty ended, the Scots continued to sell to the Americas, but the expansion of the 1830s and early 1840s was directed at previously underexploited European markets, especially France. It should be added that the Scots, dependent as they were on imported flax, benefited from the parallel reduction of duties on their raw material.

Most Irish linen did not qualify for bounties, either because it was shipped to British or European markets or because its value exceeded 1s.6d. per yard. But some manufacture of coarse cloth, notably at Drogheda and in Munster, was stimulated by the bounty and by premiums given by the Irish Linen Board. This production depended on subsidies, and their withdrawal revealed an inability to compete with Scottish producers. Some Northerners were also tempted by the bounties, to the detriment of the industry, according to one Ulster manufacturer writing in the mid-1830s:

> The bounties ... encouraged the production of low and worthless articles on the value of which the bounty became a handsome profit. Such goods were, of course, despised when brought into comparison with those of the Continent in foreign markets. A better description is now made for export ...[15]

III

Deregulation and the loss of the export subsidies, to say nothing of the removal of protective import duties on foreign linen, made the competitive environment harsher for the smaller or more distant producers such as the coarse linen manufacturers around Drogheda; and it tended to confirm the specialisation already present, of Ulster in fine linen, and East-Central Scotland in coarse. A claim made on Dundee's behalf in the 1830s, that it was shipping as much linen 'as all Ireland', drew a fierce rebuttal from Belfast's *Northern Whig*, which began with the crisp statement that 'it is well known that the Dundee or Scotch linens are of a coarse cheap description whilst ours are, in general, fine and dear'.[16] The volume of the cloth exported might be very similar, but what mattered was the value. Ulster linens, it was said, could be valued on average at 1s.6d. per yard; the Scottish linens at no more than 6d. or 7d. per yard. What this exchange underlines is the extent to which the industries had become complementary rather than competitive in their production. The differences in their products are crucial to understanding why the Scottish and Irish industries differed in two major respects, the source of flax supplied and the rate of mechanisation.

The self-sufficiency of the Irish linen industry stands in stark contrast to the Scottish experience of ever-increasing dependence on imports of flax. Scottish farmers could and did grow good flax, but as has been argued at a previous Scottish–Irish conference, the uncertainty of yields, the labour-intensive nature of cultivation and the ready availability of imports removed much incentive from this crop.[17] Imports of flax rose steadily from 7,700 tons in 1800 to 26,000 in 1829, then varied between 35,000 and 45,000 tons until the 1870s when decline set in. Two-thirds of this flax came into Dundee, with the rest being imported at Aberdeen, Arbroath, Montrose and Kirkcaldy.

Ireland in the 1850s still had around 100,000 acres in flax cultivation. Large variations in yield do not seem to have been so much of a problem as in Scotland, and Irish flax was regarded in the early nineteenth century as superior in quality to most foreign imports.[18] Yet Irish flax was not well received in Scotland when the Irish Linen Board attempted to promote it as a substitute for Baltic flax, the price of which had been driven up during the Napoleonic Wars. The Board's agent, William Marshall, reported that the Scottish mill-spinners were keen in principle to use Irish flax, but that there were a number of practical difficulties, the most serious of which was the failure of the Irish to sort and clean their flax sufficiently to prevent machinery from becoming clogged with dirt.[19] Some improvement seems to have taken place, for by the 1820s Dundee manufacturers were buying some flax grown in Cavan and elsewhere. The quantities involved, however, were not large in relation to total Scottish imports.

When mill-spinning became established in Ireland, in the 1830s, the poor preparation of Irish flax again showed itself to be a problem. Mill-spinners were obliged to import Continental flax. They also launched a campaign, first in the newspapers, then later through the Flax Supply Association, urging Irish farmers to take greater pains with the crop.[20] It is not difficult to explain why factory spinners were more exigent. Their machines were less tolerant of variations in the quality of the raw material than were those of handspinners. Moreover, handspinners working with much smaller quantities of flax could easily do some further sorting and cleaning. The persistence of handspinning in Ireland and the reliance on home-grown flax may, thus, have been related phenomena.

Yet, despite persistent criticism of Irish flax, the Irish industry did not begin to make large net imports of flax until the 1870s, well after the definitive eclipse of handspinning. Whilst it did import Continental flax from the 1830s, it is significant that much of this came from Holland, France, and Belgium, rather than from the Baltic, the source of the bulk of Scottish imports.[21] Dutch, French, and Belgian flax was the best grown, on the Continent and, as such, was suited to the fine linen production in which Ulster specialised. Supplies from these areas were limited by the growth of local linen industries which were protected by duties not only on yarn and cloth imports, but on flax exports. That the Irish industry eschewed Baltic flax in favour of home-grown flax suggests that the intrinsic quality, if not the preparation, of Irish flax was high. The differences in product mix between the Irish and Scottish industries seem to have been a major factor in determining where they obtained their raw materials.

The increasing reliance on imported flax made control of the production process by the larger manufacturers in Scotland more likely. While the weaving households were freed from agricultural work to become full-time specialists, that 'freedom' lessened their independence as dressed flax became harder to buy and the cultivation of flax by the farmers or the weavers themselves became more and more rare in the years after 1815.[22] In Ireland, by contrast, the widespread cultivation of flax in Ulster made it possible for small-scale producers to secure supplies relatively easily. What increased the influence of the larger manufacturers in Ireland, and furthered their control in Scotland, was the substitution of mill-spun yarn.

The pace of mechanisation was another area in which the Scottish and Irish industries differed. All the main processes of the linen manufacture — scutching, heckling, spinning and weaving — were eventually to be mechanised, but the Irish adoption of these changes tended to lag behind Scotland. Heckling was mechanised in Dundee much earlier than in Belfast, hand-spinning in Scotland was virtually extinct by the late 1820s whereas it persisted much longer in Ireland, and the adoption of the power-loom was much more extensive in Scotland. The common factor in all of these cases was the relative ease with which machines could be applied to the coarse fibres and fabrics in which Scotland was specialised as against the finer linens in which Ireland excelled. Important though the greater availability of labour in Ireland may have been in the persistence of hand technologies, it may be suggested that the major constraint was technological.

Take the case of power spinning. In 1838 there were only 40 spinning mills in Ireland as against 183 in Scotland and 169 in England. But there had been no lack of interest in Ireland in power spinning. The Irish Linen Board had been active — some contemporaries would probably have said lavish — in its support for improvements in spinning technology and for the diffusion of dry spinning mills. Indeed, dry spinning was widely tried in Ireland, but could not produce the fine yarns required by Irish weavers.[23] Even in the early days of wet spinning, in the 1830s, machines could not spin the finer counts. The downward trend in linen yarn prices and the drift upward in the counts spun by machine during the 1830s and 1840s bear witness to the many improvements which were necessary before handspun yarn could be supplanted in the production of fine linens.[24]

Ireland was also slow, relative to Scotland, in adopting the power loom. To some extent this lag reflected lower labour costs, particularly before the Famine. Thereafter the change in labour supply conditions did stimulate greater interest in power looms, with many Irish firms conducting trials in the early 1850s. But again, the main limiting factor was the suitability of the technique, in its current state of development, to the product mix of the Irish industry. As a well-informed contemporary put it, the small number of power looms in Ireland was 'chiefly to be attributed to the fact that so small a proportion of Irish flaxen fabrics are of that coarse and heavy description for which the power loom appears to be fitted'.[25] It took another decade and the stimulus of the cotton famine for power looms to be widely adopted in Ireland. Significantly, in Dunfermline the general use of the power loom was as 'late' as in Ireland, and for some sorts of fine linen the handloom was to prevail for decades.

IV

The changes in technology must have been a major element in the organisational transformation of linen production which took place in the early nineteenth century. By the 1820s there was already much concern in both Scotland and Ireland over the increasing dominance in the industry of entrepreneurs with wealth and power, the 'capitalists' whose firms came increasingly to control production at the expense of the independent weaver and small manufacturer.[26] In 1823 one Fife millowner thought that neither he nor any of his acquaintances could name an independent weaver, 'a Man who does nothing more than weave his own web and sell it'.[27] Yet less than ten years previously the Board of Trustees had stated that most of the linen made in Scotland was being manufactured 'by poor weavers who have not a shilling of Capital and who sell it in single webs to dealers or middle men as soon as the web is finished'.[28] Admittedly this observation is found in the context of a defence of the Stampmasters' role, but all the available evidence does point to a surprisingly fast rate of organisational change in the Scottish linen industry after 1815.

In Ireland similar changes were underway at a slower pace. In some areas, such as north Antrim, the independent weavers and linen drapers held on longer, but in most areas the control of linen production was passing into the hands of Ulster 'capitalists'. Manufacturers began to buy mill-spun yarn, first from England, then locally, and give it out to weaver-employees to be made into cloth, which was then sold (bleached or unbleached) to merchants. Unlike in Scotland, where the manufacturers had generally come up through the ranks of weavers, many Irish capitalists moved into manufacturing from either bleaching or mill-spinning. By the 1840s some Irish firms spun, wove, bleached, and marketed.[29] Such a degree of integration was rare in Scotland.

The rise of the manufacturer in Ireland coincided with increased concentration of the marketing of linen cloth at Belfast. The amount of cloth passing through the Dublin Linen Hall declined precipitously. Belfast merchants and manufacturers began to sell directly to customers, without the intervention of English factors.[30] By the 1840s it was said, with some exaggeration, that 'exporting merchants can now procure most extensive assortments of linen and cotton goods in Belfast and in most of fabrics much cheaper than in Manchester'.[31] It is tempting to argue that marketing was an important factor in the concentration of production around Belfast. The town's share in the linen trade increased well before it became an important linen-manufacturing centre, indeed while it was still occupied heavily in cotton manufacture. In Scotland this thesis seems less viable. Dundee had been the main manufacturing centre for linens for many decades, yet never quite achieved the dominance of marketing or manufacturing that its historic position might have generated. At Arbroath, Montrose and even inland Forfar, many firms, linked though they might be to Dundee through kinship, continued to hold independent positions in production and marketing. The arrival of jute, which increasingly absorbed the attention of many Dundee linen firms, only strengthened the situation of firms elsewhere in Angus and neighbouring counties. One reason why marketing may have been less important in determining the location of production in Scotland was that Scottish products were more standardised and less subject to changes in fashion.

Mechanisation and geographical concentration of production had social costs for labour in Scotland and Ireland. The long-drawn-out agony of the Scottish handloom weavers has been ably described by Dr. Norman Murray.[32] Though the wages of handloom weavers in Ireland fell in the decades before the Famine, this was more the result of general labour supply conditions in Ireland than of declining demand for their skills. After the Famine wages for weavers increased markedly. The decline of handloom weaving in Ireland was much later than in Scotland and occurred during a period when alternative employment opportunities and emigration could ease the transition.

Less attention has been paid to the effects of the decline of handspinning in Scotland, though the implications of similar developments in Ireland have been analysed in detail by Dr. Brenda Collins.[33] Factory-spun yarn took away many more jobs in the household than it created in the mills, and in doing so destabilised many households in Scotland and Ireland. The effects were arguably more severe in Scotland. They occurred earlier in Scotland, with the late 1810s and 1820s being the critical period, and were made worse by the simultaneous decline of hand-knitting, another traditional source of female employment.[34] Those who suffered most in both countries were households in peripheral areas where weaving had never taken root. In western Ireland and parts of the Highlands many families had come to rely on the earnings of women in linen spinning. When this source dried up, the women could not join the men as weavers, as was possible in parts of south Ulster and eastern Scotland. Another source of alternative employment, which was important in Ireland from the 1830s, was sewing, flowering and fancy work. It is not clear to what extent this was available to displaced spinners in Scotland in the 1820s.

V

In this essay we have examined some of the key changes in the linen industries of Scotland and Ireland during the early nineteenth century. We are well aware that much more needs to be done to elucidate the role played by the linen industry in these two economies. One finding that we want to underline, and which has implications for future research, is that by the 1830s these industries were essentially complementary, Ulster with its fine linen, Angus with its coarse. This complementarity was not total, but it does suggest that it would be more appropriate to compare their performance not with each other, but with their competitors, at home and abroad, in fabrics of similar quality and uses. By all means let us examine the Scottish and Irish industries, but as a first step towards a wider understanding of the world markets in which they had to compete — something both did with considerable success.

NOTES

We would like to thank Brenda Collins, William Crawford, and Cormac O Grada for their helpful comments on earlier drafts of this paper. Peter Solar would also like to thank the Pasold Research Fund for its support of his work on the nineteenth-century Irish linen trade.

1. The standard works on the nineteenth-century industry are still C. Gill, *The Rise of the Irish Linen Industry* (Oxford, 1925) and A. J. Warden, *The Linen Trade Ancient and Modern* (Dundee, 1864).

2. C. Gill, *op.cit.*, pp. 160–1. The description of the industries c.1780 draws on Gill and A. J. Durie, *The Scottish Linen Industry in the Eighteenth Century* (Edinburgh, 1979).

3. It is interesting to note that, according to the census, the total numbers of textile workers in Scotland and in Ulster were not dissimilar, though far fewer of the Irish workers show up in the factory returns. It would not be wise, however, to press the census figures too far, given the ambiguities in the classification of occupations.

4. See H. D. Gribbon, 'The Irish Linen Board, 1711–1828' and A. J. Durie, 'The Scottish Linen Industry in the Eighteenth Century', both in Cullen & Smout, pp. 77–87, 88–99.

5. S.R.O. Records of the Board of Trustees [BT], NG 1/60/53/5/9, 'Memorial of John Blair Millar', etc.

6. S.R.O. BT, NG 1/60/65, Notes of Meeting at Dundee, 5 Dec. 1820.

7. S.R.O. BT, NG 1/60/78, Minutes of Evidence taken before the Select Committee of the House of Lords, July 1823.

8. S.R.O. BT, NG 1/60/73, 'The Case of the Buyers and Manufacturers interested in the Proposed Repeal of the Laws', 1823.

9. C. Gill, *op.cit.*, p. 307.

10. S.R.O. BT, NG 1/3/20, letter book, 7 Feb. 1820.

11. A. J. Warden, *op.cit.*, pp. 607–8.

12. *Ibid.*, p. 669.

13. S.R.O. BT, NG 1/3/21, letter book, Secretary to Neilson & Co., Leven.

14. J. R. McCulloch, *A Dictionary, Practical, Theoretical and Historical, of Commerce etc.*, (London, 2nd ed., 1834), p. 763; A. J. Warden, *op.cit.*, pp. 635–6.

15. *Hansard Debates*, 3rd ser., 22 (1834), 1261.

16. *Northern Whig*, 14 Jan. 1836, 'Linen Trade of Belfast and Dundee'.

17. A. J. Durie, in Cullen & Smout, pp. 88-91.

18. On the variation in yields, see the Irish Agricultural Statistics from 1847. On the quality of Irish flax, see F. W. Smith, *The Irish Linen Trade Hand Book* (Belfast, 1876), p. 63, quoting James Corry's report of 1816, and *Northern Whig*, 2 Feb. 1826, 'Belfast, Its Home Trade, and Foreign Relations'.

19. P.R.O.N.I. Linen Board Papers, Report of Mr. William Marshall, 1817.

20. *Northern Whig*, 26 Dec. 1833, 'Cultivation and Management of Flax', and 20 Mar. 1834, 'To the Growers of Flax in Ireland'.

21. Dundee Trade Report Association, *Statistics of the Linen Trade* (Dundee, 1855), pp. 43–51, 115.

22. T. C. Smout, 'Centre and Periphery in History — Scotland', *Journal of Common Market Studies*, 1980, p. 266.

23. *Belfast and Ulster Directory for 1883*, p. 10.

24. H. McCall, *Our Staple Manufactures* (Belfast, 1855), p. 114.

25. Belfast Linen Trade Circular, 6 Aug. 1852, 'Irish Flax Manufactures'.

26. S.R.O. BT, NG 1/60/78.

27. Ibid.

28. S.R.O. BT, NG 1/3/19, 6 July 1814.

29. *Belfast Mercantile Register*, 2 Jan. 1844.

30. W. T. Charley, 'Linen', in G. P. Bevan, ed., *British Manufacturing Industries: Wool, Flax and Linen, Cotton, Silk*, (3 vols., London, 2nd ed., 1877), pp. 75–6.

31. *Belfast Mercantile Register*, 12 Dec. 1843.

32. N. Murray, *The Scottish Hand Loom Weavers* (Edinburgh, 1981).

33. B. Collins, 'Proto-Industrialisation and Pre-Famine Emigration', *Social History*, 7 (1982), pp. 127–46.

34. A. J. Durie, *The Scottish Linen Industry*, p. 167.

18
ASPECTS OF BANK LENDING IN POST-FAMINE IRELAND

Philip Ollerenshaw

In an article published in 1954 David Joslin wrote that London private bankers of the eighteenth century had been 'more often prejudged than investigated'.[1] The present essay argues that such a comment is equally applicable to nineteenth-century Irish banks. No part of the United Kingdom banking system has been less investigated but in spite, or perhaps because, of this the verdict of historians has exhibited a striking degree of unanimity. The banks have been criticised for being 'conservative' and for their unwillingness to assist Irish enterprise, preferring instead to channel their resources out of the country.[2] The historiography of Irish banking differs markedly from that of the Scottish banks, yet it remains relevant to emphasise that Ireland drew on the Scottish banks from the earliest days of joint-stock banking (the 1820s) and that both bank staff and banking techniques migrated to Ireland.

The structure of the Irish banking system may be briefly summarised. The largest, and the only chartered, bank was the Bank of Ireland founded in 1783. By 1850 it had lost most of its privileges and indeed suffered from some disadvantages, one of which was that it was prevented by Act of Parliament from lending on mortgage. This restriction applied to no other Irish bank and was lifted in 1860.[3] From the mid-nineteenth century the Bank of Ireland competed with its joint-stock rivals. Most of the latter had been established in two phases of bank promotion from 1824 to 1827 and from 1834 to 1838. In 1850 the Bank of Ireland and all joint-stock banks, with the exception of the Dublin-based Royal Bank, operated branch networks. Only the Provincial Bank and the Bank of Ireland had networks with approximately national coverage; three — the Belfast, Northern and Ulster — were confined to the province of Ulster; the Tipperary Joint-Stock had a small network in County Tipperary and surrounding counties; the National Bank possessed the largest branch system in 1850, although it had not yet penetrated the industrialising north-east; the smallest system was operated by the Dublin-based Hibernian.[4]

Between 1850 and 1914 the development of Irish banking was essentially based on the numerical and geographical expansion of branch networks of banks established before 1840. The total number of bank offices was probably about 170 in 1850 and had reached 800 or so by 1914.[5] There were many reasons why this increase was so rapid, but chief among them was the search for deposits, the key determinant of lending capacity and bank profitability.

Bank failure was rare in Ireland in this period, although the Tipperary Bank failed in 1856 and the Munster Bank, established only in 1864, crashed in 1885. There were even fewer new entrants: the only one was the Munster and Leinster, and this in fact was built on the wreckage of the Munster.[6] The creation of extensive branch systems enabled several Irish banks to move funds around from 'saving' to 'investing' areas even before 1850, and there is enough evidence to question a recent claim that the ability to do this in the mid-nineteenth century was peculiar to Scottish banks.[7]

The relative importance of Ireland within the United Kingdom banking system was small. One indicator of this is the level of deposits in Irish banks compared to Scotland and England and Wales. The most recent estimates are outlined in Table 1.

Even if deposits in Irish banks were not more than 7 per cent of the United Kingdom total between 1871 and 1914, it is worth pointing out that their rate of increase was higher in this period than the rates in Scotland and England and Wales. It is sometimes suggested that Irish bank deposits were 'idle' or 'sterile',[8] but a study of bank records firmly contradicts this view. Although published balance-sheet data need to be interpreted with great caution, the conclusions must be that in the later nineteenth and early twentieth centuries total advances continued to rise on trend, although at a slower rate than deposits; that discount business declined compared to overdraft business; and that investments loomed much larger in bank-asset portfolios in 1914 than they had in the 1860s. Investment of funds outside Ireland had long been a necessity for Irish banks, since securities could not be bought and sold in quantity on the small Dublin Stock Exchange without causing large fluctuations in price. For this reason purchases and sales were made via the London Stock Exchange, and the same was true of the Scottish banks.[9] Investment of bank funds served a dual purpose; it served as a liquid reserve in the event of crisis, and provided an outlet if the demand for bank credit fell below the potential supply. The evidence indicates that bank deposits increased so rapidly between c.1870 and 1914 that the demand for credit could not hope to keep pace, and this goes far to explain the increasing absolute and relative size in investments.

In any study of bank lending the limitations of the records need to be kept firmly

Table 1. Bank Deposits within the UK, 1871–1914 (£000)

	Ireland	*Scotland*	*England and Wales*	*U.K. Total*
1871	25,857 (5.8)	65,109 (14.6)	355,588 (79.6)	446,464
1881	29,761 (5.9)	78,581 (15.7)	392,760 (78.4)	501,102
1891	39,267 (6.3)	92,084 (14.7)	495,213 (79.0)	626,564
1901	48,773 (5.9)	107,350 (12.9)	676,849 (81.2)	832,972
1914	71,067 (6.4)	129,642 (11.7)	899,901 (81.0)	1,110,610

Source: Forrest Capie and Alan Webber, *A Monetary History of the United Kingdom 1870–1982*, Vol. 1 (London, 1985), p. 432.

N.B. Figures in brackets indicate percentage of U.K. total.

All figures are annual averages.

in mind. Bank records are essentially supply-side data, although their correspondence may also shed light on demand. They do not normally permit calculation of the importance of bank funds relative to other sources of credit, and it is more than likely that annual balance sheets seriously understate bank lending. This is so because the annual balance might be struck at a point in the year when lending was relatively low compared to preceding or following months. Moreover, annual balance sheets cannot show the extent to which loans were made and repaid in the period since the previous balance.[10] This is a particularly important consideration in any area where a significant amount of lending was undertaken on a seasonal basis.

In Ireland much economic activity was agricultural or related to agriculture: brewing, distilling and to some extent the linen industry are examples of the latter. Seasonal rhythms in agriculture and in other areas of the economy imply a seasonal demand for credit. This relationship has already been identified as a feature of early-modern England,[11] and it was certainly the case in Ireland before 1914. Some examples will help to clarify this aspect of bank lending.

In Ulster flax spinners frequently required credit during the flax-buying season, the autumn and winter months, and repaid the bank when the yarn had been sold. The size of sums required by spinners varied enormously: in the 1860s overdraft facilities ranged from about £2,000 for small firms to around £60,000 for giants such as the York Street Flax Spinning Co. Ltd of Belfast.[12] Millers were another group which received seasonal credit. Thus the Clonmel branch manager of the Provincial Bank normally sent a list of his customers in this trade who required the 'usual advances by way of overdraft during the grain and milling seasons' to head office in London for approval. In 1851, for example, overdraft facilities for ten millers at this branch ranged from £500 to £8,000 and totalled £38,900. Three of these customers required small advances (one for £500, two for £700) and were charged 5%; the remaining seven (£2,500 to £8,000) paid only 4% for their credit, although this differential did not always apply.[13]

Seasonal demands for credit often came from those engaged in the important provisions trade and their requirements were greatest in the winter months. One example of how a provision merchant's account fluctuated is the firm of W. and J. Campbell. The state of their account with the Ulster Bank in Belfast over the period 1854–63 is summarised in Table 2. This account may be taken as representative of many others in the provisions trade. Amongst the most extensive credit facilities afforded to a provision merchant in the 1850s was to a customer of the Limerick branch of the Provincial Bank. His discount line at 1854 was £40,000, and this relatively large sum may be explained by the fact that he was engaged in large-scale, low-risk, government contract work.[14]

Butter buyers were frequently in receipt of short-term advances, and the extent of their credit 'for the season' could be more than £10,000, although smaller sums were more typical.[15] Fishermen too might require seasonal assistance. One group of fishermen in County Cork approached the manager of the Provincial Bank in Kinsale in October 1892 for an advance of £3,000 'for the coming fishing season'. The bank's directors agreed to provide this sum 'for the season, but advance must

Table 2. Current Account of W. and J. Campbell, 1854–63 (£)

	February	*August*
1854	– 10,266	– 50
1855	– 8,661	+ 2,377
1856	– 3,116	– 89
1857	– 5,139	– 162
1858	+ 54	+ 1,176
1859	– 7,340	+ 669
1860	– 5,995	+ 1,052
1861	– 3,809	+ 932
1862	– 4,268	+ 409
1863	– 3,223	+ 1,207

Source: *Ulster Bank Half-Yearly Balances.*

be reduced at end of season and boats sold'.[16] Other occasional recipients of seasonal bank accommodation, which could be quite extensive, were importers of guano. For example, one importer in Cork City in September 1878 sought discount accommodation 'during the coming guano season' up to a limit of £43,750. The Provincial Bank in Cork agreed to discount the 'guano bills' on the personal security of the proprietor of the firm 'and the possession of the cargoes as they arrive'.[17]

It is clear from the instances already given that enterprises in many different industries required regular seasonal advances and that the banks appear to have met this need. Given the crucial significance of agriculture in the Irish economy, it is unsurprising that banks made it their business to be well-informed about agricultural conditions in those areas in which they had branches, not least because such information would enable them the better to judge creditworthiness. The Provincial Bank, for example, sent out circulars to branches, normally once a year, inquiring as to the results of the harvest; the condition and prospects of landowners, farmers and labourers; the proportion of ground under each crop; and the quantity, quality and price of each article of produce in the current year compared with previous years. Finally, bank directors wanted to know 'what opinion is entertained as to the stock of cattle, pigs &c held by farmers, and the probable amount of poor rate for the next year, and how that and other taxes and the rents are likely to be paid'.[18] Bankers appreciated more than most the interdependence of the various strata of rural society and many of the elements within the local economy. The potential for a 'domino effect' in the event of one or more bad harvests was indeed great.

The first two major downturns in post-Famine Irish agriculture were those of 1859–64 and 1877–9, and they affected the banks in a number of ways. Deposits declined and the banks moved quickly to curtail the supply of credit in rural Ireland. Amongst the first indications of apprehension was a circular sent in

August 1860 to branches of the Ulster Bank advising that due to unfavourable weather and 'gloomy prospects' for the harvest, great caution should be exercised in the discount of bills on farmers and country traders. Bill renewals and accommodation bills were to be avoided as much as possible. No new overdrafts or extensions to existing loans were to be made without permission from the directors. A similar circular was sent, as a reminder, in September 1861.[19] By the next summer bank directors had become more concerned about the state of the rural economy and tightened the screw again with the instruction that managers should abstain from discounting farmers' bills, since farmers' prospects 'are bad and we fear there may be difficulty in getting payment from them'.[20] As far as this bank was concerned the trough of the depression was reached early in 1863, and a circular of January graphically illustrates the parlous state of the country which, it judged,

> has not been in so critical a condition since the year 1847. Three successive bad harvests have reduced farmers — particularly the smaller class — to a very low ebb. The country shopkeepers, who are dependent upon the farming and labouring population, cannot collect the money due to them, while the traders carrying on business with small provision dealers in Lancashire and the North of England must have been doing a very unprofitable trade.[21]

In view of this, advances of all types were to be kept 'to the lowest possible limit'. This severe restriction of credit must have been characteristic of the early 1860s and it was certainly enforced by the Provincial Bank which was acutely aware of the impact of four bad seasons on 'the numerous class of small farmers', provision and corn merchants and millers.[22] Caution was still exercised for some time after agriculture began to improve, though it naturally gave way to easier credit conditions in the early and mid-1870s.

The downturn which began in 1877 was also accompanied by a credit squeeze. In November of that year branch managers of the Northern Bank were advised to be 'more than usually cautious' in their transactions with farmers and shopkeepers, and strict limits were imposed on accommodation. Occasional overdrafts without security were to be discontinued 'where any risk is apprehended' and managers were asked to consider how best to act on these instructions without 'losing any good business or making their management unpopular'.[23]

If the Northern began to restrict credit in 1877, by 1880 creditworthiness had evidently declined to such an extent that many branches were instructed to discount no new bills for shopkeepers or farmers unless the endorsers could be depended upon for cash payment if the acceptors failed to pay when the bill matured. The Northern was alive to the fact that if farmers were hard-pressed, the structure of agricultural credit would be jeopardised. Because this was so the bank warned managers that

> struggling shopkeepers are likely to try to get bills discounted, both to obtain ready money and to put the bank between them and their debtors to assist themselves in collecting debts. This you must not permit.[24]

These instructions related only to new bills, but additional directions urged branches to 'get rid' of farmers' and shopkeepers' bills then under discount. If any such bills were renewed, strenuous efforts were to be made to strengthen them with an additional name if this could be obtained.

The banks' reactions to agricultural depression were predictable and rational: curtailment of new advances, additional security for existing accommodation. It would be misleading, however, to give the impression that banks had to be on their guard only in acknowledged depression years or periods of scarcity. Evidence of the way in which altered market conditions might necessitate swift revision of lending policy is afforded by the Corn Trade (a term which includes all types of grain and flour). This trade was an extensive one, and the profits of merchants engaged in it depended on several factors including the weather, overseas demand and foreign competition. As far as the merchant, and to some extent the banker, was concerned a glut of grain could exercise such a downward pressure on prices that losses might be sustained. Two examples will illustrate the banks' position in these circumstances. In the summer of 1857 the Provincial Bank's directors considered that the recent fine weather and the prospect of an abundant harvest were likely to lead to a decline in the price of wheat and other grains and flour. This would adversely affect corn merchants and millers, especially those who had 'held over their stocks or made speculative purchases in anticipation of a late or deficient harvest'. A constant review was to be made of customers in this trade, generally exercising 'great caution' and ensuring that 'each is in progress of winding up satisfactorily for the season'.[25] Similar problems recurred in 1874. By June expectations of a good harvest had already caused a slight decline in wheat prices. Although stocks of wheat were not large and the demand for flour in the short term was expected to be steady, thus preventing a sudden price fall, the Provincial Bank believed that the markets were being sustained by demand from France. Since the French harvest was likely to be 'early and full' a significant fall in price was anticipated. Head office judged that the best advice to corn merchants was to 'hold only what is required for the immediate supply of his customers, while millers should buy cautiously and hold only enough to keep their concerns in work and their customers supplied with flour'.[26] Here it can be seen that the bank, while urging caution in lending, was advising those in this trade to follow a course of action which would protect themselves, and by extension the bank, from the consequences of price decline. Sometimes, however, banks could do nothing other than look on while their customers were ruined by foreign competition. Grain merchants and millers felt the full blast of North American competition in the final quarter of the nineteenth century; not surprisingly there were many bankruptcies and losses suffered by the banks. This led to a revision of lending policy. As the Provincial Bank's report for 1883 explained:

> The American trade, improved machinery and so on, had much interfered with the trade of millers. It was the custom very often for banks to advance money on the security of mills, good going concerns, which were legitimate security. Now they were obliged to refuse advances on such security.[27]

The seasonality and volatility of bank lending is a recurrent theme running through the period under review. Apart from a small number of widespread industries, bank lending to Irish industry was concentrated in a few urban centres and in north-east Ulster. In industry as in agriculture market conditions and profitability could change rapidly and lead to great expansion or contraction of credit. In linen, for example, the boom of the mid-1860s was accompanied by a massive expansion of bank credit. After the boom many linen firms failed in the tougher conditions of the later nineteenth century and the banks frequently lost money as a result. In this period there were occasions when credit to many linen firms, especially hard-pressed spinners, was severely restricted.[28]

In general Irish banks pursued a similar policy to British banks in not favouring explicitly long-term loans. A natural fear of illiquidity dictated that banks should be able to call in loans at short notice if circumstances demanded. There were of course some customers who preferred a credit facility on a longer-term basis than those who required seasonal advances. This could be achieved by means of the award of a cash credit, a technique of Scottish origin described elsewhere but adopted in Ireland as early as the 1820s. The 'textbook' cash credit, however, soon gave way to many variations, including credit facilities which the modern observer would recognise as overdrafts, secured or unsecured. Typically such overdrafts were granted on condition that they would be repaid at a few months' notice. An example of this type of advance was that provided by the Belfast Bank to the Belfast and Ballymena Railway Co. The account was opened in January 1855 with a limit of £20,000 and a further £10,000 until the opening of the Cookstown branch. Interest was fixed at 5 per cent and no repayment date was set, 'either party giving six months' notice of a change as to £20,000'.[29]

Banks encouraged borrowers actively to use their accounts and not to regard them as dead loans, although there does not appear to have been any precise definition of 'active' and 'dead' in this respect. Those overdrawn accounts deemed to be inoperative were more likely to be called in or penalised with extra interest charges. If accounts were utilised to the bank's satisfaction, there was no reason why the credit facility could not remain for many years, and the evidence from nineteenth-century Ulster certainly supports this.[30] In Ireland, as in Scotland, this was the normal method of long-term lending.

Usually a bank preferred its customers to hold accounts with one bank only since it was naturally much more difficult to assess levels of indebtedness where more than one bank was involved, but there were occasions when no objections to this were raised. A good example was the Cork Distilleries Co., incorporated in December 1867 with the merger of four distilleries in Cork City and one (the largest of the five) in Midleton.[31] In September of that year the Provincial Bank had provided £5,000 each to two of the constituent firms on the understanding that the other firms would contribute a similar amount. The other constituent firms, however, appear to have had different banks because in October 1867 Cork Distilleries asked for a temporary overdraft of £20,000 from each of the Provincial Bank, the Bank of Ireland and the Munster Bank, secured by mortgages on plant and machinery. This was granted for six months, but it may have been extended since it is known that by July 1873 each of the three banks had provided advances of £30,000. Cork Distilleries may have continued to avail themselves of extensive credit facilities from these three banks, and the Provincial Bank raised this firm's credit limit to £40,000 in 1885.[32] For a customer to have more than one banker was the exception rather than the rule, but it was probably more common in the case of very large firms.

So far some examples of lending and fluctuations in the supply of credit have been outlined. Little has yet been said about rates of interest or the nature of collateral. In the space available we can do no more than mention some of the main considerations. As far as discount rates were concerned there was a broad spectrum of charges. As a rule three-month, first-class British bills were charged the lowest rates and other bills *pro rata*. Important customers could sometimes force a bank into lowering its discount rate below that paid by smaller or less favoured firms. Again there is evidence that some four-month bills were charged the minimum rates if this was the usual practice in the trade in which they originated. Thus the Provincial Bank was prepared to discount four-month bills in 'linen districts' at the minimum rate since this was the normal period of credit in the linen trade.[33] A wide variety of rates also prevailed for overdrafts. Much depended on the security (if any) offered, the size and nature of the business, the length of time for which a loan was required, the period with which the account had been operated to the bank's satisfaction and the likelihood that a customer might take his business elsewhere if his request was refused. Some customers successfully argued their case for a reduction in overdraft rate, but the initiative for reduction always, of course, came from the customer rather than the bank.

What kind of security was required for bank credit? Here the banks were very flexible. The following advice of the Ulster Bank Head Office to its Dublin branch manager in 1885 may be taken as representative of lending attitudes in the later nineteenth century:

> It very often happens that an unsecured advance to a steady upright practical man with a moderate capital is quite as safe as a secured advance. It is for a manager in your position to discriminate such cases and not be bound in his dealings with the public by a hard and fast line that makes no allowance for special circumstances. It is no doubt a sound rule that security should be got for overdrafts, but no bank could prosper which allowed any such rule to dominate every application for an advance ... The fact of the matter is that common sense is better than any rule, and every rule must therefore in its application be made subservient to the dictates of common sense.[34]

The view of bank directors generally was that each branch should pull its weight by contributing a fair share to the overall level of lending and deposit business. This might involve, as in the case just quoted, the encouragement of a more liberal lending policy, but it might also involve restraint of a manager lending too much in relation to deposits. There does not appear to have been any predetermined maximum ratio of advances to deposits permissible at any branch; rather this was usually left to the discretion of the manager. Occasionally, directors felt obliged to point out to a manager that the advances–deposit ratio at his branch had exceeded their wishes. In 1896, for example, the manager of the Belfast Bank's Markets branch was praised for his 'zeal and general care exercised both to bills and advances', although the directors added that while no single advance was regarded as unsafe, the gross total of accommodation bore a 'very undue relation' to the resources of the branch. The figures were:

Bills	£ 28,500	Deposits	£35,800
Overdrafts	£ 84,900	Current Accounts	£42,500
	£113,400		£78,300

In the directors' opinion the manager should 'without any serious or sudden change of policy arrange to place your branch on a proper relative footing'.[35]

If the banks did not pursue a rigid policy with regard to interest rates and security, they did not always keep customers to their credit limits either. Any bank could take steps to restrict accommodation if or when discount lines or overdraft limits were exceeded. In practice limits were often broken, and in such instances banks had to trust to their own judgement. A number of reasons may be suggested as to why a bank permitted credit limits to be exceeded. One was recognition of temporary difficulties; another was fear of losing business because any customer was at liberty to go to another bank. As branch systems expanded, the opportunities for customers to switch banks increased, although this was a step not lightly undertaken. In Ulster, for example, particularly in the late nineteenth and early twentieth centuries, there were many instances of banks canvassing for business, and in such an environment it was in each bank's interest to operate with flexibility in order to maintain customer loyalty.[36] With regard to discount lines, overdraft limits and the question of security for advances, rules could be bent and conventions broken with a view to accommodating customers. It is this discretionary element which should warn us against uncritical acceptance of the view that banks were rigid, 'conservative' institutions.

While banks considered that it was in their own interest to be flexible, sometimes when they did want to reduce credit levels or call in loans they found that customers were either unwilling or unable to comply, and this was an especially serious problem if a credit was unsecured or only partially secured. It was much easier to extend credit than to try to persuade a hard-pressed customer to reduce his obligations.[37] Knowing when to forbear and when to foreclose needed both luck and good management, and these were decisions banks had to take as a matter of course. In short, historians should not assume that banks had absolute control over the level of borrowing at any one time.

This essay has attempted to show that the role of banks in post-Famine Ireland was more positive and more complex than historians have hitherto been prepared to admit. A balanced picture of banking cannot be gained from published evidence. Parliamentary enquiries in particular took evidence either from bankers or from non-bankers, but rarely from both. Furthermore, the most intensive enquiries took place after commercial crises or in depressions when banks advertised caution and customers complained about shortage of credit. As soon as the unrepresentative nature of published evidence is perceived, and the available bank records are examined, the traditional view of Irish bank lending is seen to require fundamental revision.

NOTES

1. David Joslin, 'London Private Bankers, 1720-1785', *Ec.H.R.*, VII (1954), reprinted in E. M. Carus Wilson, ed., *Essays in Economic History*, II (London, 1962), p. 340.

2. See for example Joseph Lee, *The Modernisation of Irish Society, 1848–1918* (Dublin, 1973); George O'Brien, *The Economic History of Ireland From the Union to the Famine* (London, 1921), p. 544; R. D. C. Black, *Economic Thought and the Irish Question* (Cambridge, 1960), p. 152.

3. F. G. Hall, *History of the Bank of Ireland* (Dublin and Oxford, 1949), pp. 236–39.

4. The development of branch networks after 1850 is best followed in the banking directory published within *Thom's Directory*.

5. *Report of the Departmental Committee on Agricultural Credit in Ireland* (P.P. 1914, XIII), p. 18.

6. The Munster was Ireland's first joint-stock bank with limited liability.

7. Norio Tamaki, *The Life Cycle of the Union Bank of Scotland, 1830–1954* (Aberdeen, 1983), p. 91.

8. Joseph Lee, *The Modernisation of Irish Society, 1848–1918*, p. 11 and *idem*, 'Capital in the Irish Economy' in L. M. Cullen, ed., *The Formation of the Irish Economy* (Cork, 1969), p. 53.

9. R. C. Michie, 'The London Stock Exchange and the British Securities Market, 1850–1914', *Ec.H.R.*, XXXVIII (1985), p. 62.

10. For some of these problems, see R. F. Henderson, 'Bank Credit', in Brian Tew and R. F. Henderson, eds., *Studies in Company Finance* (Cambridge, 1959), esp. p. 77.

11. B. A. Holderness, 'Credit in a Rural Community 1660–1800', *Midland History*, IV (1975), esp. p. 94.

12. See for example Provincial Bank of Ireland Court Minutes, 9 September 1864, P.B. Minute Book, Vol. 10, Allied Irish Banks Archives, Foster Place, Dublin. I am very grateful to Mr. A. St. J. Lampkin of A.I.B. for his assistance with access to these records.

13. Ibid., 10 October 1851, P.B. Minute Book, Vol. 8.

14. Ibid., 1 December 1854.

15. Ibid., 27 March 1857, P.B. Minute Book, Vol. 9.

16. Ibid., 7 October 1892, P.B. Minute Book, Vol. 14.

17. Ibid., 20 September 1878, P.B. Minute Book, Vol. 12.

18. See for example Provincial Bank Circulars to Branches, 26 September 1850, 21 October 1852, 22 October 1853, 25 October 1856, A.I.B. Archives.

19. Ulster Bank Circulars to Branches, 22 August 1860, 18 September 1861, P.R.O.N.I. D3588/2/J/1.

20. Ibid., 19 June 1862.

21. Ibid., 28 January 1863.

22. Provincial Bank Annual Report, *Bankers' Magazine*, XXIII (1863), p. 455; Circulars to Branches, 16 June 1862, 2 January 1863.

23. Northern Bank Circular to Branches, 12 November 1877, P.R.O.N.I. D3145.

24. Ibid., 19 October 1880.

25. Provincial Bank Circular to Branches, 17 July 1857.

26. Ibid., 12 June 1874.

27. Provincial Bank Annual Report, *Bankers' Magazine*, XLIII (1883), p. 916.

28. For examples see P. G. Ollerenshaw, The Belfast Banks, 1820–1900: Aspects of

Banking in Nineteenth-Century Ireland (unpublished Ph.D. thesis, University of Sheffield, 1982), ch. 5.

29. Belfast Bank Board of Superintendence, Minute Book, 8 January 1855.

30. See Ollerenshaw, Belfast Banks, chs. 3–5.

31. E. B. McGuire, *Irish Whiskey* (Dublin, 1973), pp. 250, 310, 375–82.

32. Provincial Bank Court Minutes, 6 September, 25 October 1867, 25 July 1873, 6 November 1885, 17 September 1886.

33. Provincial Bank Circular to Branches, 10 October 1856.

34. Ulster Bank, Private Letter Book, Vol. 3, 22 October 1885.

35. Belfast Bank, Secretary's Letter Book, 6 June 1896.

36. Ollerenshaw, Belfast Banks, ch. 5.

37. Ibid. For a classic example, see Provincial Bank, Court Minutes, 7 February, 10 July, 18 December 1868; 29 January, 26 February, 28 May, 12 November 1869; 17 June, 16 December 1870; 15 August, 31 October 1873; 27 March, 24 July 1874.

19
ASPECTS OF BANK FINANCE FOR INDUSTRY: SCOTLAND 1845–1914[1]

Charles W. Munn

I

In 1845 the Scottish banking system was already fairly homogeneous. There were eighteen banks of which three were the public banks:[2]

1. Bank of Scotland	Edinburgh	1695
2. Royal Bank of Scotland	Edinburgh	1727
3. British Linen Co.	Edinburgh	1746
Twelve were joint-stock banks:		
4. Commercial Bank of Scotland	Edinburgh	1810
5. National Bank of Scotland	Edinburgh	1825
6. Aberdeen Town and County Bank	Aberdeen	1825
7. Union Bank of Scotland	Glasgow	1830
8. Western Bank of Scotland	Glasgow	1832
9. Central Bank of Scotland	Perth	1834
10. North of Scotland Bank	Aberdeen	1836
11. Clydesdale Bank	Glasgow	1838
12. Caledonian Bank	Inverness	1838
13. Eastern Bank of Scotland	Dundee	1838
14. City of Glasgow Bank	Glasgow	1839
15. Edinburgh and Glasgow Bank	Edinburgh	1844
Three were provincial banking companies:		
16. Dundee Banking Co.	Dundee	1763
17. Perth Banking Co.	Perth	1766
18. Aberdeen Banking Co.	Aberdeen	1767

All eighteen banks were fairly big organisations with large numbers of shareholders, substantial capital and branch networks. Each bank had its own note issue, the only real constraint on which was the requirement to retire notes received from the note exchange.

When the government of the early 1840s was preparing legislation to impose controls on the issuing of bank notes it became clear that Scotland and Ireland would require separate treatment. Although the volume of protest from Scotland was considerably less than it had been in 1826, when the Scots had feared the loss of their £1 notes, it was nevertheless still sufficiently vociferous to impress upon Peel that any interference would be resented, if not actually opposed, because the Scots believed that their system had not displayed the same weaknesses which had been displayed in England and, therefore, did not require any amending or controlling legislation.[3]

It was evident, when the Parliamentary Bill reached its final draft that, with one important exception, the proposed legislation would do little to change the system. The provisions of the Bill which became the Act[4] in 1845 were:

a) No new banks of issue were to be formed;
b) Each existing bank of issue was to have an 'authorised issue' based on the average issue of 1844;
c) Any bank wishing to exceed the authorised issue had to back the excess with holdings of gold or silver (in defined proportions) which were to be kept in two designated offices;
d) Where two banks merged, the authorised issue of the combined concern was to be the sum of the two.

This was considerably different from the legislation passed for England and Wales in 1844 which resulted in a creeping monopolisation of the note issue by the Bank of England. Any English or Welsh banks merging or opening an office in London automatically lost their right to issue notes. Ireland, however, received similar treatment to Scotland.

The effect of the Act was to reduce the profitability of the note issues as banks gradually exceeded their authorised issues and had to back the excess pound for pound in gold and silver, but this was not a problem in the short run, for many years were to pass before the excess issues became a major portion of the total issues. In any case deposits were fast becoming more important than note issues as the major source of loanable funds. The post-1845 years, therefore, witnessed an intensification of the efforts of the banks to increase their deposit bases — hence the great growth of branch networks. Most branches in the nineteenth century were net deposit takers, i.e. deposits exceeded lending, and the result of this was that the bulk of bank lending was channelled through just a few branches — usually the Head Office and the branches in major industrial centres.[5]

When the Bank Act for Scotland was passed in 1845 it received a mixed response. Many bankers resented it as an infringement of their freedom of action — a freedom which they had enjoyed and not, so they believed, abused since the regularising legislation affecting note issues in 1765. They also felt that the Act was an unwarranted intrusion by government which went against the business ethos of the day. Yet there were others, perhaps of a more subtle mind, who believed that there was some advantage in it for them because they realised that it would be extremely difficult, if not impossible, for new non-issuing banks to be formed and to compete successfully with the existing note-issuing banks.[6] And so it proved, with the result that a competitive market situation was transformed; and freedom of entry for new banks effectively ceased. Two notable failures and a series of amalgamations in the second half of the nineteenth century further changed the nature of the system so that by 1914 the market structure of banking in Scotland had become oligopolistic. Hand-in-hand with the stable prices which usually characterise this kind of market went a list of 'Agreements and Understandings' amongst the banks whereby price competition was effectively eliminated. It was, in any case, unreasonable to expect price competition amongst banks on interest rates, but the banks' cartel also eradicated competition on charges and on innovation so that the more competitive environment characteristic of an earlier age, and of a later age, disappeared. That is not to say, however, that competition was removed completely: for, as with all market and price agreements, there were always pressures from within to soften, or even to undermine, the arrangement. But there was also an area of competition which could never be a part of any cartel, i.e. the quality of the service provided and especially the willingness to lend.

Banks were acutely aware of their self-image and felt that they had to present themselves to the public as solid, reputable, respectable and dependable. Only if they succeeded in projecting themselves in this way would they attract the degree of public confidence in their institutions which was so necessary for the maintenance and growth of their system. With a few notable exceptions the banks were highly successful in portraying the necessary image, and the growth in deposits is only one measure of this success. Yet this has created problems for historians, for the researcher who does not have access to bank archives is inevitably confronted with a series of organisations whose public image can only be described as cautious. Indeed the public utterances of bankers called to give evidence to Parliamentary Committees of Enquiry confirm this: the opportunity to speak to the Committee members was often taken as another opportunity to portray an image of quiet respectability, financial probity and prudence.

More especially, the banks (whose deposits were all short-term, mostly repayable on demand) did not wish to be seen making long-term loans, for almost the first lesson to be learned in banking was the danger of 'borrowing short and lending long'. Bankers knew, of course, that they could do some long-term lending if they had a sufficiently large deposit base. With the growth of deposits in the nineteenth century from £15m in 1825 to £35m in 1850 and £132m in 1914[7] the scope for lending larger sums to individual customers and for lending longer-term increased greatly, although bankers were not keen to advertise the fact that not all of their lending was short-term and self-liquidating.

Inevitably this has led historians to claim that banks did not lend long-term to their customers: e.g. Peter Mathias in *The First Industrial Nation* states that 'the City to a large extent had its back turned to industry';[8] and W. P. Kennedy, while conceding that banks lent long-term in the middle of the century, argues that, after the failure of the City of Glasgow Bank in 1878, which rocked British as well as Scottish banking circles, the practice of long-term lending by banks effectively ceased as financial institutions became much more conservative.[9] More generally it has led to claims that the German Kreditbanks provided a much better service of lending to their customers. Most of the criticisms which have been made refer to London-based banks or more widely to English banks. It remains to be seen how accurate these claims are when Scottish banks are examined.

II

When Scottish banking archives are examined in detail, it soon becomes evident that the public pronouncements of bankers did not always convey the whole truth: many customers obtained some very long-term loans indeed. Mostly this arose out of the peculiar, although not unusual, workings of the cash-credit system. The cash credit operated much like the modern overdraft in that a customer was given a credit line and was free to draw upon it and repay at will. Interest was charged on a daily balance basis, and if the account moved into credit, then interest, at deposit rates, was allowed on the balance.[10] If, as often happened, the customer required credit at certain times of the year but was otherwise in funds, then the deposit interest earned was offset against the interest charged for the overdrawn balance. It was, therefore, a very popular type of account. Rather interestingly, it was granted on the understanding that it was repayable on demand, and it was this fact which led bankers to claim that their lending was short-term and allowed them to maintain the illusion of self-liquidating credit. In practice, however, many of these credits continued in operation for decades. Many, of course, never moved into credit and were continually overdrawn — e.g. a customer with a credit of £10,000 might withdraw the whole amount at the start and meet his bank's requirement for turnover on the account by rapid repayments and withdrawals of, say, £2,000. The balance of the account might never fall below £8,000 and this situation might continue for many years. In this way the customer effectively obtained a long-term loan of £8,000. The related issue of importance here is that the long-term facility was obtained at short-term interest rates, i.e. there was no penalty to pay in the shape of higher rates for longer-term money.

Examples of this are to be found in the archives of the Bank of Scotland where the cash-account progressive ledgers display the account of the Shotts Iron Co. The account was opened in the mid-1820s and it is possible to trace it through to 1871. Three benchmark years were chosen in which to examine the account in detail: 1850, 1860 and 1870. These years were chosen because they were at regular intervals and did not include any crisis years. In 1850 the authorised credit was £25,000, and this was increased to £35,000 in 1860, where it still stood in 1870. The figures illustrated are the maximum outstanding balance at any point in the year and the minimum outstanding balance:[11]

	1850	*1860*	*1870*
Maximum	31,787	35,287	40,743
Minimum	22,446	18,683	24,791

The figures illustrate that there was a large part of the credit which was long-term funding, but they also prove that the amount of the credit could be exceeded, and that this did not happen only when interest was applied at the end of the year.

It must also be borne in mind when looking at these figures that the Shotts Iron Co. was probably also discounting its trade bills with the bank, although there is no physical proof of this. In a few cases where it is possible to say something about a firm's borrowing from a bank, the evidence generally shows that the volume of borrowing on discounts exceeded the funds borrowed on cash account. Also, in the same way as just described for cash accounts, the amount of bills discounted outstanding to a particular customer might never be reduced to zero so that a customer with a regular discounting facility at his bank might also obtain long-term credit in this manner.

Occasionally a bank's records make it clear that an advance was purposefully long-term. In August 1849 the Clydesdale Bank's Directors recorded a loan of £30,000 to the Dalmellington Iron Co. on the understanding that the account was to be reduced by £5,000 per annum commencing on 1 January 1851.[12] Following the progression, it appears that the account was not to be paid off finally until 1856. This kind of stipulation, however, was very unusual and it was much more common to award a cash credit without any limitation other than the customary legal form of saying that advances were repayable on demand. Yet if it was unusual to say that an advance was to be time-limited to a number of years, it was equally unusual to say that an advance was granted for a short period of time. An exception to this was the £20,000 credit to Thomas Lipton, provision merchant in Glasgow, for six to nine months, granted in 1890 by the Clydesdale.[13]

Unfortunately it is seldom possible to provide aggregates of lending by sector. The banks' own analysis of lending did not take a sectoral form until the inter-war years. Until then the banks seem to have contented themselves with ensuring that they got a good spread of business from all sectors: there is no evidence to suggest that funds were withheld from one sector of the economy in order to lend in another or that a bank, or banks, became concerned because of their over-commitment to one area of the economy. Indeed the reverse is demonstrable, for in 1855, in one of its periodic reviews, the Court of the Bank of Scotland noted that its lending business in Glasgow had grown from £490,000 in 1832 to £1,800,000 in 1855. Bad debts had been quite small at £0.2%, so it was decided to sell off £805,000 of investments; this money was 'to be employed in the discount of Commercial Bills and in Loans at Glasgow as opportunity may occur'.[14] Two of the firms to benefit from this increased provision were Barclay Curle and Co., shipbuilders, and the chemicals firm of Charles Tennant & Co.[15]

III

Another criticism sometimes made of banking is that before customers were lent money they were required to have been firmly established in business for a number of years. Again it is possible to provide several examples of companies borrowing money at, or very close to, their inception. When Sharp, Stewart & Co., locomotive builders, moved to Glasgow from Manchester in 1888 they were immediately given an unsecured overdraft of £30,000 from the Clydesdale for one year.[16] That credit appears to have been renewed, for in 1891 it was recorded that the credit was to be continued for a further year, and permission was given to go £8/10,000 beyond the limit 'for a few months'.[17] In 1903 Sharp Stewart & Co. became part of the newly formed North British Locomotive Co., and by 1913 the business was so well established that the Clydesdale was prepared to lend it £50,000 for four months at ¼% *below* bank rate.[18] Similarly Messrs. Barr and Stroud, scientific instrument makers in Glasgow, were founded in 1893, and in February of that year the Hillhead agent of the Clydesdale was in correspondence with is Head Office on the matter of a proposed overdraft of £200 or £300 for the new company, which was approved. As the firm progressed, the amount of its credit was increased in line with the company's needs.[19]

Two of the sunrise industries of the late nineteenth century which failed to shine in Scotland were electricity and motor vehicles, but here again it is possible to find examples of these industries being provided with bank credit. In 1893 the Clydesdale Bank gave a credit of £500 to the Scottish House to House Electricity Company, and this was increased to £1,000 a few months later. By August 1894 the credit was up to £4,000 and was still in operation in 1899.[20] In 1912 the Skelmorlie Electric Supply Co. was given a credit of £5,000.[21] Similarly in 1904 the Albion Motor Car Co. obtained a credit of £3,000 from the Clydesdale, and in 1911 the Argyll Motor Car Co. was awarded a credit of £20,000 at Calton Branch and a further credit of £30,000 in December 1912.[22] This firm also had money from the Bank of Scotland. It is not, therefore, true to suggest that new industries were denied access to bank funds, although it remains uncertain whether or not the volume of lending to these industries was adequate. There is, however, no evidence in the archives of the banks to suggest that requests for funds were scaled down in any way before a credit was awarded.

Other new industries financed by the banks included cinemas, and in 1912 the Savoy Theatre, Glasgow, borrowed £2,000 from the Clydesdale. This was followed in 1913 with credits to the Palace (Edinburgh) Ltd. of £7,000; the Scenic Picture House Ltd, Glasgow, £500; McDonald Bros., Picture House Proprietors, Baillieston, £300; and the grandiosely titled Scottish National Electric Theatres Ltd, Inverkeithing, £700. Perhaps most novel of all was a credit in 1913 to W. H. Ewen Aviation Co. Ltd. for £1,500.[23] A selection of credits awarded in 1913 included Ayr Harbour, engineering companies, locomotive companies, shipbuilders, building companies, shipping companies, cinemas, football clubs, warehousemen, coal companies, ships' chandlers, distillers and fruit merchants. It is certainly true to suggest, therefore, that the bulk of bank lending in 1913 was to heavy industries, although it should be remembered that steel and shipbuilding were relatively new at that time. What is demonstrably untrue is that the bankers were not lending to new and developing industries.

There are also other signs in the archives that the banks were adjusting to changes in the structure of industry. Of particular interest is the size of loans and the types of securities taken. In the early nineteenth century the typical credit was around £1,000, although discount facilities were perhaps several times as much as this. Only personal guarantees were taken for these advances, and it was extremely rare for a bank to require any more tangible security. As the century progressed, however, the demand for credits became much larger and the amounts required also grew. The result of this was that banks increasingly felt that personal guarantees were often no longer sufficient in themselves to provide the safeguards which ensured the banks' ultimate liquidity. The years between c.1830 and c.1860 were a period of experimentation with banks finding out how to lend against the security of iron warrants, warehoused goods, insurance policies and heritable property. In this they were very successful, although it took some time to iron out some of the legal niceties. The problem of how to obtain effective security over goods in a warehouse presented especial difficulty, as it occasionally happened that a bank found that the goods had disappeared despite their having been pledged to the bank. Warehouse keepers' receipts which gave effective title to the goods were the answer to this particular problem.[24]

An example of the extent to which the banks were prepared to go in helping to meet their customers' credit needs is given in the credit awarded by the Clydesdale Bank to Messrs. Lucas and Aird, railway contractors, London, in January 1892. The credit was for £90,000 and was in addition to an existing credit of £100,000. 'The security is Lucas and Airds' note (guarantee) plus fully paid shares in the West Highland Railway for the full amount of the loan; also the North British Railway Co. are to give a sealed undertaking to take over these shares at par plus 5% not later than 31 October 1893 whether the West Highland Railway be then completed or not.'[25] Much earlier in the century the Bank of Scotland had resolved to take preference shares of the Edinburgh, Dundee and Perth Railway Co. in security for their cash account of £50,000, and by 1851 that railway company had the following advances from the bank:[26]

Account	*Security*	*Amount*
No. 1 Cash Account	Preference shares	£ 52,439
No. 2 Cash Account	Debentures	10,000
No. 3 Cash Account	Preference shares	10,000
Bill	Preference shares	12,000
Loan	Debentures	25,000
		£109,439

Occasionally there are signs of banks taking anything that was offered in order to obtain some extra degree of security as, for example, when the Bank of Scotland lent £180,000 to the Fairfield Shipbuilding and Engineering Co. in 1912. The security offered was third mortgage debentures, an assignation of the reversion on heritable property, railway debenture stock, two small steamers and an assignation of debts due to the company by the Coventry Ordnance Co.[27] The Clydesdale Bank was prepared to offer similar facilities to its customers: e.g. in 1892 the credit to Carr and Co. of Carlisle, biscuit manufacturers and flour millers, was increased to £100,000 against additional security which included guarantees, stocks of flour, plant and equipment.[28] The Clydesdale's largest advance was to the Glasgow District Subway Co., and in 1896 their credit of £250,000 was increased by £60,000.[29] Unfortunately it is not clear what form the security took but the rate of interest was only 3%. There is, therefore, abundant evidence of large-scale lending by the banks supported by very flexible attitudes to security. It should be stressed, however, that most advances throughout the century continued to be made on personal securities.

Other, more subtle ways in which banks helped industry included letting their names appear on the prospectus of companies. The name of a reputable bank was thought to be a great attraction to potential investors, and in 1900 the British Linen Bank's name appeared on the prospectus of the Burmah Oil Co.[30] The Clydesdale Bank was more likely to take an underwriting participation in a new issue, and these opportunities were offered to the bank either by Baring Bros. in London or by one of the Glasgow stockbroking firms. Most of these issues were for foreign governments or railways but a few were British, and in 1912 the Clydesdale was allotted £14,200 of Scottish Iron and Steel Co. Ltd 5% Mortgage Debentures in respect of its underwriting commitment of £20,000. Clearly it was not a terribly successful issue but the underwriting system ensured that the company got its money. In this case the Clydesdale had also agreed to lend the new company £72,500.[31]

IV

Clearly, then, there is a great deal of evidence to suggest that the traditional view of bankers must be re-assessed — at least in Scotland — although it seems highly likely that there was a good deal of convergence of practice and procedure amongst banks throughout the British Isles. The British banking system was certainly structurally very different from that in Germany where the Kreditbanks acted as commercial as well as investment bankers. The evidence of this paper, however, suggests that the Scottish banks were also acting as investment bankers. The German practice was to have bankers in the boardrooms of business, but the Scottish (probably also the British) practice was to have businessmen in the boardrooms of banks. There is at least a *prima facie* case then for suggesting that Scottish businessmen got the range and quality of financial institutions which they needed, but until historians examine credit and capital from the demand side this matter will remain open to debate.

NOTES

1. The archives of the Bank of Scotland and Clydesdale Bank are the main sources for this essay. These two banks were chosen because they were so different in origin and because their archives are complementary. I am grateful to both banks for permission to quote from their records.

2. Both the National Bank and the Commercial Bank were granted a modified form of Royal Charter in 1831.

3. S. G. Checkland, *Scottish Banking: A History, 1695–1973* (Glasgow, 1975), ch. 14.

4. Separate Acts were passed for Scotland and Ireland.

5. For evidence of this, see N. Tamaki, *The Life Cycle of the Union Bank of Scotland, 1830–1954* (Aberdeen, 1983), p. 89. Professor Tamaki's findings are confirmed in the Clydesdale Bank's records.

6. C. W. Munn, 'The Development of Joint Stock Banking in Scotland, 1810–1845' in A. Slaven and D. Aldcroft, eds., *Business, Banking and Urban History* (Edinburgh, 1982), pp. 125–7.

7. S. G. Checkland, *op.cit.*, pp. 426, 428 and 745.

8. P. Mathias, *The First Industrial Nation*, 2nd ed. (London, 1983), p. 323.

9. W. P. Kennedy, 'Institutional Response to Economic Growth: Capital Markets in Britain to 1914', in L. Hannah, ed., *Management Strategy and Business Development* (London, 1975), p. 160.

10. The practice of allowing interest ceased in the mid-1890s.

11. Bank of Scotland, Cash Account Progressive Ledgers.
12. Clydesdale Bank, Directors' Minute Book, 10/8/1849.
13. Ibid., 15/10/1890.
14. Bank of Scotland, Court Minute Book, 18/6/1855.
15. Ibid., 30/5/1856 and 28/11/1858.
16. Clydesdale Bank, Directors' Minute Book, 27/6/1888.
17. Ibid., 21/10/1891.
18. Ibid., 12/2/1913.
19. Clydesdale Bank, General Manager's Note Book, 12/2/1893 and Directors' Minute Book, 10/11/1897.
20. Ibid., 17/9/1893 and 30/8/1899.
21. Ibid., 20/3/1912.
22. Ibid., 28/9/1904 and 4/12/1912.
23. Ibid., *passim.*
24. C. W. Munn, *Banking in Scotland* (Edinburgh, 1982).
25. Clydesdale Bank, Directors' Minute Book, 20/1/1892.
26. Bank of Scotland, Court Minute Book, 15/4/1851.
27. Ibid., 24/9/1912.
28. Clydesdale Bank, General Manager's Note Book, 2/11/1892.
29. Clydesdale Bank, Directors' Minute Book, 14/10/1896 and 12/5/1897.
30. British Linen Bank, Scroll Minutes, 16/1/1900.
31. Clydesdale Bank, General Manager's Note Book, 26/6/1912 and 15/7/1912.

20

SEWING AND SOCIAL STRUCTURE: THE FLOWERERS OF SCOTLAND AND IRELAND

Brenda Collins

I

In the first half of the nineteenth century in Lowland Scotland and Ulster the sewing of plain and fancy work was a major occupation among rural women. The importance of this work has been diminished by its treatment in historiography as a residual of factory-based production. Reliable and precise measurement of what was viewed as a residual is not easy; broad generalisations of the parameters of employment by contemporaries may well be as meaningful as the exactness of numbers. During the nineteenth century the industry moved from the west of Scotland to the north of Ireland. This coincided with the increased availability of and interest in employment figures as portrayed in the national censuses, giving an air of perhaps false certainty to the latter part of the period. The early nineteenth-century tambouring or embroidery which 'employed many tens of thousands of female outworkers in the countryside, almost all of them the wives and daughters of agricultural workers or unskilled labourers',[1] may not seem as statistically precise as the Irish census figures, which show that between one in four and one in nine women and girls worked in embroidery, sewing or dressmaking in every Ulster county in each decade from 1850–1914, but both convey the ubiquity of the employment. The implications of this employment in both Scotland and Ireland were to be seen not just in the income added to the family budget and spent in the community, but also in the ways in which the employment was organised, its effects on local social organisation and social relationships, and its implications for migration and emigration.

Embroidery (fancy stitches) and sewing (plain stitches and seams) were executed on fine cotton fabrics such as muslin, and on linen fabrics, both fine, like cambric, used in underwear or handkerchiefs, and thicker linens used in tablecloths, sheets and bedspreads. The various terms were whitework (white stitches on white cloth), sprigging or flowering (referring to the shape of the embroidered motif), parcelling (referring to the work organisation whereby parcels of cloth on which the work was to be executed were distributed by agents), and Ayrshire needlework (from the origin of this type of work in rural Ayrshire based on warehouses in Paisley and Glasgow).

The origins of sewing lay in the rise of the cotton trade in the late eighteenth-century west of Scotland and especially with the centralisation of the organisation of the industry through merchants and warehouses based in Paisley and Glasgow. Between 1755 and 1801 the population of the town of Paisley grew from 7,000 to 31,000 with successive concentrations of manufacture on thread, silk gauzes, lawns and cambrics even before the rise of the Paisley shawl.[2] Muslin manufacture and its embellishment by embroidery started in the 1780s as a direct attempt at emulation of highly fashionable, and therefore commercially successful, imported Indian muslins. Undoubtedly the Scottish success was due to the pooling of resources of the existing thread manufacture of Paisley with the application of fine silk weaving techniques to the production of a lower-priced cloth which was thus made available to a wider marker. Muslin manufacture and embroidery was also given stimulus by the interruption of Indian muslin imports during the Napoleonic Wars.[3]

As was to be the case a generation later in Ireland, women took up employment in flowering muslin as an alternative to spinning. The *Statistical Account* states that at Hamilton in Lanarkshire as late as 1750 large parcels of spun (linen) yarn had been sent to the north of Ireland, but the Irish 'have learnt to make good yarn to satisfy their own demands while now [1791] cotton yarn is woven by the local weavers instead of linen yarn'.[4] Hand-executed muslin embroidery thus developed alongside the mill-based output of cotton yarn and handloom production of cotton cloth, and this had important organisational implications. Where linen weaving had been undertaken by independent weavers, cotton handloom weavers operated under a putting-out system from the start, and muslin embroiderers obtained their work through the same networks. Hence it is not surprising that muslin embroidery seems to have been most prevalent in the areas where domestic cotton weaving was strongest.[5]

The organisational networks by which the wives and daughters of the villages south of Glasgow and Paisley were supplied with muslin for embroidery were based on an agency system with the headquarters at the Glasgow and Paisley manufacturers. According to the 1841 census there were 47 muslin and sewing agents in Renfrewshire, Ayrshire and Lanarkshire and doubtless many more who participated on a part-time basis. The number of manufacturers from whom the agents obtained materials is much less easy to estimate because of the ambiguity of the occupational term 'manufacturer' in the census, but an 1837 directory of Glasgow listed 25 muslin manufacturers who handled embroidery out of a total of 117 muslin manufacturers in the city.[6]

The rapid spread of sewed muslin work in the period between the publications of the *Old* and the *New Statistical Accounts* (roughly 1790s to late 1830s) was due to 'the easier, more elegant and at present more profitable employment ... [which] ... flowering muslins'[7] afforded in comparison with hand cotton spinning, an activity which was already undermined by mechanised yarn production. In some towns such as Irvine, sprigging warehouses were established where the work was done indoors, but more commonly the sewing was carried out in the sewers' own homes. It is likely that the warehouses were training schools for young girls who then continued, as adult women, to take work home from the warehouses as agencies. This can be inferred from the 1790s wage levels paid in the warehouse of 15d to 2/- per week in comparison with 4/- per week to homeworkers. Such wages generated cash incomes for many women and children 'whose work was previously unproductive ... [and rendered] ... it of still more importance to the country'.[8] This was particularly important for the married, Lowland, farm-servant class hired on a yearly or half-yearly basis and paid in kind or in ground. They enjoyed a rising standard of living down to 1815 both because of increased agricultural prices which raised the value of their earnings and because cash payments for sewed muslin work enabled them to purchase non-subsistence items of food, clothing, and furniture. Moreover, money wages for sewing appear to have risen slightly in the period to the mid-1820s. This was as much due to the rival competition for the female work-force from rural cotton spinning mills and bleachfields as it was to the high fashion demand for the products. At Kilbirnie top rates for sewing were said to be 7/- to 10/- per week; whereas, of the alternative employments in the locality, a spinning mill paid 6/-, and the bleachfields 5/- to 8/-.[9] Such wage levels also raised the wages paid to single, female farm servants, because the contributions to the family income of several unmarried daughters living at home and embroidering muslin made parents less anxious to get their daughters into farm service.

Muslin sewing also provided the means of both encouraging migration into the growing urban centres of West-Central Scotland, and also permitting a high proportion of the natural increase of the rural population to remain in the countryside. It has been estimated that between 1760 and 1800 the number of rural immigrants into Paisley was between fifteen and eighteen thousand. The Highland and Irish element in this migration began only around the turn of the century, and most of the earlier immigrants came from rural Ayrshire and Renfrew, drawn to Paisley by opportunities in the industry.[10] Glasgow's population increase of 160 per cent between 1801 and 1831 also owed much to the rural Lowland influx. At the same time, the extra income earned by the rural muslin flowerers was, as the author of the Kirkmichael contribution to the *N.S.A.* expressed it, 'a means of transmitting money from Glasgow to the country'.[11] Until after about 1860, Ayrshire, Renfrewshire and Lanarkshire remained counties with high densities of population based on a strong village/small-town structure. This stability maintained the regional distinctiveness of the area alongside the stresses of urbanisation in the central belt of Scotland, and was in marked contrast to the depopulation of some of the rural linen textile areas of Angus and Fife on the east coast in the latter part of the same period.[12]

II

The Irish side of the industry also developed out of the embryonic cotton industry around Belfast in the late eighteenth and early nineteenth centuries. As in Paisley, there were linkages with thread manufacture; John Barbour of the Plantation thread works near Lisburn (himself a native of Paisley) employed homeworkers as embroiderers using his thread. Connections between the Irish and the Scottish branches of the industry strengthened, especially after Irish sewed-muslin work grew independently of the fortunes of the Belfast cotton industry.[13] In the late 1820s the first Irish firm dealing solely in sewed muslins,

Cochranes, set up in Donaghadee, Co. Down and within a few years moved their headquarters to Glasgow. During the 1830s several Glasgow-based firms established agencies in the north of Ireland such as those of S. R. & T. Brown, and D. & J. McDonald. The former owned a sewed muslin warehouse in Belfast in 1843 which operated a sixty-hour week, comparable to spinning mills of that time. They took young girls of 10 years and upwards as apprentices, paying them 1/- or 2/- per week while they learned the trade and, after about six months' work, 4/- per week. Higher wages could be earned in the mills, but the manager of the warehouse made a status distinction between the two types of employment, claiming that most workers were 'the children of parents in a decent situation in life who would not allow of them going into the mills'.[14]

If such an establishment was typical of the urban warehouses, there was in addition another means of organising production through the establishment of training schools by local patronage of the aristocracy and clergy. There is information on very few of these in comparison with the numbers which existed, but the school at Dungannon started by the Countess of Ranfurly in the 1840s was probably typical. Its hours were shorter than in the warehouses (possibly because of the greater distances from homes to the school), but earnings were comparable for the same output.

However, by far the most important aspect of both these forms of employment was not the number of employees working indoors at any one time but the teaching of sewing skills which then continued to be undertaken by girls and women in their own homes. One sewed-muslin firm in Armagh city had employed 400 girls over the period 1837–43, and those who had left their premises continued to work at home for the warehouse. The school at Dungannon had between 50 and 60 children on its books, and a hundred more 'outside' who, 'having been trained in it [the school] are furnished with muslin to flower at home for which they are paid as when at school'.[15]

While these warehouses and schools acted as centres for distribution and collection of embroidery, the largest firms also opened up agencies throughout the north and west counties of Ulster. D. & J. McDonald of Glasgow employed an agent in the 1840s who established up to 50 training schools in Donegal, Fermanagh and Tyrone, a situation echoing the actions of the Glasgow cotton manufacturers in Ayrshire in the 1790s. At the height of that firm's prosperity in the early 1850s it was estimated that it employed 15–20,000 women and paid out £15,000 in wages every month.[16]

How important, then, was the industry? The link between the Irish and Scottish production was almost inextricable; most of the Irish work for the Scottish warehouses was said to be exported from Glasgow to London and abroad as 'Scotch work'.[17] At its peak in the 1850s, a speaker at the British Association conference claimed that there were about 50 Scots and Irish warehouse owners, who between them employed in the north of Ireland about 200,000 women and girls in embroidery and at least 4–500 agents. This may not be too unrealistic, as the Irish census figure of 1851 gives at least 125,000 workers, and the numbers employed continued to expand until 1857. The number of embroiderers in

*Table 1. Female Employment in Selected Needle and Textile Trades, Scotland and Ulster, 1841–1901***

SCOTLAND		*ULSTER*	
		1841	
Muslin and Sewing Agent	47*	No Sewed Muslin workers or Embroiderers listed	
Embroiderer	3326*	Tambour Worker	516
Muslin Manufacture	735*	Seamstress	28862
Seamstress (Renf. Ayr. Lanark. only)	6749	Spinner (flax & unspec.)	260985
Cotton Manufacture (of whom 28,000 female)	66945		
		1851	
Muslin Embroidery	2285	Embroiderer	39574
Seamstress	12971	Sewed Muslin Work	59487
		Seamstress	25566
		Spinner (flax & unspec.)	29851
		1861	
Muslin Embroidery	7224	Embroiderer	3238
Shirt and Seamstress	15054	Sewed Muslin Work	38871
Dressmaker	33066	Sewed Muslin Agent*	293
		Seamstress	42720
		Shirtmaker	7057
1891			*1901*
Muslin Embroidery	487*	Mixed Materials* (inc. embroidery)	13686
Shirt and Seamstress	7020	Dress* (inc. seamstress shirtmaking)	73623
Dressmaker	56227		

*Includes males

**Sources: Scotland, 1841 Census (P.P. 1844, XXVII), 1851 Census (P.P. 1852–3, LXXXVIII, Pt.II), 1861 Census (P.P. 1864, LI), 1891 Census (P.P. 1893–4, CVIII). Ireland, 1841 Census (P.P. 1843, XXIV), 1851 Census (P.P. 1856, XXXI), 1861 Census (P.P. 1863, LX), 1901 Census (P.P. 1902, CXXVII).

Scotland at the same time was reckoned to be 25,000, a number not greatly out of line with a projection from the 1861 census. The annual gross value of the output of sewed muslin in Ireland and Scotland together was £1 million.[18] If, in Scotland, one effect of the industry was to strengthen and stabilise the rural farming areas of Ayrshire and Lanarkshire, in Ireland the industry operated on a lower baseline; it provided a cushion against privation in bad seasons when outdoor agricultural work was scarce. The work may also have acted as a stabilising force against depopulation in the Ulster countryside, especially of young girls — an agent of McDonald's speaking of Tyrone commented on the extent to which 'a small holder, having a family of daughters, is glad to avail himself of any way of earning a living, in preference to hiring, which is considered less disreputable, besides the inexpressible joy a parent must feel in seeing himself or herself surrounded by their healthy offspring, earning a support under their own material roof . . .'[19] Finally, the income generated in each neighbourhood was one of the less seasonal inputs of cash into rural society where lack of ready cash was a severe brake on economic development. The small market town of Fintona in Co. Tyrone, for example, had, in 1855, agents acting for at least nine different sewed muslin manufacturers so that more than £200 in cash circulated there each week.[20]

There was a sudden halt to this prosperity, however, because of a combination of factors which brought an end to the hand sewing and embroidery of muslin in both countries. The immediate cause was a financial crisis in 1857 in the U.S.A. which was the destination of most of the embroidery exports. This had repercussions for Glasgow's merchants; D. & J. McDonald crashed, and others who kept afloat were overstocked with goods which they could unload only slowly onto the market. As prices were halved, the goods became more accessible to a lower-income group and lost their appeal for the rich. Meanwhile the Swiss machine embroidery industry had become productive about 1840 and the Swiss were already sending machined copies of hand-embroidered whitework to the American market. In addition, changing fashions in Britain, replacing the petticoated hooped crinoline with the more austere bustle in darker heavier colours, meant flowered muslins were *dépassé*. The outbreak of the American Civil War sealed the end of the manufacture by its interruption of cotton supplies to the Glasgow trade in the early 1860s.[21]

At least two points of contrast arise between the Scottish and the Irish sides of the industry down to the 1860s. Firstly, it seems apparent from the Scottish sources that sewing directly replaced spinning as a means of extra livelihood in rural village communities in the west of Scotland. This does not seem to have been the case in Ireland, for the chronology of the spread of sewed muslin work would not support such a contention. In particular, flowering and whitework were already widespread in Co. Down by 1820, before the demise of hand spinning, and sewing spread through Donegal, Derry and Tyrone in the 1830s. Documentation of the decline in the numbers of female spinners in Ulster is clear on an intercensal basis; in the 1841 census 261,000 spinners were recorded, while in 1851 the figure was 30,000 (one-ninth of the 1841 total), and by 1861 they were virtually extinct as a home-based hand industry.[22] However, the population decline in every county due to Famine deaths and emigration was in fact greater than the increased numbers taking up sewing. Spinning was so ubiquitous throughout all the Ulster counties that a substitute employment might have been expected to be equally widespread. Instead, however, sewing and embroidery remained spatially concentrated with more than two-thirds of the sewing and embroidery workforce in 1851 confined to the four counties of Down, Donegal, Fermanagh and Tyrone.

This spatial concentration, although a characteristic as apparent in the Scottish counties as in Ireland, is also an indicator of the second point of contrast between the two economies. While the Scottish side declined rapidly after the 1860s, the Irish production continued under another guise. In Ulster the legacy of the skills remained, used on different fabrics for different purposes, and the system of domestic outwork in Ulster continued and intensified until the twentieth century.

III

One substitute for embroidery on muslin was the move into embroidery on linens for household use rather than dress, on sheets, tablecloths, doyleys etc. A second was the development of the shirtmaking industry around Londonderry from the 1850s with its intense division of labour in the making up of the various stages of the garment. Both of these branches of sewing were grafted on to the existing system of cottage outwork. This was combined with central distribution and marketing, though the agencies became increasingly those of Irish, especially Belfast-based, warehouses rather than Scots or English.

The expansion of this production, but especially that of the fancy household linens, was entirely related to the encouragement and development of the mass middle-class market which saw the furnishing of a Victorian home as an extension of the appearance of its family members in terms of their place in respectable society. This idea was given expression and cultivated by a new phenomenon in retail purchasing, the 'department store', which marketed dry goods, 'the various cloth materials produced by the industrialization of textile manufacture and used for clothing and home furnishings'.[23] This type of business organisation originated in the U.S.A. and spread to Canada, mainland Europe and the British Isles between the 1850s and the 1890s. Many of the transatlantic stores used their connections with the Belfast linen merchants to obtain their goods. Retail firms like Robinson & Cleaver in Belfast and Switzer in Dublin and wholesale producers like Robert McBride acted as intermediaries to the international market. They employed a live-in staff to work up the patterns, but the backbone of their production was undertaken by countrywomen through agents in the rural districts of Co. Down and north-west Ulster. This minimised the fixed costs of employing girls within the warehouse and providing accommodation for them: there was a steady supply of labour available at a distance whose wages bill and output of work could be completely regulated by the volatility of consumer demand for fashionable patterns. The extent to which the embroidery and sewing production of the period 1870–1920 was completely dominated by consumer preference is summed up by the Irish consul in Portland, Oregon, who reported in 1907 to the Department of Agricultural and Technical Instruction in Ireland: 'It is the great middle-class consumption which tells . . . all other things being equal, the patterns at once decide the choice'.[24]

The progress of domestic embroidery and sewing production thus runs counter to that of most other industrial products in textiles. Generally the initial stage of production was one of domestic manufacture which was subsequently overtaken by employers attempting to control the process of production by employing their workers within factories under certain contracts of payment for working hours and conditions. In contrast the outcome of the expansion in embroidery and sewing in Ulster was precisely the opposite, its extension in the countryside.[25]

Nowhere was this rural extension more evident than in the plainer sewing side

*Table 2. Distribution by Certain Ulster Counties of Female Workers in Selected Needle Trades, 1861, 1871, 1901. Percentages of Total Numbers***

1861	Seamstresses	Shirtmakers	Embroiderers and Sewed Muslin Workers
Down	26.3	2.0	37.1
Londonderry	16.6	27.3	5.0
Tyrone	14.5	22.0	9.9
Donegal	9.6	40.0	20.7
Total nos. Ulster	42720	7057	42109
1871	Dress* (inc. seamstress and shirtmaking)	Mixed Materials* (inc. embroidery)	
Down	19.8	12.2	
Londonderry	11.1	3.6	
Tyrone	9.6	7.8	
Donegal	10.6	14.5	
Belfast	5.1	6.2	
Total nos. Ulster	83804	56262	
1901	Dress* (inc. seamstress and shirtmaking)	Mixed Materials* (inc. embroidery)	
Down	15.9	17.8	
Londonderry	12.6	3.5	
Tyrone	9.5	2.8	
Donegal	13.3	21.8	
Belfast	15.2	13.5	
Total nos. Ulster	73623	13686	

*Includes males

**Sources: 1861 Census (P.P. 1863, LX), 1871 Census (P.P. 1874, LXXIV Pt. 1), 1901 Census (P.P. 1902, CXXVII).

of the industry, especially the sector relating to underclothing for women and shirts for men. This branch of manufacture became established in north-west Ulster as early as the 1850s, and 88 per cent of the shirt workers listed in the 1861 census lived in Derry, Donegal and Tyrone. This concentration continued throughout the century.[26] The industry built on the same system of agents as had been used by the sewed muslin warehouses. Advertisements appeared in local newspapers from 1850 for shirtmakers in villages and towns such as Limavady, Claudy, Donemana, Strabane, Castlefin and Moville, and for agents to give out and take in work at these places.[27]

There were, however, two major differences between the organisation of shirt and underclothing manufacture and the organisation of whitework embroidery production. The first was in the refinement of the putting-out system in the shirt industry: outworkers were incorporated into a highly structured pattern of production whereby cut pieces were distributed for making-up. A system of proportional measurements of the body had been developed in the U.S.A. in the 1830s and 1840s which was based on the realisation that the measurements of one part of the body could be related to other measurements without the need for direct contact with individual customers. This allowed mass production of clothing and mass distribution to unknown customers. Men's shirts were the paramount example of this application because their making-up could be varied within an essentially limited number of pattern pieces. Moreover this advance was in the cutting side of the industry which always took place inside the factory and was therefore highly controlled. With the application of a cutting machine, invented in the 1860s, increased output of standard-sized pieces was possible.[28] To make up the new volume of shirt pieces into shirts required an extra input of resources, and the second difference between the shirt and underclothing manufacture and the whitework production was the former's rapid adoption of sewing-machine technology. Tillie & Henderson introduced their first batch of sewing machines into Derry city in 1856 within six years of their invention. These early machines were operated by hand and then by foot treadle, and only from the 1870s by steam power.[29] Nevertheless a hand-operated machine was estimated to perform the work of six hand sewers with proportionate increases for each technical advance.

Early sewing machines were only capable of plain sewing of seams rather than fancy stitches. Thus the making up of shirts continued to use hand and machine sewing which was conducted both in the factory and the domestic setting. Machines were supplied to women working at home on easy payment terms, eventually to become their own property. Once a woman owned her own machine, of course, she was not tied to one employer and could take work from several sources as well as using the machine for her own sewing. By the turn of the century there were three methods by which work was distributed to the outworkers. The most respectable was said to be the stations or agencies operated by the larger Derry city firms at which there were paid employees who took charge of distributing and collecting the work. In 1889 McIntyre & Hogg, for example, retained women at out-stations at Maghera, Donegal, Glenties and Kerrykeel at an average commission wage of £3–4 per month to handle the distribution of the work.[30] Other firms sent a paid servant and a cart each week to the remote districts for the women to attend at regular meeting points to deliver and collect parcels of sewing. The third way was probably the most common and also one which encountered increasing criticism from the growing body of public-service officials who were employed on the ground in Ireland. It built on the old system of agents who were generally local shopkeepers and who took a commission of about 10 per cent to give out and receive sewing parcels. This system was followed by almost all the large firms based in Belfast and the Lagan valley because it gave them local contacts in the north-west at minimum risk to themselves.

Statistics of production in the Derry shirt industry are extremely difficult to obtain with any consistency. Nevertheless in 1867 it was reckoned that 2,000 were employed within the Derry factories and 10,000 sewers in the counties of Derry, Donegal and Tyrone. In 1875 there were reckoned to be 4–5,000 indoor employees and 12–15,000 outdoor workers. By 1902 Coyne estimated 18,000 indoor employees and 80,000 in the rural districts.[31]

Output similarly rose spectacularly, from 200,000 dozen shirts *annually* in 1867, to 100,000 dozen *per week* in 1875. An associated production was that of collars, sold separately, and in 1912 it was estimated that 20 million collars were shipped annually from Derry. In 1907 the value of the Irish output of shirts, collars and cuffs was 22 per cent of the U.K. total.[32] The expansion of production was a response to that late Victorian and Edwardian phenomenon in Britain, the rise of the white-collar worker. The increasing numbers of financial and commercial clerks, civil servants and members of other professions had, as a requirement of their positions, to dress in clean white shirts with clean white collars every day.[33]

IV

Certain theories of comparative economic development might suggest that the intensification of sewing outwork in Ulster which occurred during the last quarter of the nineteenth century contrasted strangely with the diffusion of industrialisation centred on the Belfast area. However, some key modernising aspects of economic and social development, such as the growth of a railway system, which reduced distribution costs and regularised supplies and deliveries, actually strengthened the viability of the outwork system. In addition, the technical changes which might have undermined the place of the outdoor unregulated worker actually encouraged a casual labour force. Casual workers could be dispensed with when orders were low, in the knowledge that they would be there when demand picked up again. Because home workers had contractual obligations to their employers which were only loosely enforced, they also enjoyed few rights, and were mostly exempt from any state legislation regarding working conditions. This situation was made explicit in the outcome of discussions in 1912 regarding the extension of the National Insurance Acts in Ireland to sewing outworkers. This defined the agents rather than the workers as the employees who received limited benefits in return for wage deductions made by the warehouse owners.[34] In addition, homework continued in north-west Ulster despite one major modernising feature of the post-1860 period, migration to Belfast and emigration beyond. Belfast's population increased fivefold between 1841 and 1911, with much of this due to adult immigration to work in the mills, shipyards and engineering works but, even in the city, patterns of homeworking continued especially among the poorer families whose livelihood was erratic.

Why did this pattern not apply in the west of Scotland? Why did rural Ayrshire and Renfrewshire not adapt their traditions of muslin embroidery to changed fabrics and markets as the Irish did? There are parallels with the experience of the Scottish handloom weavers who, as Murray's work demonstrates, remained as an immobile ageing labour force. The younger element moved both out of the trade, and spatially, to other areas of employment opportunities, principally Glasgow, while the last generation of sewers and handloom weavers carried on in increasingly reduced circumstances until they died.[35]

Yet the Scottish pattern had something in common with the Irish after all, for, despite modernisation and industrialisation, homework continued in Glasgow and Clydeside just as it did in Belfast. The difference lay in its more or less complete transference from the countryside to inner city areas. This was a process similar to that outlined by Stedman Jones in his discussion of workshop industries in London: the effect of the Industrial Revolution on the metropolis was to accentuate its pre-industrial characteristics. Although both Glasgow and Belfast in the late nineteenth century had highly paid sections of the male workforce employed in engineering and shipbuilding, they too, like London's East End, had neighbourhoods where families were dependent on combinations of irregular low earnings from casual labour and homework.[36] It seems possible, therefore, that the crucial variable in the existence and persistence of outwork was the level and regularity of men's earnings.[37] This criterion was as valid for rural north-west Ulster, heavily dependent on male seasonal migration, as it was for Dock ward in Belfast and Bridgeton in Glasgow.

Just as the role of comparative specialisation in U.K. terms encouraged the development of the linen industry in Ulster, the intensification of sewing outwork was undoubtedly one of the linkages generated by the expansion in linen production throughout the century. In this sense, sewing in Ulster could be seen as a spread effect of industrialisation, encouraging the transfer of capital and business enterprise to a less industrialised region which thus gained access to a wider and cheaper range of goods and services. In contrast, sewing in the west of Scotland did not have sustainable linkages with the changing economic structure; instead it provided the basis for the outflow, to the Glasgow region, firstly of capital and latterly also of labour.[38] Yet in economic history there are few outright winners or losers. The long-term effects of the dual combination of sewing outwork and seasonal migration in north-west Ulster acted as a brake on economic change and diversification; at least one of the longer-term effects of the decline of sewing in the western Lowlands of Scotland was heavy emigration to north America in the early decades of the twentieth century, where the immigrants eagerly sought and could readily buy the embroidered work produced in Ulster and exported abroad.

NOTES

1. T. C. Smout, *History of the Scottish People* (London, 1969), p. 393.
2. *Ibid.*, p. 261.
3. M. H. Swain, *The Flowerers: the Origins and History of Ayrshire Needlework* (Edinburgh, 1955), p. 34; M. McCarthy, *A Social Geography of Paisley* (Paisley, 1969), *passim*.
4. *O.S.A.* (Edinburgh, 1791–7, reprint Wakefield, 1973–83), VII, *Lanarkshire*, (1973), Hamilton, p. 393.
5. *N.S.A.* (1845), V, *Ayrshire and Bute*, entries on parishes of Irvine, Kilbirnie, Tarbolton, Kilwinning.
6. Table I, and Swain, *The Flowerers*, p. 47.
7. *O.S.A.* VII (1973), *Renfrew*, parish of Erskine, p. 677.

8. *O.S.A.* VI (1982), *Ayrshire*, parish of Irvine, p. 245, and VII, (1973), *Lanarkshire*, parish of Glasgow, p. 296.

9. *N.S.A.* V, *Ayrshire and Bute*, parish of Kilbirnie, p. 717.

10. A. Dickson and W. Speirs, 'Changes in Class Structure in Paisley, 1750-1845', *S.H.R.* LIX (1980), pp. 55–62.

11. *N.S.A.* V, *Ayrshire and Bute*, parish of Kirkmichael, p. 503.

12. See M. W. Flinn, ed., *Scottish Population History* (Cambridge, 1977), pp. 466–9; M. Gray, 'Migration in the Rural Lowlands of Scotland, 1750–1850', in Devine & Dickson, pp. 104–117.

13. H. McCall, *Our Staple Manufactures* (Belfast, 1855), pp. 188–191; E. R. R. Green, *The Lagan Valley* (Manchester, 1949), *passim*; L. A. Clarkson and B. Collins, 'Proto-Industrialisation in an Irish Town: Lisburn, 1820–21', *Proceedings of the Eighth International Economic History Conference* (Budapest, 1982), mimeo.

14. Children's Employment Commission, Appendix to Second Report (P.P. 1843, XV), n 32.

15. Ibid., n 68, n 54.

16. McCall, *Manufactures*, p. 205.

17. Mr & Mrs S. C. Hall, *Ireland, its Scenery, Character etc.*, Vol. III (London, 1843), p. 85.

18. J. Strang, 'On the Rise, Progress and Value of the Embroidered Muslin Manufacture of Scotland and Ireland', *Transactions of the British Association*, 27 (1857), p. 167.

19. McCall, *Manufactures*, p. 202.

20. *Ibid.*, p. 201.

21. D. Bremner, *The Industries of Scotland*, 1868 (Newton Abbot, reprint 1969), pp. 308–9; Swain, *The Flowerers*, pp. 54–5.

22. See Table 1.

23. Deborah S. Garner, 'A Paradise of Fashion: A. T. Stewart's Department Store, 1862–75', in J. Jensen and S. Davidson, eds., *A Needle, a Bobbin, a Strike* (Temple, 1984), p. 62.

24. *Dept. for Agricultural and Technical Instruction Ireland Journal*, III, 1902–3.

25. D. Levine, 'Industrialisation and the Proletarian Family in England', *Past and Present*, 107 (May, 1985), pp. 168–203, discusses the relationship between demographic change and work organisation.

26. See Table 2.

27. W. Coyne, *Ireland, Agricultural and Industrial* (Dublin, 1902), 'The Londonderry Shirt-Making Industry', pp. 417–9; E. H. Slade, A History of the Londonderry Shirt Industry (unpublished M.A. thesis, Queen's University, Belfast, 1937), pp. 11–20.

28. According to Slade, this was an invention by an employee of the Derry firm of McIntyre and Hogg.

29. Slade, p. 28; *Report of the Commission on Factory and Workshops Acts*, Vol. II, Mins. of Evid. (P.P. 1876, XXX), qns.17323–17328.

30. P.R.O.N.I. T.3231/Ac/1, Wages Book of McIntyre & Hogg. The amount of the wage indicates the likelihood of it being based on commission but this is not actually stated.

31. Slade, p. 31; *Factories Commission*, qn.17297; Coyne, *Ireland*, p. 418.

32. Slade, pp. 31, 37; Coyne, *Ireland*, p. 418; *Census of Production*, 1907, pt. III (P.P. 1910, CIX), p. 413.

33. See G. Crossick, 'The Emergence of the Lower Middle Class in Britain', in G. Crossick, ed., *The Lower Middle Class in Britain, 1870–1914* (London, 1977). The number of white-collar male employees in G.B. rose between 1851–1911 from 144,000 to 918,000 and their proportion of the male workforce aged over 15, from 2.5% to 7.1%.

34. *Departmental Committee on the Insurance of Outworkers (Ireland)* (P.P. 1914–16, XXXI).

35. N. Murray, *The Scottish Hand Loom Weavers* (Edinburgh, 1981).

36. G. Stedman Jones, *Outcast London* (Oxford, 1971), p. 26.

37. This point is made by D. Bythell, *The Sweated Trades* (London, 1978), pp. 172–3.

38. J. Othick, 'The Economic History of Ulster: a Perspective', in L. Kennedy & P. Ollerenshaw, eds., *An Economic History of Ulster, 1820–1939* (Manchester, 1985), contains some relevant conceptual speculations on this point.

21

THE SEAFISHING INDUSTRY IN COUNTY DOWN AND ITS SCOTTISH CONNECTIONS, 1860–1939

Vivienne Pollock

Taken as a whole, the period 1860–1939 was one of progress for the seafishing industry in County Down. It witnessed a considerable strengthening of the infrastructure of the industry: road and rail communications were extended to fishing centres and fishery harbours in the region, harbours themselves were rebuilt and repaired, and major efforts were made both to initiate new markets and to increase the supply of fish to existing ones. On the operational or 'catching' side of the industry, a marked improvement took place in capital equipment, particularly in the fleet itself, and there was a pronounced shift towards the professionalisation of the local fishing population. In 1872 only 29.2 per cent of County Down fishermen derived their income solely from seafishing; in 1937 this figure stood at 43.6 per cent. By 1947 it had risen to 72.1 per cent.[1]

The initial basis for these improvements was undoubtedly the resurgence at the beginning of this period of the summer herring industry. This branch of the seafisheries had considerable national significance and continued to remain of importance in the County Down area throughout the years under review here. Nevertheless, there were times when this inherently volatile fishery showed signs of incipient collapse: the 1880s were bad years for herring fishermen everywhere, and the 1920s also saw the beginning of markedly fluctuating levels of return from herring fishing in the area. These continued into the 1930s; in 1934 the season started so badly that 'the majority of [local] fishermen contemplated laying up their boats'[2] and were only dissuaded from so doing by the unprecedented introduction of a scheme of 'minimum payment' by government to cover running costs until the situation improved. However, the local whitefisheries had been improving steadily in both performance and capacity since the turn of the century; the increase in, and increasing stability of, the returns from this sector compensated greatly for the fluctuating success of herring fishing. By the 1920s the traditional superiority of the herring in County Down was being challenged by whiting. This branch of the local seafisheries assumed enormous significance in the 1930s and 1940s, and remained from then the single most important fishery in the region until the 1970s and the emergence of the nephrops, or 'Dublin Bay Prawn', industry.

The seafishing industry in Ireland as a whole was in all respects much smaller than it was in either Scotland or England. The Irish herring industry, important as it was in relative as well as in absolute terms, never became the multi-million pound concern that it was in Scotland. The Irish whitefishing fleet paled into insignificance beside the huge fleets of North Sea trawlers that worked from English east-coast ports. The size of the seafishing industry in Ireland was also reflected in very low average figures for both productivity and value. In 1883 Spencer Walpole condemned the 'desultory operations of Irish fishermen',[3] offering as evidence estimates of average production in the United Kingdom in 1881 which suggested that the industry in England and Wales yielded six tons of fish per fisherman, in Scotland four tons, but in Ireland less than one ton.[4] From 1887 to 1911 average catch-value in the Irish commercial seafisheries failed to exceed £30 per fisherman per year (see Table 1). However, the overall performance of the seafishing industry in Ireland must be put into perspective. Pronounced regional variations in vitality existed — the Irish Fishery Board itself reported that although Ireland had over 2,500 miles of coastline, most of it lay barren as far as seafishing was concerned; for example, the herring and mackerel fisheries, which contributed over two-thirds of total fish landed, were followed on only 250 miles of littoral.[5] While the strength of commercial seafishing was significantly greater on the east coast of the country, this broad pattern was itself punctuated by even more localised differences. The presence in County Down from the 1860s of a buoyant herring industry suggests that seafishing there was of considerably more value than it was on many other parts of the Irish coast, a situation which is perhaps indicated by the increase in average catch-values calculated from the more localised landing figures available after 1922.

Assessment of the performance of these seafisheries is, however, complicated by the fact that the industry in County Down did not develop as a monolithic structure; it consisted instead of a conglomeration of different types and branches of industry which were followed in some or other combination and with varying degrees of commitment by most of the fishermen in the region. The classification of the indigenous Down industry into three main sectors — herring fishing, whitefishing, and shellfish and mollusc fishing — does not mean that these sectors either existed or developed separately; many herring fishermen were white-fishermen also, and vice versa; some who relied primarily on whitefishing turned also to mollusc fishing; while some mollusc fishermen spent part of their year herring fishing. Some possessed different boats for different pursuits, but a large proportion of the fishing vessels registered in the area over these years were entered as being used for more than one type of fishing, with 'nets and lines' being the most popular combination. Indeed, in 1927 the 'mainstay of the scattered coastal population'[6] was officially described as the 'intermediate class of boat which engages at different times of the year in shellfishing, inshore herring fishing, and in whitefishing . . . their equipment includes lobster pots, long lines, trammel nets, trawl nets and herring drift nets'.[7]

This official description relates primarily to inshore fishing, a branch of the industry which had indisputable local importance but which was of comparatively little commercial significance outside the region. Men occupied in this type of fishing would rarely have travelled far away from their home ports, and would not have stayed at sea for any great length of time. Many were part-time fishermen. The markets which they served were generally small, local and 'immediate'; their catch tended to go directly from the fishing boat to the retailer or consumer. But County Down was home also to a class of fishermen who may be called 'offshore' men. These were the fishermen who followed the fishing out of the area and who regularly spent long periods working away from their local bases. The greater size of the boats needed for this type of fishing was reflected in their greater capacity, and the markets which they served tended to be attached to central marketing networks. However, many of these offshore fishermen were inshore fishermen also at certain times in the year; many also divided their offshore activities between different types of fishing. It is therefore difficult to impose exclusive boundaries on the patchwork of fishery enterprise which comprised the commercial seafisheries in County Down.

The cornerstone of fishery activity in the region was, however, the herring. The majority of County Down fishermen turned at some time of the year and in some degree to herring fishing; indeed, much of its local significance rested on the way in which this fishery could be exploited simultaneously on a number of commercial levels and by a number of classes of fishermen. That this was so was a function, firstly, of the essential nature of the herring fishery itself and, secondly, of the type of commercial structure that obtained in the herring fishing industry.

Herring behaviour, like that of all pelagic fishes, was especially characterised by the seasonal appearance of the fish in inshore waters where they congregated in huge numbers to feed and to spawn. In location, then, herring fishing was also a seasonal affair, occurring only at those times of the year when the fish were on the move in coastal waters. In County Down, as in many other areas, the visits of the herring coincided with slack periods in agriculture, or occurred when agrarian or other pursuits could be abandoned without damage for short periods. That herring fishing was almost exclusively a night-time activity also contributed to the ease with which it could be combined with primary, land-based employment. Herring fishing was thus particularly important as a subsistence activity because it could be exploited as a supplementary as well as an alternative means of maintaining a living. For example, in nineteenth-century Caithness, 'the social value of independence on the land was realised by the use of [herring] fishing as an auxiliary'.[8] This opportunity was also of obvious use in Ireland where there was a long and enduring tradition of combining land-holding and work on the land with fishing. The relative predictability of the herring visits meant, moreover, that herring fishing could be combined at a distance with other activities; in peripheral regions this was often represented in periodic outward migration, prompted by the existence of herring fisheries elsewhere.[9] In County Down, however, herring fishing provided an incentive for local people to return; in 1923 'many of the fishermen who found employment in the merchant service in the autumn of the preceding year came back and took part in the herring fishery during the summer months and again returned to the merchant service in October'.[10]

The regularity of the herring seasons also benefited full-time fishermen. On the one hand, it allowed the local inshore fishing year to be organised 'in advance' for the maximum return. When Carlingford oyster fishermen were asked if their main fishery would profit from an extension of the official season, they replied that they 'did not care to begin oyster dredging until 1 November . . . the men here earn £2, £3 and £4 a night herring fishing, and if there was anyone out after the oysters it would be very injurious to the herring'.[11] On the other hand, local herring fishing could also be combined with offshore fishing; while Portavogie fishermen tended to spend the winter whitefishing away from home and the summer herring fishing locally, in some areas a herring fishing year was followed in which the different seasons and different types of herring fishing came in natural succession. Chambers McBride, a Kilkeel fisherman, described his fishing year (c.1920) thus:

> We went to Dunmore about St. Patrick's Day to the herring fishing and came home about the middle of June to drift for herring at Kilkeel until the first week in September. We then fished in the skiffs for the spawning herring with anchored or trammel nets. We then returned to the big boats and went drifting for herring at Balbriggan and Dundalk to the end of February.[12]

The value of herring fishing locally, in all its aspects, was considerably enhanced by the high level of commercialisation in the herring industry as a whole. This commercialisation derived and depended less upon catching the fish than on buying and selling them; it was thus superimposed rather than imposed on the general fishing operation in such a way as to allow small-scale fishermen to participate in the wider herring industry without being overwhelmed by it. This again was largely a legacy of herring behaviour. While herring fishing was and had been for centuries a highly profitable commercial enterprise, the seasonal nature of the fishery had demanded the establishment of a peripatetic fleet if the maximum return on capital investment was to be extracted from the venture. However, herring was not only a very mobile resource, it was also a highly perishable one and had therefore to be 'processed' for market within a very short space of being caught. The large travelling herring fleets originally operated either by being themselves equipped both to catch and to cure herring, or else they served a curing industry that moved around with the fish. From the mid-nineteenth century central fresh markets were also served by these journeying boats, but here too the local manifestation of the central market, in the shape of agents and buyers, also tended to be remarkably mobile. In herring fishing it was in large part the market which came to the fishermen.

The opening up of the catching sector to include small fishermen began with the introduction in the early nineteenth century of a series of bounties which were paid only on cure, instead of on catch and cure as had previously been the case. Henceforth, curers were able to obtain supplies of fish from small-boat fishermen without losing their production bounties; this was a major factor in the expansion of the Scottish herring industry[13] whose national foundation developed as a number of dispersed small-boat fleets rather than as a centrally-directed, large-boat fleet.[14] The adoption of buying by auction rather than by prior agreement severed completely the link between boat and buyer and set the final seal on the independence of the small fisherman by allowing him to compete on equal terms in a free market; this was established locally on the appearance of the herring by the arrival either of buyers for the curing industry, agents for central wet-fish wholesalers, or both.

Close proximity to a reliable and productive resource base was therefore a crucial factor in the local, long-term establishment of a commercial herring fishery. The Irish Sea was traditionally one of the prime British fishing grounds for herring and attracted fishermen from many parts of the British Isles; in the period under review here, vessels from Cornwall, from the Isle of Man, from east and west Scotland and from the rest of Ireland jostled for space with local boats in the ports and harbours of County Down. The geographical position of the area, with the ease of access it offered to the rich Channel grounds, obviously underpinned the region's prominence in the national herring industry. However, County Down also possessed in Ardglass one of the foremost Irish herring stations and the only deep-water, non-tidal harbour on the east coast of the country.[15] Ardglass had been known as a fishing centre since at least the fifteenth century;[16] its continuing success throughout the nineteenth century had been secured by the new use of its harbour by Cornish drifters after the collapse of the Manx herring fisheries in the 1820s.[17] Ardglass was the hub of local herring fishing; but it functioned also as the northernmost port of the Irish east-coast herring fisheries, as well as being a vital service port for the Irish Sea herring industry, which operated in a sea area bounded roughly by Ardglass, Howth and the Isle of Man. County Down, therefore, had not one but three interlocking herring fisheries; the purely local near-water fisheries, the local east-coast Irish herring fisheries, and the cosmopolitan national herring industry.

While it was asserted that before 1846 Ardglass was 'every year thronged with Manx, Scottish and Skerries boats',[18] evidence suggests that Scottish fishermen did not begin to visit County Down regularly until well into the nineteenth century.[19] The herring industry itself in Scotland did not begin to develop apace until the 1820s and 1830s, in an industrial acceleration that originated first on the east coast of the country.[20] By the 1840s fishermen from eastern Scotland were moving westwards, through the Firth of Forth Canal, to work herring grounds in the Minch and Lewis.[21] It is probable that this route brought them also to County Down (hence explaining the strong fishery links that were forged early between Down and east Scotland); this passage was certainly used by Cornish vessels to continue the herring season out of the Irish Sea into east Scottish waters.[22]

The regional connections which obtained in the herring fisheries were primarily a function of this shared exploitation of fishing grounds and fishery harbours by boats from many different areas. The Scottish boats which came to County Down in the nineteenth century participated, however, in a herring fishery which served only fresh markets. In the early twentieth century a new kind of Scottish connection was established locally with the introduction of the herring curing industry in County Down. This export industry, the backbone of the Scottish herring fisheries, had been breaking new ground during the late nineteenth century as new distant markets for its product were secured in the Baltic, in Russia and in the United States. It was around this time also that Scottish curers were being tempted to Ireland by the Congested Districts Board in its attempts to recreate a curing industry in the more remote areas of the country. To branch out around the coast into established herring fishing regions was a logical step for these concerns.

For herring curing, like herring fishing, was a remarkably mobile operation. All the working equipment, in the shape of barrels, salt and labour, could easily be shipped from region to region, and all the curer needed locally was a small piece of land on which to erect a shed and tables. An agreement between Davidson, Pirie & Co., Leith, and the N.I. Ministry of Commerce for land leased in Ardglass in 1925 shows how cheaply this could be obtained; three plots of the harbour cost the curing firm only £22 10s. (without taxes) for a year which ran from 1 June to 31 May.[23] Nor were barrels obtained locally; while some visiting boats came already equipped, additional supplies were brought in by sea either from or through Belfast.[24] Even the managing cooper was brought in from Scotland, but 'Scottish coopers [had] to be procured in any case, by reason of local substitutes being unavailable'.[25] And whilst there was some local supply of salt, here again a 'considerable portion' came in on the fishing vessels.[26]

The fish were gutted and packed by women — the famous 'herring girls'. They too travelled with the curers, or were brought in from other areas, local women being on the whole unwilling to do this dirty, laborious but highly skilled work. Each of the Scottish girls who came to County Down had been bound by an agent to a sum of money, the 'arles', if she followed the fishing 'from Lerwick in June, Ardglass in September, or maybe Peterhead or Fraserburgh, then on to Hartlepool or North Shields till October'.[27] There were also a number of women gutters who came regularly from Donegal and the west of Ireland, after being employed there by the curing firms.[28] This may confirm the connection between the activities of the Congested Districts Board and the establishment of the curing industry in County Down; there is no evidence of firms from other parts of Ireland working in the area, although there were Belfast and County Down firms in local competition with the Scottish.[29] The most prominent feature of the County Down curing industry, however, both before and after the First World War, was the extent to which business activity in all sectors was carried out by outsiders. Not only was a large proportion of fish caught and then cured by people from outside the region; in 1927 only three of the four salesmen required to auction it fresh were local. The other lived in Scotland.[30] Foreign representatives also played a major role in the exportation of the cured fish; in 1926 it was reported that the herring on Ardglass grounds was 'of an unusually high quality — the fish when cured was bought eagerly on the spot by the USA and Germany'.[31]

Relationships with the Scottish visitors appear to have been amicable. One Campbeltown fisherman told an Enquiry in 1893 how it was their custom to give fish for which no commercial market existed 'to old people for a fry',[32] and remarked that the Scottish 'always got on harmoniously with Irish fishermen, and with the Irish people'.[33] It must be remembered that many local fishermen would themselves have been strangers in other ports for part of the year, either on their own boats or as part of the crew of foreign boats. For example, in 1858 it was reported that 'for the last five or six years about twenty of the younger [Newcastle] fishermen get employment for the months of June and July at Anstruther in Scotland to assist in the herring fishery'.[34] Later reports mention that it was the custom of fishermen from this area to go to Scotland for July and August.[35] When the Ministry of Commerce tried, c.1920, to contact James Teggerty of Kilkeel regarding non-payment of a loan on his own fishing boat, they were told that he was 'working on the *Lull* at the minute . . . for the Dunmore East herring'.[36] The *Lull* worked regularly from Ardglass also, but she was a Scottish vessel, owned for a time jointly in Belfast and Buckie, when her master was a Buckie man, George Slater.[37] There is also firm evidence of at least one case of a fishing boat 'migrating' from County Down to Scotland; in 1922 Ernest Donnan of Portavogie lost his first-class drifter *Sally May* when she went on fire in Fraserburgh harbour, 'where she had put in on her passage home after being hired for a season to Scottish fishermen'.[38]

The closeness of the fishery connections between County Down and Scotland is emphasised by the origins of the boats which were used in the local fleet. These boats were either built locally, often to a locally-adapted 'foreign' design,[39] or, in many cases, were bought new or second-hand from outside the region. The immediate place of origin of these 'imported' boats reveals a very high proportion coming from Cornwall, the Isle of Man, and especially Scotland.[40] In addition, a large number of second-hand boats whose immediate place of origin is not known had been built in Scottish boatyards. It was also not unusual for boats to be sold 'to and fro' between Scotland and County Down; for example, the *Scotch Lass*, built in Ardrossan in 1908, was bought from Girvan in 1917, sold from Kilkeel to Portavogie in 1918, and then sold back to Girvan in 1919.[41]

The development of the County Down fleet reveals not only a preponderance of 'foreign' boats but also the emergence of distinct local preference in boat type. Kilkeel district fishermen tended to be all-year-round herring fishermen, combining participation in the Irish Sea herring industry with inshore skiff fishing in the autumn. They traditionally relied on the big Cornish-type Nickies for their main fishery. These were very fine, fleet herring boats, any potential economic disadvantage they owed to the large crews needed to sail them being offset by their increased efficiency in having a full complement of fishermen aboard to haul the heavy herring drift nets. The tendency in the Portavogie area, however, was to combine summer herring fishing with either the coastal trade or with winter white fishing; fishermen here turned to the smaller and more adaptable Manx-type Nobbies.[42] The smaller crew needed to sail these boats may have made their use in herring fishing less productive (and certainly more arduous) but it made their employment outside herring fishing much more profitable.

In the 1920s a new fishery emerged in County Down, initiated by Portavogie fishermen, in which links with Scotland assumed tremendous importance. This was the winter seine-net fishery for whiting and plaice. Reference to the use of the 'Danish Seine', as the device used in this fishery was called, appeared quite suddenly in the annual report of the Fishery Department in 1926 when 'a distinct improvement was noted in the returns from trawling, seining and lining for demersal fish'.[43] The method was certainly used in County Down before this time (the Fishery Development Commission was told in 1923 that 'more County Down boats were fishing with Danish Seine between herring seasons'[44]), and it appears likely that the Portavogie men who were the first to employ it took their example from Scottish fishermen whom they encountered in Scottish waters.[45] The method grew in local importance throughout the 1920s, with Portavogie seiners travelling regularly to grounds in Luce Bay and the Clyde and supplying to a limited extent Scottish as well as home markets.[46] However, the vital commercial break did not come for these fishermen until 1935 when Ardglass was host to a fleet of Lossiemouth seiners who brought with them to the port to handle their whiting catch five representatives of the Glasgow fish market.[47] Portavogie boats were thus encouraged to land their own catch as they had previously done. The higher prices that they secured in this central market in 1935 were made even higher in following years by 'their improved methods of handling and packing the catch, these methods being copied from the Lossiemouth seiners'.[48]

This entrance to the Glasgow fish market continued to exist when the Scottish boats no longer worked from the region. The Glasgow agents maintained their position in Ardglass, supplying boxes for the catch, arranging its transport to Glasgow, and paying for the fish on commission.[49] By preparing their whiting catch exclusively for the Glasgow market Portavogie men were able to secure not only a higher but a more regular return for their labour than if they had been supplying only local or casual markets. Furthermore, by sending fish direct on commission to Glasgow, they 'practically eliminated the middleman';[50] this made the enterprise even more profitable. By 1939 a number of Kilkeel fishermen had abandoned the winter herring for winter seine-net fishing; some even bought the more suitable Nobbies expressly for the latter purpose.[51]

The stimulus extended to quayside demand by the visits of boats from other areas had been a crucial factor also in the importance of the herring fisheries in County Down. However, just as in the whiting fishery, it was the quayside demand of central mainland markets which was attracted by the presence of a visiting fleet. The revival of the Irish Sea herring industry in the 1860s occurred at a time when a nationwide, domestic, inland market for fresh fish was beginning to consolidate. And the herring fisheries which were re-established in County Down at this time served a market which was exclusively fresh and predominantly British. These British markets were reached, however, not through a local marketing network but either through local agents of the mainland marketing network or else by 'buying-boats' which steamed directly from the fishing grounds. In 1868 Mr Brophy, one of the travelling Irish fishery inspectors, visited Ardglass at the end of the summer season and reported that although herring valued at £28,000 had been returned as sold 'in the place',

> in addition there was a large quantity of fish carried away from the fishing grounds of which no account could be taken. Two steamers from England and one from Scotland attended the greater part of the season for the purpose of conveying the fish away to Liverpool, to Holyhead, to Workington and to Glasgow ... Besides there were several buyers from across the Channel, from Belfast, from Antrim, from Armagh and Skerries who constantly bought and transmitted their purchases to their various destinations.[52]

The remark that 'demand was high' because of the presence of steamers from the 'sister country' appeared regularly in the seasonal reports for the herring fisheries in County Down harbours throughout the 1870s.[53] In 1895 it was estimated that only one-quarter of the fish taken in the Irish herring fisheries went to home markets, the rest being sold fresh to England.[54]

The short sea run from County Down to the British mainland was of tremendous importance in the establishment of these local links with the external fresh market. One consequence of this was that the spread of the railway system throughout the region was of much less significance to the development of the local herring industry than was the maintenance and improvement of steam links with the British railway system. The Coastguard in Newcastle District remarked in 1892 that 'the new railway from Ardglass to Downpatrick [did] not seem to affect the numbers of boats unloading at Ardglass'.[55] In 1926 the Fishery Inspectors commented that, because most of the herring landed at Ardglass was then taken out of the area by sea, the value that accrued to Northern Ireland Railways from herring fishing was 'not substantial'.[56] On the other hand, the establishment of the Greenore-Holyhead steam link resulted in the cumulative monthly figures for non-Irish boats using south Down harbours during the summer herring season jumping from a mere 42 in 1874 to 585 in 1879.[57]

Table 1. Average Catch Value of Irish and Northern Irish Seafishing Industry

Ireland (£s)		*Northern Ireland* (£s)	
1887	22.00	1923	39.75
1891	20.62	1927	80.71
1896	22.64	1932	51.75
1901	22.71	1936	88.74
1906	22.72	1947	336.19
1911	29.78		
1916	68.21		

These figures have been obtained from statistics presented in the Fishery Board Annual Reports. They have been calculated using the customary device of counting two part-time fishermen as one full-time fisherman (Coull, *The Fisheries of Europe, An Economic Geography* (1972), p. 130).

The emphasis placed on external markets by fishermen locally, and the local establishment of external market outlets in the more commercially-orientated sectors of the local seafisheries, had a cumulative effect on the development of central fish markets in Belfast. One would expect markets there to have relied primarily on locally caught fish. Belfast, with its rapidly growing urban population, was by the end of the nineteenth century well connected by rail to most County Down ports; speed of transport and centralised consumer demand were the two essentials in the expansion of an inland marketing network for fresh fish. However, the railway system which linked Down to Belfast was much more likely to have carried fish which had been landed in English and Scottish ports to local inland retailers than it was to have carried fish from the County Down coast to Belfast for redistribution. It is true that a proportion of locally landed fish did find its way to the city; nevertheless, these catches were 'frequently offered in a market whose requirements had already been met'[58] by fish from the British mainland. In 1925 the Ministry of Commerce entered into protracted negotiations with a Lisburn fishmonger who wanted to set up a chain of fish and chip shops and who, when asked about his supply of fish, replied that he got fresh-water fish from Lough Neagh, 'apart from supplies of seafish which he [got] from Aberdeen'.[59] In the north of Ireland, a complex marketing network for fish developed in which interior retail outlets tended to rely on fish landed outside the region for their main supply, and where most of the fish landed in the marketing hinterland of the central distributor was sent for sale in England and Scotland. In 1976 a newspaper article commented on 'how strange' it was that Northern Ireland fish used to be practically unknown in its own market:

> Ten years ago, virtually all the fish landed in Northern Ireland was either processed and shipped overseas, or transhipped fresh for sale in Glasgow. Meanwhile, retailers in Northern Ireland were supplied with fish from Aberdeen, Hull, Fleetwood and Grimsby.[60]

Perhaps the most obvious 'Scottish Connection' in the County Down seafisheries was the continued patronage of local grounds and local harbours by Scottish fishermen and the continued patronage of Scottish grounds and Scottish harbours by County Down fishermen. These links with Scotland were confirmed in the origins of many local boats and the introduction and improvement of methods of fishing. The nature of the marketing network for fish which developed locally also revealed the influence of the area's close connections with Scotland. Much of the vitality of the fishing industry in County Down resulted in the easy way in which information, ideas and markets flowed from region to region. But the continued strength of seafishing locally also rested on the fact that there were not one but two seafishing industries; County Down possessed an indigenous, home-based seafishery but was at the same time a centre for the wider, sea-based seafisheries. These existed simultaneously, creating locally an industry in which small-scale and subsistence activity and large-scale commercial enterprise complemented rather than competed with one another.

NOTES

1. Percentages abstracted from statistics issued in Fishery Board annual reports.
2. *Report of Sea and Inland Fisheries of Northern Ireland* [hereafter *RNIFB*], *1934* (Belfast, 1936), p. 30.
3. Spencer Walpole, 'The British Fish Trade', in *Handbook of the International Fisheries Exhibition, London 1883* (London, 1883), p. 47.
4. *Ibid.*, p. 48.
5. *Report of the Commissioners for the Sea and Inland Fisheries of Ireland* [hereafter *RIFB*], *1870* (P.P. 1871, XXV), p. 283.
6. *RNIFB, 1928* (Belfast, 1928), p. 27.

7. *Ibid.*

8. M. Gray, *The Fishing Industries of Scotland, 1790–1914: a Study in Regional Adaptation* (Oxford, 1970), p. 61.

9. See, for example, T. Devine, 'Temporary Migration and the Scottish Highlands', *Ec.H.R.*, XXXII, 3 (1979), pp. 353–355.

10. P.R.O.N.I. COM 43/3/4.

11. Patrick Rice, evidence to Select Committee on United Kingdom Seafisheries (P.P. 1866, XVIII).

12. Chambers McBride, quoted in *Sailing Ships of Mourne: The County Down Fishing Fleet and the Newcastle Life Boat* [hereafter *Sailing Ships*] (Newcastle, Co. Down, 1971), p. 41.

13. See Gray, pp. 27–33.

14. *Ibid.*

15. Commission on the Natural and Industrial Resources of Northern Ireland: *Report on Seafisheries and Seafishery Harbours, Northern Ireland* (Belfast, 1923).

16. J. de C. Ireland, *Ireland's Seafisheries, a History* (Dublin, 1981), p. 17 (map).

17. W. C. Smith, *A Short History of the Irish Sea Herring Fisheries in the Eighteenth and Nineteenth Centuries* (London and Liverpool, 1923), p. 13.

18. *RIFB, 1868* (P.P. 1868–9, XV), p. 590, John P. Brophy's report.

19. For example, there is no mention of Scottish visitors in the area in evidence submitted in 1836 to the Royal Commission on the State of the Irish Seafisheries although reports of Cornish and Manx visitors figure prominently.

20. Gray, pp. 39–41.

21. *Ibid.*, p. 85.

22. E. J. March, *Sailing Drifters: The Story of the Herring Luggers of England, Scotland and the Isle of Man* (Newton Abbot, 1969), p. 146.

23. P.R.O.N.I. COM 43/3/2.

24. P.R.O.N.I. COM 42/7, 1926.

25. P.R.O.N.I. COM 43/4/3, 1923–5.

26. P.R.O.N.I. COM 42/7.

27. *Sailing Ships*, p. 44.

28. *Ibid.*; see also P.R.O.N.I. COM 42/7.

29. P.R.O.N.I. COM 42/7.

30. *Ibid.*

31. *RNIFB, 1926* (H.M.S.O. Belfast, 1928). The local involvement of continental agents was a feature also of the curing industry in Scotland. Gray, pp. 50–55.

32. Unnamed witness, evidence to Interim Report of Inspectors of Irish Fisheries on Mackerel Fishing, Spring 1893 (P.P. 1893–94, XVIII), p. 417.

33. *Ibid.*

34. *RIFB, 1858* (P.P. 1859, Session 2, XIV), p. 798.

35. *RIFB, 1892* (P.P. 1893–4, XVIII), p. 314.

36. P.R.O.N.I. COM 43/1/26 and 27, Steven to Tallents.

37. Belfast Customs House, MSA Section 4 Records, (BCH) Book 3, f.95.

38. P.R.O.N.I. COM 43/3/4.

39. M. McCaughan, 'Irish Vernacular Boats and their European Connections', *Ulster Folklife*, XXIV (1979).

40. This refers to boats either bought new from elsewhere, or to boats which had their registration transferred to County Down from other regions, and noted in the official records.

41. Newry Customs House, MSA Section Records, Book 2, f.144; BCH, Book 2, f.258.

42. The prefaces 'Manx' and 'Cornish' refer here to the origin of the boat design, not to the origin of the vessels themselves.

43. *RIFB, 1926* (H.M.S.O. Belfast, 1928). This was the first annual report published regarding the Down fisheries since 1919.

44. P.R.O.N.I. COM 43/3/4, 1923.

45. H. Wood, 'Fisheries of the United Kingdom', in M. Graham, ed., *Sea Fisheries: Their Investigation in the United Kingdom* (London, 1956), p. 28. Wood dates the introduction to Britain of this method of fishing as 1921 and stresses its first use by Scottish fishermen.

46. For example, in 1929 low landings of whiting in Portavogie during the winter months were explained by local seiners landing supplies in Girvan and Dromore, Scotland. P.R.O.N.I. COM 45/22; Portavogie Returns, 1929.

47. P.R.O.N.I. AG 6/6/5; 1935 Ardglass.

48. *Ibid.*, 1938 Portavogie.

49. *Ibid.*

50. *Ibid.*

51. *Ibid.*, 1937 Kilkeel.

52. *RIFB, 1868* (P.P. 1868–9, XV), p. 590, Mr Brophy's report.

53. See, for example, *RIFB, 1873* (P.P. 1874, XII), p. 626; *RIFB, 1875* (P.P. 1876, XVI), p. 603.

54. *RIFB, 1895* (P.P. 1896, XX), p. 311.

55. *RIFB, 1892* (P.P. 1892, XXI), Coastguards' Reports.

56. P.R.O.N.I. COM 42/7, Ardglass Herring Fishery, c.1926.

57. *RIFB, 1879* (P.P. 1880, XIV), abstracted. These figures represent the total of visits per month of foreign boats, not the total number of foreign boats. If Irish boats are included, the totals are 432 visits in 1874 and 3,099 visits in 1879.

58. *Sailing Ships*, p. 10.

59. P.R.O.N.I. COM 43/3/2.

60. *Belfast Newsletter*, 11 May 1976.

22

LABOUR IN SCOTLAND AND NORTHERN IRELAND: THE INTER-WAR EXPERIENCE

Graham Walker

It is an oversimplification to say that the Irish settlement of 1921–22 was the making of the Scottish Labour movement and the breaking of its Ulster counterpart, but it nonetheless contains a significant amount of truth. The removal of the Irish issue from the forefront of British politics was of great importance to Labour's attempts to weld together an electoral machine in Lowland Scotland of both Protestant and Catholic (overwhelmingly of Irish descent) workers; on the other hand, the nature of the settlement confronted the Labour movement in the new Northern Ireland State with formidable obstacles to the development of class-based politics. The fortunes of both movements were thus destined to be very different in the inter-war period. It should be noted that here the term 'Labour movement' covers what might be called the orthodox or 'reformist' set of Labour organisations, political and industrial: namely, in Scotland, the Labour Party, the Independent Labour Party (I.L.P.), and the trade unions; and in Ulster, the Belfast Labour Party (1917–24), the Northern Ireland Labour Party (from 1924), the I.L.P., and the trade unions.

I

Before the First World War Irish political organisation in Scotland, based on the United Irish League (U.I.L.), generally lent its support to the Liberal Party. During the war the situation was radically changed by the Easter Rising of 1916 and its aftermath, an episode which effected a virtual sea change in Irish opinion towards the republican separatism of Sinn Fein. In the 1918 election in Ireland Sinn Fein emerged overwhelmingly victorious. Ireland had entered a new phase of intensified and heightened national aspirations, and military confrontation with Britain followed in the latter part of 1919. This Anglo-Irish war was to provoke Labour into emerging as the party most clearly in support of Irish self-determination; its campaign on the issue grew in parallel with the 'Black and Tan' atrocities in Ireland.

Labour in Scotland, in effect the I.L.P. at this time, was in the forefront of this campaign with numerous 'Hands Off Ireland' rallies. The U.I.L., and leading figures in the Glasgow Catholic community, such as the newspaper editor Charles Diamond, now came to co-operate closely with Labour and to advise Catholic electors to vote for the party at local and national elections during the period 1918 to 1922. The effects of the growing Labour/Catholic alliance were to be seen in the local election results in Glasgow in the years 1920–22 in which wards with large Irish Catholic communities swung noticeably behind Labour.[1] However, the swing had still to be shown at national level, where Labour had yet to establish itself solidly. In the November 1922 election this hurdle was scaled with greater conviction in Glasgow than in any other part of the United Kingdom, as Labour, in the form of the I.L.P., took ten seats out of fifteen. The Irish 'machine', inherited from the U.I.L. and now marshalled by adroit political managers such as Patrick Dollan, formed the background of the Labour vote in several constituencies.

Many in the Irish community in Scotland may have disparaged it, but the Anglo-Irish Treaty of December 1921 effectively removed the Irish question from British politics while providing for its escalation into civil war in Ireland itself. Consequently, by the November 1922 election there was little political point in an Irish campaign in the context of British politics. Irishmen were now killing Irishmen and the reaction of exiles, from Scotland to America, was one of despair and sadness rather than of indignation and agitation. Partition was an established fact, and the unsavory spectacle of civil war in the south undermined the moral case which might have been put against it.

Labour's backing for the Irish cause during the Anglo-Irish war had been instrumental in winning it the support it needed. However, the issue's removal from British politics was arguably a greater benefit, for it largely defused the potential sectarian conflict which might have been aroused had the matter continued in a violent way to be intractable. On the one hand, the Irish Catholic community became more receptive to the main issues in Labour's programme which concerned the alleviation of the deleterious social and economic conditions that affected it disproportionately. Secondly, Labour was able to direct its appeal to the Protestant working class on the same issues without the risk of alienating its support by an emphasis on Ireland.

Ulster, of course, was at the centre of the whole imbroglio of the Irish question. In Belfast and elsewhere Labour faced the daunting prospect of attempting to build class unity in conditions of institutionalised sectarianism in the workplace, and sharp residential segregation along religious lines.[2] Most important of all, sectarianism was the expression of a division in which class was subordinate to the claims of nationalism and ethnic identity. The Ulster Unionists' resistance to Home Rule was a cross-class phenomenon which many Labour spokesmen were too ready to view simplistically as a bourgeois plot for selfish economic ends.[3]

Belfast Labour did have a tradition of 'Labour Unionism' as personified by William Walker, one of its most outstanding pre-war personalities. Walker was anti-Home Rule and favoured the integration of the Irish Labour movement with that of the rest of Britain. However, his influence had waned by around 1912 when James Connolly's concept of an Irish Workers' Republic separate from Britain was claiming an increasing number of adherents. In effect Belfast Labour took something of a middle way before the war by embracing the cause of Dominion Home Rule. In the immediate post-war years the Belfast Labour Party opposed partition while trying to minimise the issue's significance at a time of social and economic unrest. Its showdown with the Protestant workers, however, was not to be long delayed.

Both the Scottish and Ulster Labour movements took shape against the background of the development of their respective economies. In both places there was a pronounced bias towards heavy industry which, as Dickson has noted for Scotland, pointed up the particular significance of skilled workers and their importance to Labour.[4] In both places craft sectionalism was strong and skilled/unskilled divisions were very clear. Hepburn has detailed the religious character of the occupational hierarchy and the residential pattern in Belfast,[5] while McLean has argued that skilled and unskilled were rigidly segregated into different residential areas in Glasgow.[6] 'Red Clydeside' was largely a skilled workers' phenomenon, stemming as it did from struggles against wartime dilution of labour in heavy engineering. In January 1919 both Belfast and Glasgow witnessed skilled engineering workers' strikes for shorter working weeks. These failed to achieve their declared aims, but the strike in Belfast almost paralysed the city for three weeks, while in Glasgow the 'Bloody Friday' riot in George Square raised the spectre of Bolshevism in establishment circles. In Glasgow, however, the skilled workers played a crucial part after the war in Labour's political breakthrough, while in Belfast the historical conjuncture of the Protestant skilled workers' self-assertiveness and the political crisis engendered by the national question yielded a violent sectarianism which shaped the new Northern Ireland state.

It has been argued that 'Red Clydeside' was far from revolutionary,[7] and it is clear that the rent and dilution struggles were of themselves limited in aim. However, this recognition may hinder appreciation of the cumulative effect of the different struggles, protests, controversial arrests and deportations, rows over censorship, and growing public awareness of radical personalities. As Bob Morris has argued, the fundamental changes in the housing market wrought by the rent struggle, the increasingly important role played by the trade unions at State level, and the circulation of socialist ideas, constituted, in the context of 1918–20, a revolution of a kind.[8] It was a revolution which turned the skilled labour force, for the most part, to the politics of Labour and to a much closer association of interest and comradeship with the unskilled than had existed before the war.

Housing was perhaps the main issue which cemented this alliance, an issue which struck so close to home that it might be said to have overshadowed doubts held by some Protestant workers regarding the widespread support in the Labour movement for Sinn Fein in the period of the Anglo-Irish war. The rent struggle of 1915 was still a vivid memory and the people involved then were overwhelmingly the skilled 'respectable' working class from mainly Protestant areas such as Govan and Partick.[9] In the period 1918–22 Labour launched a veritable housing crusade in the West of Scotland. Uproarious scenes in the Glasgow Corporation took place as Labour members sought to publicise the wretched state of working-class housing in the city. In August 1920 there was another rent strike against proposed increases, and it was again strongest in the 'skilled' districts.[10] However, housing was an issue which won the votes of skilled and unskilled, Protestant and Catholic.

That sectarianism was a factor in Glasgow political life, and a threat to Labour, is shown clearly in contemporary accounts of elections and constituency characteristics. In 1920 Willie Regan, organising secretary of the Glasgow I.L.P., wrote a report on the local elections in which he referred to several instances of 'Orange and Green' conflict.[11] Of the Provan ward of the city, for example, he wrote: 'our two labour candidates had to compete with two Irish nominees who stole our political thunder. This allowed a "Good Government" candidate, who commanded the Orange vote, to secure first place'. So echoes of Ireland were certainly heard in Scotland at this time and Labour *did* have problems with them. However, these problems seem to have been more significant at local rather than national level. Moreover, they are likely to have been of greater concern to people in 1920 during the height of the Anglo-Irish war than in late 1922 after the Anglo-Irish Treaty had been put into effect. In any event, the momentous result of 1922 could not have been achieved without the Irish Catholic 'machine' as well as extensive Protestant working-class support. Much of this support must have come from the skilled workers who were of considerable significance in an economy dominated by heavy industry.

In Belfast, in contrast to Glasgow, the skilled workers reached no such 'concordat' with the unskilled to the political or industrial benefit of the Labour movement. Large numbers of the unskilled were Catholic and Nationalist (or Republican), and the dilution which had taken place in the Belfast shipyards during the war had been viewed by many Protestant workers in terms of Catholic infiltration. This situation was exacerbated by the sectarian form of protest adopted by those Protestant ex-servicemen who returned from the war to find themselves out of the skilled jobs which they regarded as their preserve. The Labour movement, despite increased trade-union membership during the war, had to compete with the Ulster Unionist Labour Association (U.U.L.A.) for the attention of the skilled workers. The U.U.L.A. was set up in 1918 for the express purpose of strengthening the pan-class unity of the Unionist bloc and of spiking the guns of Labour. Unionist propaganda against the Labour movement linked it unequivocally with Sinn Fein. Despite this, Labour appeared to be making inroads in January 1920 when the Belfast Labour Party won ten seats on the City Council. However, it had skilfully avoided committing itself on the National question, and it soon became clear that it would be forced to confront the issue. In July 1920, a week after a 'twelfth' speech by Sir Edward Carson in which he classed Labour alongside Sinn Fein as Ulster's 'enemies', a series of violent expulsions from the shipyards of both Catholic workers and Protestant Labour men took place. It was the prelude to a two-year period of communal strife which provided the new State with a bloodstained birth and an edifice of sectarianism on which ethnic and not class politics were to be erected.

II

The inter-war period brought serious economic problems to both Scotland and Northern Ireland.[12] As staple industries declined or fluctuated erratically, unemployment became more widespread. Alleviation of the problem in both places was largely due to the regalvanising effect of rearmament in the late '30s. In the context of the international crisis, both areas were particularly vulnerable due to their dependence on shipbuilding, engineering and textiles, all of which were export-oriented industries. New domestic consumer industries sprang up in the south of England, helping to generate economic and demographic trends which had recurrent and damaging effects on Scotland and Northern Ireland. As these new industries grew people moved south, where the consumer market expanded; while unemployment in Scotland and Northern Ireland produced a lack of purchasing power which in turn hindered the investment needed in both regions. The response of the Scottish Labour movement was very much determined by an acceleration of the process of absorption, both politically and industrially, into the wider British Labour structure; of primary influence in Northern Ireland were the constraints and impediments imposed by the nature of devolved government.

Scottish Labour's political breakthrough in 1922, combined with the advent of economic recession, led the movement into a greater involvement in British politics and closer co-operation with the British Labour movement as a whole. 'Red Clydeside's' ten M.P.s may have journeyed to Westminster with Home Rule for Scotland on their lips, but it was not long before the broader demands of the British political system dominated their minds. As the 1920s wore on, Scottish Home Rule slid down Labour's list of priorities. The realities of the situation seemed to conspire against it. The crucial social and economic problems of the day were posed in a British context and thus seemed to beg a Labour response appropriate to the United Kingdom as a whole. As has been noted mainly by critics, Scottish Labour's integration with British Labour paralleled the economic developments of the time whereby Scottish capital and Scottish industry became increasingly bound up with British economic policy.[13] Structurally, more Scottish trade unions became British-based: mergers and amalgamations increased and the centralisation process invariably shifted the centre of gravity south. It has been noted that, by 1925, three out of five Scottish trade unionists were members of British unions, and that many of the unions which remained based in Scotland were co-ordinating their efforts with British unions in the spheres of collective bargaining and negotiations over pay and working conditions.[14]

Economic conditions reinforced Scottish Labour's 'British' approach. While the economy, and particularly the Scottish part of it, was sluggish or worse, suggestions of Home Rule seemed self-indulgent. The economic crisis of the early 1930s induced a more pronounced reformist caution and largely stifled the urge towards radicalism. The radicals of the I.L.P. repudiated the conservatism of the broader Labour movement in this respect and disaffiliated in 1932. This had particularly profound effects in Scotland where Labour's organisation was heavily based on local I.L.P. branches, and the rebuilding which subsequently took place had the effect of bringing the Scottish organisation even closer into line with that of the movement in Britain as a whole. Trade union organisation in Scotland was weakened by unemployment, industrial decline and emigration south; it too moved to a position of closer dependence on the national movement.

As Scotland's staple industries floundered and new industries were conspicuous by their absence, Labour looked to the state for remedies. The 1930s saw an unprecedented concern with regional planning. Groups and committees on industrial development were set up and reports and surveys proliferated. However, significant positive action did not follow. Investment continued to flow south and overseas: government aid to traditional industries was sufficient only to slow down their decline; Scotland continued to rely on an economic basis which lacked the diversification necessary for prosperity. Labour's call for economic renewal was loud and strident; its defence of the old industries in which much of its support remained was equally spirited.[15] But such was the incompatibility of these objectives at a time of international economic stringency that Scottish Labour effectively fell between them. Its leadership struck an ambiguous pose: articulating grievances in an attempt to raise class consciousness, while identifying itself with a policy of central planning dependent on new investment.

Scottish Labour also saw its task as securing the best possible set of social security and welfare benefits for its supporters. This acted as another factor in reinforcing identification with the British Labour movement and the British State. Whatever the attractions of an independent Scotland to Labour leaders, or the disquiet felt at the dependence on London as a financial capital, the 'safety net' provided by the state in respect of social security, imperfect though it was, acted as a strong deterrent against any rash moves to break the union or even to resist the process of integration. This question of social benefits will also loom large in our assessment of Northern Ireland Labour's predicament. Scottish Labour, faced with economic depression and gearing itself increasingly towards pragmatic measures, sought not to stir Scottish nationalist unrest, but to steer a nationalist consciousness towards the attainment of political, social and economic ends within the United Kingdom.

Throughout the inter-war period the Labour movement in Northern Ireland attempted to make its appeal to the working class on social and economic questions alone. The Northern Ireland Labour Party (formed 1924) was effectively 'neutral' on the national question, declining to take up an unequivocal pro-union or anti-partition position. There were important struggles within the movement on this issue, but in general Labour attempted to circumvent the national question by adopting an approach and a programme very much in line with that of the British Labour movement.[16] In this it failed. In its role as 'third party' in Northern Ireland politics, Labour found itself under attack from both Unionism and Nationalism, and could not build a sufficiently broad base among either the Protestant or the Catholic working class. Its best performance, electorally, in this period came in 1923 when it secured three seats in the Northern Ireland Parliament. A political culture which revolved around the one issue of whether or not Northern Ireland should be part of the United Kingdom was no place for the party since its social democratic concerns became almost an irrelevancy. That this should have been so was arguably the product of the way the national question had been settled in 1921. Partition of itself was not necessarily a barrier to the development of class politics across the religious divide; devolved government in the new Northern Ireland state effectively was. The Northern Ireland Parliament at once became the means through which the province's British status could be continually expressed. As a result it was an institution which, on the whole, alienated nationalists. Labour was not, therefore, participating in a 'normal' parliamentary democracy. Moreover, the effects of devolved government *in practice* further deepened Labour's sense of impotence, and it is to this issue that we will now turn.

It became clear almost from the time of the state's establishment that Northern Ireland would not be financially self-sufficient. Under the terms of the Government of Ireland Act it was envisaged that Northern Ireland's very limited tax revenue would not only provide for its expenditure but also leave something over and above to be paid as an 'Imperial contribution' to the British Treasury. Economic conditions after 1921 undermined such notions and the two governments were soon locked in negotiations over more suitable arrangements. What emerged allowed Northern Ireland to maintain standards of social security and welfare benefits which kept 'step by step' with the rest of Britain. This was of vital importance to the Unionist government, and its ramifications for Labour were far-reaching. The Unionist government did not encourage devolved government to be seen as much more than a way of reaffirming Britishness.[17] It was not in its interests to do so. Unionists, it may be remembered, had not asked for a regional parliament. They had not accepted it in any spirit of constitutional adventure or willingness to embark on innovative politics. The first government led by Sir James Craig set the tone: a policy of 'step by step' to maintain British standards in a province committed to a 'British way of life'.[18]

The extent to which Northern Ireland marched 'step by step' with Britain has been well discussed and detailed.[19] Certainly, the Province lagged noticeably behind Britain as a whole in terms of housing, health and education provision. However, as David Johnson has recently pointed out, Northern Ireland's performance has often been inappropriately judged in relation to the overall figure for the United Kingdom. Taken in comparison with Wales or Scotland, Northern Ireland's position may be put into better perspective.[20] Indeed, in regard to such social benefits as unemployment insurance Northern Ireland kept in line, probably at the cost of reducing its scope for investment and expansion in other areas. The maintenance of parity in the realm of social security was of enormous political importance to the Unionist government. It enabled it to claim that British standards were being attained and that the working class was sharing the benefit of the Union.[21] The Unionist Party's image was one of commitment to such standards coupled with an emphasis on what it saw as traditional 'Ulster' values of thrift, self-reliance and industriousness. It was a dual appeal to the majority's traditional sensitivities, and it was an appeal which effectively outdistanced a party such as Labour which started with the handicap of its equivocal stance on the constitution.

In such circumstances Labour turned to championing the potential of devolved government. It attacked the government for not making the most of its opportunities, for not being bold and pioneering. Harry Midgley, the Labour leader at Stormont in the 1930s, condemned the government's 'traditional complex' in regard to Westminster and the British government.[22] For Midgley and Labour, the Unionists were using 'step by step' as an excuse for not applying themselves to the particular problems of Northern Ireland.[23] The government replied to criticisms of economic policy by arguing that Northern Ireland was not an economic unit, that it was effectively bound up with the U.K. economy as a whole and that its scope for innovation was therefore extremely limited.[24] Where Labour's criticisms fastened on to practical details of social and economic policy, it was usually British government policies which were the real targets. Thus Ulster Labour's frequent attacks on the limited scope of unemployment insurance and on the means test in the 1930s[25] were really echoes of a critique developed by the British Labour movement. The Northern Ireland government simply claimed that it could do no more than reproduce British policy. For Labour in Northern Ireland all of this added up to an overwhelming sense of frustration.[26]

Whether the Northern Ireland government was as powerless as it often claimed is a matter of debate. Some commentators have reiterated Labour's criticisms of the 1930s: that it failed to make the most of the powers it did have.[27] The government, for example, had responsibility for industrial development and regional planning. In addition, it certainly could have used its powers to ensure that local authorities provided better housing and education standards. By maintaining social security benefits at the British level, the Northern Ireland government placed such a burden on its finances that little or nothing was left for programmes of industrial development and economic expansion. There was no money to induce new industries to set up in the province, although it should be said that the amount of money needed for such inducements would have been beyond the Northern Ireland government even if it had cut welfare benefits. As for the province's staple industries, their inter-war plight was so closely linked to international developments that the government probably did as much as it could.[28]

Maybe the government's 'step by step' approach was not in the province's best economic interests — although this is by no means clear — but it certainly was in the government's best political interests. Social and economic problems always came a poor second to the constitutional issue in Northern Ireland political life. This was ensured by the government's determination to present devolution as a means of consolidation, not experimentation. The government was generally content to leave the important social and economic decisions to Westminster where, in effect, Northern Ireland had only a muted voice. Northern Ireland Labour in the inter-war years was thus a party and a movement in limbo, cut off from the wider British movement whose outlook it shared, and locked in a provincial form of politics which blunted its appeal.

III

Having overcome sectarian problems to secure a working-class base of support which was to prove durable, Labour in Scotland went on to become an integral part of a British Labour response to the economic severity of the inter-war period. This response was for the most part a defensive and cautious rearguard action which forced the departure into the wilderness of the more cavalier crusading radicalism of the I.L.P. The taint of 'wildness' with which the Clydeside I.L.P.

had imbued Scottish Labour was gradually replaced by a steadier pragmatism which took its cue from the South. Notions of Scottish Home Rule came to be viewed as untenable in the light of those economic realities which rendered Scotland's fate so inexorably bound up with that of England. Religious sectarianism continued to be an important feature of the social life of west-central Scotland, and Labour's ability to win support from both the Protestant and Catholic working class was more severely tested at local than at national level. However, the broader context of U.K. politics had the effect of diluting the force of such issues. In the absence of the Irish question, sectarian passions could draw on very little outside the realm of local politics. Labour might thus be said to have benefited politically from the effects of greater U.K. integration, even if the economic effects of such a process were of questionable benefit to Scotland as a whole.

While Scottish Labour was being sucked into a British framework which threatened its distinctiveness, it could at least feel that it played a role in the process by which the country was governed. For Labour in Northern Ireland there was no such role to play. It was not built into the structure of the British Labour movement — although the bulk of trade unionists in Northern Ireland belonged to British-based unions — and could operate only as a provincial party. As such, Labour in Northern Ireland found that the Unionist government's conception of devolution and its policy of 'step by step' all but removed the provincial basis for class politics. Whether it was unwilling or unable (or both) to do otherwise, the Unionist government effectively left Northern Ireland socially and economically in the hands of Westminster. This had the effect of reinforcing the division over the national question as the central issue in the State's politics, and thus intensifying sectarianism.

The inter-war period for Scottish Labour was thus marked by the experience of integration with its attendant benefits and problems. For Labour in Northern Ireland, on the other hand, the experience was one of dislocation and acute frustration.

NOTES

1. See Iain McLean, *The Legend of Red Clydeside* (Edinburgh, 1983), p. 180.
2. See A. C. Hepburn, 'Belfast 1871–1911: Work, Class and Religion', *Ir. Ec. & Soc. Hist.*, X (1983), pp. 33–50.
3. See H. Patterson, *Class Conflict and Sectarianism* (Belfast, 1981), *passim.*
4. T. Dickson, ed., *Scottish Capitalism* (Edinburgh, 1982), p. 247.
5. Hepburn, *loc.cit.*
6. McLean, *op.cit.*, pp. 177–181.
7. *Ibid., passim.*
8. R. J. Morris, 'Skilled Workers and the Politics of the Red Clyde', *Journal of the Scottish Labour History Society*, 18 (1983), pp. 6–17.
9. See J. Melling, *Rent Strikes* (Edinburgh, 1983), esp. ch. 2.

10. McLean, *op.cit.*, p. 170.

11. *Forward*, 13 November 1920.

12. For analyses of the respective inter-war economies, see B. Lenman, *An Economic History of Modern Scotland* (London, 1977), ch. 7, and D. S. Johnson, 'The Northern Ireland Economy 1914–39', in L. Kennedy and P. Ollerenshaw, eds., *An Economic History of Ulster 1820–1939* (Manchester, 1985).

13. Dickson, *op.cit.*, ch. 6.

14. M. Keating and D. Bleiman, *Labour and Scottish Nationalism* (London, 1979), p. 94.

15. See articles by Patrick Dollan and Tom Johnston respectively in *Forward*, 27 January 1934, and 16 March 1935.

16. The N.I.L.P. modelled its constitution on the British party.

17. See D. Birrell and A. Murie, *Policy and Government in Northern Ireland* (Dublin, 1980), *passim.*

18. See quotation in P. Buckland, *The Factory of Grievances* (Dublin, 1979), p. 150.

19. See Birrell and Murie, *op.cit.*, and Buckland, *op.cit.*

20. Johnson, *loc.cit.*

21. See Craig's declaration at Stormont, *N.I. House of Commons Debates*, XVI, 36–7, 18 Dec. 1933.

22. *Ibid.*, XVI, 1384–5, 3 May 1934.

23. *Ibid.*, XVI, 80, 19 Dec. 1933.

24. See, for example, J. M. Andrews' statement at Stormont, *Debates*, XVI, 97–8, 19 Dec. 1933.

25. See Midgley's criticisms at Stormont, *Debates*, XVI, 1919–20, 29 May 1934.

26. See Midgley's despairing outburst, *Debates*, XVI, 1486, 9 May 1934.

27. See Birrell and Murie, *op.cit.*, esp. p. 289ff.

28. Johnson, *loc.cit.*

23

INFANT MORTALITY IN INTER-WAR NORTHERN IRELAND[1]

B. M. Browne and D. S. Johnson

I

In the third quarter of the nineteenth century Ireland had the lowest rate of infant mortality in Europe. This was partly a result of its relatively low level of urbanisation. But it may also have been a consequence of the high nutritional standards of its people compared to countries with similar proportions of urban population.[2] Though rates fluctuated, there is no discernible trend in the level of infant mortality until the 1890s when, for reasons which are unclear, it rose slightly, peaking at 109 per 1,000 between 1897 and 1900. Developments in the counties which later became Northern Ireland paralleled those in the country as a whole. They were higher, though, reflecting the fact that the north-east was more urbanised than the rest of the island. Still in 1901, at 112 per 1,000, infant mortality in the province, though above that in the rest of Ireland (96), was well below Scotland (129) and England and Wales (151).

Subsequently the relative position of Northern Ireland deteriorated both in relation to other parts of the United Kingdom and to the rest of western Europe.[3] As Figure 1 illustrates, the reason for this was the failure to maintain the reduction in rates achieved in the early years of the inter-war period. Although from 1918–23 infant mortality in Northern Ireland fell by 24 per cent, matching the record in England and Wales, there was little subsequent improvement until the Second World War.[4] Meanwhile rates in Scotland and England and Wales declined steadily.

In the end we have no convincing explanation for the rapid fall in infant mortality between 1918 and 1923, though it was a development paralleled in the rest of the United Kingdom. It may have been a result of the post-war boom which continued to have a beneficial effect, through accumulated savings, even after it ended in late 1920.[5] Equally it may have been the extension of the scope of the provisions for unemployment and health insurance in the immediate post-war period. The latter could have led to a 'one off' improvement in the condition of those classes at the bottom of the social scale where infant mortality was most prevalent.[6] Because we have no entirely satisfactory explanation of the fall in infant mortality in the immediate post-war years, we will confine our analysis to the reasons why infant mortality failed to decline significantly in the period from the early 1920s to 1939.[7]

So far we have been discussing infant mortality as if it was a cause of death. It is sometimes treated as such; and often, in the Northern Ireland context, mentioned

Figure 1
INFANT MORTALITY IN BRITAIN & IRELAND 1882–1939

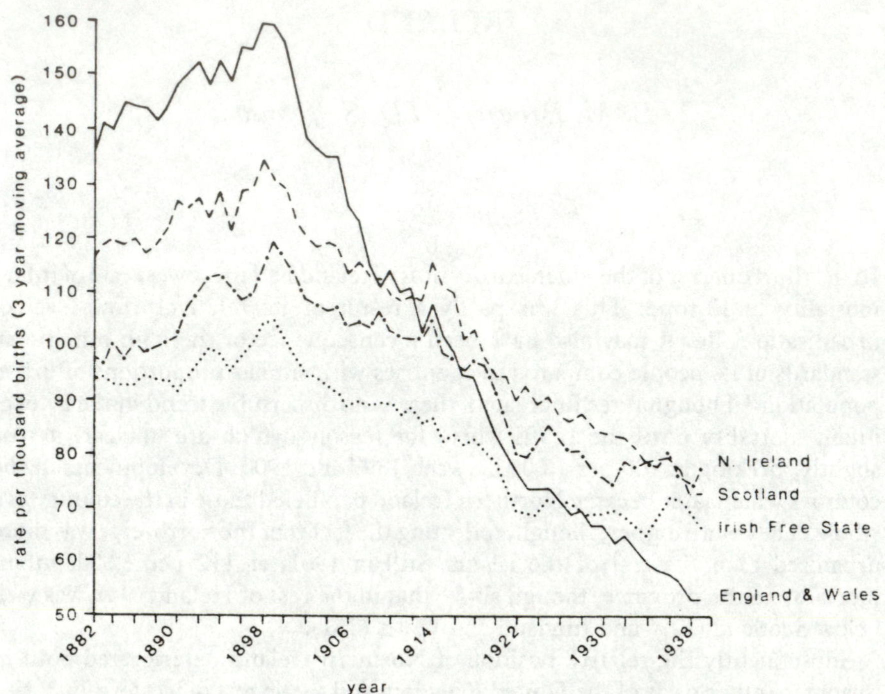

Sources: Annual Reports of the Registrar General (Ireland) 1882–1920; Annual Reports of the Registrar General (Northern Ireland) 1922–1939; Ulster Year Books 1926–1947; B. R. Mitchell & P. Deane, *Abstract of British Historical Statistics* (Cambridge, 1971), pp. 36–37.

in the same breath as tuberculosis, to show the relatively poor health in the province. It was, of course, no such thing, being simply the aggregate of deaths from the various diseases affecting children under the age of one. As Figure 2 shows, it is possible for the contributions of these diseases to move in opposite directions. Even this oversimplifies the problem, because the definition of infant mortality, with a cut-off point of one year, is arbitrary. During the inter-war period, the death rate of children between six and twelve months fell, while neo-natal mortality (children dying in their first month of life) increased.[8] Thus, the only way we can understand why infant mortality fell between 1918 and 1923, and more importantly why it ceased to fall significantly thereafter, is to examine its constituent elements. We will consider these in ascending order of importance.

Tuberculosis was not a major cause of infant death: its main impact came in later life. The overall pattern in the disease's decline after the Great War was mirrored among infants, the rate falling from 2.5 per 1,000 in 1919 to 0.9 in 1938. In contrast to the experience of adults, most infant deaths were non-pulmonary, tubercular meningitis accounting for the largest proportion.[9] Tuberculosis was primarily a function of poor housing conditions and bad diet, spread via droplet infection in

Figure 2
NORTHERN IRELAND: INFANT MORTALITY BY DISEASE

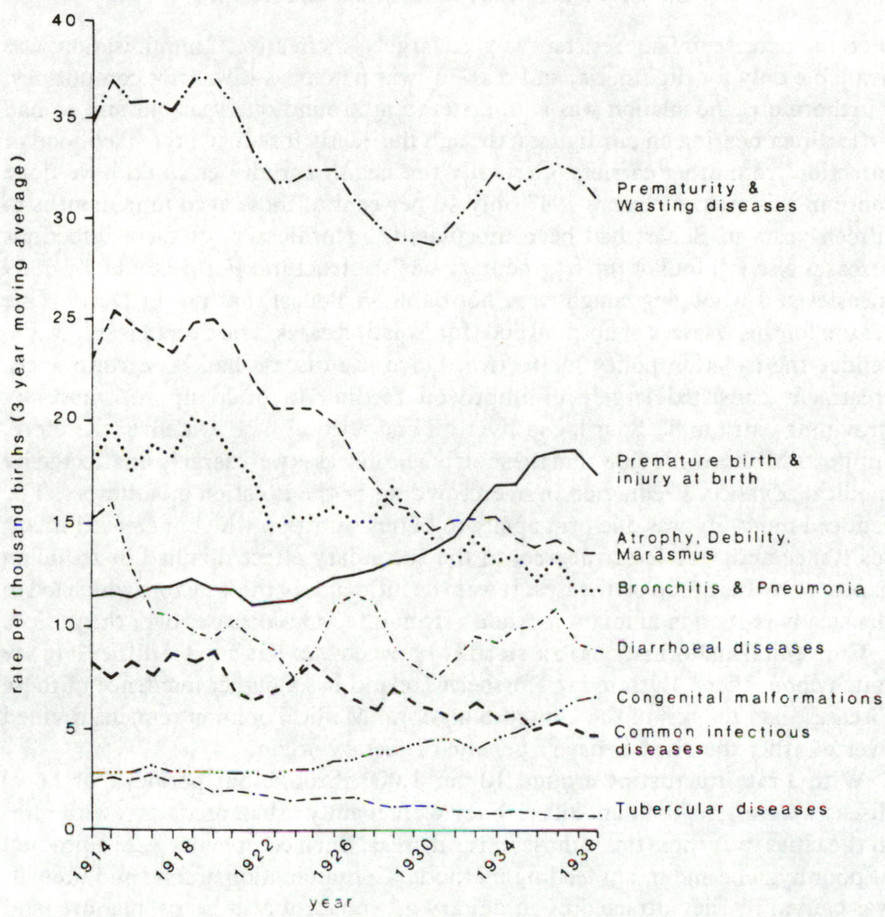

Source: Annual Reports of the Registrar General (Northern Ireland) 1922–1939.

overcrowded and ill-ventilated accommodation, striking particularly those of weak constitution. Infants were also susceptible to infection from contaminated cow's milk, and McKeown considers the level of abdominal tuberculosis to be a good yardstick of the quality of the milk supply.[10] Initially constituting around a quarter of all deaths from tuberculosis, this fell from a peak of 0.6 per 1,000 in 1918 to 0.1 in 1938. The fall was most marked after 1927, when the government established a system of licensing for the production of Tuberculin Tested milk. This guaranteed that the herd was free from tubercle *bacilli*.

The common infectious diseases comprised smallpox, scarlet fever, diphtheria, measles, influenza and whooping cough. Smallpox can be disregarded as there were no recorded deaths from it, while mortality from diphtheria and scarlet fever was low, never above 0.3 per 1,000 between the wars. Measles and influenza came in epidemics, so while mortality was usually low it could rise dramatically, as in 1918 when influenza deaths reached a peak of 4.6 per 1,000, and in 1935 when mortality from measles peaked at 4.7. The biggest killer within this group was whooping cough, usually running at a rate of between 3 and 6 per 1,000, and frequently responsible for more deaths than all other infectious diseases combined. Medical activity, consisting of immunisation, isolation and improved diet to increase infant resistance, was largely ineffective. Immunisation was available only for diphtheria, and take-up was patchy as it was not compulsory. Furthermore, inoculation was administered at around one year old and so had little direct bearing on our figures, though indirectly it reduced the likelihood of infection from other carriers. Certainly the health authorities could have done more in this area. As late as 1943 only 40 per cent of those aged nine months to fifteen years in Belfast had been inoculated.[11] Notification of these infectious diseases also fell foul of the fragmentary health structure. For example, by 1939 measles and whooping cough were notifiable in Belfast, but not in Derry. One reason for this was lack of hospital beds for isolation cases. The overall result was to render the isolation policy ineffective. Once the disease had been contracted, treatment consisted largely of improved feeding to build up resistance by providing extra milk, Bovril, cod liver oil and Virol.[12] The evidence, therefore, supports McKeown's view that these airborne diseases were largely unaffected by medical advance, a reduction in overcrowding or the isolation of sufferers. The reduced mortality was due principally to better nutrition which increased infant resistance and, to a lesser degree, to the secondary effect this had in reducing exposure to this group of diseases. It was the influence of these factors which led to the steady reduction in infant mortality from infectious diseases over the period.

Congenital malformations rose steadily between the wars but it is difficult to say much about them. Even today Northern Ireland has a higher incidence of these diseases than the rest of the United Kingdom. Medical opinion remains divided over whether the diseases have a genetic or dietary origin.

With a rate fluctuating around 10 per 1,000 through our period, diarrhoeal diseases were a major infant killer. They were mainly urban predators, with rates in the cities over three times those in rural areas. Such complaints were a product of poor hygiene and infant feeding methods. Contamination of food and utensils was caused by flies attracted by insanitary ash-pits, rubbish heaps, manure, and infrequently emptied privy middens. Although the installation of water-closets proceeded rapidly in urban districts between the wars, poor water and sewage systems ensured the persistence of insanitary dry conservancy systems in many rural areas. Personal hygiene was difficult as many houses had no baths, let alone adequate hot water supplies. For example, as late as 1943 two-thirds of houses in Derry[13] and 90 per cent of those in Carrickfergus were without baths.[14] Probably more critical were feeding methods. In 1911 the Medical Superintendent Officer of Health for Belfast attributed the higher urban mortality from diarrhoea to the greater incidence of artificial feeding amongst the working classes,[15] an observation confirmed by Bigger in 1917.[16] An inquiry by the Medical Officer for Cork found that of infants who died from diarrhoea in 1935 and 1936, 90 per cent had been artificially fed, mostly on cow's milk.[17] A later study of infant mortality in Belfast found considerable discrepancy in feeding practices between those babies who died and a control group of surviving infants.[18] While 75 per cent of children in the control group were breast-fed at the time of the first month, the figure for the mortality group was 50 per cent. By the third month the figures had fallen to 62 per cent for the control group and 34 per cent for the mortality group. This gap persisted throughout infancy, and while the study did not correlate feeding with cause of death, it indicated that artificially fed babies were less likely to survive infancy than their breast-fed counterparts. Some indication of the proportion of babies breast-fed between the wars exists, though evidence is scanty. A study of all births in Belfast in 1915 found that in the first four months of life 70 per cent were entirely breast-fed, 20 per cent were fed on a mixture of breast and bottle and 10 per cent were artificially fed.[19] The 1941/2 inquiry found that the proportion of babies entirely artificially fed during the first six months had risen to 25 per cent.[20] Throughout our period, then, a growing minority of mothers were exposing their children to the risk of gastro-intestinal disorder through artificial feeding. This risk came from two directions. Firstly, cow's milk was a major source of infection, especially in hot weather. T.T. milk afforded some defence but pasteurisation was the real solution. This process faced several obstacles. Inefficiently done, it increased the risk of infection. A greater hindrance was the opposition of a public who felt that the process destroyed vitamins and ruined the milk's taste.[21] Medical opinion was divided (none of the hospitals in Belfast took pasteurised milk even in 1943). The consequence was that pasteurisation was not compulsory until after 1945. Thus a major source of infection lay untouched. The second area of risk lay in lack of adequate sterilisation of bottles and teats, through ignorance or carelessness, and in the use of dummy teats.[22] Fluctuations in diarrhoeal deaths were, therefore, largely determined by the weather, the purity of the milk supply and the extent of artificial feeding.[23] Nevertheless the absence of any fall in the rates between the wars must be ascribed to governmental inactivity with regard to the compulsory pasteurisation of milk and the education of mothers in feeding practices and domestic hygiene.[24]

Bronchitis and pneumonia claimed the second largest number of infant lives in 1918 with a rate of over 20 per 1,000, and remained a major threat to infant life until 1939. Again medicine made no real inroads on these diseases so we must look to increased resistance through better nutrition and environmental improvements to explain a fall in mortality. The latter was emphasised by Bigger who stressed the inimical effect of dampness in houses and stuffy, ill-ventilated rooms. Such conditions were caused by the 'dearness of fuel', which reduced the incentive to ventilate and encouraged the heating of one room only. Temperature changes, consequent upon the removal of infants to cold, damp bedrooms for the night or their being taken outside, insufficiently clothed, on cold, wet days, encouraged the contraction of pneumonia and bronchitis. Belfast had the highest death rates in Ireland from these diseases; this was attributed in part by the Medical Superintendent Officer of Health for the city to the common practice of mothers carrying inadequately clad babies early in the morning to the homes of 'minders' who looked after the infants while the mothers were at work. From a peak of 1918 bronchitis and pneumonia fell rapidly to 1922, and then stagnated before beginning a steady fall in the late '20s which lasted until 1939. Since there were no significant medical developments, these trends can largely be explained by improved housing and the state of the economy. Northern Ireland benefited from the post-war boom which enabled the working classes to purchase more fuel, clothing and foodstuffs, reducing the incidence of bronchitis and pneumonia in the population as a whole, and particularly amongst infants. The decline after 1929 was probably due to improved housing conditions. Half the new houses built between the wars were completed in the period 1928–32, and while these would not all have gone to those previously in the worst accommodation, there was a considerable 'trickling down' effect. Occupancy density decreased between 1926 and 1937, the reduction being greatest in urban areas.[25] Here, too, bronchitis and pneumonia declined most.

Regarded separately, wasting diseases and prematurity ranked first and third in their contributions to infant mortality in 1918, the former at the higher level. Thereafter their relative positions changed and by 1939 were reversed. Mortality from wasting diseases fell rapidly from 1918 to 1930, but only slowly thereafter. Conversely, deaths from prematurity fell slightly to 1922 and then increased steadily to 1937, the rise becoming steeper in the 1930s. So after 1922 the two moved in opposite directions, a pattern which is difficult to explain. Most likely, classification of these deaths was arbitrary, differentiation between the two conditions being difficult.[26] The relative movements in the figures may reflect changes in the diagnostic practices of doctors rather than in the incidence of the diseases. While the Registrar General's reports make no mention of a formal change in classification, there is evidence to support the possibility of an informal shift in practice. Both diseases claimed most victims within the first months of life and were characterised by the infant's failure to thrive. Medical observers have commented on the vagueness of the terms. Thus McKeown asserts that around 1900 premature birth had no consistent meaning and later disappeared as deaths in this category were transferred to other causes.[27] Likewise Bigger described atrophy, debility and marasmus as 'a heterogeneous collection of names which signify little', maintaining that further examination would reveal that the real causes were either improper feeding leading to starvation or enteritis, or else prematurity.[28] Combining the two sets of figures, a different picture emerges. From a high rate of 37 per 1,000 in 1918 and 1919, mortality from these diseases shared in the general fall to 1922, when it steadied at under 32 per 1,000. Improvement followed in the second half of the '20s but was superseded by a deterioration from 1930 to 1936, which then tailed off before 1939. Prematurity is primarily a consequence of the mother's condition, while the survival of a premature child is largely dependent upon post-natal care.[29] Heavy work, domestic or industrial, can precipitate labour. The health of the mother and particularly her nutritional state is, therefore, important in determining the birth weight and health of the child, and its chances of survival.[30] But good obstetric care, before and during labour, and a high standard of medical care for the premature infant are also critical in reducing deaths.

The physical condition of many mothers and the standards of obstetric care were poor in Northern Ireland. Maternal mortality increased from 5.9 per 1,000 births in 1922 to 6.6 per 1,000 in 1938, and in 1936 the Northern Ireland figure was double that for England and Wales. Evidence given to the Maternity Services Committee in 1939 and to the 1944 Select Committee on Health Services demonstrated the medical officers' concern about the nutritional state of many mothers.[31] This was clear from the poor condition of the teeth of expectant mothers — much worse than in Britain and a consequence of calcium and vitamin deficiency. Prematurity, according to the Belfast Medical Superintendent Officer of Health, was a result of the mother's poor diet, excessively closely-spaced childbearing (particularly among Catholics) and employment close to and soon after confinement. Family income therefore played a part in determining prematurity. Richer families had stronger, better-fed mothers either not working or able to withdraw from the labour force well before confinement. The impact of the post-war boom must go some way towards explaining the sharp fall in mortality from prematurity from 1918–22. Similarly, economic improvement in the later 1920s helps to explain the second dip in deaths from prematurity before the impact of the recession raised mortality in the 1930s. But in addition to economic factors the absence of any major development in obstetric services had a significant bearing on deaths from prematurity. A series of inquiries during the Second World War condemned the record in this area.[32] Midwives were found to be badly trained, poorly paid and severely overworked. There were, outside Belfast, for 152 dispensary districts only 199 midwives, employed part-time by Boards of Guardians. They were available free of charge only to the destitute poor, but also undertook additional private work to supplement their income. The result was that some midwives attended, annually, double the recommended number of confinements.[33] Ante-natal supervision was largely confined to Belfast; even there it was limited. The Maternity Services Committee found that 'vast numbers of women in Belfast and throughout the province do not receive any ante-natal care'.[34] Belfast was also alone in providing home helps and meals for expectant mothers, services which the 1944 Inquiry recommended should be extended along with post-natal care and child welfare clinics. The deficiencies in obstetric care strongly suggest that it made little impact on infant mortality from prematurity.

II

The reasons for the high level of infant mortality in 1938 — and for the failure of the rate to fall during most of the inter-war period — are complex. As Winter has shown, there was no simple relationship between unemployment and income changes in the various regions of the United Kingdom, and infant mortality. In south Wales, for example, which had the highest unemployment rates in the country, infant mortality fell relative to that in the nation as a whole.[35] Yet income differentials cannot be discounted. As Webster has recently re-emphasised, there was a marked difference in rates of infant mortality between social classes.[36] A medical survey by the Ulster Society for Economic Research in Belfast in February 1937 confirmed that this was the case in the city.[37]

As we have suggested, the rise in incomes in the immediate post-war period led to lower infant mortality. However, conclusions remain uncertain. It is clear that income levels for the majority of the Northern Ireland community rose in the period from the mid-1920s to the late 1930s. Yet infant mortality did not fall. Perhaps the paradox can be resolved in the following way. As we have noted, children were in the greatest danger in the first months of life. If a child managed to survive to the age of six months, it stood a better chance of further survival in 1938 than in the early 1920s. Therefore, a child over six months could benefit from the generally improving economic conditions in the province. Children under the age of six months, and especially those under the age of one month, stood less chance of survival in 1938 than fifteen years earlier. At these early stages of life, the quality of medical services was more important than were economic circumstances. We would, therefore, place considerable weight in explaining the failure of infant mortality to fall on the lack of improvement in medical facilities and the poor hygiene prevalent in the province. The latter was partially a consequence of poor ante- and post-natal care and lack of advice for mothers.

Why were medical facilities in the province inferior to, and slipping further behind, those in the rest of the United Kingdom? First, there were the financial constraints which were a permanent feature of the province's administration between the wars. Unlike other depressed regions of Britain, Northern Ireland had, basically, to live off its own revenue. Its difficulties were compounded by the decision to maintain 'parity' with Britain in certain areas of the social services (unemployment and sickness benefits and old age pensions) and the derating of agricultural land, which proved relatively more expensive in the province than in Britain. The result was that little money was available for improvements in medical facilities, even if there had been the will. And there was little evidence of much will. As has recently been shown, in the late 1930s Belfast Corporation spent over three times as much on libraries as on child and maternity services.[38] The problem was exacerbated by the fragmentary and cumbersome structure of the medical services.[39] While Britain established a Ministry of Health in 1919, health in Northern Ireland came within the ambit of five different ministers.[40] Lack of central direction was compounded at local level by overlap between local district councils and the Poor Law dispensary system. The outcome was less duplication of services than abdication of responsibility.[41] Discrepancies between areas also arose, as in disease notification, immunisation and milk pasteurisation noted earlier. Standards varied widely in different parts of the province. The overall result was that Northern Ireland fell well behind England and Wales in the provision of personal health services.[42] No doubt wider economic conditions played a part in determining movements in infant mortality. But in the absence of *major* advances in family income and home circumstances, particularly among the unemployed, it was largely the lack of improvement in the quality and availability of medical care and advice which determined the survival or otherwise of the infant in the inter-war period.

NOTES

1. This essay is a considerably shortened version of the paper presented at the Conference. The original paper dealt both with infant mortality and fertility control. It argued that the fall in the birth rate in the six counties (later Northern Ireland) began

around the turn of the century and was more marked among Protestants than Catholics. The argument was supported by correlations, at Poor Law Union level, between the proportion of Catholics in the population and the level of marital fertility. By 1911 this relationship was significantly positive (r = 0.67). It also used data from the 1961 *Fertility Report* for Northern Ireland which showed that, for marriages contracted prior to 1919, mean completed family size for Catholics was 5.98 compared to 4.28 for Protestants. We noted that during the inter-war period, while there was a fall in fertility in both religious denominations, this differential widened and was marked in all social classes and age groups. (See also C. O Grada, 'Did Ulster Catholics always have Larger Families?', *Ir. Ec. & Soc. Hist.*, XII (1985), pp. 79–88). We further suggested that the main form of birth control was neither appliance methods nor *coitus interruptus*, but increased abstinence from sexual intercourse. In this way family size was restricted without involving conflicts with Christian principles, as perceived at the time by both Catholics and Protestants. We would like to thank Richard Johnson for helping with many of the calculations on which the paper is based.

2. The Scandinavian or southern European countries, for example.

3. See J. M. Winter, 'Infant Mortality, Maternal Mortality and Public Health in Britain in the 1930s', *Journal of European Economic History*, VIII (1979), pp. 439–62.

4. The bulk of this fall came in urban areas. In Belfast and Derry, containing one-third of the province's population, infant mortality fell by 30 per cent, compared with 17 per cent for the remainder of the province.

5. Winter stresses the role of full employment and higher real wages in reducing infant mortality during the war through a rise in levels of nutrition, particularly among the unskilled and semi-skilled (especially women). J. M. Winter, 'The Impact of the First World War on Civilian Health in Britain', *Ec.H.R.*, XXX (1977), pp. 487–503. However, in Northern Ireland most of the fall in infant mortality occurred *after* the war rather than during it. Winter provides no adequate explanation of the rapid decline in mortality in Britain in the immediate post-war years.

6. Winter feels this helped to prevent any severe deterioration in public health in the 1930s. J. M. Winter, 'Infant Mortality, Maternal Mortality and Public Health in Britain in the 1930s', p. 462.

7. Collins implies that the fall between 1917 and 1927 was attributable to annual grants of roughly £5,000 on child welfare schemes after 1921. However, this sum was surely too small to have caused the decline in infant mortality shown in Figure 1. Anyway, the war began before the grants were made. Mary Collins, The Public Health and Medical Services in Northern Ireland 1921–48 (unpublished M.A. thesis, New University of Ulster, 1978), p. 19.

8. Although annual figures fluctuated wildly, deaths of children before the age of one month averaged 31.9 per 1,000 live births between 1922 and 1924, compared to 35.6 between 1936 and 1938. Over the same period, deaths of children 6–12 months fell from 19.8 per 1,000 to 14.9. Child mortality — deaths between the ages 1-4 — also fell from 11.2 per 1,000 children living in 1925/27 to 7.4 per 1,000 in 1936/38.

9. This struck at the central nervous system and was mainly contracted from human carriers.

10. T. McKeown, *The Modern Rise of Population* (London, 1977), p. 111.

11. *Report of Select Committee on Health Services in Northern Ireland* 1944 (HC601) Minutes of Evidence, p. 128.

12. *Ibid.*, p. 320.

13. *Ibid.*, p. 145.

14. *Ibid.*, p. 178.

15. H. W. Baillie, *Annual Report on the Health of the County Borough of Belfast* (Belfast, 1911), p. 87.

16. E. Coey Bigger, *Report on the Physical Welfare of Mothers and Children* IV. *Ireland* (Dublin, 1917), p. 13.

17. *Report of Medical Officer of Cork* (Cork, 1936), pp. 28–32.

18. James Deeny and Eric Murdock, 'Infant Mortality in the City of Belfast', *Journal of the Statistical and Social Inquiry Society of Ireland*, XVII (1943–4), pp. 221–40.

19. Marion Andrews, 'Report on Maternity and Child Welfare in Belfast County Borough', in E. Bigger, *Report on the Physical Welfare*, p. 133.

20. In this study an infant is considered breast-fed if the major part of its diet was breast milk.

21. The Medical Officer of Health for Belfast noted in his 1926 report that of 14 samples of so-called pasteurised milk, 6 contained living *bacilli coli*, which indicated contamination, probably from cow manure. Quoted in *Report of Chief Tuberculosis Officer* (Belfast, 1927), p. 20. For a fuller discussion of the influence of milk on infant mortality, see M. W. Beaver, 'Population, Infant Mortality and Milk', *Population Studies*, XXVII (1973), pp. 243–54.

22. See E. Bigger, *Report on the Physical Welfare*, p. 13.

23. See B. Thompson, 'Infant Mortality in Nineteenth-Century Bradford', in R. Woods and J. Woodward, eds., *Urban Disease and Mortality in Nineteenth-Century England* (London, 1984), pp. 120–47.

24. In contrast, there was a decline in deaths from diarrhoea in England and Wales between the wars which Winter ascribes to purer milk. The improvement was not due to government intervention but to the concentration of milk production in large companies producing to high standards. Maternal ignorance was a contributory influence but should not be overplayed. It fails, for instance, to explain why infant mortality in some rural areas was below that of Social Class I in urban areas. C. Dyhouse, 'Working Class Mothers and Infant Mortality in England, 1895–1914', *Journal of Social History*, XXII (1978–9), pp. 248–267.

25. Occupancy density fell from 1.01 persons per room in 1926 to 0.91 persons in 1937. D. S. Johnson, 'The Northern Ireland Economy, 1914–39', in L. Kennedy and P. Ollerenshaw, eds., *An Economic History of Ulster, 1820–1939* (Manchester, 1985), p. 210.

26. See A. S. Wohl, *Endangered Lives: Public Health in Victorian Britain* (London, 1983), p. 16.

27. McKeown, *Modern Rise*, pp. 144–5.

28. Bigger, *Report on the Physical Welfare*, p. 16.

29. See F. B. Smith, *The People's Health, 1830–1910* (London, 1979), pp. 65–135, and Wohl, *Endangered Lives*, pp. 10–42.

30. McKeown, *Modern Rise*, p. 144.

31. *Report of Maternity Services Committee on Maternal Mortality and Morbidity in Northern Ireland*, Cmd. 219 (1943), p. 24. *Report of Select Committee on Health Services*, Minutes of Evidence, p. 506.

32. See Report of Maternity Services Committee, Select Committee on Health Services, and Report of Dr. Thomas Carnwath to the Special Committee of the Belfast Corporation on the Municipal Health Services of the City (Typescript, Queen's University Library, Belfast, 1941).

33. *Report of Select Committee on Health Services*, Minutes of Evidence, p. 376. E. McCamley, The Development of Personal Health Services in Northern Ireland 1920–49 (unpublished M.A. thesis, New University of Ulster, 1982), p. 40.

34. Report of Maternity Services Committee, p. 15.

35. J. M. Winter, 'Infant Mortality, Maternal Mortality and Public Health in Britain in the 1930s', p. 446.

36. Charles Webster, 'Healthy or Hungry Thirties?', *History Workshop*, XIII (1982), pp. 110–129.

37. H. Scott Booker, 'Poverty and Infantile Mortality in Belfast: Report by the Ulster Society for Economic Research', *Ulster Medical Journal*, VII (1938), pp. 99–105.

38. See E. McCamley, 'The Development of Personal Health', pp. 41–2.

39. R. J. Lawrence, *The Government of Northern Ireland* (Oxford, 1965), p. 128.

40. These were Labour, Education, Home Affairs, Finance and possibly Commerce.

Report of Select Committee on Health Services, p. 710.

41. As Carnwath noted in his survey of Belfast: 'The council is not quite certain of what it is doing in this field, whether it is worth doing, or whether they are the people to do it'. Carnwath Report, p. 26.

42. Carnwath Report, p. 26.

24
INDUSTRIAL POLICY IN SCOTLAND AND IRELAND IN THE INTER-WAR YEARS

Mary E. Daly

At first glance the inter-war economies of Scotland and the Irish Free State would seem to have had relatively little in common and this is particularly true of their respective industrial sectors. While Scotland boasted a highly-developed industrial sector, industry accounted for only 13.3 per cent of the workforce of the Irish Free State in 1926. Scotland had much more in common with Northern Ireland which also boasted significant shipbuilding and textile industries. During the inter-war years, however, both economies sought to generate new industrial employment: Scotland's efforts were motivated by a need to replace jobs lost in traditional heavy industry, while Ireland was engaged in building up a weak industrial sector.

Both Scottish and Irish industry had evolved under a virtually identical political and economic system characterised by *laissez-faire* and free trade. The changes of the inter-war years led to the emergence of heretical proposals such as tariff protection, increased state intervention and a demand for new structures and institutions. Among the problems apparently faced by industry was a shortage of long-term capital — a problem of allegedly greater consequences for smaller firms.[1] Efforts to establish new institutions specifically designed to meet industrial credit needs in both Scotland and Ireland met with a lack of support from their respective banking sectors. Of the two, the Irish banking system was perhaps tied to the City of London to a greater extent than its Scottish counterpart. Independence had done nothing to break the traditional links. Irish banks clung to their policy of only providing short-term capital. Unlike the British banks who advanced long-term loans under the state-guaranteed Trade Facilities Act, the Irish banks refused to lend under the similar Trade Loans (Guarantee) Act, thus rendering the measure almost useless until 1932.[2] The Industrial Trust Co., an industrial bank which was shunned by the commercial banks, ultimately foundered because of highly speculative investments in the British and U.S. stock markets.[3]

Scottish banks proved no more adventurous than their Irish counterparts. In the past they had boasted a tradition of independence from the English system and a history of more innovative practices, but this would seem to have ended by the inter-war period, perhaps because of closer institutional links with English banks. During these decades Sydney Checkland has noted no evidence of Scottish bankers advocating alternative economic or monetary policies. Efforts to obtain support for a Scottish-based institution to provide long-term capital for small and medium-sized firms foundered when the Scottish General Managers responded that they 'regretted they could not see their way to recommend the scheme to their banks'. They also rejected a proposal to provide finance to enable Scottish contractors to tender for overseas business.[4] While Scottish companies had access to new London-based institutions such as Credit for Industry, it remains uncertain to what extent they were beneficiaries. Evidence suggests that Scotland received less than its due share of financial resources, both public and private, during these years.

The changing industrial climate gave rise to various promotional and lobbying groups. Irish industry, because of a combination of nationalism and previously adverse conditions, would seem to have been far ahead of Scottish industry in this respect. An Irish trade mark was established by the Irish Industrial Development Association in the first decade of the century, contemporaneous with a number of local industrial development associations, of which the Dublin Industrial Development Association, subsequently the National Agricultural and Industrial Development Association, was the most notable.[5] There is no evidence of corresponding Scottish institutions existing before 1931 when the Scottish Development Council was established.[6]

The major difference between these countries lay in the role and attitudes of government. Ireland had full political and economic autonomy within the limitations which its small size, relative poverty and lack of indigenous resources presented. Scotland's economic policies were determined at Westminster with little if any attention being paid to specific Scottish interests. Irish independence brought little immediate change to economic policy. The Cumann na nGaedhal government subscribed to the continuation of Ireland's traditional trading links with Britain and, placing its major emphasis on promoting agriculture, sought to maintain an open, low-cost economy. To this end it fought shy of tariff protection, and although some tariffs were introduced they were embarked upon with considerable reluctance. Each application was subjected to detailed inquisition by a Tariff Commission composed of three otherwise very busy men, who apparently favoured free trade.[7] Decisions were delayed for three or four years and many applications were rejected. They considered applications only from existing industries, and proposals for protection with a view to establishing new industries were not entertained.

Irish attachment to free trade was undermined in the autumn of 1931 when Britain adopted protection. By this stage Irish agricultural interests were no longer totally committed to free trade and the government was forced to introduce legislation providing for the imposition of emergency duties. However, the Cumann na nGaedhal government used the measure sparingly,[8] unlike their successors, the Fianna Fail government of 1932. The latter were committed to protection, not merely as a response to international depression, but as a conscious device to develop an Irish industrial sector. Their programme included the unrealistic goal of maximising both industrial and agricultural self-sufficiency, a commitment that Irish industry should, as far as possible, be under native control, and a desire to decentralise industry and to maximise the use of indigenous resources.

The key man in this programme was Sean Lemass, the Minister for Industry and Commerce, who exercised quasi-dictatorial power in the realm of industrial policy, power which was restricted only by the pragmatic pressure of business negotiations and hardly at all by the parliamentary process. He and his officials determined the criteria for granting tariff protection and tariff levels with minimal outside supervision. Tariffs, trade loan guarantees, licences to foreign businesses and duty-free import licences were used to attract industry to Ireland much as grants and tax concessions are employed in more modern times, with the important distinction that the cost of these measures was hidden from the public and that much of it was borne by the consumer. Boot and shoe laces were subjected to duties of 100 per cent in order to attract a Leicester firm to Ennis, Co. Clare. The duty on coffin mountings was increased from 33 to 66 per cent to protect a state loan guarantee of £2,000, while the Ever-Ready battery company was granted additional protection provided that it favoured male employees at the expense of women. Consumer goods were relentlessly tariffed or, if this proved ineffective, subjected to quotas in the pursuit of employment. Denture wearers and the purchasers of second-hand shoes were among the 1934 victims.[9] The overwhelming majority of tariffs were initially imposed under emergency legislation which precluded their discussion in the Dail, and although they were subsequently regularised in the Finance Bill the sheer volume — an estimated 1,947 by 1937 — limited the possibilities of debate. Lemass could also waive tariffs by granting duty-free import licences to favoured plants, while he alone determined the criteria whereby foreign businessmen were given licences to operate plants in Ireland — licences which were never subjected to Dail supervision.[10]

Lemass used these powers to shape Irish industry, the only constraint being the availability of projects from either Irish or foreign businessmen. Control of Manufacture Act licences were used to shift foreign businesses to the west of Ireland; residence permits from the Aliens Office were granted or refused depending on the nature of the proposed industry and its preferred location. A permit could hang on manufacturing women's rather than men's clothing, or on locating at some distance from Dublin. While favoured firms were assisted, those not in favour were punished. One firm which contravened the spirit, if not the letter, of the Control of Manufactures Act was denied duty-free import licences unless explicitly approved by Lemass and was refused the right to run a sponsored programme on Radio Eireann in the later 1940s.[11] One firm could be favoured at the expense of another, while import licences were used during the Economic War to channel purchases of capital equipment to non-English firms.[12]

In addition the state could facilitate access to capital resources. The Trade Loans Guarantee Acts were expanded in scope, emerging as an Irish solution to the capital needs of smaller businesses though some larger firms also benefited. The state-controlled Industrial Credit Co. was established to provide long-term finance for industry. In practice its capital resources proved insufficient for a substantial loans business but it underwrote a host of new Stock Exchange issues, many of them ironically for what were effectively foreign firms such as Ranks

(Ireland) Ltd. During the 1930s, whether motivated by patriotism or by the profits accruing from protection, there was a major upsurge in investment on the Irish Stock Exchange with the total value of issues launched in the years 1932–36 amounting to £6.5m. compared with a total stock market value of £3.25m. in 1932.[13] Some of the capital resulted from the realisation of foreign investments by Irish stockholders; the remainder reflected the channelling of money hitherto held in secure savings (such as Post Office accounts) into industrial investment. While large investors were of undoubted significance, patriotism, plus the desire to assist the establishment of local industry, attracted investors of modest means. Virtually every town established an industrial development association to lobby for 'its' factory and this body generally raised not inconsiderable sums for investment in any prospective industry. The shareholders in the Portlaoise firm, Irish Worsted Mills, included shopkeepers, professional men, the local convent, engine drivers, mental hospital staff and widows.[14]

The result was the creation of a heavily-protected, high-cost industrial sector which was very dependent on government. The negative aspects of this policy were many: the belief that every town was entitled to only one factory and the mass recruitment of a workforce unused to industry which resulted in low productivity and poor-quality products. Manufacturers were protected by the high level of protection. The major loser was undoubtedly the consumer, perhaps to a lesser extent the taxpayer. However, the policies were instrumental in creating a considerable number of jobs. Industrial employment rose from 162,400 in 1926 to 217,500 in 1938. These jobs proved particularly valuable at a time of negative emigration and helped stem poverty and social discontent.

In contrast to the Irish experience, Scottish industry was largely left to fend for itself. Protection was introduced in 1931 but this was of limited benefit to the largely export-oriented Scottish industrial sector. By switching the emphasis to the domestic market, tariffs gave increased importance to Scotland's distance from the lucrative south-east and led to greater unwillingness to locate plants in areas of weak consumer demand. Board of Trade figures for the 1930s show that the primary momentum of new industrial investment lay in the greater London area, the south-east and the midlands. Scotland was a net loser with a total of 34 factories opened and 14 extended in the years 1932/33 while 66 were closed. Nationally 1,109 new factories were opened and 269 extended while 829 closed down.[15]

Government policy in the early 1930s did nothing to check this tendency. Perhaps it is unrealistic to expect alternative action, given unemployment rates in 1932 of 13.5 and 14.3 per cent in London and the south-east. Efforts to channel industry to more depressed areas were at total variance with the non-interventionist philosophy of the National Government which sought the solution to unemployment in tariff protection, voluntary industrial restructuring, lower interest rates and the re-establishment of business confidence. The history of industrial transference schemes in the late 1920s when unemployed workers were shifted from depressed regions to the south of England indicated the political difficulties in discriminating between workers. Few transferees were placed in private employment and ultimately most were engaged in public works schemes. Once unemployment began to rise in the autumn of 1928, however, local workers were preferred; transference had broken down by the summer of 1930.[16]

British tariff policy did not afford the same possibilities for political direction of industry as existed in Ireland. The emergency tariffs of 1931 were soon replaced by a general tariff of 10 per cent. Higher tariffs could be imposed only on the recommendation of the Import Duties Advisory Committee, an independent body chaired by businessman Sir George May.[17] While its work resulted in some upward trend in tariff levels, British tariffs were considerably below Irish levels. In 1937, with Irish tariffs measured on an index of 100, Britain's stood at 64.9.[18] The I.D.A.C. used its tariff granting powers somewhat half-heartedly to restructure the British steel industry, but there is no evidence that it was conscious of the regional dimensions of its decisions.[19] The power to award tariffs does not appear to have been used to channel industry to depressed areas such as central Scotland.

As in Ireland, tariff protection brought an influx of foreign businessmen who established British plants; yet there was no apparent attempt to direct them to specific locations. The majority settled in the greater London area, close to major markets where they could rent factories on new industrial estates. The late 1930s brought a further influx of foreign businessmen, mostly Jewish refugees from central Europe, some of whom were attracted to depressed regions by the availability of financial assistance and factories for rent, but only 3.7 per cent of foreign manufacturing firms established in Britain in the years 1918–44 were located in Scotland and they accounted for a mere 0.7 per cent of the employment provided by such firms.[20]

Regional divergences in unemployment and industrial development received little attention until the end of 1933 when statistics indicated that unemployment had fallen by over 20 per cent in London and the south-east but by less than 10 per cent in Scotland and Wales. The social problems of long-term unemployment, plus a highly emotive series of articles published by *The Times* under the title 'Places without a Future',[21] led the government to commission a series of regional studies, including one dealing with central Scotland. These were not the first such surveys. In 1931 a number of British universities produced government-commissioned regional reports, including one on south-west Scotland by Glasgow University. This report exuded an optimism which was in marked contrast with those from other areas, expressing confidence in the area's economic diversity and ability to attract new industries; but it was short on concrete proposals.[22] The primary concern of the 1934 studies was more social than economic. They placed undue confidence in agricultural smallholding as a possible source of new employment, while the only industries discussed were those based on indigenous resources, despite the footloose nature of new expanding industries. On government instructions the Scottish report was confined to Lanarkshire, which resulted in a highly artificial discussion of unemployment in mining villages without reference to the ability of Glasgow to absorb surplus workers.[23] It was also testimony to the government's desire to minimise the impact of these studies, a desire which was confirmed by the ensuing legislation. Two Commissioners were appointed to deal with the problems of the re-named Special Areas, one for Scotland, the other for England and Wales. However, their activities were severely circumscribed. Their remit was limited to the areas covered by the reports and they were precluded from aiding schemes normally assisted by local authorities or from embarking on programmes of public works. Assistance to industry was specifically excluded.[24] The Commissioners were thus unable to remedy major infrastructural defects, such as inadequate roads, and confined their early activities to agricultural allotments, clearing slag heaps, providing playgrounds, holidays for children and assisting district nursing schemes.

While the actual impact of such measures verged on the trivial, the Commissioner for England and Wales pressed for more extensive powers. His third report in November 1936 — which coincided with his resignation, reputedly due to frustration — demanded the institution of specific measures to attract industry to the Special Areas. He urged an end to restrictions on assisting profit-making businesses and controls over new factory development in London.[25] This report, combined with pressure from some government back-benchers and public opinion, resulted in the provision of state finance for loans to industry; the building of industrial estates; and rent, rates and tax concessions to new firms; while in a separate gesture Lord Nuffield established a personal fund to help industry in the Special Areas.

The appointment of a Scottish Commissioner should have been of particular benefit to the area. In fact the reports of the Scottish Commissioner, Sir Arthur Rose, are much less informative than those of his English and Welsh counterpart and show no evidence of pressure for change.[26] Both Commissioners found their work subjected to lengthy scrutiny by hostile ministers and officials. While both the Scottish Development Council and the Scottish Office pressed for extended economic aid their efforts were largely ignored, perhaps because unemployment in the Scottish Special Area was below that in Wales or England.[27]

Despite these limitations industry in Lanarkshire could seek finance from three different funds. The Special Areas Reconstruction Association (S.A.R.A.) provided loans of up to £10,000 for small businesses, while a Treasury Fund of £2m. was available for larger projects. Lord Nuffield's Trust fund of £2m. provided both loan and share capital on a less stringent basis. Scotland fared relatively poorly in the allocation of these funds. In the first year of operation Scotland received only 13 per cent of the total sum allocated despite accounting for over 21 per cent of Special Areas' unemployment. Its share ranged from a mere 2 per cent of the Treasury Fund to 13 per cent of Nuffield Trust resources. The suspicion that Scotland was treated in a less generous fashion is supported by the fact that the Nuffield Trust recovered 93 per cent of its Scottish loans compared with 72 to 77 per cent in Wales, Cumberland and the North-East. Only S.A.R.A. with a separate Scottish office which allocated 24 per cent of total resources gave Scotland a sum proportionate to its share of unemployment. These three funds were credited with creating a mere 2,886 jobs in the period 1937/8.[28]

Industrial estates which provided purpose-built factories at competitive rents were perhaps the most effective form of assistance. The Scottish estate at Hillington was the second largest. Its location close to Glasgow docks proved attractive and by May 1939 a total of 87 factories had been let, of which 78 were in production employing 1,500 workers. While the industries attracted were primarily small, employing mainly female labour, they contributed to a diversification of the area's industrial structure. The other measures available, tax and rates concessions, were regarded with considerable hostility by the Treasury and seem to have been awarded in a niggardly manner, though few new companies would have been liable for income tax in their early years of operation.[29]

The Special Areas financial measures did not operate for a sufficient length of time to permit considered evaluation of their effectiveness. Of the three funds, the Nuffield Trust, with its more relaxed conditions and the ability to provide advice and management assistance, was the most effective. S.A.R.A. which operated under the auspices of the Bank of England seems to have been unduly rigid in its criteria. The Treasury Fund was spent on expensive capital-intensive projects in heavy industry and was mainly allocated to politically sensitive areas such as Jarrow and south Wales. Those promoting Welsh industrial development stressed that they were handicapped by the lack of an industrial bank similar to the Irish Industrial Credit Co. while the state aids available in Northern Ireland, which provided grants towards site costs, factory rentals, interest-free loans and five years' income tax remission, were deemed superior to those available in the Special Areas.[30]

Unemployment in Scotland, Wales and the North of England fell steadily in the later 1930s primarily as a result of the rearmament programme which led to a recovery in traditional heavy industries. Rearmament provided an ideal opportunity to channel resources to peripheral regions on both strategic and economic grounds. By March 1936 it was agreed that, price and other factors being equal, contracts should be allocated to areas of above-average unemployment; yet evidence suggests that the armed services favoured the more developed areas. However, political pressure ultimately bore some fruit. The proportion of defence contracts allocated to special and scheduled areas (areas of above-average unemployment which were less severely affected than the Special Areas) rose from 12 per cent in 1936/7 to 31 per cent in the first half of the financial year 1937/8. In March 1937 Scotland was allocated government factories with a total value of £6m. while the Clyde benefited from naval rearmament.[31] The sharp reduction of Scottish unemployment was therefore ultimately attributable, not to industrial diversification, but to a revival of traditional sources of employment.

Both Scotland and the Irish Free State shifted from a free trade to a protectionist economy during the 1930s. The Irish administration, however, was singularly more vigorous in using the powers which tariffs presented to direct industrial policy. In contrast to Britain, where the share of industrial production and insured workers accounted for by London and the south-east rose, the proportion of industrial production located in Dublin and other major cities fell, while the Irish government also managed to curb the advance of women in the industrial workforce.

The late 1930s produced contrasting experiences for Scottish and Irish industry. While Scotland benefited from the British government's rearmament programme, newly-protected Irish industries faced a number of serious problems. The momentum of the protectionist programme had been exhausted with tariffs and quotas covering virtually the whole domestic market in basic consumer goods. Efforts to extend protection to intermediate goods — such as textile yarns — led to conflicts with established industry. The Anglo-Irish Trade Agreement of 1938 marked the apparent end of the unquestioning commitment to self-sufficiency, though World War Two gave this policy a new lease of life. Despite the differences in industrial structure, much of the contrast between the two economies lay in their political circumstances. The comparative lack of interest devoted to Scottish unemployment and industrial decline is evident. Scottish interests were not examined at Westminster or in the press in the way that public attention focused at different times on the problems of South Wales, Jarrow or Cumberland. Sydney Checkland, writing of Glasgow in the '30s, noted the inability 'to mobilise business interest in regional recovery to any great degree'.[32] In the independent Irish Free State the self-conscious need to demonstrate the reality of political autonomy brought intense activity in the sphere of economic policy. Whether it was of any greater long-term benefit than the apparent Scottish indifference is, however, a moot point.

NOTES

1. The so-called Macmillan Gap, named from its analysis in the *Committee on Finance and Industry* (P.P. XIII, 1930–1, Cmd.3897).

2. Mary E. Daly, 'Government Finance for Industry in the Irish Free State: the Trade Loans (Guarantee) Acts', *Ir. Ec. & Soc. Hist.*, XI (1984), pp. 73–93.

3. University College, Dublin, Archives Dept., Blythe Papers, P 24/475, Industrial Trust Co.

4. S. G. Checkland, *Scottish Banking, A History, 1695–1973* (Glasgow, 1975), pp. 473–4.

5. For D.I.D.A.A. and N.A.I.D.A., see National Library of Ireland, MSS.16243–5.

6. R. H. Campbell, 'The Scottish Office and the Special Areas', *Historical Journal*, 22 (1979), p. 175.

7. Ronan Fanning, *The Irish Department of Finance* (Dublin, 1978), p. 205.

8. James Meenan, *The Irish Economy since 1922* (Liverpool, 1970), p. 141.

9. For Ever-Ready, cf. Dept. of Industry and Commerce (DIC), Trade and Industries Division, TID 1207/166. For background to 1934 tariff schedules, cf. State Paper Office, S.2920.

10. M. E. Daly, 'An Irish-Ireland for Business? The Control of Manufactures Acts, 1932 and 1934', *I.H.S.*, 24 (1984), pp. 246–72.

11. D.I.C. TID 1207/653.

12. P.R.O. T.160/744 14026/2, Anglo-Irish Negotiations, 3 Feb. 1936.

13. *Report of Commission of Inquiry into Banking Currency and Credit* (Dublin, Stationery Office, 1938), paras. 129, 431.

14. D.I.C. TID 19/145, Inds. A.R. 303.

15. Board of Trade, *Survey of Industrial Development, 1933*, Table II.

16. P.R.O. Cab. 27/438, 23 June 1930.

17. J. C. Carr and W. Taplin, *A History of the British Steel Industry* (Oxford, 1962), p. 495.
18. W. J. L. Ryan, 'Measurement of Tariff Levels for Ireland', *Statistical and Social Inquiry Society Journal*, XVIII (1948–9), p. 130.
19. Carr and Taplin, *op.cit.*, pp. 495–508.
20. Christopher M. Law, *British Regional Development since World War One* (Newton Abbot, 1980).
21. *The Times*, 20–22 March 1934.
22. *An Industrial Survey of South-West Scotland*, made for the Board of Trade by the University of Glasgow (1932), p. 191.
23. Ministry of Labour, *Reports of Investigations into the Industrial Conditions in Certain Depressed Areas*, 1933–34, Cmd.4728.
24. Mary E. Daly 'Government Policy and the Depressed Areas in the Inter-War Years (unpublished D.Phil. thesis, Oxford University, 1978), ch. 5.
25. *Third Report of the Commissioners for the Special Areas (England and Wales)*, (1936–7, Cmd.5305).
26. There are four Scottish Reports, (1934–5, Cmd.4958; 1935–6, Cmd.5089; 1935–6, Cmd.5245; 1937, Cmd. 5604).
27. Campbell, 'Scottish Office and the Special Areas', pp. 175–83.
28. P.R.O. Cab. 27/578, D.A. Report on Financial Assistance, 9 March 1938.
29. Daly, thesis, ch. 6.
30. *Ulster Yearbook, 1938* (Belfast, 1939).
31. T. Balogh, 'Economic Policy and Rearmament in Britain', *Manchester School*, VII (1936).
32. S. G. Checkland, *The Upas Tree: Glasgow, 1875–1975* (Glasgow, 1976), p. 41.

25

STRUCTURAL CHANGE AND DIVERSIFICATION IN IRELAND AND SCOTLAND

R. B. Weir

I

The international depression between the wars severely disrupted the highly specialised industrial and agricultural structures which had developed in Ireland and Scotland during the second half of the nineteenth century. Both countries experienced relative decline measured in terms of income per head (Tables 1 and 2).

Table 1. Per Capita Incomes[1]

	(A) United Kingdom £	*% change*	*(B) Irish Free State* £	*% change*	*(C) Scotland* £	*% change*
1926	92.5	—	51.9	—	82.2	—
1929	98.4	6.4	54.9	5.9	87.9	6.9
1931	88.2	-10.4	50.1	-8.7	73.3	-16.6
1933	84.4	-4.3	45.4	-9.3	72.3	-1.4
1936	96.5	14.3	51.9	14.3	85.6	18.4
1939	114.2	18.3	57.7	11.3	98.9	15.5

Table 2. Relative Incomes (%)

	(A) IFS/UK (i)	*(ii)*	*(B) IFS/SCOT*	*(C) SCOT/UK*
1926	56	55	63	89
1929	56	57	63	89
1931	57	61	68	83
1933	53	58	63	86
1936	54	52	61	89
1939	51	49	58	87

Note: For sources and basis of the estimates see note 1.

Whilst membership of the club of relatively disadvantaged regions of the British Isles was nothing new for most Irish people, for many Scots it was; and this has exercised a profound influence on the interpretation of Scottish economic history. High unemployment, exacerbated by changes in migration, and falling incomes characterised much of the period, producing a variety of attempts to alter the existing economic structure and to develop new specialisations.

The meaning and implications of structural change were not the same in each country. For Scotland and Ulster structural questions were primarily associated with the high degree of dependence on the heavy industries and with the inability to develop new industries on a scale sufficient to absorb resources released by older forms of manufacturing. Although Scotland and Ulster had a larger proportion of their labour forces engaged in agriculture than average for the United Kingdom (9.5% and 26.0% respectively in 1921),[2] and although agriculture continued to release labour, structural change was concerned mainly with change *within* the manufacturing sector. By contrast, in the Irish Free State it embraced two issues. One was the balance of output *within* agriculture between pasture and tillage; the other, the overall balance between agriculture and industry. With less than 5% of the labour force employed in manufacturing industry 'the industrialisation of Ireland had still to take place'.[3] Despite a strong conviction, pre-dating independence, 'that the absence of industries impoverished the national life, economically, socially and spiritually',[4] the ability of the Free State government to do anything about the overall balance of the economy was highly contingent on policy towards the structure of output within agriculture. For the first decade of the Free State's existence Cumann na nGaedhal settled policy in favour of pastoral products and their export to the British market, a policy which assumed that the prosperity of agriculture would provide an expanding market for Irish industry and which, because of the need to minimise farmers' costs, required the adoption of a very cautious approach to tariff protection for industry.[5] Such protection as industry received was less concerned with the creation of new industries than with the survival of existing ones.[6] From 1932, with the election of a Fianna Fail government, both agricultural and industrial policy changed radically. Self-sufficiency, industrialisation and rural regeneration formed three elements of a social design that was unique to the Free State.

Despite the different meanings and implications of structural change there are elements of comparison, if only that few of the attempts to develop new specialisations proved particularly successful. The main purpose of this essay is to consider the explanations that have been offered for this lack of success. Before this can be done, however, there are two issues concerning comparative work in the inter-war period which merit discussion.

II

The first, and most basic, is that the chronological boundaries created by the two world wars mean rather more to Scottish than to Irish economic history. Scottish economic historians, to judge by their textbooks, have been content to operate within these boundaries and the Scottish economy, particularly its industrial sector, is described as either 'under pressure', or 'troubled', or in 'an Age of Crisis'.[7] With Scotland enmeshed in a continuing economic and political union, and economic policy determined in Westminster, Scottish economic historians have been more concerned with the results rather than the formation of policy.[8] Two major justifications exist for interpreting Scottish economic history within this chronological framework. One is the difficulty created for the Scottish economy by the break-up and ultimate collapse of the international trading system; the other is the failure of successive governments to escape from economic orthodoxy and to produce coherent solutions to the depression. The restoration of the international economy after 1945 and the marked shift in attitudes to economic management during the Second World War changed the terms on which Scotland's economic problems could be dealt with, even if they did not solve them. The inter-war years can thus be justified as a distinct period for the study of Scottish economic history.

A similar case is less easy to make for Ireland. The beginning of the inter-war period is dominated by political events — the struggle for independence, partition and the civil war — whose analysis imposes a quite difference character on the writing of Irish economic history. The economic history of the Free State involves a much greater concern with the formation of policy and the constraints on policy makers.[9] It is far less pessimistic than Scottish economic history, an observation which is surprising given the lower level of income and the awesome problems the newly independent state faced. The difference lies in the tendency of Scottish historians to view the inter-war period from the commanding heights of late nineteenth-century industrial success. This perspective, shared by Welsh historians,[10] is understandable but has the effect of making subsequent economic history look unduly bleak and causes all sorts of difficulty when an attempt is made to reconcile the apparent paradox of a poor industrial performance with a long-term rise in the standard of living.[11] Irish historians may stress that 'in economic matters continuity not change was . . . the order of the day'[12] but their perspective is one in which political independence offered the prospect of solving economic problems inherited from the nineteenth century; the commanding heights ahead may have been formidable but at last they were ones which a parliament in Dublin could choose either to scale or to avoid.

Nor does the end of the inter-war period mark a significant discontinuity in Irish economic history. The economic policies adopted by Fianna Fail in 1932 had a long-run continuity, stretching well beyond 1939. The ultimate failure of these policies came in the economic crisis in the Republic in the mid-1950s, and the publication of the Whitaker Report, *Economic Development*, in 1958 marks the real break with the past and a more appropriate terminal date.[13]

III

A second feature which makes comparative work more complex is Lloyd George's settlement of the Irish question. A full comparative study of Scotland and Ireland would need to incorporate the economic consequences of three different systems of government: a self-governing dominion in the Irish Free State with full constitutional power to shape its own economic destiny; a devolved government in Ulster with most of the vital economic powers 'reserved' to the imperial government; and, in Scotland, a region with no local autonomy, part of a highly centralised system of government.

How have historians interpreted the economic consequences of these different systems? In the case of the Free State it is necessary to distinguish between policy before and after 1932. During the first decade of the State's existence the exercise of economic power was carried out under considerable constraint. Sovereignty was limited by the need to establish political legitimacy, the fiscal system and the continuing close economic relationship with Great Britain.[14] The nineteenth-century legacy of close economic integration through capital, labour and product markets could not easily be cast off, and an economic policy which further encouraged pastoral farming and eschewed wholesale protection for industry reflected this.[15] Recognition of underlying economic realities thus produces an interpretation of the period from 1922 to 1932 which is remarkably similar to that of the Irish economy in the second half of the nineteenth century where resource endowments and access to markets determined the pattern of specialisation.[16]

From 1932 Fianna Fail attempted to break that pattern of specialisation. Agricultural support was directed towards tillage rather than pasture, the small farmer rather than the large, the home market rather than export. Industrial policy also underwent radical change with a high tariff wall to encourage import substitution and legislation to restrict foreign ownership of manufacturing industry.[17] The value judgements behind these policies — the type of society they were meant to produce — were unique and offer no comparison with Ulster or Scotland. The results may, however, have been less radical than the policies. Events, particularly the Anglo-Irish tariff war, soon proved that the bonds of economic interdependence could not be easily broken without material damage to both parties.[18] This judgement applies more to agriculture than to industry and, at least to an outsider, industrial policy looks much more daring and innovative than anything attempted in Britain in the 1930s. If the policy is viewed as that of a country coming late to industrialisation and seeking to offset profound competitive disadvantages, it impresses. In a much more difficult economic environment than faced Cumann na nGaedhal industrial employment increased, though not all of the increase occurred in the protected industries, and its exact extent remains a matter of considerable statistical uncertainty.[19]

Protection had its disadvantages: the new industries had difficulty operating outside the protected market, prices were high, and an anti-competitive frame of mind may have developed amongst Irish businessmen, though this does not look very much different from the imperfections of competitive behaviour so studiously cultivated by much of British industry during the 1930s. These disadvantages have to be weighed against the long-run effects of past free trade policy on the Irish economy and the evidence that protection permitted the development of some of the fundamental requirements for industrialisation such as a pool of skilled labour and managerial competence.[20] Protectionism has not been short of critics, but their criticisms have been made from the standpoint of the relative economic success in the 1960s that followed trade liberalisation and the type of society that Fianna Fail sought to create. The former perspective may underestimate contemporary economic problems; the latter may overstate the respective merits of two very different leaders, De Valera and Lemass.[21] In one way it is curious that Fianna Fail's policies should have received such critical treatment, for Buckland's study of devolved government in Ulster shows that the greater freedom possessed and exercised by the Free State compared very favourably with the North's limited powers. The vitality of the Free State may just have been an 'impression', not an actuality, but it nevertheless suggests the need for assessment of the Free State's economic policies to recognise the more dependent relationship of its northern neighbour.

Devolution in Ulster owed little to long-term considerations of the benefits of regional government and everything to 'the Imperial government's desire to extricate itself from Ireland in the face of strident Irish republicanism'. Economic issues relating exclusively to Northern Ireland were devolved but in all important economic matters, such as the exchange rate, tariff protection and trade agreements, effective sovereignty lay with Westminster. Northern Ireland could not develop a regional economic policy, even had economic orthodoxy and fatalism allowed it. Legislation was introduced in 1932 and 1937 to encourage the development of new industries but it failed to broaden Northern Ireland's industrial base. Weaknesses in the legislation and opposition from the Ministry of Finance and from existing industry both contributed, but the fundamental reason for failure was that Northern Ireland was competing on unequal terms with distressed areas in Britain and with the Free State. British M.P.s were anxious to see that Northern Ireland did not benefit from devolution more than their own distressed areas. Buckland concludes that Ulster was ill-placed to offset its natural economic disadvantages of distance from markets and absence of raw materials.[22] His characterisation of Northern Ireland as 'the factory of grievances' seems apt; the Free State, whatever the long-run consequences of the policies adopted in 1932, never presents the same impression of a government with so little competence to manage its own economic affairs. Yet, what both had in common in the 1930s was a continuing high degree of dependence on Britain. Beneath the veil of the constitutional settlement of 1920–1922 was an underlying economic reality where existing specialisations endured and where forms of government had less impact than might have been predicted.

IV

Scotland, like Northern Ireland, had an old industrial structure and there are some striking similarities in the explanations that Scottish historians have offered for the restricted development of new industries. R. H. Campbell has argued that new industrial development was limited by exogenous factors such as distance from major markets in the south of England and the inability of the heavy industries to supply the raw materials and semi-processed goods required by the new industries, an argument common to Ulster. Failure was not, however, wholly due to exogenous factors: 'the production of consumer goods . . . was inhibited by the refusal to adopt the mass production methods essential for success'.[23] Slaven argued that the depression both debilitated the staple industries and cut off new developments, making regeneration even more unlikely. This argument was based on Beardmore's unsuccessful diversification into automobiles and aircraft. The former industry was given especial significance: it was 'the real growth leader' and its absence exacerbated existing constraints on new industries arising from lack of suitable factories, good industrial sites, relevant skills, inter-industry linkages, suitable demand trends and effective government support.[24] Buxton has also argued that 'emphasis on traditional sectors meant a corresponding neglect of new developments'. On the demand side, the contraction of the basic industries resulted in a slow growth of real income which impeded diversification and the development of new industries dependent on the domestic market.[25] On the supply side, the new trades found it difficult to obtain capital, and the low profitability of the older sectors made them reluctant to diversify.[26] A combination of supply and demand side factors or, in Lenman's words, 'a series of mutually reinforcing interlocked factors', inhibited the new industries and condemned Scotland to economic failure.[27]

Whilst historians have produced a lengthy catalogue of possible explanations for Scotland's economic failure, they have not cast their net quite as wide as did contemporaries. J. H. Bowie in *The Future of Scotland*, published in 1939, saw deficiencies in the educational system, banking, research effort, and local and central government. His severest strictures were reserved for Scottish businessmen who, as a class, 'have demitted their function and given up the struggle'. A retreat from 'the rough-and-tumble of business' had drained entrepreneurial talent whilst at the same time capitalists had become increasingly averse to risk: 'finance there is in Scotland in plenty, but those who own or control it show little desire to put it to industrial hazard'. In Bowie's view it was not only individual enterprise that had failed but collective effort too. The structure of Scottish industry had been moulded by individualism and this had made it less adaptable to modern demands; on the other hand, collaborative effort was impossible because 'Scotsmen are the world's worst co-operators'. Given the extent and scale of these inadequacies it was scarcely surprising that Bowie saw a major role for the state in the restructuring of Scottish industry, a conclusion that many historians have shared whilst recognising the dead hand of economic orthodoxy on policy.[28]

Bowie's critique serves as a useful reminder that the origins of Scotland's inter-war difficulties may not have lain solely with economic factors and that any comprehensive explanation will need to incorporate political, social and psychological characteristics. His criticisms of the behaviour of Scottish businessmen have been a feature of later historical assessment. Harvie has probably come closest to Bowie's position:

> If the inter-war British economy was imprisoned in the strait-jacket of financial orthodoxy, the position was aggravated in Scotland by the dominance of the magnates from the traditional heavy industries, family dynasties which were keener to protect their own status and power than to experiment in new fields.[29]

Dissensions between old industrialists and new, in Harvie's view, hampered the work of the two new institutions, the Scottish Development Council and the Scottish Economic Council, founded during the 1930s to promote industrial regeneration. The old school of business, represented by men such as Sir James Lithgow, Sir William Weir, Sir Andrew Duncan, Lords Maclay and Inverforth,

Lord McGowan and Sir Robert Horne, had an attitude of 'unveiled hostility' to the new consumer-goods industries: '"sheltered" industries was the contemptuous epithet they used'. Harvie's criticisms of the heavy-industry magnates support his argument that 'the weakness of the Scots economy was largely the result of decisions taken in Scotland by Scotsmen while the economy was still prosperous and largely autonomous', but it is difficult to know how to interpret these criticisms in the absence of any discussion of the context in which decisions were taken.[30] Lithgow's views on the sheltered industries are surely misrepresented, for 'sheltered' was not a term of abuse but the adjective used to describe industries that were less exposed to foreign competition.

A more sympathetic appraisal of business leadership is contained in R. H. Campbell's specialised study of Scottish industry. Campbell considers the methodological issues involved in discussion of structural change and warns against the dangers arising from the use of hindsight: only judgements by standards accepted by contemporaries produce a satisfactory historical interpretation. This caution is directed against the theory of overcommitment, and emphasises the desirability of taking account of the general evaluation of economic prospects by contemporaries when judging the action of individual firms. Using the annual *Glasgow Herald Trade Review* as his barometer of contemporary opinion, Campbell shows the gradual acceptance amongst industrialists by the 1930s of the desirability of change. Rationalisation was increasingly advocated and there was a growing belief that industrial recovery could only be expected from an increased output from the new industries. Whilst this shift in contemporary opinion legitimates criticism of the inadequacy of the movement towards structural change, especially the limited objectives of rationalisation and the failure to provide compensatory growth in new industries, a different form of short-term analysis, also rooted in contemporary thinking, justified the policy common amongst businessmen in the heavy industries of 'wait and see', that is, a policy of pursuing such opportunities as arose from increased defence expenditure. Campbell's justification of this policy rests largely on his belief that 'no alternative strategy was obvious'. Further, the degree of consensus necessary to change the industrial structure was lacking. Rationalisation plans, for example, were impeded by 'the entrenched opposition of powerful personalities; the sheer complexity ... of the industrial structure; the costs — private and social — of change'. Finally, 'wait and see' had its ultimate justification in the survival of an industrial structure which met later defence needs. 'This achievement,' in Campbell's view, 'is as relevant as some of the more critical evaluations of the failure to move adequately towards a different industrial structure.'[31]

V

This limited survey of the literature on the inter-war Scottish economy suggests some general observations. Firstly, many of the explanations for the limited development of new industries in Scotland — the small size of the domestic market, transport costs, imperfections in the capital market, inappropriate labour skills and entrepreneurial deficiencies — appear also in the literature on Irish economic history. But an abundance of explanation is matched by an absence of formal testing: the fact that economic revival was difficult seems to constitute adequate proof.[32]

Secondly, nearly all the empirical evidence comes from the heavy industries. With most heavy industry located in the West of Scotland this imparts a decidedly occidental bias to Scottish economic history; in Ulster the bias lies to the opposite point of the compass. Whether it presents an accurate picture of structural change is another matter. George O'Brien once likened the Irish Free State to 'Scotland . . . with Glasgow and the Clyde left out' (the comparison was made in an article celebrating the economic *progress* of Ireland — has anyone ever written in the same way about Scotland?).[33] Without wishing to argue that Scottish economic history should be written without the West of Scotland, structural change should include more than the manufacturing sector and more than one region. Scotland was not a one-sector economy. The service sector accounted for an increasing proportion of employment — 37% in 1931 as against 33% in 1921 — and provided a majority of the new jobs in Scotland, even though part of it — public administration and defence — suffered a greater loss of employment than any industry within the manufacturing sector, including shipbuilding and marine engineering (Table 3).

Table 3. Employment Gains in Scotland, 1921–1931

SIC	*Rank*	*Industry*	*Numbers*
23	1	Distributive trades	64,643
25	2	Professional and scientific services	43,620
20	3	Construction	32,862
26	4	Miscellaneous services	26,059
22	5	Transport and communications	16,628
11	6	Vehicles	10,419
3	7	Food, drink and tobacco	9,199
18	8	Paper, printing and publishing	5,516
19	9	Other manufacturing industries	3,120
24	10	Insurance, banking, financial and business services	2,582
16	11	Bricks, pottery, glass, china	1,934
8	12	Instrument engineering	1,052
17	13	Timber furniture	818
9	14	Electrical engineering	787
21	15	Gas, water and electricity	675

Source: Calculated from Census Tables in C. H. Lee, *British Regional Employment Statistics, 1841–1971* (Cambridge, 1979).

Views on the service sector vary. Buxton omits it from his discussion of structural change on the grounds that the size of the service sector was determined by the growth of the primary, extractive and manufacturing industries,[34] a line of causation which Lee, using data for the Victorian period, rejects in favour of variations in income.[35] Whatever the causation, what is striking (and this applies equally to the growth of the service sector in the Irish Free State and in Ulster)[36] is how little is known about these new forms of employment. It is also legitimate to question whether the experience of the heavy industries will ever offer useful insights into the problems faced by entrepreneurs in the new industries (in both the service and manufacturing sectors), industries which allegedly had quite different characteristics from the old.[37]

Thirdly, ever since H. W. Richardson put forward the theory of 'over-commitment', a theory whose multiple parenthood makes it impossible to test, the discussion of structural change has been couched in terms of industries rather than firms. In Scotland where government played a more limited role than in the Free State, only tentatively coming round to the acceptance of the need for a policy on new industries in the 1930s,[38] structural change was dependent on the decisions of private businessmen. Although collective reorganisation was attempted in some industries, aided and abetted by public intermediaries such as the banks, it is not usually industries which bring about structural change but the decisions of individual firms. The point may seem pedantic and definitional, but it is important for shaping the perception of the problem. In the absence of intervention by government or the banks, the creation of new industries could only come about in three ways: by the emergence of new firms, by the diversification of existing firms, and by the appearance of foreign-owned firms. Recognition of this provides a convenient classificatory scheme for examining the development of new industries and the factors which shaped investment decisions. Attitudes to foreign ownership, for example, were quite different in the Free State and in Scotland, whilst in both Scotland and Ireland the limited development of large-scale firms may have contributed to the lack of diversification.[39]

Finally, whilst historical judgement must be related to contemporary opinion, there is no unique source for such opinion: different sources may yield different opinions. The point may be illustrated by Dickson's use of the records of the Glasgow Chamber of Commerce which show no evidence of any thinking about new industry, though plenty of belief in the efficacy of wage reductions as a cure for unemployment.[40] How then does the historian select the appropriate criteria for evaluating the actions that incorporated these opinions, and what is the appropriate time period over which actions should be judged? It may be that much of Scottish industry died through emphasising the short run and that it was those, 'the best people', who looked to the long run who flourished.[41] But how long was the long run? To have hung on till rearmament may have been an achievement but it contributed little to the resolution of Scotland's structural problems. It was the unresolved nature of structural issues, problems which were postponed until after 1945 for a new generation, that was the most common experience of Scotland and Ireland during the inter-war years.

NOTES

1. The following sources were used for Table 1: Col.A, United Kingdom: C. H. Feinstein, *Statistical Tables of National Income, Expenditure and Output of the U.K., 1855–1965* (Cambridge, 1972), Table 9; Col.B, Irish Free State: G. A. Duncan, 'The

Social Income of the Irish Free State', *Journal of the Statistical and Social Inquiry Society of Ireland*, 16 (1939–40), as cited in J. W. O'Hagan, 'An Analysis of the Relative Size of the Government Sector: Ireland 1926–52', *Economic and Social Review*, 12, I (1980), pp. 17–35; Col.C, Scotland: A. D. Campbell, 'Changes in Scottish Incomes, 1924–49', *Economic Journal* (June 1955), Table 1, p. 226. Population figures from B. R. Mitchell and P. Deane, *Abstract of British Historical Statistics* (Cambridge, 1962), Table 3, p. 10, and B. R. Mitchell and H. G. Jones, *Second Abstract of British Historical Statistics* (Cambridge, 1971), Table 2, p. 5. Feinstein's U.K. estimates and Duncan's Irish Free State estimates are the most comparable and show G.N.P. at current factor cost. The basis of Campbell's estimates is different and is explained in the original article. In Table 2, Col.A(ii) shows Crotty's estimates of relative per capita income at constant prices; see R. D. Crotty, *Irish Agricultural Production* (Cork, 1966), Table 19, p. 131 and Table 32, p. 156.

2. C. H. Lee, *Regional Economic Growth in the U.K. since the 1880s* (London, 1971), Table C5, pp. 230–1.

3. J. W. O'Hagan and K. P. McStay, *The Evolution of Manufacturing Industry in Ireland* (Dublin 1981), p. 12.

4. J. Meenan, *The Irish Economy since 1922* (Liverpool, 1970), p. 315.

5. D. S. Johnson, 'The Economic History of Ireland between the Wars', *Ir. Ec. & Soc. Hist.*, I (1974), pp. 49–61.

6. O'Hagan and McStay, *op.cit.*, p. 14.

7. See R. H. Campbell, *Scotland since 1707* (Oxford, 1971), p. 249; C. Harvie, *No Gods and Precious Few Heroes, Scotland 1914–1980* (London, 1981), p. 35; B. Lenman, *An Economic History of Modern Scotland* (London, 1977), p. 206.

8. An exception is R. H. Campbell, 'The Scottish Office and the Special Areas', *Historical Journal*, 22, I (1979), pp. 167–83.

9. See, for example, T. K. Daniel, 'Griffith on his Noble Head: The Determinants of Cumann na nGaedheal Economic Policy, 1922–32', *Ir. Ec. & Soc. Hist.*, III (1976), pp. 55–65.

10. See K. O. Morgan, *Rebirth of a Nation: Wales, 1880–1980* (Oxford, 1981), pp. 210–240.

11. See Harvie, *op.cit.*, p. 35.

12. F. S. L. Lyons, *Ireland since the Famine* (London, 1971), p. 588.

13. The contrast between pre- and post-1958 appears in several recent books. See, for example, T. Brown, *Ireland: A Social and Cultural History, 1922–79* (Dublin, 1982), pp. 241–66; J. Lee and G. O'Tuathaigh, *The Age of de Valera* (Dublin, 1982), pp. 129–63.

14. Lyons, *op.cit.*, pp. 588–90; T. K. Daniel, *loc.cit.*, pp. 56–60.

15. Lyons, *ibid.*

16. *Ibid.*

17. M. Daly, 'An Irish-Ireland for Business?: the Control of Manufactures Acts, 1932 and 1934', *I.H.S.*, XXIV (1984), pp. 246–72.

18. Lyons, *op.cit.*, pp. 602–4.

19. This view of Ireland has been argued by E. O'Malley, 'The Decline of Irish Industry in the Nineteenth Century', *Economic and Social Review*, 13 (1981), pp. 21–42. I am extremely grateful to David Johnson for pointing out that the increased coverage of the Census of Production resulted in an overstatement of the number of people employed in industrial occupations. For discussion of the point, see D. S. Johnson, *The Interwar Economy in Ireland* (Dundalk, 1985), pp. 29–30.

20. J. Meenan, 'Irish Industry and Industrial Policy, 1921–43', *Studies*, (1943), pp. 208–19; W. J. L. Ryan, 'Protection and the Efficiency of Irish Industry', *Studies*, (1954), pp. 317–26; Daly, *loc.cit.*, p. 272; for anti-competitive behaviour amongst British businessmen see W. H. Reader, *Imperial Chemical Industries: A History*, II (London, 1975); Meenan, *loc.cit.*, pp. 145–58.

21. The contrast between de Valera and Lemass has been most sharply drawn in J. J. Lee, ed., *Ireland, 1945–70* (Dublin, 1979).

22. P. Buckland, *The Factory of Grievances: Devolved Government in Northern Ireland, 1921–39* (Dublin, 1979), pp. 1, 4, 12, 55.

23. Campbell, *op.cit.*, p. 273.

24. A. Slaven, *The Development of the West of Scotland, 1750–1960* (London, 1975), pp. 200–8.

25. N. K. Buxton, 'Economic Growth in Scotland between the Wars: The Role of Production Structure and Rationalisation', *Ec.H.R.*, XXXIII (1980), pp. 538–55; S. G. E. Lythe and J. Butt, *An Economic History of Scotland* (Glasgow, 1975), p. 216.

26. Buxton, *loc.cit.*, p. 549.

27. Lenman, *op.cit.*, p. 225.

28. J. H. Bowie, *The Future of Scotland* (Edinburgh, 1939), pp. 134, 143, 179, 180; the very limited account taken by the banks of structural problems is discussed in S. G. Checkland, *Scottish Banking: A History, 1695–1973* (Glasgow, 1975).

29. C. Harvie, *Scotland and Nationalism* (London, 1977), pp. 115–6.

30. *Ibid.*, pp. 112, 172.

31. R. H. Campbell, *The Rise and Fall of Scottish Industry* (Edinburgh, 1980), pp. 151, 169–70, 181–2.

32. An attempt has been made to test inter-industry linkages in Britain; see N. von Tunzelman, Britain's New Industries between the Wars: an Input-Output Approach, unpublished paper, and his chapter, 'Structural Change and Leading Sectors in British Manufacturing 1907–68', in C. P. Kindleberger and G. di Tella, eds., *Economics in the Long View, Essays in Honour of W. W. Rostow* (New York, 1982), Vol.II.

33. G. O'Brien, 'The Economic Progress of Ireland 1912–62', *Studies*, pp. 544–5.

34. Buxton, *loc.cit.*, pp. 544–5.

35. C. H. Lee, 'The Service Sector, Regional Specialisation, and Economic Growth in the Victorian Economy', *Journal of Historical Geography*, 10 (1984), pp. 139–55 and 'Modern Economic Growth and Structural Change in Scotland: the Service Sector Reconsidered', *Sc.Ec.&Soc.Hist.*, 3 (1983), pp. 5–35.

36. Meenan, loc.cit., Table 2.1, p. 41. Occupational classifications differ between Scotland and Ireland but the service sector in the Free State accounted for 35.4% of employment in 1926 and 36.7% in 1936.

37. von Tunzelman, *loc.cit.*, pp. 6–9.

38. Campbell, *op.cit.*, pp. 167–83.

39. Compare the views of foreign ownership in Daly, *loc.cit.*, and J. H. Dunning, *American Investments in British Manufacturing Industry* (London, 1958), pp. 41–5; C. E. Heim, 'Industrial Organisation and Regional Development in Inter-War Britain', *Journal of Economic History*, XLIII (1983), pp. 931–50 and 'Regional Development and National Decline: Responses to the Regional Problem in Inter-war Britain', paper presented to the Anglo-American Conference on the Decline of the British Economy, Boston University, 1983.

40. T. Dickson, ed., *Scottish Capitalism* (Edinburgh, 1980), p. 257.

41. S. B. Saul, 'The Shortcomings of Scottish Industry', *Sc. Ec. & Soc. Hist.*, I (1981), pp. 76–81.

INDEX